Improving Global Environmental Governance

The experience of environmental governance is approached in *Improving Global Environmental Governance* from the unique perspective of actor configuration and embedded networks of actors, which are areas of emerging importance. The chapters look at existing Multilateral Environmental Agreements (MEAs) and the broader constellation of partially networked institutions to better understand the involvement of individual actors and how to deepen the networks that include them to generate more effective governance.

The book covers a wide range of issues pertaining to environmental governance including trans-boundary air pollution, marine pollution, biodiversity and ozone depletion. It also examines partnerships as a hybrid case of emerging modes of environmental governance. These partnerships are a recent form of actor configuration that warrant attention for dealing with global environmental threats in order to better understand the full potential of actor configurations in the absence of state involvement. In order to test applicability to on-going but stalled processes, the book applies the approach to one of the most difficult issues we face: climate change.

By addressing key questions in this important area, the book provides new perspectives in the nexus between agency and architecture in environmental governance in the twenty-first century.

Norichika Kanie is Associate Professor at the Tokyo Institute of Technology, Japan, and Research Fellow at the United Nations University Institute of Advanced Studies.

Steinar Andresen is Research Professor at Fridtjof Nansen Institute, Norway, and a Professor II (part time) at the Pluricourts Centre of Excellence at the University of Oslo, Norway.

Peter M. Haas is Professor of Political Science at the University of Massachusetts Amherst, USA.

Routledge Research in Global Environmental Governance

**Improving Global Environmental
Governance**
Best practices for architecture and agency
*Norichika Kanie, Steinar Andresen and
Peter M. Haas*

Improving Global Environmental Governance

Best practices for architecture and agency

Norichika Kanie, Steinar Andresen and Peter M. Haas

Routledge
Taylor & Francis Group

LONDON AND NEW YORK

First published 2014
by Routledge
2 Park Square, Milton Park, Abingdon, Oxfordshire OX14 4RN

and by Routledge

711 Third Avenue, New York, NY 10017

First issued in paperback 2014

Routledge is an imprint of the Taylor & Francis Group, an informa business

British Library Cataloguing in Publication Data
A catalogue record for this book is available from the British Library

Library of Congress Cataloging-in-Publication Data
Improving global environmental governance : best practices for architecture
and agency / [edited by] Norichika Kanie, Steinar Andresen, Peter M. Haas.
    pages cm – (Routledge research in global environmental governance)
    Summary: "By addressing key questions in this important area, the book
    provides new perspectives in the nexus between agency and architecture
    in environmental governance in the twenty-first century" – Provided by
    publisher.
    Includes bibliographical references and index.
    1. Environmental policy – International cooperation. 2. Environmental
    protection – International cooperation. 3. Environmental economics.
    I. Kanie, Norichika, 1969– II. Andresen, Steinar. III. Haas, Peter M.
    GE170.I48 2013
    333.7–dc23   2013015924

ISBN 978-0-415-81176-7 (hbk)
ISBN 978-1-138-89907-0 (pbk)
ISBN 978-0-203-58936-6 (ebk)

Typeset in Times New Roman
by HWA Text and Data Management, London

Contents

Illustrations

Figure

Tables

Contributors

Steinar Andresen is a Research Professor at the Fridtjof Nansen Institute (FNI) in Norway and a Professor II (part time) at the Pluricourts Centre of Excellence at the University of Oslo. He has been a visiting fellow at the University of Washington (1987–8), a part-time position as visiting senior fellow at IISA 1994–6, visiting research fellow at Princeton University 1997–8, professor at the Department of Political Science, University of Oslo (2002–6) and a visiting research fellow at Brookings Institution, Washington DC, fall 2012.

Graeme Auld is an Associate Professor at Carleton University in the School of Public Policy and Administration, and also holds an appointment at the Institute of Political Economy. He is a Research Fellow with the Carleton Centre for Community Innovation and a Faculty Associate at the Governance, Environment, and Markets Initiative at Yale University. His research examines the emergence, evolution and impacts of non-state and hybrid forms of global governance across economic sectors, particularly fisheries, agriculture and forestry.

Benjamin Cashore is a Professor of Environmental Governance and Political Science at Yale University's School of Forestry and Environmental Studies, and holds a courtesy appointment in Yale's Department of Political Science. He is director of the Governance, Environment, and Markets Initiative at Yale (GEM); Director, of the Yale Program on Forest Policy and Governance; coordinator of the International Union of Forest Research Organization's Task Force on International Forest Governance and Editor-in-Chief, *Forest Policy and Economics.*

Pamela S. Chasek is Professor of Political Science and Director of the International Studies Program at Manhattan College. She is the author and editor of several books and numerous articles on international environmental policy, including most recently *The Roads from Rio: Lessons Learned from Twenty Years of Multilateral Environmental Negotiations* (2012) and *Global Environmental Politics*, sixth edition (2013). She is also the executive editor of the *Earth Negotiations Bulletin*, a reporting service on United Nations environment and development negotiations.

Peter M. Haas is a Professor of Political Science at the University of Massachusetts Amherst. He received his PhD in 1986 from MIT, and has been at UMASS since 1987. He has held visiting positions at Yale University, Brown University, Oxford University, and the Wissenschaftszentrum, Berlin. He has published on international relations theory, constructivism, international environmental politics, global governance, and the interplay of science and international institutions at the international level.

Masahiko Iguchi is a PhD Candidate and a Researcher at the Graduate School of Decision Science and Technology at Tokyo Institute of Technology, Japan. He is also affiliated with Keio University and Sophia University as an adjunct lecturer. He is co-author with Norichika Kanie and Masachika Suzuki of 'Fragmentation of international low-carbon technology governance: an assessment in terms of barriers to technology development' (2013) in *Global Environmental Research* vol.17(1).

Norichika Kanie is an Associate Professor at the Graduate School of Decision Science and Technology, Tokyo Institute of Technology, Japan, and also a Senior Research Fellow at the United Nations University Institute of Advanced Studies (UNU-IAS). He serves as a scientific steering committee member of the Earth Systems Governance project and as the chair of the Working Party on Climate, Investment and Development at the OECD. He has held a visiting position at Sciences Po, Paris. He received his PhD from the Keio University.

José Antônio Puppim de Oliveira is Assistant Director and Senior Research Fellow at the United Nations University Institute of Advanced Studies (UNU-IAS). He is particularly interested in researching the political economy of environmental governance and policy implementation at different levels, looking at how global policies are translated into local policy implementation.

Stefan Renckens is a PhD candidate in Environmental Politics at Yale University, School of Forestry and Environmental Studies. His doctoral research deals with explaining the interactions between European Union policy and non-state environmental and social regulation in the areas of biofuels, fisheries, organic agriculture and fair trade. Other research projects deal with the emergence, uptake and evolution of private governance, and the governance of electronic waste.

Casey Stevens is a PhD candidate in the Department of Political Science at the University of Massachusetts-Amherst. His dissertation explores the forces that contribute to resilient governance in regional biodiversity governance projects. He is co-author with Peter M. Haas and Casey Stevens of 'Environmental Governance' (2011) in *Governing the Air: Science-Policy Interactions in International Air Policy* published by MIT Press and edited by Rolf Lidskog and Goran Sundquist.

Olav Schram Stokke, is based at the Department of Political Science at the University of Oslo and is also a Research Professor at the Fridtjof Nansen Institute, where he was Research Director from 1997–2003. He has been affiliated to the Centre for Advanced Study at the Norwegian Academy of Science and Letters, the International Institute of Applied Systems Analysis, and the University of Tromsø.

Stacy D. VanDeveer is an Associate Professor at the University of New Hampshire. His research interests include international environmental policymaking and its domestic impacts, the role of expertise in policymaking, and the politics of consumption and environmental and human rights degradation in global commodities markets. He co-edits the journal *Global Environmental Politics* (MIT Press). He has authored and co-authored over 70 articles, book chapters, working papers and reports, and six co-edited books on international and comparative environmental politics.

Preface

The idea for this book emerged during the project that lead to the creation of the book, *Emerging Forces in Environmental Governance* in 2004 (UNU Press). The project that produced the book ended in 2002 as it aimed at providing insights into the World Summit on Sustainable Development in 2002 in Johannesburg, but discussion about remaining tasks followed soon after. A few years later an opportunity arose when Peter, Steinar and myself got together to discuss concretely the idea of a new project to address issues related to emerging actors and environmental governance. While actual functioning of actor configurations has always been of academic interest to us, there was also practical concern around the time of the discussion with regard to the direction of the "beyond Kyoto" climate change institution. Following the initial conversation, a brainstorming meeting was held at the United Nations University office in New York in early 2007, when we came up with a clearer idea about the structure and focus of the project – identifying the best and worst practices of environmental governance in terms of configuration of actors. We figured that tri-continental leadership of Asia, the Americas and Europe makes the project even more legitimate by bringing different perspectives into the project.

The initial phase of the project was devoted to the development of methodological, conceptual and organizational framework, including identifying chapter authors for each governance component. After several rounds of discussion, we had the final planning session at the UNU office in New York from 18–20 February 2009. In that year, invitations were sent to the chapter authors and the project officially commenced. Apart from internet-based communications, a few meetings of the whole group were held back to back with International Studies Association annual conventions, in New Orleans in 2010 and in Montreal in 2011. The Great East Japan Earthquake and the Fukushima Daiichi Nuclear Power Plant Disaster hit Japan in 2011 and destroyed many things, including the process of the project. I can still recall the Montreal meeting in March 2011, when I decided to return to my family in Tokyo even before our presentation took place at the convention, as the situation after the explosion of the nuclear power plant was getting very serious. Still, we succeeded in bringing together contributions from the chapter authors and in drawing conclusions out of them during 2012. They were presented on a few occasions later that year and early in 2013.

The Introduction summarizes lessons from the experience of international environmental governance (IEG), and brings about conceptual framework for better understanding the best and worst practices in global environmental governance. We focus on the role and performance of different political actors and their networks in the activities of five governance components: agenda setting, negotiation, compliance, implementation and resilience. In addition, we investigate private partnerships as an alternative model of actor configurations, which has received increased importance in recent years. Chapters 2 to 7 address different governance components and private partnerships. The case studies span a variety of different environmental challenges. The cases selected are those that the principal investigators assigned to each component regarded as most salient for addressing the questions about the actors engaged in performing the components they studied. Each chapter does not describe the regimes in detail, but rather concentrates on the description of best and worst practices in terms of the perspective of actor configuration. Instead, a summary outline of the regimes is provided in the Annex. Before drawing a general conclusion, we present a chapter focusing on climate change, discussing whether the insights can improve the current global governance related to the issue of climate change. In the concluding chapter, we also propose a possible way forward to solve the climate issue.

We are grateful for the funding provided by Grant-in-Aid for Scientific Research(B) by the Ministry of Education, Culture, Sports, Science and Technology (MEXT), Japan (grant number 20310023), the Global Environmental Research Fund of the Ministry of Environment, Japan (S-6 and S-7), and the Mitsui & Co. Ltd. Environmental Fund. They supported the project in different stages. Towards the end of the project, our discussion was further facilitated by the funding provided by the Japan Foundation Center for Global Partnership (CGP).

A draft of the Introduction was presented at the Amsterdam Conference on Earth System Governance on 2 December 2009, the Transnational Conflicts and International Institution Unit, WZB in November 2009, the UMASS Amherst Department of Political Science Institutions and Governance workshop on 3 August 2010, Princeton University Niehaus Center on Globalization and Governance Workshop on International Relations and Climate Change on 19 February 2011, and the International Studies Association Meeting in Montreal on 17 March 2011. We thank Professor T.V. Paul and McGill University Department of Political Science for providing space for our workshop in Montreal. A draft of the conclusion was presented at the Yale Conference on Climate Change Governance without the United States, 9–10 November 2012, and the Earth System Governance Tokyo Conference, 28–31 January 2013. We appreciate all the comments and questions provided at these occasions. We are particularly grateful for the comments provided by Charli Carpenter, Marc Levy, Ron Mitchell, Craig Murphy, MJ Peterson, Jesse Rhodes, and Oran Young.

Thanks to IDDRI and SciencesPo, Paris, for their congenial support during his one-year stay in Paris from 2009 to 2010. The Marie Curie International Incoming

Fellowships of the European Commission, under the proposed project GAIA – Governance and Agents in Institutional Architecture on Climate and Energy – generously supported the entire duration of his stay in Paris. Peter Haas is grateful to the Wissenshaftzentrum Berlin.

Much administrative support was provided throughout the duration of the project. Thanks are due especially to Kanako Morita, Jun Oshima, Noriko Takemura, Motoko Fujii, Maki Koga, Maki Sato, Akira Ichikawa and the administrative staff at the Tokyo Institute of Technology. Masahiko Iguchi helped us at the final stage of the project when we were desperately in need of assistance in formatting and obtaining final information from the authors.

Putting this volume together has been a lot of fun. As we enjoyed working on the project, we hope readers will also enjoy the book.

On behalf of the co-authors,

Norichika Kanie
Tokyo, March 2013

1 Introduction

Actor configurations and global environmental governance

Peter M. Haas, Steinar Andresen and Norichika Kanie

The study of international environmental governance is now a well-established field of study, in political science and across other disciplines. Recent findings in International Environmental Governance (IEG) have emphasized the emergent equivalent of a division of labor amongst actors involved in environmental governance (Biermann and Pattberg 2012). Elsewhere in international relations (IR) attention has focused on the prevalence of transnational public–private partnerships and networks (Keohane and Nye 1971; Keohane and Nye 1974; Hall and Biersteker 2002; Kahler 2009; Schaferhoff *et al.* 2009) and even a new global pluralism (Cerny 2010). In this book we aim to move beyond a concern with partnerships of non-state actors, and of state and non-state actors, to develop a framework research program that will look at the effects of different configurations of political actors on environmental governance. As a consequence we seek to develop hypotheses about best and worst governance practices, as well as raising some suggestive puzzles that may advance our understanding of the interplay of political actors in environmental governance, and their ability to exercise agency. That is, what kinds of partnerships are most conducive to effective environmental governance, and what kinds are likely to inhibit effective environmental governance? Harold Saunders, a US diplomat, insightfully wrote: "Remember, policy isn't made on paper, it's a continually changing mix of people and ideas" (Saunders 2005: 45).

This chapter summarizes lessons from IEG, and helps develop a research protocol for better understanding best and worst practices for global environmental governance. It focuses on the role of different political actors performing five governance components for addressing international environmental issues: agenda setting, rule making, compliance, implementation and resilience. It also investigates non-state partnerships and an alternative model of actor configurations. The volume stresses actors, agency, and networks. In conclusion, it asks what can be learned about IEG and proposes hypotheses on best and worst practices in environmental governance for further research. It is not just another effectiveness study. Rather, it seeks to develop a new focus on the interconnections between actors and actor groups in IEG, and discuss whether the insights can improve the current global governance system for climate change.

The lack of political will is often mentioned as an explanation for weak environmental governance. Our argument is that through the clever mobilization of political actors to perform governance components, states may be induced to develop a stronger will to cooperate and protect the international environment. This volume analyzes green pluralist governance, trying to better understand the extent to which configurations of different actor groups contribute to, or inhibit, better international environmental governance.

The contemporary context

Globalization in many of its guises constitutes an ontological transformation of the contemporary international system. In this introductory chapter we consider two key features of globalization: the proliferation of actors, and the growing international concern about governance of shared and transboundary environmental threats. These features shape the politics of IEG, and to some extent are more clearly visible in IEG than other global issues, thus providing a laboratory for understanding contemporary international relations more generally.

While "globalization" itself remains contested, the core driving forces which shape choices and understandings within the current setting are widely believed to include the following features (Grande and Pauly 2005; Biermann and Pattberg 2008; Cerny 2010):

1   The nation state has lost a monopoly over the sovereign control of policy.
2   Most actors believe that transboundary and global threats require cooperation.
3   There is a large-scale diffusion of non-state actors who participate in the decision-making process. MNCs, IOs, scientific networks and NGOs are actor groups that compete for attention in international diplomacy, as well as seeking to influence states.
4   Uncertainty is the dominant systemic condition facing actors.
5   Decisions are taken through multi-level governance that entails vertical, horizontal, temporal and networked linkages across and between scales.

Global environmental problems require some degree of collective governance for their management. Kennette Benedict provides a useful definition of the current application of "global governance" (2–3; Benedict 2001: 6232) which is also shared with the Commission on Global Governance (The Commission on Global Governance 1995: 2–3):

> a purposeful order that emerges from institutions, processes, norms, formal agreements, and informal mechanisms that regulate action for a common good. Global governance encompasses activity at the international, transnational and regional levels, and refers to activities in the public and private sectors that transcend national boundaries.

Governance entails a procedural component of administrative activities which diplomats frequently perform when designing institutional arrangements. Some of these components were initially identified as the 3Cs (cooperative environment, capacity building and building concern) by Haas *et al.* in 1993 (Haas *et al.* 1993), but the list has subsequently been extended and elaborated. Such components are now regarded as administrative activities that are performed in effective international governance, rather than phases of environmental governance, as in practice they overlap and there is no clear linear sequence with which they were performed (Kingdon 1995; The Social Learning Group 2001). These activities include agenda setting, issue framing, rule making, enforcement and assessment (Haas 2004; Kanie and Haas 2004; Speth and Haas 2006). Mark Zacher identifies a similar list of activities performed in United Nations governance of economic issues (Zacher 1999). We refer to a similar set of activities as governance components. We avoid the term "functions" in order to avoid confusion with functional analysis, as there is no clear analytic reason why states or other actors would value these functions. They remain analytic categories to focus our research.

A governance focus entails a shift in analytic scrutiny from the policies that may contribute to better management of the environment to the architectural design of collective action processes. While policy analysts argue about the appropriate policies for better management, considering the full array of governance components helps to understand the conditions under which integrated management is more likely to be widely applied. The United States National Research Council's Committee on the Human Dimensions of Global Change observes (Brewer and Stern 2005: 42):

> Analyzing environmental governance as a problem of institutional design is useful because it reframes the central governance question from one of selecting a single best governance strategy (e.g. choosing between top-down regulation and market oriented policies) to one that considers a full range of governance options and seeks to match institutional forms to specific governance needs.

In practice, these governance components are performed by a number of different groups of actors, including governments (or states), international organizations (IOs), multinational corporations (MNCs), nongovernmental organizations (NGOs), and scientists and scientific networks. Most effective governance in practice utilizes synergies from different groups that utilize institutionalized tensions amongst the parties, such as NGOs and MNCs in joint regulatory arraignments that yield more binding results than MNCs desire, and command stronger compliance than NGOs are able to achieve through selective political campaigns. As Grande and Pauly observe, the diffusion and influence of non-state actors has grown both in numbers, and in influence (Pauly and Grande 2005: 286; Betsill and Corell 2008).

To a large extent, IEG writings presaged the more general insights about globalization for the rest of IR. Some of the seminal IEG works were published in the early 1990s, identifying many of the general ontological features of the international political system which were mentioned above (Hurrell 1992; Choucri

1993; Choucri 1993a, 1993b; Haas 1993; Zürn 1998; Patterson 1999; Mitchell 2002; Dauvergne 2005; Betsill *et al.* 2006; Haas 2008). More recent work in IEG remains focused on aggregate reviews and comparisons of regimes (Young 1997; Zürn 1998; Breitmeier, Young *et al.* 2006; Young 2009) and does not break the regimes down into more discrete governance components, as we propose to do. While there is analysis in the literature of the involvement of individual actor groups (Biermann and Pattberg 2012), none looks at the positive and negative consequences of different configurations.

The 1992 United Nations Conference on Environment and Development (UNCED), with its parallel NGO congress, provided the foundations for the participation of a variety of actor groups in governance. A key recent finding is the wide array of actors that participate in governance, and the different components that governance entails. In addition, it has been demonstrated that the presence of scientific networks (epistemic communities) and strong international organizations yield distinctively comprehensive negotiated outcomes and more effective regimes (Meyer 1997; Andresen *et al.* 2000; Miles 2002; Haas and Kanie 2004; Busch, Jorgens *et al.* 2005; Haas 2007). Networks have proven to be more effective than formal hierarchical designs in providing compliance with international regimes as well (Victor *et al.* 1998; Oberthur and Gehring 2006).

In short, over the last thirty years there has been a significant shift in terms of practice and academic attention to the widespread involvement of multiple non-state actors in the activity of global governance. Recent findings from outside IEG confirm these broad foundational observations. Outcomes – in terms of framing and negotiated settlements – vary by institutional venue (Feinberg 1988; McNamara 2004; Alter and Meunier 2006; Alter and Meunier 2009), and institutions vary by membership, so that actor variation influences outcomes. Recently Abbott and Snidal have talked about the variation of effects that can be explained by analyzing configurations of actor groups (Abbott and Snidal 2009). While most analysts have looked at the effect of individual groups, or at most two groups, we focus on the configurations of multiple different political actors.

The significant research question remains, *which actors and combinations of actors are best at performing which governance components, and under what circumstances will they be able to perform those components?*

Actors and networks

A distinct set of categories of political actors, or actor groups, has emerged over the last thirty years. In addition to traditional nation states, international organizations (IOs), nongovernmental organizations (NGOs), multinational companies (MNCs), and scientists have all emerged as significant actors in IEG. In the following section we specify typical characteristics of each actor group, describing their general motivations, resources, preferred political strategies, and impacts. Given the extensive empirical and theoretical focus on agency in IR and IEP, identifying the salient political feature of each political group seems warranted.

In this section we summarize the important classes of actor groups in IEG, and provide theoretically informed deductive theorizing about their likely preferences and behavior. We focus on the missions and resources available to each actor group in order to derive their likely independent behaviors. Configurations are then designed based on affinities between actor groups, and also to take advantage of creative adversarial relations (such as between NGOs and MNCs in compliance and enforcement). In addition we provide links to secondary literature and empirical studies to confirm that most of the actor groups behave consistently with the presumed patterns.

By focusing on the participation of actors we seek to accomplish three analytic tasks. One, is to take an analytic stance that stresses agency rather than structure. Second, we hope to complement the extensive literature on functions of governance with a political understanding of who performs or executes governance components, and who is capable of performing them. Third, the behavior of particular actors informs the political impulse behind the performance of governance components. Certain configurations, or partnerships, presumably, will provide the political impulse behind better or worse performance of governance components.

States

States remain the legitimate sovereign actors in IEG, and although the significance of states in IEG has been reduced, their role should not be underestimated. Yet states are increasingly losing the ability to exercise control over activities within their own territories, and thus have to rely on consultations with other actors to ensure that policies are achieved. Moreover, states are, by choice or not, ceding authority in IEG to other actors.

Most IR theorizing about states presumes that they act rationally, based on accurate cost/benefit assessments of the likelihood that their environmental policy reforms will be reciprocated by others and that the jointly faced environmental problem will be resolved in a way that the net benefits exceed the costs to each country (Sprinz and Vaahtoranta 1994; Underdal 1998). Because IEG is a collective action problem, smaller countries are only likely to support governance measures if stronger countries set the pace, as otherwise their own unilateral efforts will fail. The only exceptions are what Arild Underdal calls "leadership through unilateral action," in which middle powers exert leadership by showing example, but then often those countries rely on the relatively strong power of coalition they belong to, or on structural power such as the EU (Underdal 2004; Kanie 2003). Still, while behavioral research demonstrates that some countries behave as "leaders" whereas others remain "followers" or on the sidelines, it is difficult *ex ante* to specify which countries will follow which role. Nonetheless, without some countries exercising leadership, meaningful governance is unlikely (Andresen and Agrawala 2002). While state leadership may be an important factor in providing international public goods, the determinants of state leadership – indeed of political *will* – follows from the configuration of influences on the states.

Environmental nongovernmental organizations (ENGOs)

Environmental nongovernmental organizations (ENGOs) have become common-place participants in international environmental diplomacy, becoming frequent participants at international meetings, and being invited to cooperate with project development as well as delivery (Weiss and Gordenker 1996; Fox and Brown 1998; Betsill and Corell 2008) and are analytically similar to the broader universe of all NGOs. In the following paragraphs ENGOs refer to specifically environmental NGOs, whereas NGOs relates to the properties of all NGOs. By ENGOs we refer to individual not-for-profit non-state-based organizations that are interested in environmental protection. They are distinct from networks of such organizations mobilized around a common goal or belief (transnational actor networks), and are less formally organized or strategically motivated than social movements and groups that share a broader set of political values or identities (Tarrow 1994; Della Porta and Diani 2006). Civil society lacks the homogeneity of individual ENGOs, and is probably best analytically treated as a disparate array of NGOs, or network of similar NGOs (Rohrschneider and Dalton 2002; Bartelson 2006).

ENGOs encompass a vast array of political actors performing different components, from domestic consciousness raising and development efforts (as is common in LDCs), to international pressure, lobbying and education at international conferences and negotiations (Chasek 1995; Chasek 2001; Yamin 2001; Fisher 2004; Betsill and Corell 2008; Chasek and Wagner 2012; Gulbrandsen and Andresen 2004). Weiss and Gordenker provide a broad conceptual taxonomy of three components performed by NGOs (Weiss and Gordenker 1996): activist NGOs that engage in publicity campaigns; more establishment and administrative NGOs that carry out projects on the ground; and think-tanks.

ENGOs can be treated as organizations that seek to advance their mission through the acquisition of material resources. Specific ENGOs vary as to whether they develop principled missions which they seek to pursue, or whether they choose their missions strategically based on the potential availability of resources for that niche. Regardless, the basic constraints under which NGOs principally operate are economic. Few NGOs have stable funding sources, so are dependent upon foundations, foreign-aid agencies, and member contributions for financial support. Consequently the NGOs are faced with incentives to differentiate themselves for funders, and to constantly present themselves as offering a new agenda or approach. Thus they face incentives to exaggerate risks, and to engage in high-profile demonstrations and publicity events to attract media attention. It is important to note the difference between Western European based ENGOs and the US ENGOs as the former often receive substantial financing from the government. It has been argued that they are more integrated in decision-making as well as more influential than their US counterparts (Vig and Faure 2004).

The primary resources available to NGOs consist of their ability to mobilize and educate mass publics on behalf of their principled beliefs, often through transnationally coordinated campaigns (Keck and Sikkink 1998), national lobbying, and providing information to weak delegations at international meetings (Betsill and Corell 2008). It has been argued that lobbying at the domestic level is often more effective than international lobbying and that think-tank strategy of providing information and work on the "inside" is often more effective than the activist strategy (Andresen and Skodvin 2008; Gulbrandsen and Andresen 2004).

Significant examples of NGO participation in governance include the anti-MAI (multilateral agreement on investment) movement, anti-landmines movement, as well as how FIELD supported AOSIS in the UNFCCC negotiations. A clear counterfactual underscores the NGO influence in climate change diplomacy. Although the overall influence may have been very modest, the impact is greater when they were in alliance with states (in this case, the US Clinton administration); without the legal support of FIELD, AOSIS wouldn't have had the discursive legitimacy in negotiations to push the issue, and the UNGA would not have supported the initiative (Gulbrandsen and Andresen 2004; Graz and Nolke 2008).

Multinational corporations (MNCs)

The private sector and in particular multinational corporations (MNCs) also play a key role in environmental governance. Surprisingly few MNCs played high-profile roles before the World Business Council on Sustainable Development was mobilized by Stephen Schmidheiny for the 1992 Rio Earth Summit, possibly because most companies tended to discount international regimes coming from the UN, and preferred to rely on their existing networks of lobbying at the national level.

MNCs potentially play significant roles in international environmental governance, through their control over environmental technologies, and decisions about R&D and investment in future technologies. Ultimately, the decision about what kind of factory and how clean it will be rests on calculations taken at the level of the firm.

Firms, of course, are rational economic actors that seek to maximize long-term profits. In practice this means that there is some degree of heterogeneity amongst firms and their preferences (Murphy 2004; Shanahan and Khagram 2006). Large, low- cost and profitable companies will favor environmental protection, as it will help them consolidate market positions vis-à-vis higher cost, less efficient or profitable firms. Conversely, less productive firms will be resistant to anything that will add to their production costs. Moreover, global firms are most likely to be responsive to pressure in markets in which they are most exposed and where consumers are more environmentally inclined. For instance, Greenpeace adroitly deployed its Brent Spar campaign against Shell in Germany, where consumers were greener and Shell was reliant for a relatively large share of its profits, rather than in the UK, where Shell had its headquarters but consumer concern was more muted and market exposure was less (Dickson and McCulloch 1996; *Financial Times* 1995).

Because of their economic orientation, firms prefer market oriented policies. By and large companies have preferred to support voluntary sectoral guidelines for environmental governance, working at times with the UNEP industry liaison office in Paris, which lays out best environmental practices (BEPs) and best available technologies (BATs) for particular sectors. They argue that such voluntary guidelines are better over time, by not locking companies into potentially obsolete technologies and inhibiting R&D. On the other hand, voluntary guidelines such as these have no enforcement mechanisms, and, as Harrison and Vogel have found, actual adherence to social standards by companies are mixed (Harrison 1999; Vogel 2005). Ultimately their primary goal is to maximize profits, and accountability rests on shareholders. Prakash's work on ISO standards finds that these standards have led to internal reorganization and profits for the ISO certifying companies, but there is little evidence of actual change in environmental outcomes (Prakash and Potoski 2006a, 2006b).

Corporate environmental responsibility appears to vary by types of company. For instance, the energy industry is split on climate change, with BP, Shell and Texaco now recognizing climate change science and calling for GHG reductions, while Exxon continues its denial (Saeverud and Skjaerseth 2007). The corporate leaders – those that endorse strong uniformly applied environmental standards and apply them in their own actions – are those that are economically profitable, have strong brand identification, and rely on environmentally concerned consumer markets in the North as well as the emerging low-carbon market in the South for a large proportion of their profits. These companies tend to call for environmental governance, and apply uniform corporate practices throughout their activities worldwide, as well as seeking to impose them on other companies throughout their supply chains (Levy and Prakash 2003; Levy and Newell 2005; Prakash and Potoski 2006a, 2006b; Auld *et al.* 2008).

International organizations (IOs)

International institutions, or as we address in the current usage, international organizations (IOs), also play a significant role in IEG. IOs operate in two ways. First is through their contextual effects, by providing incentives for states and other actors within their aegis. This is the argument laid out by most scholars of international institutions (Keohane and Martin 1995; Koremonos *et al.* 2001; Hawkins *et al.* 2006). Strong IOs can place issues on the agenda through publicity and convening conferences, shape negotiated outcomes, and promote compliance.

It remains an ongoing debate within the IR literature as to why some IOs are strong and others are weak. Is it a matter of state choice at the founding, the configuration of actors and their networks in the domain in which the IO operates, through some skillful leadership of the secretariat to carve out a new niche over time, or what? For instance, the UNCSD was designed to be weak, whereas the World Bank and UNEP were designed with more autonomous leeway to evolve over time in ways that were not directly controlled by member states (Haas 1990; Biermann and Siebenhuner 2009).

A second way of looking at IOs is as deliberative actors capable of agency. The secretariats have motivations and resources that they choose to apply to environmental governance (Haas and Haas 1995; Biermann and Siebenhuner 2009). Such IOs are able to inform IEG in several ways: they help set agendas, they inform national positions and thus shape the form of negotiated outcomes, and help to diffuse ideas through governments, other IOs, and even other actors with whom they interact. Thus they enjoy an indirect yet ultimately transformative effect on IEG by developing and transferring new ideas.

Determining whether IOs are likely and able to exercise agency on their own is a function of their administrative properties (Haas 1990; Haas and Haas 1995; Biermann and Siebenhuner 2009). IOs with institutional autonomy from member states, strong executive leadership, adequate budgets, professional secretariats, and porous organizational boundaries that facilitate information flow with epistemic communities are most likely to be active autonomous actors in IEG. IOs with an independent secretariat and access to broader expert knowledge outside the IO have been capable of learning and of steering the behavior of their member states (Haas and Haas 1995; Biermann and Siebenhuner 2009).

Organized science

Organized science of course plays a key role in environmental governance as well. Influential individuals like Al Gore and Gro Harlem Brundtland have both endorsed scientific management as a guideline for environmental governance, and such views about the need for scientific input to environmental decision-making is widespread amongst policy makers. Science is particularly important in the agenda setting. It is hard to envisage how various environmental problems would have been discovered in the absence of science. Moreover, it is equally hard to envisage environmental management in the absence of scientific knowledge. The alternative is that management should be based on only political and economic factors. This is not to say that science is necessarily very influential on management decisions as science is not the only legitimate decision premise to consider. It has been documented fairly well, however, that if scientific consensus is attained, the chances of scientific influence increases considerably (Haas 1990; Andresen *et al.* 2000; Haas 2008; Haas and Stevens 2011). Generally, scientific influence also increases, the more politically "benign" the problem, while the scientists often face an uphill battle when problems are malign (Andresen and Skjærseth 2007).

The key role of scientists in epistemic communities has been given particular emphasis. Work on epistemic communities has demonstrated their necessary role in promoting more effective agendas and negotiated settlements. Under conditions of uncertainty by state decision makers and when epistemic communities exist, the decision makers are likely to delegate to the experts and derive agendas and policy alternatives from them (Haas 2013). Further work on institutional design for epistemic communities has demonstrated that epistemic communities are most effective when they are mobilized through standing, independent, international and interdisciplinary environmental panels (Haas 2004). As such they tap into knowledge from beyond individual scientific disciplines, yet do not get subsumed within civil society or captured by other actors.

Networks

A key question for our analysis is how configurations of actors organize themselves. Governance is increasingly networked (Ansell and Weber 1999; Coleman and Perl

1999; Castells 2000, 2005; Slaughter 2004; Weber *et al.* 2007; Jordana *et al.* 2011; Levi-Faur 2011). Networks are distinct from hierarchies (and anarchies) because lower level units can make choices about policies and associations occurring at higher levels – the state or at the international level (Eilstrup-Sangiovanni and Jones 2008). Some putative virtues of networked governance are their efficient communication and information processing, as well as their scalability by transferring information and resources across scales and scope, while remaining immune to hierarchical control. Networks are much more adaptive to changes in the world, resilient because of their internal redundancies and the persistence of institutional arrangements over time, and conducive to learning due to the reflective and reflexive nature of many of the network members. Oran Young argues that complex systems are better managed through networks, as networks are able to generate more diffuse information, and avoid organizational capture (and are thus more resistant to collective action problems) by special interests (Young 2010). The key feature of networked governance is its emergent properties.

Networks are not just a combination of actors, but form an entirely new set of political influences. The whole may be greater than the sum of the parts, and the interactions of the parts (either actors' participation or the performance of governance components) can trigger social mechanisms and outcomes beyond the potential of the individual forces. For instance, social learning is a possible emergent property of networked multilevel governance.

Despite the intuitive notion that networks are robust and sustainable social institutions, this may not be the case in IEG. Networks have mobilized around specific treaties, rather than around regimes, and overall governance is heavily differentiated. Given the relative paucity of informed non-state participants in agenda setting and negotiating settlements, networks may prove fragile as individuals are scooped up for issues that command more resources. For instance, climate change, biodiversity and the millennium ecosystem assessment were competing to recruit experts. The epistemic community that was influential in developing the land-based sources protocol in the Mediterranean in 1980 drifted away, as institutional resources dried up and more professional opportunities appeared for dealing with other global environmental threats.

Globalization implies greater network linkages, as well as greater numbers of actors involved in governance (Kanie and Haas 2004; Grewal 2008; Haffner-Burton, Kahler *et al.* 2008; Siebenhuner 2008; Kahler 2009).

In this project we ask several sets of questions about how the configuration of actor groups is organized. Not all configurations need be networks, although networks are organizationally superior institutional arrangements because they are more enduring. We ask:

1   Are actors involved together on an ongoing basis as a network, or are the configurations merely a brief organization of convenience, such as is the case with Sabatier's advocacy coalitions (Sabatier and Jenkins-Smith 1993)? Networks are closer to concepts of community or *gemeinschaft*, whereas brief coalitions are closer to concepts of *gesselschaft*.

2   By what means or techniques is collective action sustained within the grouping of actors? How do they exchange information, raise resources, and interact in ways that expedite their performance of governance configurations?

3   Who do various actor groups believe should be members of the network, and who shouldn't be members? This question is elaborated below in the discussion of resilience and legitimacy. The underlying question is with whom actor groups would be willing to be associated when engaged in international environmental governance.

4   Which actors serve as hubs in the networks? Are all actor groups equal?

5   What is the glue that holds configurations together?

6   Did the configurational network have a significant influence over the governance component? Was the influence beneficial or negative?

Few works on networks have meaningfully answered these questions about the nitty gritty of how they are organized. We seek to relate the work on configurations to the networks literature in order to augment its insights into the organization of diffuse actors seeking to pursue collective action. Partnerships, discussed separately, are a special form of configuration and network.

Governance components and partnerships

Overall environmental governance has to do with the development and enforcement of collective obligations to deal with particular problems. As noted, to a large extent this has been approached analytically through studies of the effectiveness of international regimes. Various approaches have been developed, but we shall not go into the merits and shortcomings of them here as this is *not* another "effectiveness project." We use the insights gained from the many existing comprehensive studies; although there are nuances in the picture, generally there is agreement in the research community as well as among policy makers on the performance of various regimes. Our approach here is that governance is not a homogeneous activity. Recent studies have clearly demarcated distinct governance components which must be performed in order for environmental governance writ large to be effective (Clark *et al.* 2001; Haas and Kanie 2004). As we have listed before, these governance components include: agenda setting, negotiations, compliance, implementation and resilience. While there is no linear sequence to their performance – they are often concurrent or even cyclical – good environmental outcomes are associated with good performance of each (Kingdon 1995; Clark *et al.* 2001). Another distinct feature in recent developments in environmental governance is the increasing number of partnerships between and among actor groups (Clapp 1998; Bernstein and Cashore 2007; Chan and Pattberg 2008). Although different from the concept of governance components, partnerships are a crosscutting governance phenomenon that emerges in all components of governance, as well as across them, and influence overall governance effectiveness. In this sense, attention has to be paid to partnerships as well in the absence of any state involvement.

We remain agnostic about the path dependence or lock-in effects of each component, or of the larger-scale political involvement of actors from any one component to others. These path-dependent questions will remain open empirical questions, to be addressed further upon the completion of more focused studies on the performance of each component by different configurations of actors. Agenda setting is most likely to have a close connection to negotiations, because agenda setting helps establish the array of choices over which actors fight, as well as privileging the institutional venues in which negotiations will occur. Compliance may also positively contribute to implementation by increasing the number of actors pressuring states and other actors to enforce their commitments on the ground, as well as providing more resources for implementation. The causal distance between agenda setting and implementation or enforcement is probably too long to make a discernible difference. Compliance and implementation may have a feedback effect on agenda setting as actors reflect and learn about the concrete difficulties associated with addressing the environmental problems in question (Majone and Wildavsky 1978), although this causal link is not pursued in the chapters.

Agenda setting

Agenda setting is the process of collectively identifying a set of problems that require some actions by delimiting (or denoting) the salient features of an environmental threat for collective attention following, or anticipating, a catalyzing crisis. Agenda setting helps establish the frame within which problems are addressed: defining the parameters of meaningful action as well as delimiting the array of appropriate representation in terms of presumptive institutional venues and actors who should participate in governance. Without a good agenda-setting process, problems will not be efficiently defined, and governance will probably be ineffective because it will not address the core problems. Key for good agenda setting is an agenda that reflects political and technical realities, and a broad enough coalition formed through the conferences to keep political momentum afoot. Technically, an accurate agenda should avoid false positives and false negatives. False positives – false alarms – divert scarce resources and undermine the legitimacy of the governance efforts. False negatives – missed problems – allow problems to grow and also undermine the legitimacy of governance efforts. Good agenda setting requires a means for assessing claims about potential environmental harm, and publicizing the accurate assessments.

Good agenda setting has both a technical and a political component. It generates an agenda which is subsequently confirmed: both accurately identifying threats as well as confidently rejecting issues which are not threats. In addition it identifies problems that are politically tractable for collective management. Bad agenda setting, in turn, consists of agendas that are inaccurate.

In the agenda-setting chapter, agenda setting is treated as a long-term iterated process that develops over the span of a regime. Thus it is a matter of trial and error correction, where better agenda setting is related to the involvement of salient stakeholders and actor groups able to articulate stronger political and technical agendas.

Agenda setting can be seen as a sequential process (Mitchell 2009), but it can also be seen as a less-linear development of continuous processes. In practice, one can think of cases of linear or sequential agenda setting (i.e. ozone and LRTAP), cyclical agenda setting (i.e. Baltic), and parallel (such as climate change). The sequential process is a standard linear one, where the agenda is set and then decisions are taken subsequently based on that agenda. Cyclical processes involve continued interactions between the components, with the agenda being modified over time in light of changes in other components. Parallel is where each of the components is occurring simultaneously. Most agenda setting is continuous when viewed over time, as new problems emerge requiring attention and the modification of prior governance arrangements. The analysis here is based on the linear and cyclical experience.

Judging whether an agenda is "good" or "bad" can be done in two ways.[1] The determination can be done *post-hoc*, to see if the warnings were supported by subsequent events.[2] Second, judging agenda setting can be done procedurally, whether the putative problems were recognized and presented in a way consistent with the inter-subjective consensual understandings of the relevant policy communities.

Negotiated settlements

Negotiated settlements involve the process by which parties create collective arrangements for environmental management, be they hard law, soft law, or voluntary commitments. Although various types of partnerships and other new approaches are becoming increasingly important, the traditional "hard-law" MEAs are still the dominant mode of negotiation (Andresen *et al.* 2012). While states usually play a small role in the agenda-setting stage, they are the key actors in this stage (Andresen and Agrawala 2002). Focusing on the process of negotiations represents a large branch of international relations studies through negotiation theory (Hopmann 1996; Zartman 1994). Traditionally these scholars focused on states as "crystal balls" pursuing their national interests as rational unitary actors. This approach is still a large school in international relations, not least through the use of game theory. The rational choice approach may be useful in giving an initial overview of actors' main interests and positions and thereby predicting whether an agreement will be reached or not. However, in an increasingly globalized and complex world, additional perspectives are needed in order to assess how these processes evolve and what will eventually result from them (Hovi *et al.* 2003). Two-level games, state-society relations as well as leadership all loom large in more recent studies of complex international negotiations. This does not mean that we should underestimate the significance of the role played by the states in this particular phase as they – not the non-state actors – are the legitimate (elected) actors representing their respective constituencies.

Good settlements are those that mobilize political commitments of will and resources to dealing with the problems in a successful way. Bad ones are likely to inhibit subsequent progress, or reward opponents of meaningful cooperation. What determines the one or the other? Clearly that is a very complex question and cannot be answered generally as one size does not fit all. However, often the distribution between "pushers" and "laggards" is crucial (Miles *et al.* 2002). While the pusher seeks ambitious solutions, the laggard drags its feet. The more and stronger the (state) pushers, the greater the chances for a successful outcome of the negotiations. If the laggards dominate, we are bound to come closer to the "law of the least ambitious program" (Underdal 1980). The subsequent key question is what decides the distribution of laggards and pushers and by what mechanisms – if any – can it be influenced in a "positive" manner? Here we assume that the influence and inclusion of various non-state actors described above may make a difference in how states perceive their interests and how they choose to deploy their capabilities on behalf of those interests. In short, the involvement of non-state actors in negotiation may itself explain whether individual states become pushers or laggards, or if states' roles change (Sprinz and Vaahtoranta 1994; Connolly 1999).

Compliance

Compliance measures entail a variety of mechanisms to ensure that parties live up to their obligations. To study compliance is important because even seemingly "good" negotiation processes are no guarantee of success unless solid compliance mechanisms are elaborated (Victor *et al.* 1988; Chayes and Chayes 1993; Mitchell 1993; Young 1999; Dai 2002). Put crudely, there are two sets of approaches to secure compliance, "the carrot" approach and "the stick" approach (Mitchell 1993; Weiss and Jacobson 1998). The former yields various forms of assistance based on the assumption that this is a necessary condition for weaker parties, mostly in the South, in order to secure compliance. Towards that end, technological assistance and/or different funding mechanisms are provided for. The alternative or supplementary approach is based on the premise that some kind of punishment or threat of punishment is needed in order to secure compliance. Based on experiences from most major MEAs, it seems that the former mechanism is more effective than the latter, although threats of trade sanctions sometimes seem to have some effect (Victor *et al.* 1998; Barrett 2003). It may also be that various forms of "shaming" and "blaming" performed by ENGOs may be more effective than the formal sanctions provided by the MEA (Stokke *et al.* 2005). Our assumption is that some kind of assistance is needed to secure compliance in global agreements. In some instances ENGOs may play an important part in this process. If sanctions are to be used they have to be credible and carefully designed.

Other mechanisms are important to secure compliance as well. These can include information to deter noncompliance, or positive incentives to encourage compliance through capacity building. Good compliance measures are those that generate rule adherence, whereas bad ones deter compliance, or have no effect. A very practical low-key approach to contribute to good compliance is linked to national reporting and verification. Unless you have reasonably accurate and reliable information on relevant national data, the effectiveness of any measures adopted will be seriously hampered. Especially in the South, there may be difficulties in providing reliable data. Assistance in building national data inventories and capacity building by various types of expertise may therefore be necessary. However, countries in the South may sometimes be cautious in allowing foreign expertise to get access to what they may regard as sensitive data (Victor *et al.* 1998). Independent verification of national reports therefore remains a challenge.

Although good compliance performance normally points towards higher effectiveness, this is not always the case. The diagnosis of the problem may be wrong, as was the case in the Whaling Commission in the 1950s. Overall most Parties complied, but as long as the quotas set were far too high, the large whales were still depleted (Andresen *et al.* 2000). Moreover, compliance is often based on self-reporting and is not necessarily reliable.

Implementation

We need to address actual domestic implementation on the ground in order to fully understand the real effects of the regime. There are obvious overlaps between compliance and implementation as both deal with the extent to which rules and regulations adopted are actually followed up in practice. However, while compliance mostly deals with provisions elaborated at the international level, and is a favorite study of international lawyers, implementation is what is actually done at the domestic level to live up to international commitments. That is, domestic implementation is essentially the outcome when measuring regime effectiveness – behavioral change by relevant target groups caused by the regime in question. The extent to which implementation is successful is a function both of the will and ability of the actors concerned (Victor *et al.* 1998; Skjærseth 2000; Haas 1998, 2000; Checkel 2001). If the political will to live up to obligations is lacking – as witnessed in many international regimes – the effectiveness of the relevant regime is bound to be low. More interesting and relevant both politically and analytically is that even though political will is present, the ability to deliver on the ground is often hampered by vertical and horizontal disintegration among domestic institutions (Hanf and Underdal 1996; Heggelund *et al.* 2005).

What lessons stand out from various regimes in terms of performance in terms of implementation and why are some successful while others fail? One obvious explanatory factor is that some problems are much more "malign" than others. Crudely put, if costs are high and up-front affecting powerful actors while benefits are spread and diffuse, the chances for effective implementation are strongly reduced (Hanf and Underdal 1996). As climate change is a typically "malign" problem we need to control for problem structure when we apply lessons from other regimes in terms of implementation. In short, lessons from a regime regulating a "benign" issue area cannot simply be transposed to the climate regime as the two may simply not be comparable. For instance, the stratospheric ozone regime may not be a good model for climate change governance, although the stratospheric ozone regime does look more benign with the benefit of hindsight. At the domestic level, strong states can generally be expected to perform better than weak states – irrespective of issue area. Also, chances of good performance increase if the target groups affected are included early in the decision-making process – preferably also in the negotiation delegation. We will also look at the inter-linkage between implementation and compliance by studying how mechanisms to improve compliance can also help improve implementation. For example, measures to improve capacity building in weak states through the assistance of international organizations as well as ENGOs may contribute to improved implementation.

Resilience

Lastly, good governance must be resilient. It must be able to persist over time, past the initial political configurations that gave rise to regime creation. Less attention has been paid to resilience than the performance of other governance components. We define resilience here as the governance institution persisting over time and being able to accurately respond to new challenges. Resilience is akin to adaptive governance.

Resilience takes two forms in our research. One is an institutional form, as analyzed in the resilience chapter. The question here is whether resilience varies by institutional design. The second approach to resilience looks at the political dimension of resilience: namely the extent to which the actor configurations are seen as legitimate by those who are subject to influence by them.

Jutta Brunnee and Stephen J. Troope argue that "authoritative decisions, those which states will voluntarily comply with, come from processes which are legitimate and reflect shared understandings about values and causal mechanisms" (Brunnee and Toope 1997: 32). In practice this means that the collective procedures and the decision-making process of each actor group must be regarded as legitimate to all groups, and to their members (Cohen and Sabel 2006). In particular, for a governance arrangement to be resilient it must be regarded as legitimate by the majority of the significant producers of the environmental problem in question, including states, and who are willingly controlling their own behaviors at the international and domestic levels.

Legitimacy is a social fact, subject to the perceptions of those who are being asked to subordinate themselves to the choices taken by actor groupings (McNamara 2010). Yet, legitimacy remains a contested and vague concept (Bodansky 1999; Raines 2003; Bernstein 2004, 2011; Bernstein and Cashore 2007; Koppell 2010; Weale 2011). Opinions vary on what constitutes legitimacy, from processes, outputs, outcomes, to effects. For example, authors cite a transparent process (Keohane 2001), outcomes that are seen as fair (Young 1991; Mitchell *et al.* 2006), outcomes informed by socially authoritative actors (Dunlop 2000), if the outcomes are regarded as working (Vibert 2007), adversarial processes (Majone 2009) if the participatory arrangements are politically acceptable to the dominant states (Keohane 2002), to multidimensional measures of legitimacy that combine elements of each (Fung 2006).

In short, for governance arrangements to be resilient they must be perceived to be legitimate to the major actors involved in performing the governance components. Such perceptions can vary by actor; and indeed even possibly vary over time. Whereas weak states may value legitimacy according to measures of process, stronger states may measure it according to outcome measures. Non-state actors could value governance arrangements in terms of the underlying norms expressed, the degree to which they gain material benefits from participation, or have their own representative roles reinforced or legitimized through the governance arrangements.

Rather than specifying *ex ante* a measure of legitimacy, we ask each author to investigate what measures of legitimacy are cited by the actor groups within particular governance components.

Partnerships

In addition to the aforementioned five governance components, another factor which influences effectiveness of the performance of governance components is the emerging practice of partnerships. Numerous types of partnerships between actor groups have been explored in IEG. Partnerships or configurations of broad-based actor groups were part of the Rio Agenda 21 and Johannesburg outcome (Andonova 2010; Pattberg, Biermann *et al.* 2012). New types of market-based public–private and MNC–NGO partnership institutional arrangements have been widely entertained, particularly since the 2002 Johannesburg Summit. The reasons for this new focus are not clear, varying probably from continuing globalization, and the growing influence of non-state actors; as well as state dissatisfaction with regulatory environmental regimes and the growing post-Cold War dominance of market-based paradigms for all manner of issues on governance; or reluctance of the US to be engaged in MEAs. In practice, these partnerships take the form of multi-actor networks organized around particular issues, concurrently performing all governance components. Their form can vary from state–NGO–MNC, NGO–MNC to state–MNC partnerships (Andonova and Levy 2003; Schaferhoff *et al.* 2009).

This chapter looks at the distinctive features of non-state market-based partnerships. Such actor configurations are a recent form of actor configurations that warrant attention for dealing with global environmental threats, to better understand the full potential of actor configurations in the absence of state involvement.

Methods

This volume focuses on the determinants of good and bad governance in the performance of particular governance components. It is very much a plausibility probe to better appreciate the utility of applying a focus on configurations of actors, and to better understand and improve patterns of global environmental governance.

In this regard each chapter has a different dependent variable. In the conclusion we seek to aggregate these findings to a broader set of insights about international environmental governance, and apply those findings to climate change governance and discuss future governance architecture. While some authors may draw links between governance components, the research design for this project is primarily intended to focus on the determinants of effective governance of each component. The combination of governance components and the case of environmental governance practices are shown in Table 1.1.

Our presentation is based largely on qualitative research, looking at focused comparative case studies in the aggregate, and process tracing for individual regimes. In designing the research, we hoped for a multi-methods endeavor that would include large-*n* statistical studies of participation and performance effectiveness. However, given the vast numbers of potential actors, we could not find any meaningful databases that would allow us to measure or analyze independent and dependent variables in a statistically rigorous fashion. Most of the major existing data bases lack such discriminating coding (Mitchell 2003; Breitmeier *et al.* 2006; Oberthur and Gehring 2006; Breitmeier *et al.* 2011).

Our broad research enterprise has far too many variables to empirically test with confidence. There are at least fifteen possible configurations for each governance component, given the various combinations of actor groups that can conceivably perform the governance component. The numbers grow geometrically when we disaggregate the actor groups.

As there are no large-*n* data bases that code for participation, this enterprise is conceived of as a plausibility probe: articulating clear hypotheses/propositions and testing them in hard cases. Miles *et al.* follow a similar approach of focused comparative case studies, while confirming our sense that configurations of actors matter (Miles 2002).

Each chapter weighs hypotheses about the extensive secondary literature on IEG, and is based on considerations of the motivations and resources of each actor group. The descriptions of the empirical domain are drawn from authoritative sources in IEG. Hypotheses are drawn from all major schools of thought in international relations. Testing of the hypotheses should thus advance our understanding through developing overlapping findings from different research traditions, as well as developing further lines of inquiry about multilevel networked governance. The additional research queries are intended to refine the hypotheses and to clarify the domains in which each hypothesis is likely to operate.

Because our research design focuses on actor configurations within discrete governance components, we are unable to meaningfully address some key questions about international environmental governance. We cannot fully look at cross-scale effects. Moreover we cannot meaningfully consider dynamic effects over time or between governance components, because the analysis focuses on how governance components are affected by the configurations of actors within

Table 1.1 Cases covered in the volume

	Agenda setting	Negotiation	Compliance	Implementation	Resilience	Private governance
The Forest Stewardship Council						×
Marine Stewardship Council						×
Fair-trade Labeling Organization						×
E-Stewards Initiative						×
Convention on Long-Range Transboundary Air Pollution	×					
Convention on the Protection of the Marine Environment of the Baltic Sea Area	×					
Montreal Protocol on Substances that Deplete Ozone Layer and The Vienna Convention for the Protection of the Ozone Layer		×		×		
UN Convention to Combat Desertification		×		×		
Convention on the Prevention of Marine Pollution by Dumping of Wastes and Other Matter			×			
International Convention for the Prevention of Pollution from Ships			×			
Convention on the Future Multilateral Cooperation in North-East Atlantic fisheries			×			
Norwegian–Russian Joint Commission on Fisheries			×			
The Convention on Biological Diversity and the Cartagena Protocol on Biosafety		×		×	×	
Man and the Biosphere Programme					×	
The Conservation on International Trade in Endangered Species of wild Fauna and Flora				×	×	

each one. Nonetheless, because of the novelty and potential benefit of this analysis, the limited scope of this research design still appears warranted.

Based on existing IEG work, and insights from IR theory, we now offer some hypotheses about best and worst practices of environmental governance. We also augment these hypotheses with some queries which may focus attention on some key fruitful policy and theoretical questions to clarify our understanding of multilevel networked environmental governance. The following hypotheses about best and worst practices follow from our understandings of the nature of different actor groups, discussed above.

Hypotheses

Agenda setting

Most agenda setting comes from national laboratories and individual scientists. Most of the major monitoring sources – satellites, ships, networks of land-based laboratories – are administered by states and universities. Their work is publicized, amplified and simplified by NGOs, the media, and international assessment processes. IOs often help coordinate these networks. For the purpose of this study the media is treated as part of the private-sector actor group.

Agenda setting best practices hypothesis: Good agenda setting comes from combinations of science, NGOs, media and IOs.

Peer review can confer confident results, but entails a delay in providing prompt early warning of new threats. Epistemic communities should be involved in designing the networks to assure that the proper things are being monitored. Scientific diagnosis is often simplified to be made policy relevant by ENGOs and IOs.

Agenda setting worst practices hypotheses:

1   Agenda setting solely by ENGOs is likely to yield skewed results.
    ENGOs are likely to exaggerate risks and stress false positives. This follows from the description of ENGOs' constraints and motivations above as actors.
2   Agenda setting solely by MNCs is likely to yield skewed results.
    MNCs are likely to minimize risk, stress false negatives and underreport true positives. This follows from the description of MNCs' constraints and motivation above as actors.

Negotiated settlements

Negotiated settlements take many forms. Here we focus on hard law based on treaties between states.

Negotiated settlements best practices hypotheses:

1   The stronger the influence of pusher states, the higher the chances of effective negotiated settlements. Pusher states can provide capacity-building inducements to garner support from countries that need assistance.

2   The stronger "insider" NGOs lobby, the higher the chances of effective negotiated settlements. Insider ENGOs work for strong MEAs, but their influence can be expected to vary with the nature of the problem. Influence will often be modest in "malign" issue areas but can be higher in more "benign" issue areas.
3   Strong international organizations and epistemic communities are likely to generate effective negotiated settlements.

Such arrangements may have a dynamic effect on other governance components as well. Strong international organizations and epistemic communities may also engender learning by states and other IOs, and thus lead to more resilient collective management arrangements. If the epistemic community is primarily natural scientists, the negotiated settlements will be regulatory. If the epistemic community is primarily economists, the negotiated settlements will be market based.

Negotiated settlements worst practices hypotheses:

1   Negotiations in the absence of state leadership or strong international organizations will lead to ineffective least-common denominator outcomes.
2   Negotiated settlements conducted under the auspices of weak IOs, in the absence of any other actors, are likely to yield ineffective outcomes.
3   Treaties strongly influenced by activist ENGOs will take the form of principled declarations or moratoria and not be effective.

Compliance and implementation

Compliance is widely regarded as the weak reed of environmental governance. Treaties may have many strong components, but compliance procedures are often weak. Despite the fact that many treaties include provisions for arbitration and sanctions, and possibly even third-party inspections, these provisions are seldom invoked.

Compliance best practices hypotheses:

1   Vigorous capacity building by IOs or developed states can render more effective compliance in developing countries with weak states. Separate funding mechanisms, especially the Global Environmental Facility (GEF), may be most effective at facilitating compliance.
2   Independent scientific networks can provide impartial data about compliance, and thereby improve effectiveness via voluntary compliance by the verified. Similarly, good reporting and verification mechanisms, including direct and close contacts between national enforcement agencies, increase the chances of higher effectiveness. However, well-designed mechanisms are likely to operate by the active involvement of participating actor groups, rather than by dint of pure institutional design.
3   MNCs that anticipate net discounted benefits will comply and contribute to more effective compliance. Firms that will only enjoy benefits from

compliance in the future will be less likely to actively promote compliance than those who will enjoy more immediate benefits.

Compliance worst practices hypotheses:

1   No "activist" NGO involvement provides weak compliance by states and/or MNCs.
2   MNC involvement without countervailing pressure provides weak compliance.
3   Self reporting and no independent verification (by weak IOs or Business/ Industry groups) provide weak and inaccurate compliance.

Closely related to compliance is implementation. Compliance does not guarantee actual on-the-ground domestic enforcement. In order to fully understand the effects of the regime, we need to look into implementation.

Implementation best practices hypotheses:

1   Vigorous capacity building by IOs or developed states is likely to render more effective implementation in developing countries. Because weak states find it difficult to comply and implement international obligations, this same hypothesis applies for each component.
2   States with strong administrative capacity are likely to implement more effectively than weak states.
3   Implementation of multilateral commitments by states and business will be stronger if sub-national actors and stakeholders were included in negotiations. However, such involvement may have an effect on shaping the nature of the commitments which they are implementing, by design or through mere outputs.
4   Shaming and blaming by NGOs, amplified by media, may render higher effectiveness.
5   Scientific reporting can build or reinforce state implementation.

Implementation worst practice hypotheses:

1   Weak administrative capacity (of those who implement) renders low implementation.
2   Net discounted losers (MNCs) without countervailing forces (i.e. NGOs, IOs and science) will lead to low implementation.
3   If relevant stakeholders are not included in policy making and negotiations, implementation is likely to be low.
4   The higher the political and economic stakes involved, the lower the likely implementation.

Resilience

Truly resilient arrangements will have to reflect the legitimacy desires of all the major participating actors. The following hypotheses amplify these insights.

Resilience best practice hypotheses:

1   Major contributors (states, MNCs) to the problem need to be a part of the governance arrangements, either directly or indirectly, in order for the arrangements to be resilient.
2   The involvement of both strong IOs and epistemic communities is likely to foster resilient governance.

Resilience worst practice hypotheses:

1   Unrestrained NGO activities will weaken resilience.
2   Weak IOs combined with the absence of epistemic communities are likely to yield unresilient governance, as there will be no institutional memory.
3   The absence of key actors renders no resilience.

Networked partnerships

New types of market-based public–private and MNC–NGO partnership institutional arrangements have been widely adopted, particularly since the 2002 Johannesburg Summit. In practice these partnerships take the form of multi-actor networks organized around particular issues, concurrently performing all governance components.

Market-based partnerships best practice hypotheses:

1   MNCs and NGOs in an adversarial setting are likely to yield demanding guidelines.
2   Certificate schemes work best when there is third-party verification.

Market-based partnerships worst practices hypotheses:

1   IOs and MNCs are likely to develop relatively weak (undemanding) market-based guidelines.
2   Soft negotiated arrangements without any form of third-party oversight are likely to yield unverifiable and ineffective governance.
3   State and MNCs partnerships are unlikely to have discernible environmental impact.

Conclusion

Understanding current patterns of multilevel networked governance requires an analysis of the configurations of actors performing environmental governance components. In this chapter we offered a number of hypotheses regarding best and worst practices in the design of governance components to improve overall environmental governance drawn from existing studies on international relations. The hypotheses will be discussed in the ensuing chapters and the findings will be applied to understanding and improving climate change governance.

Multilevel networked governance may also generate emergent properties. The analytic Catch 22 of studying emergent properties is how can one theorize about unintended or unpredictable consequences of social interactions? We have laid out some hypotheses about processes that are likely to engender such change, which we will then investigate empirically.

Notes

1   In this chapter good and bad are judged in terms of improving environmental quality of the given issue area.
2   For this class of cases a Cassandra effect is unlikely to influence the judgment of agenda setting. Because environmental harm is almost certainly likely to occur after early warning signs are observed, and because protecting the environment requires behavioral change, merely announcing the likelihood of a threat is unlikely to lead directly to behavioral change and thus one would not observe bad agenda setting.

References

Abbott, K. W. and Snidal, D. (2009) 'The Governance Triangle', in W. Mattli and N. Woods, *The Politics of Global Regulation*, Princeton, NJ: Princeton University Press, 44–88.

Alter, K. J. and Meunier, S. (2006) 'Nesting and Overlapping Regimes in the Transatlantic Banana Trade Dispute', *Journal of European Public Policy*, 13(3), 362–382.

Alter, K. J. and Meunier, S. (2009) 'The Politics of International Regime Complexity', *Perspectives on Politics*, 7(1), 13–24.

Andonova, L. B. (2010) 'Public–Private Partnerships for the Earth', *Global Enviornmental Politics*, 10(2), 25–53.

Andonova, L. B. and M. A. Levy (2003) 'Franchising Global Governance, Making Sense of the Johannesburg Type II Partnerships', in O. S. Stokke and Ø. B. Thommessen, *Yearbook of International Co-operation on Environment and Development 2003/2004*, London: Earthscan Publications, 19–31.

Andresen, S. and Agrawala, S. (2002) 'Leaders, pushers and laggards in the making of the climate regime', *Global Environmental Change*, 12, 41–51.

Andresen, S. and Skjaerseth, J. B. (2007) 'Science and Technology: From Agenda Setting to Implementation', in D. Bodansky, J. Brunnee and E. Hey, eds, *The Oxford Handbook of International Environmental Law*, Oxford: Oxford University Press, pp. 182–205.

Andresen, S., Boasson, E. L. and Honneland, G. (2012) *International Environmental Agreements*, London: Routledge.

Andresen, S., Skodvin, T., Underdal, A. and Wettestad, J. (2000) *Science and Politics in International Environmental Regimes*, Manchester: Manchester University Press.

Ansell, C. K. and Weber, S. (1999) 'Organizing International Politics: Sovereignty and Open Systems', *International Political Science Review*, 20(1), 73–93.

Auld, G., Bernstein, S. and Cashore, B. (2008) 'The New Corporate Responsibility', *Annual Review of Environment and Resources*.

Barrett, S. (2003) *Environment and Statecraft*, Oxford: Oxford University Press.

Bartelson, J. (2006). 'Making Sense of Global Civil Society', *European Journal of International Relations*, 12(3), 371–396.

Benedict, K. (2001) 'Global Governance', in N. J. Smelser and P. B. Baltes, eds, *International Encyclopedia of the Social and Behavioral Sciences*, New York: Pergamon Press, pp. 6232–6237.

Bernstein, S. (2004) 'Legitimacy in Global Environmental Governance', *Journal of International Law & International Relations*, 1(1–2), 139–166.

Bernstein, S. (2011) 'Legitimacy in Intergovernmental and Non-state Global Governance', *Review of International Political Economy,* 18(1), 17–51.

Bernstein, S. and Cashore, B. (2007) 'Can Non-state Global Governnance be Legitimate?' *Regulation & Governance*, 1, 347–371.

Betsill, M., Hochstetler, K. and Stevis, D., eds (2006) *Palgrave Advances in International Environmental Politics*, London: Palgrave.

Betsill, M. M. and Corell, E., eds (2008) *NGO Diplomacy*, Cambridge, MA: MIT Press.

Biermann, F. and Pattberg, P. (2008) 'Global Environmental Governance: Taking Stock, Moving Forward', *Annual Review of Environment and Resources*, 33.

Biermann, F. and Pattberg, P., eds. (2012) *Global Environmental Governance Reconsidered*, Cambridge, MA: MIT Press.

Biermann, F. and Siebenhuner, B., eds (2009) *Managers of Global Change*, Cambidge, MA: MIT Press.

Bodansky, D. (1999) 'The Legitimacy of International Governance', *American Journal of International Law*, 93(3), 596–624.

Breitmeier, H., Underdal, A. and Young, O. R. (2011) 'The Effectiveness of International Environmental Regimes: Comparing and Contrasting Findings from Quantitative Research', *International Studies Review*, 13(1), 1–27.

Breitmeier, H., Young, O. R. and Zurn, M. (2006) *Analyzing International Environmental Regimes*, Cambridge, MA: MIT Press.

Brewer, G. and Stern, P. C., eds (2005) *Decision Making for the Environment*, Washington, DC: National Academies Press.

Brunnee, J. and Toope, S. J. (1997) 'Environmental Security and Freshwater Resources', *American Journal of International Law*, 91(1).

Busch, P.-O., Jorgens, H. and Tews, K. (2005) 'The Global Diffusion of Regulatory Instruments: The Making of a New International Environmental Regime', *The Annals of the American Academy of Political and Social Science*, 598, 146–167.

Castells, M. (2000) *The Rise of the Network Society*, Malden, MA: Blackwell Publishing.

Castells, M. (2005) 'Global Governance and Global Politics', *PS*, 9–16.

Cerny, P. C. (2010) *Rethinking World Politics*, Oxford: Oxford University Press.

Chasek, P. (1995) 'Environmental Organizations and Multilateral Diplomacy', in J. P. J. Muldoon, *Multilateral Diplomacy and the United Nations Today*, Boulder, CO: Westview Press.

Chasek, P. S. (2001) *Earth Negotiations: Analyzing Thirty Years of Environmental Diplomacy*, Tokyo: United Nations University Press.

Chasek, P. S. and Wagner, L. M., eds (2012) *The Roads from Rio*, Washington DC: RFF Press.

Chayes, A. and Chayes, A. H. (1993) 'On Compliance', *International Organization*, 47(2), 175–206.

Checkel, J. T. (2001) 'Why Comply', *International Organization,* 55(3): 553–588.

Choucri, N. (1993a) 'Environmentalism', in J. Krieger, *The Oxford Companion to Politics of the World*, New York: Oxford University Press, 267–271.

Choucri, N. (1993b) *Global Accord*, Cambridge, MA, MIT Press.

Chan, S. and P. Pattberg (2008) 'Private Rule Making and the Politics of Accountability', *Global Enviornmental Politics* 8(3): 103–121.

Clapp, J. (1998) 'The Privatization of Global Environmental Governance: ISO 14000 and the Developing World', *Global Governance*, 4(3), 295–316.

Clark, W. C., Eijndhoven, J. V. and Jager, J. (2001) *Social Learning and the Management of Global and Transboundary Risks*, Cambridge, MA: MIT Press.

Cohen, J. and Sabel, C. F. (2006) 'Global Democracy?' *New York University Journal of Law and Politics*, 37, 763–797.

Coleman, W. D. and Perl, A. (1999) 'Institutionalized Policy Environments and Policy Network Analysis', *Political Studies,* XLVII, 691–709.

Connolly, B. (1999) 'Symmetrical Rivalry in Common Pool Resources and European Responses to Acid Rain', in J. S. and G. E. S. Barkin, *Anarchy and the Environment*, Albany, NY: SUNY.

Cooper, A.F., Higott, R.A. and Nossal, K.R. (1993) *Relocating Middle Powers: Australia and Canada in a Changing World Order*, Melbourne: Melbourne University Press.

Dai, X. (2002) 'Information Systems in Treaty Regimes', *World Politics*, 54, 405–436.

Dauvergne, P. ed. (2005) *Handbook of Global Environmental Politics*, Cheltenham: Edward Elgar.

Della Porta, D. and Diani, M., eds (2006) *Social Movements*, Malden, MA: Blackwell.

Dickson, L. and McCulloch, A. (1996) 'Shell, the Brent Spar and Greenpeace: A Doomed Tryst?' *Environmental Politics*, 5(1), 122–129.

Dunlop, C. (2000) 'Epistemic Communities, A Reply to Toke', *Politics*, 20(3), 137–144.

Eilstrup-Sangiovanni, M. and Jones, C (2008) 'Assessing the Dangers of Illicit Networks', *International Security*, 33(2), 7–44.

Feinberg, R. E. (1988) 'The Changing Relationship Between the World Bank and the International Monetary Fund', *International Organization*, 42(4), 545–560.

Financial Times (July, 1995) *Brent Spar: A Strange Affair*, London: Financial Times Energy Publishing.

Fisher, D. R. (2004) 'Civil Society Protest and Participation', in N. Kanie and P. M. Haas, *Emerging Forces in Environmental Governance*, Tokyo: UNU Press, 176–202.

Fox, J. A. and Brown, D. L., eds (1998) *The Struggle for Accountability: The World Bank, NGOs, and Grassroots Movements. Global Environmental Accord: Strategies for Sustainability and Institutional Innovation,* Cambridge, MA: MIT Press.

Fung, A. (2006) 'Varieties of Participation in Complex Governance', *Public Administration Review*, 66, 66–76.

Grande, E. and Pauly, L. W., eds (2005) *Complex Sovereignty: Reconstituting Political Authority in the Twenty-first Century*, Toronto: University of Toronto Press.

Graz, J.-C. and Nolke, A., eds (2008) *Transnational Private Governance and its Limits*, London: Routledge.

Grewal, D. S. (2008) *Network Power*, New Haven, CT: Yale University Press.

Gulbrandsen, L. and Andresen, S. (2004) 'NGO influence in the Implementation of the Kyoto Protocol: Compliance, Flexibility Mechanisms, and Sinks', *Global Environmental Politics*, 4(4), 54–75.

Haas, E. B. (1990) *When Knowledge is Power*, Berkeley: University of California Press.

Haas, P. (1993) 'Epistemic Communities and the Dynamics of International Environmental Cooperation', in V. Rittberger, ed., *Regime Theory and International Relations*, Oxford: Oxford University Press, 168–201.

Haas, P. (2004a) 'Addressing the Global Governance Deficit', *Global Environmental Politics,* 11(4), 1–19.

Haas, P. (2004b) 'When Does Power Listen to Truth? A Constructivist Approach to the Policy Process', *Journal of European Public Policy,* 11(4), 569–592.

Haas, P. M. (1990) *Saving the Mediterranean, The Politics of International Environmental Cooperation*, New York: Columbia University Press.

Haas, P. M. (1998) 'Compliance with EU Directives', *Journal of European Public Policy*, 5(1), 38–65.

Haas, P. M. (2000) 'Choosing to Comply', in D. Shelton, ed., *Commitment and Compliance*, Oxford: Oxford University Press.

Haas, P. M. (2007) 'Epistemic Communities', in D. Bodansky, J. Brunnee and E. Hey, *The Oxford Handbook of International Environmental Law*, New York: Oxford University Press, 791–806.

Haas, P. M., ed. (2008) *International Environmental Governance*, Aldershot: Ashgate.

Haas, P. M. (2013) 'Ideas, Experts and Governance. The Role of Experts', in M. Ambrus, K. Arts, E. Hey and H. Raulus, *International Decision-Making: Advisors, Decision-Makers or Irrelevant?* Cambridge: Cambridge University Press.

Haas, P. M. and Haas, E. B. (1995) 'Learning to Learn: Improving Global Governance', *Global Governance*, 1(3), 255–284.

Haas, P. M. and Kanie, N., eds (2004) *Dynamics of Multilateral Environmental Governance*, Tokyo: United Nations University Press.

Haas, P. M. and Stevens, C. (2011) 'Organized Science, Usable Knowledge and Multilateral Environmental Governance', in R. Lidskog and G. Sundqvist, *Governing the Air*, Cambridge, MA: MIT Press, 125–161.

Haas, P. M., Robert, O. K. and Levy, M. A., eds (1993) *Institutions for the Earth: Sources of Effective International Environmental Protection. Global Environmental Accords Series*, Cambridge, MA: MIT Press.

Haffner-Burton, E. M., Kahler, M. and Montgomery, A. H. (2008) 'Network Analysis for International Relations', *American Political Science Association Annual Meeting*, Boston.

Hall, R. B. and Biersteker, T.J., eds (2002) *The Emergence of Private Authority in Global Governance*, Cambridge: Cambridge University Press.

Hanf, K. and Underdal, A. (1996) 'Domesticating International Commitments: Linking National and International Decision-making', in O. R. Young, ed. *The International Political Economy and International Institutions, Vol.2* Chelterham: Edward Elgar.

Harrison, K. (1999) 'Talking with the Donkey: Cooperative Approaches to Environmental Protection', *Journal of Industrial Ecology*, 2(3), 51–72.

Hawkins, D. G., Daniel, D. A. L., Nielson, L. and Tierney, M. J., eds (2006) *Delegation and Agency in International Organizations*, Cambridge: Cambridge University Press.

Heggelund, G., Andersen, S. and Ying, S. (2005) 'Performance of the Global Environmental Facility in China', *International Environmental Agreements: Politics, Law and Economics*, 5(3), 323–348.

Hopmann, P. T. (1996) *The Negotiation Process and the Resolution of International Conflicts*, Columbia: University of South Carolina Press.

Hovi, J., Skodvin, T. and Andresen, S. (2003) 'The Persistence of the Kyoto Protocol: Why Other Annex 1 Countries Move on Without the United States', *Global Environmental Politics*, 3, 1–24.

Hurrell, A. and Benedict, K., eds (1992) *The International Politics of the Environment: Actors, Interests, and Institutions*, Oxford: Clarendon Press.

Jordana, J., Levi-Faur, D. *et al.* (2011) 'The Global Diffusion of Regulatory Agencies', *Comparative Political Studies*.[Issue and vol nos. and page referenes missing.]

Kahler, M. ed. (2009) *Networked Politics*, Ithaca, NY: Cornell University.

Kanie, N. (2003) 'Leadership in Multilateral Negotiation and Domestic Policy: The Netherlands at the Kyoto Protocol Negotiation', *International Negotiation,* 8(2), 339–365.

Kanie, N. and Haas, P., eds (2004) *Emerging Forces in Environmental Governance*, Tokyo: UNU Press.

Keck, M. E. and Sikkink, K. (1998) *Activists Beyond Borders*, Ithaca, NY: Cornell University Press.

Keohane, R. O. (2001) 'Governance in a Partially Globalized World', *American Political Science Review*, 95(1), 1–13.

Keohane, R. O. (2002) 'Global Governance and Democratic Accountability', *Miliband Lecture London School of Economics,* 35.

Keohane, R. O. and Martin, L. L. (1995) 'The Promise of Institutionalist Theory', *International Security*, 20(1), 39–51.

Keohane, R. O. and Nye, J. S. (1974) 'Transgovernmental Relations and International Organizations', *World Politics*, 27(1).

Keohane, R. O., Joseph S. and Nye, J. S., eds (1971) *Transnational Relations and World Politics*, Cambridge, MA: Harvard University Press.

Kingdon, J. (1995) *Agendas, Alternatives and Public Policy*, Boston, MA: Addison Wesley.

Koppell, J. G. (2010) *World Rule*, Chicago, IL: University of Chicago Press.

Koremonos, B., Lipson, C. and Snidal, D. (2001) 'The Rational Design of International Organizations', *International Organization*, 55(4), 761–799.

Levi-Faur, D. (2011) 'Regulatory Networks and Regulatory Agentification', *Journal of European Public Policy,* 18(6), 810–829.

Levy, D. L. and Newell, P. J. eds (2005) *The Business of Global Environmental Governance*, Cambridge, MA: MIT Press.

Levy, D. L. and Prakash, A. (2003) 'Bargains Old and New: Multinational Corporations in Global Governance', *Business and Politics*, 5(2), 131–150.

Majone, G. (2009) *Europe as the Would-be World Power*, Cambridge: Cambridge University Press.

Majone, G. and A. B. Wildavsky (1978) 'Implementation as Evolution', in H. E. Freeman, *Policy Studies Annual Review*, Beverly Hills, CA: Sage, 103–117.

McNamara, K. (2004) 'The Institutional Dilemmas of Market Integration', in M. Doyle and E. C. Luck, *International Law and Organization: Closing the Compliance Gap*, Lanham, MD: Rowman & Littlefield.

McNamara, K. R. (2010) 'Constructing Authority in the European Union', in D. D. Avant, M. Finnemore and S. K. Sell, *Who Governs the Globe?* Cambridge, Cambridge University Press.

Meyer, J. W. (1997) 'The Structuring of a World Environmental Regime', *International Organization*, 51(4), 623–651.

Miles, E. L. (2002) *Environmental Regime Effectiveness: Confronting Theory with Evidence*, Cambridge, MA: MIT Press.

Mitchell, R. (2002) 'International Environment', in T. Risse, B. Simmons and W. Carlsnaes, *Handbook of International Relations*, Thousand Oaks, CA: Sage Publications, 500–516.

Mitchell, R. B. (1993) 'Compliance Theory: A Synthesis', *Review of European Community and International Environmental Law,* 2(4).[Page range missing]

Mitchell, R. B. (2003) 'International Environmental Agreements: A Survey of their Features, Formation, and Effects', *Annual Review of Environment and Resources,* 28, 429–461.

Mitchell, R. B. (2009) *International Politics and the Environment*, London: Sage

Mitchell, R. B., Clark, W. C. *et al.*, eds (2006) *Global Environmental Assessments: Information and Influence*, Cambridge, MA: MIT Press.

Murphy, D. D. (2004) *The Structure of Regulatory Competition*, Oxford: Oxford University Press.

Oberthur, S. and Gehring, T. (2006) *Instititonal Interaction in Global Environmental Governance,* Cambridge, MA: MIT Press.

Pattberg, P., Biermann, F. *et al.*, eds. (2012) *Public–Private Partnerships for Sustainable Development*, Cheltenham: Edward Elgar.

Patterson, M. (1999) 'Interpreting Trends in Global Environmental Governance', *International Affairs*, 75(4), 793–802.

Pauly, L. W. and Grande, E. (2005) 'Reconstituting Political Authority: Sovereignty, Effectiveness and Legitimacy in a Transnational Order', in L. W. Pauly and E. Grande, *Complex Sovereignty,* Toronto: University of Toronto Press.

Prakash, A. and Potoski, M. (2006a) 'Racing to the Bottom? Trade, Environmental Governance, and ISO 14001', *American Journal of Political Science*, 50(2), 350–364.

Prakash, A. and Potoski, M. (2006b) *The Voluntary Environmentalists*, Cambridge: Cambridge University Press.

Raines, S. S. (2003) 'Perceptions of Legitimacy and Efficacy in International Environmental Management Standards', *Global Enviornmental Politics*, 3(3), 47–73.

Rohrschneider, R. and Dalton, R. J. (2002) 'A Global Network? Transnational Cooperation among Environmental Groups', *The Journal of Politics*, 64(2), 510–533.

Sabatier, P. A. and Jenkins-Smith, H. C., eds (1993) *Policy Change and Learning: Advocacy Coalition Approach*, Boulder, CO: Westview Press.

Saeverud, I. A. and Skjaerseth, J. B. (2007) 'Oil Companies and Climate Change', *Global Enviornmental Politics,* 7(3), 42–61.

Saunders, H. (2005) *Politics is About Relationships*, Basingstoke: Palgrave.

Schaferhoff, M., Campe, S. *et al.* (2009) 'Transnational Public–Private Partnerships in International Relations', *International Studies Review*, 11, 451–474.

Shanahan, S. and Khagram, S. (2006) 'Dynamics of Corporate Responsibility. Globalization and Organization', in G. S. Drori, J. W. Meyer and H. Hwang, *Globalization and Organization: World Society and Organizational Change,* Oxford: Oxford University Press, 196–225.

Siebenhuner, B. (2008) 'Learning in International Organizations in Global Environmental Governance', *Global Environmental Politics*, 8(4), 92–116.

Skjærseth, J. B. (2000) *Linking International and Domestic Pollution Control*, Manchester: Manchester University Press.

Slaughter, A.-M. (2004) *A New World Order*, Princeton, NJ; Princeton University Press.

Speth, J. G. and Haas, P. M. (2006) *Global Environmental Governance*, Washington, DC: Island Press.

Sprinz, D. and Vaahtoranta, T. (1994) 'The Interest-based Explanation of International Environmental policy', *International Organization*, 48(1), 77–105.

Stokke, O., Hovi, J. and Ulfstein, G., eds (2005) *Implementing the Climate Regime – International Compliance*, London: Earthscan.

Tarrow, S. (1994) *Power in Movement*, Cambridge, Cambridge University Press.

The Commission on Global Governance (1995) *Our Global Neighborhood.*

The Social Learning Group (2001) *Social Learning and the Management of Global Environmental Risks*, Cambridge, MA: MIT Press.

Underdal, A. (1998) 'Explaining Compliance and Defection', *European Journal of International Relations,* 4(1), 5–30.

Underdal, A. and Young, O. R., eds (2004) *Regime Consequences*, AA Dordrecht: Kluwer.

Vibert, F. (2007) *The Rise of the Unelected*, Cambridge, Cambridge University Press.

Victor, D. G., Raustiala, K. and Skolnikoff, E. B., eds (1988) *The Implementation and Effectiveness of International Environmental Commitments*, Cambridge, MA: MIT Press.

Vig, N. and Faure, M. (2004) *Green Giants. Environmental Policies of the U.S. and the EU,* Cambridge, MA:MIT Press.

Vogel, D. (2005) *The Market for Virtue*, Washington, DC.: Brookings.

Weale, A. (2011) 'New Modes of Governance, Political Accountability and Public Reason', *Government and Opposition*, 46(1), 58–80.

Weber, S., Barma, N., Kroenig, M. and Ratner, E. (2007) 'How Globalization Went Bad', *Foreign Policy,* January/February, 48–54.

Weiss, E. B. and Jacobson, H. K., eds (1998) *Engaging Countries*, Cambridge, MA: MIT Press.

Weiss, T. G. and Gordenker, L., eds (1996) *NGOs, The UN, and Global Governance*, Boulder, CO: Lynne Rienner.

Weiss, T. G. and Leon, G., eds (1996) NGOs, *The UN, and Global Governance*, Boulder, CO: Lynne Rienner Publishers.

Yamin, F. (2001) 'NGOs and International Environmental Law', *RECIEL*, 10(2), 149–162.

Young, O. R. (1991) 'Political Leadership and Regime Formation', *International Organization*, 45(3), 281–308.

Young, O. R., ed. (1997) *Global Governance: Drawing Insights from the Environmental Experience. Global Environmental Accord: Strategies for Sustainability*, Cambridge: Cambridge University Press.

Young, O. R., ed. (1999) *The Effectiveness of International Environmental Regimes*, Cambridge, MA: MIT Press.

Young, O. R., ed. (2009) *Institutions and Environmental Change*, Cambridge, MA: MIT Press.

Young, O. R. (2010) *Emergent Patterns in Intenational Environmental Governance*, Cambridge, MA: MIT Press.

Zacher, M. (1999) *The United Nations and Global Commerce*, New York: United Nations.

Zartman, W. (1994) *International Multilateral Negotiation: Approaches to the Management of Complexity*, Proquest Info & Learning.[Place of publication missing.]

Zürn, M. (1998) 'The Rise of International Environmental Politics: A Review of Current Research', *World Politics*, 50(4), 617–649.

2 Agenda setting at sea and in the air

Stacy D. VanDeveer

Introduction

Agenda setting, from impact identification to action item construction, involves a host of issues that are "the stuff" of international relations – and of politics. As greater numbers of actors bring their interests and goals to research and political debates about particular issues, a host of complex social processes are involved including the construction of knowledge, consensus, concern and a sense of urgency, as well as processes of social mobilization, the diffusion of norms and ideas, and the definition and articulation of storylines about causality, blame and the possibilities of collective action around a set of possible policy options. Throughout these processes agents frame issues in ways consistent with their beliefs and interests. These frames and the discourses that carry and structure them continuously interact with larger social institutions. For example, framing environmental issues in regional, pan-European terms in recent decades "fits" well within larger discourses about the construction of European institutions to address common problems in Europe and achieve the benefits of collective action at the continental level (VanDeveer 2004; Balsiger and VanDeveer 2010, 2012). In short, agenda setting – what works and what does not achieve particular ends – is a set of complex social processes embedded in larger, ongoing social and political institutions and dynamics.

This chapter briefly describes two complex environmental cooperation regimes: Baltic Sea cooperation aiming to reduce marine pollution and engender more sustainable development in the Baltic region, and cooperation based at the United National Economic Commission for Europe seeking to reduce long-range transboundary air pollution (LRTAP) and its ecological, human health and economic impacts. The structure and content of densely institutionalized transnational networks within each regime help to explain agenda setting politics over time, with LRTAP remaining dominated by highly technocratic actors and discourses while Baltic cooperation has expanded greatly in terms of actor and institutional diversity – and in terms of the types of knowledge brought to bear in regional politics.

A recent analysis of the "international emergence of environmental problems" (Mitchell 2009: 81–82) argues that agenda setting involves transitions through stages from the identification of anthropogenic environmental impacts, to anthropogenic environmental problems, to an international environmental discussion item, to an international environmental action item. While this formulation suggests more linearity than complex social interaction likely produces, it does call attention to the bases of scientific and technical information often involved in identifying a phenomenon as an anthropogenic impact, as well as the construction of such an impact as a "problem." This more complex notion of agenda setting in international environmental politics thus includes research and knowledge construction (with an accompanying construction of causal understandings), as well as framing processes among a host of diverse actors. Mitchell's notion of agenda setting also asks analysts to assess how issues are introduced into international and transnational discussions among actors of all types, and how they may move from items of discussion and debate to items associated with specific policy actions. Around environmental issues such as acid rain and marine pollution, these processes began in earnest in the late 1960s and early 1970s (with longer historical roots for some aspects, of course) and have continued apace for over 40 years.

The case discussions, each covering over 40 years of international cooperation history, are each presented in three eras to facilitate comparison. Next, the chapter turns to discussions of actor configuration in each regime and agenda setting dynamics and practices. These two sections draw particular attention to the roles of scientific and technical assessment institutions, institutionalized networks and institutional linkages across multiple cooperation fora.

Sea and air examples

Case materials draw on two areas of international, regional environmental cooperation: marine pollution reduction around European regional seas, with particular focus on the Baltic Sea regimes, and agreements under the auspices of the UNECE long-range transboundary air pollution regime (LRTAP). These two regimes offer considerably more than two MEA cases, as each has been developing multiple types of agreements since the 1970s. Each area offers examples of well developed, often consensus based cooperation among a diverse set of well networked actors, and areas of cooperation where consensus and action were more difficult to achieve. One advantage of drawing on the extensive empirical experience (and extensive scholarship) related to these two areas of international environmental cooperation is the ability to trace changes in agenda setting dynamics over time. For example, after air and water pollution were framed and generally understood as problematic in terms of both ecological and human health – a construction that indeed took considerable time and resources to achieve within and beyond scientific and policymaker communities – the issues under debate become considerably more technically and scientifically complex over time.

The long history of environmental debate, civil society action and policy development also reveals, however, that some issues are much more difficult to push into the "action needed" column than others. One reason may be extreme technical and social complexity, as illustrated in LRTAP debates about smog, VOCs and multi-pollutant interactions. Also, opponents of policy action are better organized, well-funded, and politically and socially more salient and influential around some issues than around others. We see instances of years of success by such actors in keeping some issues off the international action agenda. Examples of this latter category include the many years of scant attention within regional seas cooperation to particularly economically (and politically) important industrial or economic sectors such as the pulp and paper industry around the Baltic Sea, or the substantial contributions of tourism and mobile sources to Mediterranean marine pollution and coastal zone degradation (VanDeveer 2000; Auer 1996; Kutting 2000).

Baltic regional cooperation

Baltic regional environmental cooperation has existed for almost 40 years, beginning as a rare attempt to construct and institutionalize environmental policy-making and scientific and technical cooperation across the Cold War's East–West divide in the early 1970s.[1] This history makes Baltic regional environmental cooperation one of the oldest and most active cases of international environmental cooperation, offering lessons for both scholars and practitioners of environmental politics (VanDeveer 2011). After 40 years, Baltic regional cooperation is extensive, including various manifestations of formal, informal, intergovernmental and non-governmental collaboration, primarily involving and driven by actors from the region. As with many international environmental regimes, the region's national actors (state and non-state) are asymmetrically engaged – with long histories of leadership by Swedish, Danish and German individual and organizational actors, for example. To organize analysis and highlight agenda setting developments and dynamics over four decades, the case material below is organized into three eras.

Reaching across the Baltic (1960s–1980s)

Bilateral and multilateral environmental protection arrangements for the Baltic date back to the late 1960s, but international groups of scientists began studying the Baltic Sea in the early twentieth century. By the 1960s and early 1970s, such study had become substantially more regionalized, outlining priorities for regional research (Dybern 1980; ICES 1974). The 1974 Helsinki Convention was the first regional international agreement limiting marine pollution from both land- and sea-based sources, whether air- or water-borne. It established the Baltic Marine Environmental Protection Commission, known as the Helsinki Commission or HELCOM. Over time, HELCOM came to sit at the center of the Baltic Sea environmental regime and the extensive set of scientific and technically-based and state-based regional networks it entails. In negotiating the 1974 treaty, some states in the region were so concerned with protecting their sovereignty and security that they exempted coverage of coastal waters – by far the most polluted – from the convention

HELCOM functions as a secretariat to administer and implement the Convention, beginning operation immediately after the 1974 signing. During the interim period (1974–1980), Finland and Sweden provided the resources necessary to support the maintenance of international cooperation and remained leading states, backing HELCOM's development, portending the central importance of lead, sponsor or pusher states in Baltic regional cooperation over the subsequent decades. Detailed analysis of the regional treaty negotiations and the many activities of HELCOM appear elsewhere (Koskenniemi 1993; Haas 1993; Hjorth 1992, 1993; VanDeveer 1997; Westing 1989; Selin and VanDeveer 2004). Though analysts do not all use the terms "network" or advocacy coalitions, they agree that cooperation within groups that included Nordic state officials and marine scientists from around the region helped to drive state interest in establishing and maintaining early regional intergovernmental environmental cooperation around the Baltic Sea.

Several important aspects of scientific consensus drove state officials' environmental concerns, shaped regional negotiations and early cooperation activities. For example, the Baltic Sea has a comparatively long water replacement time (50 percent replacement takes approximately eight years) and it was a region of substantial industrialization, urbanization, and shipping and naval activities (Zmudzinski 1989; Koskenniemi 1993; Westing 1989). In other words, pollutants discharged into the sea remain and accumulate for many years. By the late 1960s, scientists from multiple disciplines and from across the region's states generally agreed that the sea was dangerously degraded, and that international cooperation was required to address such concerns (Hjorth 1993; ICES 1970). Of most concern were increasing inputs and ambient levels of toxins, and increasing nutrients such as nitrogen and phosphorous (eutrophication) and the decreased oxygen levels associated with these inputs. The combination of these concerns led to the inclusion, in the 1974 agreement, of air and water based pollutants and early technical focus on urban waste and industrial effluents, offering early evidence of scientific and technical (S&T) influence on the regional political agenda. In short, the treaty focused on the individual hazardous substances about which the scientific researchers were most concerned.

Yet, the exclusion of coastal waters in the first treaty's coverage – later rectified in the 1992 treaty – offers a clear example of the limits of S&T consensus. The coastal zone, where pollution damages are the most obvious and generally the most severe – was excluded from coverage because of the overlapping security and sovereignty concerns of state officials. Also exempted from coverage was the military sector. Also, S&T knowledge did not engender regional cooperation on its own. The establishment of inter-state cooperation was spurred by the 1972 Stockholm Convention, in which Swedish and Finnish officials and experts pushed for Baltic regional cooperation, and the subsequent resolution of the East–West stand-off over the (non)recognition of East Germany by Western states and the related emergence of the *detente* era (Rytovouri 1980; Hjorth 1993; VanDeveer 1997). Thus, Cold War political contexts and dynamics shaped both the opportunities for regional cooperation and the forms it took in negotiations, and the high profile meeting of political leaders in 1972 spurred the region's leaders toward negotiations for the original agreement.

HELCOM established itself as a center of S&T assessment in the early years of the Baltic cooperation regime. As the secretariat for the conventions, it administers the many meetings and programmatic activities under the auspices of the formal agreements among states (treaties, resolutions, declarations, recommendations, etc.). These roles place HELCOM at the center of broad environmental cooperation and environmental science efforts in the region (VanDeveer 1997, 2011), making it a centrally important forum in which the region's S&T experts share and jointly assess information and construct consensus-based knowledge, and shape future directions of their shared research agendas. This makes HELCOM a source of, anchor for, and focus of a variety of environmental policy networks that have developed to address a range of issues including pollution from ships and ports, land-based pollution, and habitat protection. Leading states such as Sweden and Finland often respond to HELCOM-identified S&T knowledge or data gaps by funding research intended to address stated needs. Hjorth (1993) argues that a "scientific-technical strategy" of populating working groups, committees and sub-committees with S&T experts illustrates the expert influence on the early work of HELCOM. As noted below, this strategy of populating S&T committees and working groups with national experts as a way of driving S&T and policy agendas simultaneously is common to the lead states in both air and marine pollution cooperation (see also Selin and VanDeveer 2003).

HELCOM's working groups operated by consensus among the state-appointed S&T participants, using a "lead country" principle where experts from a state with a particular interest and experience with the substance or practice under discussion examines and reports out about domestic monitoring and regulatory practice. Such information provides a basis for proposed joint measures, which are issued as recommendations. Recommendations are voluntary, but they must be adopted unanimously by all states. Lead states tend to push for regional standards based on their domestic practice, that are higher than regional norms. Thus lead country dynamics tend to drive up regional standards, because the states with the most regulatory experience tend to serve as the lead parties. They also reduce the possibility for states without a particular sector or practice to push for regulation that disadvantages those states with said sector or practice. Early work focused on reducing pollution from ships, ports and off-shore installations, combating spills, and monitoring and assessing land-based pollution into the seas. Discussion of these issues, and resultant recommendations, illustrate the dominance of scientific and technical discourse and participation. Denmark, Sweden and the Federal Republic of Germany (FRG) emerged as environmental leaders, with Finnish officials often seeking to articulate compromise positions between the leaders and the laggards (Haas 1993).

Transforming Baltic Europe (late 1980s–early 2000s)

The period from 1988 to 1992 saw enormous changes in political and economic institutions in the Baltic region and across Europe, as Soviet-style state socialism collapsed across Central and East Europe even as the states of the Baltic region were embarking on a thorough updating of the 1974 Helsinki Convention.

In 1992, the region's states adopted a second convention. During times of dramatic political change, S&T experts networked within HELCOM activities in conjunction with the region's environmental lead states and used the convention revision process to address some institutional deficiencies of the first convention – such as the exemption for coastal waters – and to write some of the voluntary recommendations into the revised, binding treaty. This process was enhanced by increasing ministerial-level regional cooperation and collaboration around the Baltic, creating an increasingly "thick" institutional and organizational situation in Baltic regional cooperation. Peter Haas (1993) called attention to regular ministerial conferences – every few years – as a "new institution" in Baltic regional environmental protection. Institutionalizing periodic ministerial meetings is an idea picked up from the North Sea regime, where meetings in 1984 (in Bremen) and 1987 (in London) produced joint declarations with ambitious joint pollution-reduction goals (Haas 1993; Skjaerseth 2000). These conferences generally garner media attention and result in new announcements of common goals. In a way, Baltic cooperation went back to its origins, having initially been spurred by the 1972 Stockholm conference.

Among the most important decisions taken at the ministerial meetings was the 1988 joint ministerial declaration establishing a 50 percent emissions reduction goal for emissions of nutrients and hazardous substances. Since 1998, most HELCOM activity and many of the subsequent recommendations have been in pursuit of goals set at high profile ministerial meetings. Ministers at a 1992 Diplomatic Conference adopted a resolution establishing, within the HELCOM structure, a permanent Programme Implementation Task Force (HELCOM PITF) to initiate, facilitate, and coordinate the implementation of the Baltic Sea Program. The fact that many of HELCOM's changes – including the inception of periodic ministerial conferences, the 1992 Convention, organizational expansion and restructuring, and the launching of a joint implementation program – occurred simultaneously yielded mutual compatibility and a sort of synergistic momentum among these changes. The HELCOM Secretariat and individuals within HELCOM subsidiary bodies – the central organizations of the regime and the bearers and promulgators of the regime principles and norms – directed much of the regime change through their participation in the inter-state negotiations (including drafting and redrafting proposals). Throughout these processes, HELCOM activities were at the center of dense regional networks of individuals and organizations, functioning both as a center of scientific and technical assessment and as a center for collaborative policy making (VanDeveer 2011). This period also sees environmental advocacy organizations more explicitly included in HELCOM work. In fact, with the political changes in the former communist countries, environmental activism was explicitly encouraged and often funded by Western states or the European Union).

In terms of agenda setting, participating S&T experts continued to influence important aspects of the political agenda, as they raised awareness about ongoing challenges with both toxic inputs and nutrient loading (mostly from agriculture). However, the direction of this influence changes somewhat in this period. Rather than largely quiet S&T work in HELCOM committees resulting in recommendations, we see the more high profile goal setting at ministerial meetings (with somewhat more arbitrary numerical goals such as 50 percent reduction) shaping HELCOM activities. S&T research and cooperation within HELCOM bodies often becomes more in service to the broader and more ambitious goals. The topics about which ministers set goals (nutrient and toxics reduction, for example) are those of most interest to S&T networks, but the goals are largely selected via ministerial negotiations.

The integration of EU organizations and institutions in the Baltic region occurs at multiple levels of environmental governance from the ministerial level down into the national and subnational level bureaucracies. In the environmental policy area, national and subnational authorities may have links to personnel or organizational bodies with the EU Directorate which administers and helps develop environmental policy. Also, the EU is a formal member of the 1992 Helsinki Convention. This places a voting representative from the EU Commission at the table with the state representatives on HELCOM. Furthermore, EU policy officially insists on the "harmonization" of national environmental policy with EU policies as a condition of EU membership, which had an enormous impact on Baltic states' environmental policy agendas (Selin and VanDeveer 2004; Carmin and VanDeveer 2005). In the Baltic region, these candidates (all of which became EU member states) included Estonia, Latvia, Lithuania and Poland. In all four, environmental officials and parliamentarians moved to bring their countries' environmental law and regulations into line with EU policy (OECD 2000; Selin and VanDeveer 2004).

The introduction of the EU as an important Baltic actor and funder/donor also shaped cooperation goals with the Baltic regime. During the late 1990s and early 2000s, officials around the region often prioritized issues and actions perceived to simultaneously improve the Baltic environment and further the harmonization goals of EU applicant states. Initiatives often attempted to combine capacity-building goals and implementation goals, such that more attention was paid to the assessing and improving the impact of common goals, standards and measures. EU assistance to Central and Eastern European countries commonly focused on technical assistance projects such as studies, training, and technical advice. Over time, the EU has provided environmental assistance only for projects and policies contributing to the goals of approximation of EU legislation. For example, PHARE was part of the broader donor network and its funds often contributed to projects in cooperation with various multilateral development banks, particularly through a Project Preparation Facility established by donors in Central and Eastern Europe in 1993 as a coordination mechanism to enhance aid efficiency. EU funds also paid for a large report comparing EU and HELCOM policies and recommending amendments and changes to HELCOM recommendations to bring them into line with EU policy (HELCOM 2001; Selin and VanDeveer 2004). The region's S&T researchers generally supported such changes, in part because of the perception that EU environmental policies were generally more stringent and, perhaps, more likely to be fully implemented by the region's EU-bound states. EU programs, together with donor organizations and multilateral development banks, were actively involved in international cooperative efforts for the Baltic Sea, providing financing, for example, for individual projects, and to different degrees have also been involved in broader agenda-setting exercises such as the Joint Comprehensive Environmental Action Program (JCP) set up in 1992 and updated in 1998 under HELCOM (see Gutner 2002; Auer and Nilenders 2001).

Seeking regional sustainability around the Baltic in the early twenty-first century

After 40 years of environmental cooperation, chief threats to Baltic Sea environmental quality remain eutrophication and toxic substances, substantial marine activities (shipping and resource exploitation) and biodiversity loss (Kern 2011). Active transnational civil society groups and networks are engaged in activities related to each of these issues, drawing on, and often networked with, the region's S&T experts. Substantial progress has been made in reducing toxic inputs at sea and from land based sources (Westing 1989; Selin and VanDeveer 2004), but much remains to be done.

By the 2000s, Baltic cooperation remained heavily influenced by ongoing S&T research and the densely institutionalized connections of regional researchers with state officials, but participation in these networks and the regional agenda have expanded substantially. Issues such as local and urban sustainability and historical preservation joined the more traditional antipollution agenda of the regime (Joas *et al.* 2008; Kern 2011), as civil society and local public sector actors have joined the networks and succeeded in getting lead states to push these issues regionally. Ministerial meetings, one of the institutional innovations of the 1980s and early 1990s, continued to shape regional agendas in the 2000s. Meetings in 2001, 2003, 2007 and 2010 all illustrate this pattern. The 2007 ministerial meeting in Krakow saw the launch of a detailed HELCOM Baltic Sea Action Plan, setting goals and initiating programs to substantially cut pollution in the region by 2020. At the 2010 ministerial meeting, HELCOM countries presented implementation plans for the 2020 goals and passed a set of recommendations intended for further collective implementation of the 2007 action plan.[2] These meetings are attended by representatives of dozens of public and NGOs, and hundreds more are involved in the stakeholder meetings and discussions about goal setting and implementation. Participation has expanded well beyond S&T researchers and state-appointed experts. However, environment ministers are not the only ones who now meet regularly around the region. In addition to regular Prime Ministerial meetings, ministers from Defense, Health, Transport, Economic/Finance and Culture, to name a few, hold high-profile conferences. Ministers use these meetings to leverage bureaucratic power at home, setting interim and long-term goals for common policies. In addition, many of the non-environmental ministerial meetings seek to address aspects of regional sustainability, and it is common for HELCOM and some other regionally networked environmental actors to be represented as such gatherings.

Baltic regional environmental cooperation is now densely networked and institutionalized beyond HELCOM. Regional Baltic environmental protection efforts constitute an institutionally dense web of connections – including parliamentarians and other policymakers, scientific and technical groups, advocacy NGOs of many kinds, and professional organizations from the region (Joas *et al.* 2008; Kern 2011; VanDeveer 2011). These many overlapping networks and initiatives regularly interact with HELCOM activities and individual participants, and HELCOM's scientific and technical reports and the policy recommendations and requirements are regularly used by actors throughout the other networks and organizations.

Lastly, continuing EU influence is illustrated by the 2009 launch of the EU Strategy for the Baltic Sea Region. The strategy pulls together a set of environmental and development goals under the auspices of EU cohesion goals and initiatives. It coordinates co-financing from a number of EU sources with those from the region's states and a number of other international organizations and development banks. By mid-2011 some 80 projects were included in the strategy. Of these, many seek to implement HELCOM action plans and EU goals simultaneously around the region. This work illustrates that EU officials, and Baltic regional lead states working through the EU, are now among the most important influences on regional agendas.

CLRTAP

The Convention on Long Range Transboundary Air Pollution (CLRTAP) was signed in late 1979, and entered into force in 1983 under the auspices of the United Nations Economic Commission for Europe (UNECE) in Geneva. The convention was the product of several years of growing concern among scientific and technical researchers and civil servants and the persistence of a small number of leading state officials. CLRTAP cooperation proceeded through a framework convention-protocol model, now common in international environmental politics. As a framework convention, CLRTAP established a basis for continuing research, information sharing and policy making. Eight subsequent CLRTAP protocols have been negotiated to date, including those on finding and conducting monitoring and scientific research, and addressing environmental problems associated with pollutants such as sulfur, nitrogen, VOCs, heavy metals and persistent organic pollutants. CLRTAP cooperation and the science underlying it are the subject of an extensive analytical literature (see, e.g. Levy 1993; Selin 2010; Selin and VanDeveer 2003; Farrell and Jager 2006; Social Learning Group 2001; Lidskog and Sundqvist 2012; VanDeveer 2006a, 2006b; Wettstad 2002). Annex X includes more detailed information about the ratification status of CLRTAP protocols and their environmental goals. Like the Baltic case above, CLRTAP agenda-setting case material below is organized into three eras.

From scientific concern to a convention in the 1970s

CLRTAP formation can be traced to the "discovery" of acidifying precipitation by scientists in Western Europe and North America in the late 1960s and early 1970s, as an aspect of growing scientific and public concern about the impacts of air pollution. Much of the framing and discourse for LRTAP issues was established within OECD technical cooperation beginning in the 1960s, the 1972 UNCHE in Stockholm, and early public warnings about acidification issues by scientists as echoed by environmental activists (VanDeveer 2006). As such, ideas and knowledge about long range air pollution were a product of S&T and public official interaction from the beginning, as participants in these early discussions served as "knowledge brokers" (Litfin 1995) integrating facts and values in interpretation as participants in the co-production (Jasanoff and Wynne 1998) of S&T knowledge, politics and social order. The early movers in the transboundary air pollution debates were Swedish scientists and officials (Oden 1968; Cowling 1982; McCormack, 1997; Levy 1993). These researchers began to connect insights across several disciplines and to state publicly (and publish) their concerns about pollutants moving long distances and across borders, with serious and negative impacts in pollution-importing countries. These conclusions were internationalized and legitimized in OECD assessments (VanDeveer 2006b). In fact, it was within the OECD work that the term "long range transboundary air pollution" was established. Swedish and Norwegian scientists and officials, seeing their country as negatively impacted by such pollution, used the 1972 Stockholm conference and other smaller inter-state and scientific venues to raise awareness about the issue and push other countries to establish international cooperation efforts (VanDeveer 1998). From the initial phase, S&T knowledge and interstate policymaking tended to be shaped most by Western European and Nordic (and some North American) scientists and S&T trained policymakers.

The UNECE was chosen as the institutional venue because it was one of the very few that included states from both East and West. Lead state dynamics were clear in the negotiations, as Sweden, Norway, Denmark and Finland pushed for a strong convention – based on their status as victims of others' pollution – and the UK, West Germany, and others were more reluctant. Importantly, from the beginning, lead states in the cooperation tended to combine significant investment in S&T research and data collection with an explicitly politicized expectation that they were net importers of others' damaging pollution. The resulting LRTAP convention's general goals of increasing scientific and technical cooperation and endeavoring to limit and reduce transboundary pollution over time through further, more specific cooperation goals and institutions was largely consistent with the scientific and technically framed anti-pollution political agenda of the time, including substantial uncertainties about the quantities and distances traveled of transboundary pollutants. As in the Baltic region, Cold War political dynamics played a role in launching negotiations, the selection of UNECE as the venue and for aspects of the treaty negotiation outcomes, including making accommodations for Soviet reluctance to gather and share the same types of data on pollution emissions and transportation expected by (and of) other states.

Lead states, science and protocol development (1980s and 1990s)

CLRTAP's first protocol established a treaty-based funding stream for monitoring and evaluation of pollution, with subsequent protocols on sulfur, NOx, VOCs and sulfur (again). These agreements sought to address emissions and transboundary movement of significant components and precursors to acidifying precipitation and smog. Concern about the acid rain issue, and the perceived need to have much better monitoring data, animated the LRTAP political agenda, and these were the subjects of the early protocols. The existence of a protocol on monitoring, data gathering and analysis resulted – importantly – in ongoing work to standardize (as much as possible) the generation and sharing of much of the data underlying S&T cooperation bodies. The early CLRTAP pollution-specific protocols set common, time-specific reduction targets for all parties. In other words, they set baseline years and called on all signatories to reduce emissions by the same amount. In contrast, the multi-effects/multi-pollutions protocol on acidification, eutrophication and ground-level ozone, adopted in Gothenburg 1999, sets a series of variable national emission-reduction targets for each pollutant for each state (Wettestad 2002). The Gothenburg protocol is also based on the critical loads concept, which was first used in the 1994 second sulfur protocol. The concept of critical loads denotes an attempt at establishing a critical environmental threshold (or exposure level) below which no harmful effects occur. Emission reductions are divided among countries on a regional basis in an attempt to minimize the costs for the region as a whole while meeting set environmental and human health targets for all parts of the region (Tuinstra *et al.* 2006; Grennfelt and Hov 2005; Bäckstrand 2001).

CLRTAP's discourse was heavily science and technology based from its inception, with technically oriented working groups of experts in frequent consultation with state officials – particularly state officials from the sub-group of states often driving the negotiating and reporting agendas (VanDeveer 1998, 2004, 2006a, 2006b). Integrated assessment modeling, particularly critical loads modeling and mapping, have been central to the policymaker–technical expert interactions for over 20 years. While the critical loads concept, modeling and mappings are not highly complex by the standards of mathematical modelers, they remain the purview of those with particular types of S&T training. Furthermore, the models include some embedded attempts to optimize (or at least to lower) costs of policy goals under discussion, thereby remaining salient to state officials and their concerns. Over time, the LRTAP agenda has grown more technically complex as policy discussions followed scientific research into the interactions between multiple pollutants. The group of lead states expanded over time, with the lead states generally having among the largest and most actively engaged scientific and technical communities on LRTAP-related issues. Northern/West European leadership in both policy spheres and scientific communities continues, apparent in the S&T committees and working groups and in the patterns seen around state negotiating behaviors (VanDeveer 1998, 2006a, 2006b).

Europeanizing air pollution politics (late 1990s to the present)

As the formerly communist states of Central and Eastern Europe and the former Soviet Union experienced economic, political and social transitions in the 1990s and 2000s and the drive by many of them to join the European Union accelerated, EU policymaking debates and agendas became increasingly linked and influential in CLRTAP institutions and outcomes (Carmin and VanDeveer 2005; Selin and VanDeveer 2003, 2012). Parallel to CLRTAP policy making, the EU has become increasingly active on air pollution abatement issues. Compared to CLRTAP's transboundary environmental focus, the EU often focuses more on local human health aspects, sometimes in collaboration with the World Health Organization. Whereas some EU air policy dates back to the 1970s, the main policy developments began in the early 1980s, greatly accelerating in the 1990s and 2000s. Current EU air policy sets standards for ambient air quality, establishes national emissions ceilings (NECs) for acidification and eutrophication, regulates emissions from stationary sources, targets emissions from road vehicles and ships, and seeks to reduce emissions of VOCs. Greater EU engagement on air policy issues, with the EU's greater enforcement capabilities and its significant funding levels for policy-related S&T research meant that many of those engaged in LRTAP-related, policy relevant research within the LRTAP regime actively participating in EU developments.

The development of the Gothenburg Protocol and subsequent efforts to implement it, in conjunction with the EU's creation of NECs for all member states, greatly accelerated EU-CLRTAP linkages (Selin and VanDeveer 2003, 2012). In both venues one sees a similar set of lead states and heavy reliance on the scientists and environmental activist organizations which initially grew up around LRTAP. The effort to revise the Gothenburg Protocol with more stringent emissions ceilings and to potentially add commitments to reduce short-lived climate change forcers like black carbon and tropospheric ozone (and their precursor pollutants), are likely to further expand the number and scope of the already significant governance and actor linkages between CLRTAP and the EU. CLRTAP remains both an important venue for scientific, technical and political air pollution abatement work, and an influential part of European air pollution linkage politics even as the EU has greatly expanded its air pollution work. By now, states, individuals and various organizations seeking to influence transboundary air pollution politics are commonly engaged in both venues, and both venues rely heavily on the same body of S&T knowledge and researchers (Selin and VanDeveer 2003, 2012). As CLRTAP membership grew to include states across much of the former Soviet Union, CLRTAP programs have increasingly prioritized S&T and state capacity building across the Caucuses and Central Asia as vehicles for the improvement of air pollution data, assessment, and research and policy across this large group of new independent states.

Actors and configurations: mature, institutionalized networks

Densely networked and institutionalized connections among actors operate at both international and national levels around the Baltic and LRTAP regimes. In fact, much of the body of knowledge and information that moves between state actors does so via NGO and S&T actors working to set agendas and influence outcomes. The co-production of S&T knowledge for politics and policymaking is much in evidence in both cooperation regimes. Nevertheless, evidence suggests that shaping the preferences of state institutions and actors remains the most important leverage point for shaping the international agenda over the years. The one, partial, exception here is that particular sets of S&T information (like the RAINS model of atmospheric transport and deposition) influence international-level discussions and then shape the states via international interaction (including the "selling" of such information at the state level). A major difference between the cases, to note here, is that the Baltic networks have grown much more diverse and expansive in terms of local level, professional and transnational participation over the last 20 years, while LRTAP networks remain considerably more constrained to a smaller, more closed state and non-state set of networked communities involving mostly people with considerable scientific and technical training and facility with quantitative models.

Networks, leaders and asymmetry

In both cases one sees multiple, overlapping networks through which a diverse set of actors seek to shape the political agenda and institutional designs. Individuals and the organizations with which they work are both well connected. Over time, substantial resources have been invested in these networks, including regular meetings, establishing and maintaining network based organizations, email lists, chat rooms and online groups, and so on. Organizations pool resources and co-sponsor reports, research, workshops and public campaigns, even lobbying funders on each other's behalf occasionally. Here again the state connections are important to note, but they tend to persistently overlap with non-state actors. Individuals move between state and non-state sectors and to/from the state and expert/analysts organizations, blurring some of the lines between public and civil society sectors and between state and international organizations (Selin and VanDeveer 2003). Furthermore, lead states tend to populate both international S&T working groups and policy assessment bodies with their nationals, as a way to drive agendas toward higher standards (Selin and VanDeveer 2003, 2004). In fact, in both regimes, leading NGOs also hail from lead states and are well connected with them, often serving to drive civil society agendas and lead state preferences in similar directions. Frequent, iterated interaction within networks appears to help construct general agreement among participating actors on both information/knowledge and on policy options across S&T, NGO and civil service agencies. Over time, this influences the details of the international institution agendas.

Analytical literature on international environmental politics has often focused substantial attention on international regimes and transnational networks (Börzel 1998; O'Neill 2009; Selin and VanDeveer 2009; Steinberg and VanDeveer 2012; VanDeveer 2011). The Baltic region plays host to both robust environmental cooperation regimes and a burgeoning and unusually mature set of policy networks encompassing efforts to clean up and protect the Baltic Sea and its associated regional environment (Hjorth 1992, 1993; Joas *et al.* 2008; VanDeveer 1997, 2000, 2002, 2011; Gutner and VanDeveer 2001). Generally speaking, a number of important trends in Baltic regional cooperation stand out. These trends include deepening and expanding regional environmental cooperation, much of which occurs under the auspices of a regional anti-pollution treaty and the international cooperation regime that surrounds it. This regional cooperation incorporates multiple levels of governance across public, civil society and private sectors in a densely institutionalized and networked set of transnational relations.

The Baltic region also displays growing, but asymmetric, regional economic and political interdependence and a substantial increase in the role and influence of the European Union (EU). However, in most cases Russia remains the least integrated of the region's states and societies into regional multilateral cooperation efforts of all kinds (VanDeveer 1997, 2002; Selin and VanDeveer 2004). Because many Baltic regional environmental recommendations and initiatives are voluntary (and well beyond the commitments in the binding convention), Russia's laggard status can coexist with robust regional cooperation. Russia neither obstructs, nor enthusiastically joins many ongoing programs. Swedish and Finnish participants, in particular, tend to try to "do what they can" to involve their S&T and public sector Russian colleagues in the St. Petersburg region, while acknowledging the long-standing asymmetries in both capacity and commitment.

In CLRTAP, long-standing state and civil society leaders continue to drive the agenda, while Southern and Eastern European and Central Asian states often lag, resisting new initiatives and newer protocols. But CRLTAP leaders have come to view the regimes as a primary vehicle to build air pollution S&T and policy capacities in laggard states, in partnership with EU programs which can drive implementation among member states and fund capacity building among CLRTAP's non-EU members.

Network structure

Environmental networking and policy advocacy are highly developed around the Baltic Sea, having accrued decades of experience. Networks are generally horizontally organized, meaning that information generally flows between or across actors outside (or around) organized hierarchies (VanDeveer 2011). However, the highly institutionalized inter-state and transnational environmental cooperation seen in the Baltic region adds a greater element of hierarchy to Baltic environmental policy networks – largely because many of the networks are maintained by formal state, intergovernmental and non-governmental organizations. As such, the "mature" nature of the regional environmental policy networks around the Baltic Sea gives them a relatively high degree of organizational structure and hierarchy. Various environmental policy networks discussed below are centered around a small set of influential intergovernmental organizations or around a host of active non-governmental organizations. Because issue areas are dynamic, overlapping and nested, so too are the networks. There is not one, single Baltic regional environmental network – nor even one regional network for combating marine pollution in the Baltic Sea. Rather, various networks play direct and important roles in developing and diffusing norms and sets of scientific and technical information about environmental priorities and ways of addressing them. However, the networks' successes are more difficult to measure in terms of their environmental impact on the ecological quality of the Baltic Sea itself.

In LRTAP, somewhat smaller and more S&T dominated networks shape work plans and agendas. A long-standing group of air pollution experts and transport and deposition modelers centered around the International Institute for Applied Systems Analysis has long been influential. Among NGOs, perhaps the most consistently engaged is a group originally called the Swedish NGO Secretariat on Acid Rain, founded in 1982. The group is now called AirClim: Air Pollution and Climate Secretariat. The name change reflects the evolution of long range air pollution scientific and political agendas from an early focus on acidification to a broader concern for a larger set of air pollution and climate change challenges that traverse borders. The group's publication, Acid News, has long been among the most authoritative publications on air pollution policies and issues, presenting broadly accessible scientific and technical information. So, while LRTAP's agenda has expanded substantially over the last 30 years, its focus remains on policymaking in response to high profile scientific and technically backed concern about air pollution that crosses international borders.

From the earliest discussions and debates about environmental pollution in the Baltic Sea to contemporary debates about the myriad environmental challenges within the region, transnational networks of scientific and technical researchers have been actively engaged and organized. These networks are often centered around professional associations and organizations, many of which have regular international meetings, workshops and conferences. Of particular historical importance are the Baltic Marine Biologists, the Conference of Baltic Oceanographers, the International Council for the Exploration of the Seas (ICES), UNESCO programs and committees, and a host of pan-Nordic organizations and programs for international scientific and technical research and exchange. Many of these groups were first to develop policy networks and to begin to advocate regional international environmental cooperation around the Baltic (VanDeveer 1997).

In addition to the scientific networks, regional cooperation, both multilateral and bilateral, exists among environmental activists and a multitude of professional organizations (such as port authorities, city officials and other sub-national governing bodies). Importantly, these groups function as transboundary conduits for specific types of expertise and/or values, principles and policy norms among the countries in the region (Heisler and VanDeveer 1997). Many of these groups engage in professional development or "capacity building" activities with their members, promote public environmental education, and compile and distribute environmental information. Transnational norms are diffused into domestic spheres through discourse communities and social learning within regional networks and organizations (VanDeveer 1997; Andonova and VanDeveer 2012).

Groups such as the Union of Baltic Cities, the ECOBALTIC Foundation, HELCOM PITF's working group on Public Awareness and Environmental Education, and the Baltic Sea Region On-Line Environmental Information Resources for Internet Access (BALLERINA) initiative all have multinational NGO and NGO-public sector public awareness and environmental education programs. These programs include large and diffuse public awareness raising and narrowly tailored education and professional training programs. For example, a number of state, university, intergovernmental and NGO organizations are coordinating "An Agenda 21 for the Baltic Sea Region" to formulate and attempt to implement an action plan for sustainable development in the region. The initiative, like many around the Baltic region, involves public, private and civil society actors, seeking to enhance collaboration between diverse groups across all three sectors (Joas *et al.* 2008; Kern 2011).

Baltic environmental protection efforts constitute an institutionally dense web of connections – including parliamentarians and other policymakers, scientific and technical groups, advocacy NGOs of many kinds, and professional organizations from the region. Regional organizations designed explicitly to build and expand regional networks and cooperation activities of all kinds are sponsored by groups of universities, intergovernmental organization, environmental NGOs, Nordic states – and by a host of private sector actors such as the regional chamber of commerce and sector-specific industry associations. Subnational public officials participate in an extensive set of regional organizations and networks, linking public officials, private sector actors and NGOs in regional issue-specific networks around such issues as wastewater treatment, urban pollution, parks protection, ports management and pollution, and so on. Also, a small number of regionally organized networks focus on specific marine and wildlife species protection and management. In addition, many regional groups and organizations are linked to larger pan-European and global institutions. As Kern (2011) makes clear, both the nongovernmental and intergovernmental initiatives have moved toward more concerted attempts to enact and engender sustainable development ideas over time, seeking to integrate environmental protection with broader economic and social development goals.

Baltic regional environmental actors and networks are shaped by the involvement of other international organizations (and a host of their constituent organizational bodies) including the EU. With the governance changes across the formerly communist Central and Eastern Europe and the former Soviet Union, and the drive toward EU membership in 2004 of Estonia, Latvia, Lithuania and Poland, the EU role in the Baltic region increased substantially. While the EU is hierarchically organized, its involvement in the Baltic region helps to produce and support regional sub-networks, each centered on their various program areas active in the region.

Actors in the Baltic environmental networks spend a great deal of their time and resources expanding the networks and institutionalizing their links to one another. Over time, one can identify a clear trend toward increasing routinization and formal organization within the networks. Given the policy goals of most of the network actors and their need for material and information resources, it is generally in their interest to maintain and expand their ties within the network and sub-networks. This often leads, in the Baltic case, to the increasing formalization of networks into formal organizations with physical locations, small staffs, budgets and program areas and at least minimal sets of rules and decision-making procedures. Furthermore, the regional web of interconnected individuals, groups and organizations grows increasingly dense – with highly overlapping participation. The region has seen an increasing number of formally established regional organizations. Formal organizations yield many of the material ramifications of deepening regional integration and networking, including mailing lists and email lists and list-servers, websites, regular meetings of representatives and participants from around the region, increasing hierarchy among individuals and roles within the organizations, and shared decision-making procedures. The production of increasing amounts of information products – printed publications and electronic versions, for example – make the boundaries of the network ever more difficult to identify because (for instance) it is not possible to determine the total number of information users/receivers. Finally, increasing institutionalization is also evident in the more abstract realm of social institutions such as regionally shared principles, norms and discourses. For example, the precautionary and polluter-pays principles have been rapidly diffused throughout the region, having inspired the creation of pollution, consumption and resource extraction taxes, and engendering changes in many states' legal definition of pollution toward more precautionary and probabilistic definitions (VanDeveer 1997).

Engaged LRTAP actors have generally not invested much time and energy expanding their networks and involving an ever growing set of diverse actors and issues. Instead, influential LRTAP states (lead states, often called) and S&T and NGO actors like IIASA analysts and the AirClim Secretariat have focused more on influencing the policymaking discussions among LRTAP state parties and with the EU Commission. Facilitating such a focus is that the lead or pusher states in both LRTAP and the EU air policy debates tend to be the same, offering lead actors opportunities to venue shop for their ideas and policy priorities (Selin and VanDeveer 2003, 2012).

A final focus of actor activity discernible within the Baltic environmental policy networks involves the regional diffusion or dissemination of resources, norms and processes (or procedures) among actors. Actors distribute material resources and information across the network. For example, NGOs in the transition countries regularly receive financial and technological support from their counterparts in the wealthier Baltic States such as Sweden and Germany. Various actors work within networks to solicit, raise, supply and/or expend material resources such as funding, physical equipment, in-kind services, expertise and data of various kinds. The offices of virtually all active environmental policymakers and advocates in the region contain numerous directories of their respective counterparts around the region and a myriad of internationally sanctioned manuals for their respective areas of policy interest. Regionally networked actors also disseminate principles, norms and procedures for environmental policy, and increasingly standardized organizational processes for activities such as information gathering and distribution, fund raising, and project development (Connolly and Gutner 2000). Such regional diffusion dynamics include dissemination of models for organizational development, policy advocacy strategies, public access to information and environmental policy implementation, thereby linking the diffusion activities to the advocacy and institutionalization activities discussed above.

The "implementation turn" on international agendas

Networked actors' records in producing new commitments from state officials and new regional institutions has been impressive, but widespread regional implementation of international environmental commitments remains mixed. The mature, institutionalized networks around Baltic environmental protection issues suggest that networks may be better at driving the distribution and diffusion of material and ideational resources than they are at producing ground-level implementation. For example, transnationally networked actors move information and material resources around the region, shaping consensus on scientific, technical and environmental policy issues resulting in the issuance of joint "recommendations" by the region's states. Work on such recommendations has produced regionally standardized norms and principles (e.g. polluter pays, precautionary approaches, and emissions standards) and highly technical sets of regulatory practices for many types of facilities and industries. In CLRTAP, years of work to produce new protocols often resulted in years of refusal to ratify on the part of some states, and very scant evidence of implementation and compliance among some ratifiers.

Networked actors – those in the public and civil society sectors – are aware of their weakness on the implementation side. As a result, goals of actors constituting the networks have also evolved over time, and are increasingly focusing on outcomes such as implementation review procedures, strengthening of existing domestic policies, and capacity building exercises. In other words, one can see in both regimes a kind of "implementation turn" in the political agenda, as many participating actors work to push implementation of previously stated commitments higher on the agenda of the engaged states. In both regimes, organizational bodies have been tasked since the 1990s – under pressure from S&T, environmental NGO and lead state actors – to more specifically review and assess information about implementation of agreed commitments, in an attempt to raise implementation rates. In the Baltic, implementation task forces, joint implementation assessment and long lists of pledges and individual projects have been repeatedly organized to drive all participating states to prioritize needed policy changes and investments toward implementation. In CLRTAP, joint implementation review among states and extensive S&T and public sector capacity building have been organized. These efforts were pushed to the front of political agendas in both regimes by combinations of lead state, S&T, and environmental NGO activism that repeatedly called for a much greater focus on implementation of announced goals.

Networked regional knowledge communities

The diverse, and often fractious networks through which consensual knowledge is created in both regimes and through which NGO, state and research agenda are co-produced has helped to keep environmental action and policy-making effectiveness on regional political agendas for decades. Active epistemic communities are present, and clearly influential, in both regional regimes. But an important clarification is warranted here. Namely, the epistemic communities cannot be understood as single, coherent groups whose members always hold a single set of consensus positions – about policy or scientific and technically based causal models.

If epistemic communities in each case are understood as communities of knowledge production – meaning communities that include debate and some degree of shared ideas of knowledge creation and legitimization – then they are clearly influential in each region. In CLRTAP, where they tend to be smaller and more technically based (and elite vetted), one sees a rather tight-knit set of experts. Yet, even in such a group, differences on integrated assessment model assumptions, methods and/or outputs, for example, exist and often persist over time. In the Baltic region, where regime-connected networks include many more participants across very different civil society, state, and private sector organizations – with a vast array of professional and educational differences – it is much more difficult to even speak of a (singular) epistemic community. Rather, one sees a series of overlapping, connected communities – perhaps characterized best as "networked communities." So, while some may labor over setting detailed technical standards for urban run-off, or pulp and paper industry practices, others campaign for and debate historical preservation and culturally grounded ideas about the nature of sustainable development in the Baltic region, or its sub-regions.

Conclusions: lead states and institutionalized networks

In marine pollution politics and in LRTAP, the cooperation of leading states and small groups of leading state civil servants with S&T researchers and civil society actors is central to understanding why actors with the highest domestic regulatory standards so often shape (sometimes even dominate) international agenda setting. These leading states lend staff to international institutions, sponsor large quantities of the research and modeling (and the conferences and meetings where consensus is constructed), and build and sustain networks designed to achieve policy commitments that bring other jurisdictions up to their high standards – akin to Vogel's trading up and DeSombre's "Baptist and bootlegger" dynamics (Vogel 1995; DeSombre 2000). In both cases, the lead role of a subgroup of lead states, usually in close cooperation with S&T and non-state actors of various types, often manage to move new issues on the common political agenda. Certainly at the international level, leader/pusher states appear quite influential (a phenomenon identified in global politics associated with the Landmines ban, for example, and other issues outside the environmental area).

In neither regime does one see extensive dominance of particular actor groups of agenda setting, though in both cases environmental lead states tend to have the most influence on the agenda. In other words, those states which often already have higher environmental standards than many other participants tend to frame discussions of common policies in both fora. Furthermore, they tend to invest most in S&T data, research and knowledge creation and their nationals often have substantial influence on S&T assessment bodies. Certainly, however, Baltic regional environmental cooperation captures public imagination more than does LRTAP. In part, this appears to result from the highly technical and state-centric nature of the formal cooperation under UNECE.

A caveat regarding generalizing from both cases is their regional framing. That is, it may be important that both "regional regimes" are predominately situated within Europe, where regional integration and decision-making institutions are increasingly seen as the norm, rather than an exception. I remain uncertain what to make of the importance, in agenda setting and framing, or the regional frame of both cooperation institutions and of the S&T knowledge (text, images, membership, etc.) that is central to the discursive and policy agendas in both cooperation regimes. Nearly all participating civil society and S&T actors endorse, use and promulgate the regional framing of marine and air pollution ideas and norms in each regime. In fact, many actors have sought to reproduce the perceived success of each regional regime in other regions of Europe and around the globe. And yet, most states and societies pollute their own coastal waters much more than their neighbors – and most produce the great majority of their own air pollution. Experience around the Mediterranean and Black Seas, for example, suggests that most people should demand more from their own governments, rather than place their hopes in international cooperation institutions if they want identifiable ecological improvement (VanDeveer 2000).

For over 30 years, environmental protection advocates (scientific researchers, environmental activists, and some state officials) have pushed national and international officials to create and maintain organizations for regional cooperation among overlapping groups of scientific researchers, national and municipal policymakers, non-governmental environmental activists and, more recently, private sector actors. VanDeveer (2000) argues that, in the earliest stages of regional anti-pollution efforts, actors are concerned largely with "getting organized" for transnational and interstate cooperation. Here actors attempt to overcome significant political obstacles to multinational cooperation (such as high level political conflict between states) and they tend to be focused on building common institutions for regularized scientific and technical cooperation, the provision of environmental policy advice, multilateral policymaking, and the construction of broad-based consensus positions (e.g. "the sea is being polluted by

X, Y and Z substances" or "air pollution is traveling across international borders and damaging distant environments"). At this stage, actors engage in activities analogous to those described by Keck and Sikkink (1998) in their discussion of human rights networks. That is, actors use the networks to define and increase awareness of "problems."

Establishing, maintaining and expanding regional networks are goals in themselves and means to attain other outcomes: namely, the construction of regionally institutionalized interactions around an issue area, the establishment of formal regional organizations for interstate and transnational cooperation of many kinds, and environmental protection. Networked Baltic regional actors have been tremendously successful at creating and expanding regional networks, organizations and common policies. Such networks appear to keep environmental issues – older ones and new, emerging concerns – on the social, political and S&T researchers' agendas.

Baltic environmental cooperation is highly institutionalized at multiple levels of governance, including the following forms of cooperation: interstate (bilateral and multilateral), inter-bureaucratic, subnational-to-subnational (regional and local), scientific and technological, private sector and NGO. Agenda setting within this extensive environmental cooperation therefore involves a large set of overlapping environmental policy networks in the region. Lead states and environmental advocates, using the same S&T discourses, helped push the regionalization of more ambitious goals via periodic ministerial conferences. Lead states, pushed by and in cooperation with environmental advocates, successfully used these meetings (a de facto regional institution, since they persist over time) to shape the regional environmental political agenda. These regional environmental policy networks have been successful in disseminating material resources and processes throughout the region, including their involvement in gathering and distributing information, funds and equipment, and creating and diffusing norms about environmental priorities and ways of addressing them.

The literature on policy networks contains little discussion regarding whether or not such dynamics should be treated as one decentralized "regional environmental network" or many linked networks and sub-networks. Yet, even in the LRTAP case, who exactly is to be termed "in" knowledge or epistemic networks and who is "out" remains problematic. In agenda setting, the influence of particular images, discourses or policy frames is therefore likely to vary substantially across networks or parts of the many engaged communities.

If research on agenda setting dynamics within the context of densely institutionalized transnational networks research is to advance understanding of the relationship of international factors to domestic policy and behavior, more attention to the co-production of S&T and political knowledge, and to growth implementation concerns, is likely to be required. Research on the domestic implementation of international rules and norms makes clear that international agreements do not simply implement themselves (O'Neill *et al.* 2004). Implementation itself may well need to be a major part of the international agenda, to drive states and other actors to make it a priority. Numerous factors may facilitate and/or inhibit implementation, including regime/agreement design, organizational capacities at various levels of organization, intervening domestic institutions, and the presence of implementation review mechanisms. As lead states and NGOs learn more about how to get implementation on international agendas – in addition to new issues and commitments –they are likely to demand more focused attention on it. What are the connections between transnational policy networks and implementation of agreed standards? Mediterranean regional pollution control efforts provide a cautionary tale. The Mediterranean region is home to a very active transnational environmental policy network (Haas 1990). Networked actors have been an important force in pushing for and creating a multitude of regional environmental protection organizations and institutions in the past 30 years and more. Yet, in many cases little environmental improvement has been witnessed (Kutting 2000; VanDeveer 2000; EEA 1999).

Kern (2011) argues that transnational environmental networks for political action are proving to be important influences on sustainable development debates and initiatives across the Baltic region, but networked actors face substantial obstacles in their attempts to move political, social and economic institutions toward the realization of sustainability. For three decades, research on CLRTAP has demonstrated that a scientific and technically framed political agenda has helped to keep state officials negotiating around specific policy goals and challenges related to particular air pollution issues. But explaining why particular S&T-based ideas dominate S&T communities of actors may be harder than explaining the political agenda. In both regimes, however, the combination of committed, concerned leading state institutions and iterated investments in the generation and organization of S&T knowledge for policymaking has proved very influential in inter-state and transnational agenda setting over time.

Notes

1 The section draws on VanDeveer 2011 and 2004; Selin & VanDeveer 2004; and Gutner & VanDeveer 2001.
2 All documents and declarations are available on the HELCOM website.

References

Andonova, L. and VanDeveer, S.D. (2012) "EU Expansion and Internationalization of Environmental Politics in Central and Eastern Europe", in P. Steinberg and S.D. VanDeveer, eds., *Comparative Environmental Politics*, Cambridge, MA: MIT Press, 287–312.

Auer, M. (1996) *Crafting an Agreement: Negotiations to Reduce Pollution from the Nordic Pulp and Paper Industry, 1985–89,* PhD dissertation, Yale.

Auer, M. and Nilenders, E. (2001) "Verifying Environmental Cleanup: Lessons from the Baltic Sea Joint Comprehensive Environmental Action Programme", *Environmental Planning C* (19), 2001, 881–901.

Bäckstrand, K. (2001) *What Can Nature Withstand? Science, Politics and Discourses in Transboundary Air Pollution Diplomacy*, Lund: Lund Political Studies 116.

Balsiger, J. and VanDeveer, S.D. (2010) "Regional Governance and Environmental Problems", in R.A. Denemark, ed., *International Studies Encyclopedia*, Oxford: Wiley-Blackwell.

Balsiger, J. and VanDeveer, S.D. (2012) "Navigating Regional Environmental Governance", *Global Environmental Politics* 12(3), 1–17.

Börzel, T.A. (1998) "Organizing Babylon: On the Different Conceptions of Policy Networks", *Public Administration* 76, 253–73.

Carmin, J. and VanDeveer, S.D., eds. (2005) *EU Enlargement and the Environment*, New York: Routledge.

Connolly, B. and Gutner, T. (2000) "Policy Networks and Process Diffusion: Environment for Europe", paper presented at the International Studies Association Conference.

Cowling, E. (1982) "Acid Precipitation in Historical Perspective", *Environmental Science and Technology* 16(2), 110A–123A.

DeSombre, E. (2000) *Domestic Sources of International Environmental Policy*, Cambridge, MA: MIT Press.

Dybern, B.I. (1980) "The Organizational Pattern of Baltic Marine Science", *Ambio* 9(3–4), 187–93.

EEA (1999) *State and Pressures of the Marine and Coastal Mediterranean Environment*, Environmental Issues Series No. 5, Copenhagen: EEA.

Farrell, A.E. and Jäger, J. (2006) *Assessments of Regional and Global Environmental Risks: Designing Processes for the Effective Use of Science in Decision Making*, Washington, DC: Resources for the Future.

Grennfelt, P. and Hov, Ø. (2005) "Regional Air Pollution at a Turning Point", *Ambio* 34(1), 2–10.

Gutner, T.L. (2002) *Banking on the Environment*, Cambridge, MA: MIT Press.

Gutner, T.L. and VanDeveer, S.D. (2001) "Networks, Coalitions and Communities: Capacity Building in the Baltic Region", conference paper, International Studies Association Annual Convention, Chicago, IL, February 20–4.

Haas, P.M. (1990) *Saving the Mediterranean: The Politics of International Environmental Cooperation,* New York: Columbia University Press.

Haas, P.M. (1993) "Protecting the Baltic and North Seas", in Peter M. Haas, Robert O. Keohane and Marc A. Levy, eds., *Institutions for the Earth*, Cambridge, MA: MIT Press.

Heisler, M.O. and VanDeveer, S.D. (1997) "The Diffusion of Virtue? International Institutions as Agents of Domestic Regime Change", paper presented at the 1997 annual meeting of the Northeast Political Science Association, Philadelphia, 13–15 November.

HELCOM Project Team on Hazardous Substances (2001) "The Implementation of the 1988 Ministerial Declaration on the Protection of the Marine Environment of the Baltic Sea Area with regard to Hazardous Substances", HELCOM.

Hjorth, R. (1992) *Building International Institutions for Environmental Protection: The Case of Baltic Sea Environmental Cooperation*, Linkoping, Sweden: Linkoping Studies in Arts and Sciences.

Hjorth, R. (1993) "Baltic Environmental Cooperation: The Role of Epistemic Communities and the Politics of Regime Change", *Cooperation and Conflict* 29(1), 11–31.

ICES (International Council for the Exploration of Seas) (1970) "Report of the ICES Working Group on Pollution of the Baltic Sea", *ICES Cooperative Research Report*, Series A. No. 15, Copenhagen: ICES.

ICES (International Council for the Exploration of Seas) (1974) "Research Programs for Investigations of the Baltic as a National Resource with Special Reference to Pollution Problems", *ICES Cooperative Research Report*, No. 42, Copenhagen: ICES.

Jasanoff, S. and Wynne, B. (1998) "Science and Decision Making", in S. Rayner and E. Malone, eds., *Human Choice and Climate Change, Volume 1: The Societal Framework*, Columbus, OH: Battelle Press, pp. 1–88.

Joas, M., Jahn, D. and Kern, K. (2008) *Governing a Common Sea: Environmental Policies in the Baltic Sea Region*, London: Earthscan.

Keck, M.E, and Sikkink, K. (1998) *Activists Beyond Borders; Advocacy Networks in International Politics*, Ithaca, NY: Cornell University Press.

Kern, K. (2011) "Governance for Sustainable Development in the Baltic Sea Region", *Baltic Studies Journal* (42)(1), 21–35.

Koskenniemi, M. (1993) "Environmental Cooperation in the Baltic Region", *Tulane Journal of International and Comparative Law* 59(1).

Kutting, G. (2000) *Environment, Society and International Relations*, London: Routledge.

Levy, Marc (1993) "European Acid Rain: The Power of Toteboard Diplomacy", in Peter M. Haas, Robert O. Keohane and Marc A. Levy, eds., *Institutions for the Earth: Sources of Effective International Environmental Protection,* Cambridge, MA: MIT Press, 75–132.

Lidskog, R. and Sundqvist, G., eds. (2012) *Governing the Air: The Dynamics of Science, Policy and Citizen Interaction*, Cambridge, MA: MIT Press.

Litfin, K. (1995) "Framing Science: Precautionary Discourse and the Ozone Treaties", *Millennium: Journal of International Studies* 24(2), 251–77.

McCormack, J. (1997) *Acid Earth*, 3rd edn, London: Earthscan.

Mitchell, R.B. (2009) *International Politics and the Environment*, London: Sage.

Oden, S. (1968) "The Acidification of Air and Precipitation and Its Consequences in the Natural Environment", *Ecological Community Bulletin* No. 1, Stockholm: Swedish National Science Research Council.

OECD (2000) "Environmental Performance Reviews (1st Cycle): Conclusions and Recommendations: 32 Countries (1993–2000)", *OECD Working Paper on Environmental Performance*, Paris: OECD.

O'Neill, K. (2009) *The Environment and International Relations*, Cambridge: Cambridge University Press.

O'Neill, K., Balsiger, J. and VanDeveer, S.D. (2004) "Actors, Norms and Impact: Recent International Cooperation Theory and the Influence of Agent-Structure Debate", *Annual Review of Political Science* (7), 149–75.

Rytovuori, H. (1980) "Structures of Détente and Ecological Interdependence", *Cooperation and Conflict* (15)(2), 85–102.

Selin, H. (2010) *Global Governance of Hazardous Chemicals: Challenges of Multilevel Management*, Cambridge, MA: MIT Press.

Selin, H. and VanDeveer, S.D. (2003) "Mapping Institutional Linkages in European Air Pollution Politics", *Global Environmental Politics* 3(3), 14–46.

Selin, H. and VanDeveer, S.D. (2004) "Baltic Sea Hazardous Substances Management: Results and Challenges", *Ambio* (33)(3)(May), 153–60.

Selin, H. and VanDeveer, S.D., eds. (2009) *Changing Climates in North American Politics*, Cambridge, MA: MIT Press.

Selin, H. and VanDeveer, S.D. (2012) "Institutional Linkages and European Air Pollution Politics", in Rolf Lidskog and Goran Sundqvist, eds., *Governing the Air*, Cambridge, MA: MIT Press, 61–92.

Skjærseth J.B. (2000) *North Sea Cooperation: Linking Internationl and Domestic Pollution Control*, Manchester: Manchester University Press.

Social Learning Group (2001) *Learning to Manage Global Environmental Risks*, Vols. 1, 2, Cambridge, MA: MIT Press.

Steinberg, P.F. and VanDeveer, S.D., eds. (2012) *Comparative Environmental Politics: Theory, Practice and Prospects*, Cambridge, MA: MIT Press.

Tuinstra, W. (2008) "European Air Pollution Assessments: Co-production of Science and Policy", *International Environmental Agreements: Politics, Law and Economics* 8(1), 35–49.

Tuinstra, W., Hordijk, L. and Kroeze, C. (2006) "Moving Boundaries in Transboundary Air Pollution Co-production of Science and Policy Under the Convention on Long Range Transboundary Air Pollution", *Global Environmental Change* 16(4), 349–63.

VanDeveer, S.D. (1997) "Normative Force: The State, Transnational Norms and International Environmental Regimes", Doctoral Dissertation, University of Maryland, College Park.

VanDeveer, S.D. (1998) "European Politics with a Scientific Face", *ENRP Discussion Paper E-98-9*, Kennedy School of Government, Harvard University.

VanDeveer, S.D. (2000) "Changing Course to Protect European Seas: Lessons after 25 Years", *Environment* 42(6)(July/August), 10–26.

VanDeveer, S.D. (2002) "Environmental Cooperation and Regional Peace: Baltic Politics, Programs and Prospects", in Ken Conca, ed., *Environmental Cooperation and Regional Peace*, Baltimore: Johns Hopkins University Press.

VanDeveer, S.D. (2004) "Ordering Environments: Organizing Knowledge and Regions in European International Environmental Cooperation", in S. Jasanoff and M. Long-Martello, eds., *Earthly Politics: Local and Global in Environmental Governance*, Cambridge, MA: MIT Press, 309–34.

VanDeveer, S.D. (2006a) "Assessment Information in European Politics: East and West", in Ronald B. Mitchell, William C. Clark, David W. Cash and Nancy Dickson. eds., *Global Environmental Assessments: Information and Influence,* MA: MIT Press, 113–50.

VanDeveer, S.D. (2006b) "European Politics with a Scientific Face", in Alex Farrell and Jill Jaeger, eds., *Assessments of Regional and Global Environmental Risks*, Washington, DC: Resources for the Future, 25–63.

VanDeveer, S.D. (2011) "Networked Baltic Environmental Cooperation", *Journal of Baltic Studies* 42(1), 37–55.

Vogel, D. (1995) *Trading Up: Consumer and Environmental Regulation in a Global Economy*, Cambridge, MA: Harvard University Press.

Westing, A., ed. (1989) *Comprehensive Security in the Baltic: An Environmental Approach,* London: Sage Publications.

Wettestad, J. (2002) *Clearing the Air: European Advances in Tackling Acid Rain and Atmospheric Pollution,* Aldershot: Ashgate.

Zmudzinski, L. (1989) "Environmental Quality in the Baltic Region", in Arthur H. Westing, ed., *Comprehensive Security in the Baltic*, London: Sage.

3   Lessons learned in multilateral environmental negotiations

Pamela S. Chasek

Negotiations represent the process by which parties create collective arrangements for environmental management, including hard law, soft law or voluntary commitments. As noted in the introductory chapter, although various types of public–private partnerships and other new approaches are becoming increasingly important, the traditional "hard law" multilateral environmental agreement (MEA) is still the dominant form of international environmental governance. But this is no easy feat. Global environmental issues, which combine scientific uncertainty, citizen and industry activism, politics and economics, may be among the most complicated and challenging to resolve. In environmental negotiations, the characteristics of the actors, the issues and the outcome all point to the need for strategies and processes that may be different from those used in other multilateral negotiations, such as those on arms control, trade or peace. The negotiations themselves are both complex and time-consuming. They are usually preceded by extensive scientific fact-finding. The debate then centers on various response strategies, although political rivalries and national sovereignty concerns often get in the way. Any solution is constrained by the costs of deploying new technologies and concerns about the fair allocation of the costs involved (Chasek 2001: 2).

What determines the nature of the outcomes of these negotiations? Good settlements are those that mobilize political commitments of will and resources to deal with the problems in a successful way. Bad ones are likely to inhibit subsequent progress, or reward opponents of meaningful cooperation. What determines one or the other? What roles do different actors play in this regard? What configurations of actors improve or inhibit the outcome? If actors are organized as a network, does it significantly affect the course of the negotiations? This chapter will seek to examine these questions to determine any correlations between roles of actors and outcomes of multilateral environmental negotiations.

To examine the roles of actors and networks in the negotiation of MEAs, this chapter examines three different case studies: the 1987 Montreal Protocol on Substances that Deplete the Ozone Layer, the 1994 UN Convention to Combat Desertification, and the 2000 Cartagena Protocol on Biosafety. Each of these cases involved different states playing different roles, and different nonstate actors and networks (including non-governmental organizations (NGOs), business and industry groups, the scientific community, and intergovernmental organizations).

Finally, the subject matter covers the breadth of MEAs from a global commons/ chemicals issue (ozone depletion) to biodiversity, technology and trade (biosafety) and to a land management/economic development issue (desertification).

This chapter will first briefly examine the process of multilateral environmental negotiations and then look at the different actors involved, through the framework of the three cases. The chapter will then analyze the configurations and networks of actors and elaborate some lessons learned.

Process of multilateral environmental negotiations[1]

Multilateral negotiation can be defined as the process of simultaneous negotiation by three or more parties over one or more issues that aims at agreement acceptable to all participants (Touval 1991: 351). Within this context, multilateral environmental negotiations still have their own set of distinguishing attributes.[2]

First, there are multiple issues. What appears to be a relatively straightforward environmental issue, such as protecting the ozone layer, soon turns out to have important economic, social, and political implications. Second, there are multiple roles of the actors involved, including pushers, who try to produce an ambitious agreement that is consonant with their own interests, and laggards, who oppose or resist a strong agreement. Sjöstedt *et al.* (1994: 11) argue that actors can also play additional roles including conducting, defending and cruising. Conductors seek to produce an agreement from a neutral position. Defenders are single-issue participants and cruisers are filler, with no strong interests of their own. Third, there is the difficulty in arriving at decisions. Parties to multilateral negotiations usually find themselves confronted with a procedural trade-off between efficiency, fairness or legitimacy, meaning recognition by all participants that their interests and views have been taken into account in the resulting decision (Hopmann 1996: 247). As a result, the most common decision rule has been the attainment of consensus – a decision rule in which, essentially, abstention is an affirmative rather than a negative vote (Zartman 1994: 5). Pressure to accept consensus language is often so high that parties may agree to the text at the eleventh hour so as not to be blamed for the failure of the negotiations.

While states play the primary roles in determining the outcomes, they are not the only actors. Non-state actors – intergovernmental organizations, NGOs, corporations, and the scientific community – seek to influence the positions of individual state actors, the international negotiation process, and the outcomes. Group dynamics and networking also play an important role in the process, especially with regard to coalition formation, the role of interpersonal relationships, the development of leadership, and the institutional context within which many multilateral negotiations take place (Chasek 2001: 25).

Actors and networks

As noted above, one of the key elements that determine the outcomes of multilateral environmental negotiations is the different types and roles of actors and networks in the negotiations. This multiplicity of actors helps to set the global environmental agenda, and initiate and mediate the process of regime formation. Since the conduct of international negotiations within the United Nations system is still mainly the prerogative of national governments, states remain the most important actors. Pusher states are able to influence the process by calling for the negotiations, through the provision of funding and the scheduling of negotiating sessions and intersessional workshops to educate other participants, contributions to trust funds to encourage the participation of developing countries, and the development of draft negotiating texts.

International organizations, including secretariats, are also influential participants in multilateral environmental negotiations. They may supply information needed to clarify issues, summarize proceedings and undertake systematic comparison of key elements in national position papers. According to Scott (1985), the role of international organizations and secretariats can range from a purely technical and servicing nature to an "activist" approach. With regard to the former, Benedick points out (1993: 224) that international organizations as secretariats are essential for the logistical tasks of convening meetings, developing or commissioning background documentation, and providing translation and similar activities. The secretariat provides continuity for negotiations that may stretch through numerous sessions over a period of years, during which there may be considerable turnover among government negotiators.

But international organizations can go beyond a secretariat function. According to Biermann *et al.* (2009: 47), international bureaucracies can influence the behavior of other actors by changing their knowledge and belief systems. It may help determine which issues the international community will address through its influence on the agenda for global action. During negotiations, international organizations may also participate as actors, providing independent and authoritative information on a global environmental issue. In some cases, delegations prefer the technical/servicing role, because an activist secretariat may be inimical to their interests. In some cases, international organizations can have their own agendas and try to influence the negotiations in such a way that their desired outcome is guaranteed. Sometimes this agenda can be ideological in nature and other times it can be practical, such as a means to guaranteed continued employment of staff (Young 1993).

A third type of participant is the non-governmental organization. NGOs can include public advocacy groups, environmental organizations, development and social welfare organizations. The rate of participation of NGOs in environmental negotiations has increased in recent years. Not only do they have unprecedented access to the negotiations themselves, they also play roles in the agenda setting and implementation of the resulting agreements, as described in other chapters in this volume. NGOs influence MEA negotiations in various ways, including: issue definition; lobbying governments at international negotiations; proposing draft text to be included in treaties and agreements; and providing scientific and technical information, and assisting in capacity building, especially to developing country delegations but also to secretariats and others (Chasek *et al.* 2013).

Knowledge and information are a key source of power for NGOs in world politics, according to Betsill and Corell (2008: 23). They argue that in international environmental negotiations NGOs often use their specialized knowledge in the hope of modifying actions taken by state decision-makers and/or altering how they define their interests. Such knowledge is a particularly valuable resource since government delegates, especially from developing countries, often turn to NGOs for help in understanding the nature of the problems and the implications of various policy alternatives under consideration. Knowledge and information enhance NGOs' perceived legitimacy in negotiations and may open up opportunities for influence. NGOs use tactics very similar to those used by states in order to exert influence on the negotiations. Persuasion is the most widely used, but NGO diplomacy may also involve more coercive measures, including threats and "blaming and shaming" in the hope of getting support for their positions (Betsill and Corell 2008: 23).

The importance of scientific evidence and expertise in the politics of many global environmental issues cannot be ignored. Indeed, a significant degree of scientific understanding and consensus has sometimes been a minimum condition for serious international action on an issue (Chasek *et al.* 2013: 28). Over the past three decades, an international network of cooperating scientists and scientific institutions has become an actor on the negotiating scene. In some cases, scientists have counterbalanced the industrial lobby, worked closely with government officials and assumed responsibility for the implications of their findings for policy options (Chasek 2001: 28). Informal networks of experts can also contribute to regime design and effectiveness by strengthening the knowledge base on which regimes can be designed and can operate (Biermann *et al.* 2009: 47).

Corporations, including business, industry and the media, have been active in multilateral environmental negotiations for many years. Like NGOs, representatives of corporate interests lobby during negotiations primarily by providing information and analysis to the delegations most sympathetic to their causes. They may also facilitate or delay, strengthen or weaken global environmental regimes by direct actions that have an impact on the environment. They may take these actions unilaterally or based on agreements reached with their respective governments. Such actions can be crucial to a government's ability to commit itself to implementation of a treaty (Chasek *et al.* 2013: 98). The media can be the major influence on public opinion on both the negotiations and the issue under negotiation. Public opinion can then influence the position of government delegations, in some cases more than others.

Organization of case studies

International environmental negotiations over the past 30 years have typically included different configurations of the major different types of actors described in the previous section. Closer examination of the negotiations of the 1987 Montreal Protocol on Substances that Deplete the Ozone Layer, the 1994 UN Convention to Combat Desertification, and the 2000 Cartagena Protocol on Biosafety provides useful insights into these configurations.

Each case elaborates the different actors who participated in the negotiations. Within each section, the different roles are highlighted along with the active actor configurations during the negotiations.

Montreal Protocol

The Montreal Protocol on Substances that Deplete the Ozone Layer was designed to reduce the production and consumption of ozone depleting substances in order to reduce their abundance in the atmosphere, and thereby protect the earth's fragile ozone layer. The original Montreal Protocol was negotiated in 1986 and 1987, adopted on 16 September 1987 and entered into force on 1 January 1989. The nature and relationship between the actors reflect this time period when negotiations were dominated by developed countries with limited participation by other groups. In addition, the case of the Montreal Protocol illustrates quite clearly that economic implications and national environmental policies often have the largest influence on the roles and networks of actors.

States. During the original Montreal Protocol negotiations in the 1980s, the United States, which at that time accounted for more than 40 percent of worldwide chlorofluorocarbon (CFC) production, played a pusher role in the negotiations in part because it had already banned CFC use in aerosol spray cans, a large percentage of total use at that time, and wanted other states to follow suit. However, for an international ozone-protection policy to succeed, it was essential that all states producing and consuming CFCs come to consensus.

During the 1986–1987 negotiations, the pusher states – a coalition that included Canada, Finland, Norway, Sweden, Switzerland and the United States – initially advocated a freeze followed by a 95 percent reduction in production of CFCs over a period of ten to 14 years. The laggards – the European Community (EC), Japan and the Soviet Union – collectively represented nearly 60 percent of worldwide CFC production but doubted the science, wanted to preserve their industries' overseas markets, and wished to avoid the costs of adopting substitutes. The laggards eventually proposed placing a cap on production capacity at current levels. Pusher states argued that a capacity cap would actually allow for an increase in real CFC production because European producers could increase real production while maintaining their current capacity, gaining economic benefits from the regime. Consistently rejecting this proposal, pusher states issued a series of counter proposals before eventually offering a 50 percent cut as a final compromise. As late as April 1987, the EC would not accept more than a 20 percent reduction, but relented in the final days of negotiations. The evolution of the pusher-state position reflected the need to include the Europeans in the Protocol. A regime that did not include countries responsible for 40 percent of global production could not succeed. Thus, they believed it was better to compromise at 50 percent cuts and hope that these could be increased in light of future scientific information than to have the EC outside the regime (Chasek *et al.* 2013).

Large developing countries, including Brazil, China, India and Indonesia, formed another potential coalition of laggards. Their bargaining leverage stemmed from their potential to produce very large quantities of CFCs – a situation that would eventually eviscerate the effectiveness of any regime.[3] Although most developing countries were cruisers and did not play an active role early in the regime's development, they eventually used this leverage to secure a delayed control schedule and precedent-setting financial and technical assistance.

International organizations. The key international organization actor in the Montreal Protocol negotiations was the United Nations Environment Programme (UNEP) and within these negotiations, UNEP played different roles. For example, UNEP contributed to the scientific discussions by co-sponsoring research with NASA, NOAA and the US Federal Aviation Administration, and the World Meteorological Organization. While this role is similar to that of the role of the scientific community (see below), UNEP was responsible for creating this network of scientific actors to inform the process. UNEP also played a secretariat role by convening the Montreal Protocol negotiations as well as a series of workshops prior to the negotiations. During the negotiations, UNEP started playing a more activist role as then UNEP Executive Director Mostafa Tolba took over as mediator when a deadlock emerged between the protagonists. Tolba took the initiative in the form of written communications incorporating proposed compromise language and informal consultations to narrow the gap on central issues (Széll 1993; Benedick 1991). In the post-agreement negotiations, it was UNEP, specifically Tolba, who convened the first meeting in 1988 to consider practical details of implementing the Montreal Protocol. In 1990, Tolba circulated for consideration a "personal" proposal for revisions of the protocol's control measures in response to the latest scientific information about the role of these chemicals and the pace of ozone depletion. Tolba had hoped that his efforts would promote greater consensus on the measures (Benedick 1991). He continued to hold informal consultations prior to and during the Meeting of the Parties in London in June 1990. According to Benedick (1993: 225), Tolba "risked taking personal positions, he initiated ideas and advanced concerns that might otherwise have been overlooked, and he in effect made UNEP a subtle advocate for governments and populations not represented in the formal negotiation."

Following the negotiations of the protocol, UNEP assumed the role of host of the Ozone Secretariat servicing the scientific bodies and the annual Meetings of the Parties. The Ozone Secretariat has become the hub of the ozone regime and is credited with the smooth cooperation with parties around the world, including the 110 national Ozone Units that have been created following ratification of the Montreal Protocol. The resulting network, facilitated by the Secretariat, provides for efficient communication flows between national authorities that are responsible for implementation, which ultimately feeds back into the intergovernmental processes (Bauer 2009a: 235). The Secretariat, especially its Executive Director, has also actively "interfered" with the intergovernmental negotiations either to facilitate consensus among parties or to seek ways for them to comply with existing commitments under the Protocol (Bauer 2009a: 237). Thus, the Ozone Secretariat, while still a part of UNEP, could be considered a subordinate unit of UNEP. Bauer (2009a) argues that the Secretariat has made its own contributions to the development of the ozone regime, particularly by facilitating highly constructive intergovernmental negotiations, both "on stage" and behind the scenes.

NGOs. When the Montreal Protocol was negotiated, NGOs did not have as much access as they did during the MEA negotiations that took place after the watershed 1992 Earth Summit in Rio de Janeiro that opened up negotiations to greater NGO participation. During the Montreal Protocol negotiations, NGOs were permitted to participate as observers, if they were qualified in fields related to protection of the upper atmosphere. NGOs were not permitted to table proposals and the Chair asked for their views only after the participating governments had given theirs. As a result NGOs remained largely silent during formal negotiating sessions, making no more than occasional, short statements. They sat and listened carefully to the proceedings and used what they learned to brief the press and lobby legislators and Ministers back home before the next round of negotiations. The use of press briefings, the tactic used by most of the North American and European environmental NGOs, resulted in more headlines in the Western media, which helped shaped public opinion (Széll 1993: 39). Among the more active NGOs were the Green movement in Germany and the United Kingdom, and the Natural Resources Defense Council in the United States (Hampson 1995: 257). During the negotiation of the 1987 Protocol, developing country NGOs were largely absent.

American NGOs, led by the Natural Resources Defense Council, were much more active than European NGOs. As a result, the European negotiators were more influenced by industry than environmentalists. According to Benedick (1991: 28), the US State Department encouraged US environmental organizations to motivate their European counterparts to offset the influence of industry in the EC. Thus, while the negotiations were underway, US NGOs traveled to Europe and Japan to try to form a network with local NGOs to take a stand on protecting the ozone layer.

Scientific community. Members of the scientific community actually created the impetus for the Montreal Protocol when two scientists at the University of California, Sherwood Rowland and Mario Molina, advanced the theory that chlorofluorocarbons might be damaging the ozone layer. Initially, scientists, industrialists and politicians were skeptical, but by May 1977, UNEP decided that the threat of ozone depletion was serious enough to require international action. But the scientific community remained uncertain about the effects of CFCs. Scientific advice ranged from warnings that the problem was potentially extremely serious to cautions against overreacting to the situation (Széll 1993: 32). The lack of scientific consensus in the 1970s and early 1980s led to a weak Vienna Convention for the Protection of the Ozone Layer with no specific obligations for protecting the ozone layer.

However, by the mid-1980s scientific evidence confirming ozone depletion was becoming clearer and more compelling. In particular, in May 1985, scientists with the British Antarctic Survey published data that sent shock waves through scientific and political communities. Their observations pointed to a 40 percent decrease in total ozone over Antarctica during each austral spring since the 1960s (Széll 1993: 33). This scientific evidence proved to be just what a network of scientists, NGOs, pusher states and UNEP needed to enable governments to reach agreement to reduce production and consumption of five CFCs and three halons in 1987 in Montreal. And it was scientific evidence again in 1988 that became more conclusive and led to tighter control measures beginning as soon as the protocol entered into force in 1989.

Business and industry. In the case of the Montreal Protocol negotiations, the American and European chemicals industries had different perspectives on the necessity for international regulations. US companies seemed more willing to adapt to changing scientific knowledge and public perceptions. Although DuPont had declared in 1975 that restrictions on CFCs "would cause tremendous economic dislocation," producers in the United States, responding to consumer pressure, had moved to develop new propellants for spray cans even before the Montreal Protocol negotiations began. Even though these substitutes proved more economical than CFCs, for several more years European chemical companies persuaded their governments that replacing CFCs in aerosols was unfeasible (Benedick 1991: 31).

By 1986, many influential US business leaders had realized that the risk of ozone depletion would not go away. Pressures for new controls were mounting among environmental groups and in Congress. Just prior to the start of negotiations, the Alliance for Responsible CFC Policy, a coalition of about 500 US producer and user companies, issued a policy statement supporting international regulation of CFCs. Reflecting differences within the business community, the statement did not endorse a specific set of controls, but recommended additional scientific research, development of alternatives and substitutes for CFCs, and the establishment of a "reasonable" global limit on the future rate of growth of CFC production and consumption (Benedick 1991: 32). This policy change, which broke industry's transatlantic united front on the eve of the negotiations, contributed to tensions between American and European corporations who attended the negotiations. For their part, the primary objectives of the European companies were to preserve market dominance and avoid for as long as possible the costs of switching to alternative products. These views were reflected in the position of the European delegates, who sometimes even included industry representatives on their official delegations to the negotiations. American industry representatives were only observers (Benedick 1991: 33). Yet there was a much larger presence of industry representatives both on and off official delegations than there were environmental NGOs, enabling them to have much more influence throughout the negotiations.

Thus the division amongst business and industry groups broke an industry hold against CFC restrictions, which gave government delegates the necessary leeway to reach agreement on the Protocol. If the Alliance for Responsible CFC Policy in the US had maintained a position expressing skepticism about the linkages between CFCs and ozone depletion, it is unlikely that the US would have been able to take the lead in the negotiations and enable the compromises that led to eventual adoption of the Montreal Protocol.

Networks. The Montreal Protocol negotiations demonstrate the utility of networks of actors in promoting international environmental regulation. In this case, a small group of scientists succeeded in framing the situation in a way that made precautionary measures look very reasonable and in institutionalizing a set of legal norms which could be used by the pro-regulatory forces in the mid-1980s (Grundman 1999: 8). The core of this network was made up of scientists, staff of government agencies in pusher states, international organizations, and environmental NGOs. The scientists, who did not have sufficient consensus in their own community, needed the support of powerful allies such as the Natural Resources Defense Council, the National Academy of Sciences, the media, US government agencies, including the Environmental Protection Agency and NASA, and, at the international level, by UNEP, the World Meteorological Organization (WMO) and other pusher states. This policy network raised public awareness about consequences of CFC emissions for stratospheric ozone and put pressure on negotiators to control these substances. This network has continued to cooperate on ongoing research and advocacy work to influence governments during post-agreement negotiations and the strengthening of the ozone regime.

Cartagena Protocol

The Cartagena Protocol on Biosafety addresses the safe transfer, handling and use of living modified organisms (LMOs) that may have adverse effects on biodiversity, taking into account human health, with a specific focus on transboundary movements of LMOs. It includes an advance informed agreement (AIA) procedure for imports of LMOs for intentional introduction into the environment, and also incorporates the precautionary approach and mechanisms for risk assessment and risk management. The Protocol was negotiated between 1996 and 2000, adopted on 29 January 2000 and entered into force on 11 September 2003.

States. As was the case in the Montreal Protocol negotiations, the roles of states in the negotiation of the Cartagena Protocol on Biosafety were similarly based on economic implications of the proposed regulation of LMOs that cross national borders. In this case, the European Union (EU) members played the role of pusher states, calling for a precautionary approach to modern biotechnology. The laggards, called the Miami Group (named after the city where the group first met), consisted of the world's major grain exporters outside the EU (Argentina, Australia, Canada, Chile, the United States[4] and Uruguay). The Miami Group argued that the trade restrictions on LMOs would harm the multibillion-dollar agricultural export industry, creating unnecessary and excessive procedures and financial costs (Chasek *et al.* 2013). The Miami Group, therefore, had little incentive to conclude a treaty that would impose such regulation (Depledge 2000). The remaining industrialized countries were somewhat isolated and eventually formed a new "compromise" group (Depledge 2000). This group provided a home for Japan, Mexico, Norway, Republic of Korea and Switzerland, joined later by New Zealand and Singapore. Two other coalitions formed during the negotiations, including the Central and Eastern European Group and the Like-minded Group (the majority of developing countries).

The gulf between coalitions ran deep. While for most developing countries the purpose behind the biosafety protocol was to promote human well-being, the industrialized nations argued for the protection of biodiversity for its own sake. While the Miami Group saw nothing inherently problematic about genetic modification, others raised ethical questions and appealed to the precautionary principle. Trade issues also aroused strong passions, with developing countries and the EU more comfortable with trade regulation than other industrialized countries (Depledge 2000).

International organizations. In contrast to the activist role of UNEP and the Ozone Secretariat during the Montreal Protocol negotiations, UNEP and the Biodiversity Secretariat played a more low-key role during the negotiations of the Cartagena Protocol. UNEP is responsible for the overall management of the Convention on Biological Diversity (CBD) Secretariat, but when the Secretariat relocated to Montreal in 1996, UNEP's role in the process diminished (Mee 2005: 246). While the Secretariat remains dependent on UNEP for financial and support services and appointment of the executive secretary, the Secretariat has become the information hub for the biodiversity regime. In this respect, the Secretariat has gained a high level of trust among the negotiators and selected audiences of its publications and information campaigns (Siebenhüner 2009: 281). As the Secretariat became more independent, UNEP had less political influence on the negotiations. In fact, since the CBD is often considered to be more than "just an environmental convention" (Le Prestre 2002), it has attracted the attention of UNDP and UNESCO, who have called for closer linkages with the achievement of the Millennium Development Goals (Mee 2005: 246).

A number of international organizations, including UNEP, the UN Food and Agriculture Organization (FAO), the World Health Organization (WHO), and the UN Industrial Development Organization (UNIDO), worked with a group of 15 experts to prepare a background document on the need for a biosafety protocol for an *ad hoc* group of experts nominated by governments, which was established in 1994 by the first meeting of the CBD Conference of the Parties (COP) (CBD 2003). During this period, UNEP also prepared a set of Technical Guidelines on Biosafety, which was promoted by Norway and the UK in 1994 as a voluntary framework. The UNEP Guidelines were intended to provide a technical framework for risk management commensurate with risk assessment, without prejudice to the development of a biosafety protocol by the COP of the CBD. While the UNEP Guidelines were not always supported by NGOs and developing countries (Ling 1998), they provided a basis for negotiations during the work of the *Ad Hoc* Working Group on Biosafety. Other international organizations also had created biosafety information systems, including UNIDO's Biosafety Information and Advisory System, UNEP's International Registry on Biosafety and the OECD's BioTrack. Nevertheless, during the actual negotiations, all of the relevant international organizations played a low-key role, often acting behind the scenes by providing information and technical expertise.

Even the Biodiversity Secretariat and the Executive Secretary shied away from an openly activist role throughout the negotiating process. Instead, the Biodiversity Secretariat collated the necessary scientific research and disseminated it to delegates and prepared the other documentation necessary for the negotiation of the protocol. The Secretariat was also supportive in keeping parties at the negotiating table despite conflicting interests, heterogeneous cultural backgrounds and different levels of expertise (Siebenhüner 2007). According to Siebenhüner (2007:12), its "balanced and continuous efforts in facilitating dialogues and negotiations on the issue of biosafety contributed to the successful adoption of the protocol. However, it [was] the weak and imprecise formulations in the protocol that enabled hesitant countries to join."

NGOs. Unlike the Montreal Protocol, there were many environmental NGOs participating in the negotiation of the Cartagena Protocol, ranging widely in size and geographic distribution. During the pre-negotiation phase, a relatively small number of NGOs, such as Greenpeace International, Friends of the Earth International, and Third World Network, were present at the biosafety meetings. Their common policy goal was to endorse the immediate need for a protocol and to establish a mandate to start negotiations on such an agreement right away. Their common aim as well as their small number made it easy for them to form a network and organize meetings and workshops, cooperate, and discuss and work out a common position at this stage of the process. Larger NGOs and NGO networks, such as Third World Network, Greenpeace, Worldwide Fund for Nature International, and Friends of the Earth International, worked together with smaller NGOs, such as Acción Ecológica, the Australian GeneEthics Network, Diverse Women for Diversity, Ecoropa, the Edmonds Institute, the Council for Responsible Genetics, and the UK Food Group (Burgiel 2008: 78).

NGOs tried to influence government representatives by lobbying delegates in the hallways, during lunch and at other possible occasions. They also promoted their views, positions and policy-relevant information by organizing forums and handing out material to delegates (Arts and Mack 2003: 24). During the early stages of the negotiations, NGOs had the ability to access the formal discussions both in written and verbal form, although there were some closed contact groups. However, as was the case with the Montreal Protocol and other negotiating processes, the number of opportunities to access the floor was limited for non-state actors and, therefore, NGOs generally worked collaboratively to maximize input through joint statements, other lobbying activities and position papers (Burgiel 2008: 78).

NGO access to the negotiations diminished as time progressed. In 1998 at the fourth meeting of the Biosafety Working Group (BSWG), the Bureau took a decision that NGOs and industry groups could only participate as observers without the right to speak or intervene in the negotiations. They were still allowed to give statements at opening and closing plenaries. At BSWG-5 later in 1998 governments placed further restrictions on NGOs and industry representatives barring them from initiating direct contact with delegates (either orally or through written materials) during formal negotiating sessions and allowing the Co-Chairs of the working group to restrict their access. Towards the end of the negotiations (BSWG-6 in 1999 through the resumed Extraordinary COP in 2000 that adopted the protocol, discussions were conducted either as closed meetings of "Friends of the Chair" or in the "Vienna Setting" with two representatives for each of the five major negotiating blocs. These formats effectively shut out NGOs from the formal negotiations and limited their ability to participate and lobby governments. However, while their ability to influence the actual negotiations was limited, through their statements and position papers they could take a proactive stand on what should be included on the agenda (and thereby the Protocol), particularly with regard to liability, the precautionary principle and the scope, including all living modified organisms (Burgiel 2008: 78–80; Arts and Mack 2003: 25).

During the final stages of the negotiations, NGOs put together press releases, held demonstrations and worked on raising public awareness of the dangers of genetically modified organisms. Inside the conference rooms, they were busy lobbying government delegates wherever possible. NGOs also continuously handed out information to delegates or deposited it on the tables in the hallways, trying to strengthen their arguments through both science and knowledge. In particular, some NGOs, such as Third World Network, the Edmonds Institute, the Institute of Science in Society (ISIS) and the Rural Advancement Foundation International (RAFI), released a variety of scientifically-based reports and briefings (Arts and Mack 2003).

Scientific community. The biosafety negotiations were faced with no scientific consensus on the nature of biosafety. According to Depledge (2000: 160), for every scientist warning against the hazards of genetic modification, there was another proclaiming its merits. While the Food and Agriculture Organization and the World Health Organization have addressed the health issues through the Codex Alimentarius Commission, there was no other international scientific body addressing the safe transfer, handling and use and environmental impacts of LMOs. Negotiators were presented with "extreme science" from both sides: warnings of "Frankenstein foods" and "suicide seeds" from scientists in the environmental community and promises of a hunger and pesticide free world from industry scientists. As a result, government delegates could not agree whether genetic modification was really a problem and negotiated in the face of scientific uncertainty about adverse impacts of the transfer of LMOs and the role for precautionary decision making (Gupta 2000: 27). Scientists from research institutions and universities were generally accredited to the negotiations as NGOs, and scientists from the biotechnology industry were accredited as representatives of business and industry. As a result, their contributions were part of the networks they established with these two groups.

Business and industry. Industry representatives took great interest in the biosafety negotiations. Representatives generally came from industry associations, such as the Biotechnology Industry Organization (US), BIOTECanada (Canada), EUROPABIO (Europe), the Global Industry Coalition, the Green Industry Coalition, the Green Industry Biotechnology Platform, Japan Bioindustry Association, American Seed Trade Association, the International Chamber of

Commerce, as well as some of the larger biotechnology and seed companies, such as Cargill, DuPont, Merck, Monsanto, Novartis and Pioneer Hybrid. The level of industry presence was a clear indication of the trade and economic interests at stake in the protocol's negotiation (Burgiel 2008: 89).

Industry representatives were subject to the same restrictions as environmental NGOs (ENGOs) during the meetings, but they were also less vocal and less likely to provide proposed text for negotiation or influence the agenda, other than to oppose discussion of issues of direct concern to them (e.g., liability and labeling). This was quite similar to the activities of the European and Japanese industry representatives in the Montreal Protocol negotiations. Industry representatives also served as resources for delegates, explaining biotechnology issues and concerns and hosting lunchtime briefings and side events on the application of specific biotechnologies. These events often focused on the role of biotechnology in the developing world (Burgiel 2008: 89).

By the end of BSWG-5 in 1998, industry representatives had organized themselves into a network under the umbrella of the Global Industry Coalition (GIC), which presented consensus industry positions. The GIC included approximately 2,200 companies in more than 130 countries, from sectors including agriculture, food production, human and animal health and the environment. The GIC sought to limit the purpose of the Protocol to protecting biodiversity and to avoid negative impacts on trade. They also stated that a poorly conceived protocol would undermine economic development by denying biotechnology's benefits to developing countries, compromise established scientific processes for evaluating LMOs, impede technology transfer and research cooperation, and hinder generation and sharing of biotechnology's benefits (Burgiel 2008: 91–92).

Without the presence of industry groups at the negotiations there would not have been as close scrutiny of how provisions under the Protocol would affect business practices on the ground. This impact was most clearly visible in the areas of the Protocol's scope, and documentation and labeling requirements. Industry representatives formed a network with the Miami Group, argued against a strict identification and documentation system, and opposed liability and redress provisions. They believed that the latter would have a negative economic impact on industry. In addition, industry groups wanted to limit the scope of the Protocol so that the advance informed agreement procedure would be limited to only those LMOs for direct introduction into the environment, thereby waiving possible onerous restrictions on LMOs for food, feed or processing, LMOs in transit and for contained use, and pharmaceuticals.

Networks. The Cartagena Protocol negotiations, like the Montreal Protocol, demonstrate the utility of networks of actors on both sides of the international environmental regulation debate. In this case, the issue was framed differently by two different networks – a network of states who were wary of biotechnology led by EU members, some scientists and many environmental NGOs on the one side and major grain exporting states, pro-biotechnology scientists and industry representatives on the other side. As a result, one could argue that without networking with industry representatives, the positions of the Miami Group might have been less stringent, potentially resulting in a protocol that was more protective of the environment and more restrictive to trade in LMOs (Burgiel 2008). At the same time, scientists and NGOs who were arguing for precaution were able to get their position across – even when they were shut out of the final phase of the negotiations – by networking with the EU and some African states that were in the room.

United Nations Convention to Combat Desertification

The UNCCD was the first MEA to be adopted after the Earth Summit in Rio and was also dubbed the first "sustainable development convention." The UNCCD was negotiated in 1993–1994, adopted on 17 June 1994 and entered into force on 26 December 1996. The convention recognizes the physical, biological and socioeconomic aspects of desertification, the importance of redirecting technology transfer so that it is demand-driven, and the involvement of local communities in combating desertification and land degradation.

States. The negotiation of the United Nations Convention to Combat Desertification was less about the economic interests of developed countries, as was the case of the Montreal and Cartagena Protocols. In fact, the negotiations revolved not around commitments to environmental conservation actions but around economic and social development issues of concern to developing countries, especially in Africa. As a result, these negotiations were largely along North–South lines, rather than between different groups of industrialized countries with the developing world playing merely a cruiser or supporting role. On the one side, the African countries were pusher states, having lobbied for a global treaty at the Earth Summit in 1992. The African Group was supported by the Group of 77 (G-77) and China.[5] As the largest developing country coalition in the United Nations, the G-77 provides the means for the developing world to articulate and promote its collective economic interests, enhance its joint negotiating capacity on all major international economic issues in the United Nations system, and promote economic and technical cooperation among developing countries (Najam 2004). On the other side were the developed countries, negotiating under the moniker "The OECD Group." These countries were members of the Organization for Economic Cooperation and Development (OECD) and received coordination support from the OECD, particularly the Club du Sahel that provides development assistance to a number of Sahelian African countries suffering from desertification and drought. The OECD, as an international organization, played a role of a deliberative actor, helping to inform national positions of its members and to shape the form of the negotiated outcomes. As a funding organization, the Club du Sahel also had influence over the positions of some of the African countries, particularly in the Sahelian region of Africa.

The Africans shaped the negotiations by presenting detailed draft text for every section of the treaty. They argued, with the support of the G-77 and China, that external debt burdens and commodity prices, among other international economic policy issues, affected their ability to combat desertification. The OECD Group argued that those North–South economic issues should be negotiated only in other international forums. They did agree to general obligations to "give due attention" to the trade and debt problems of affected countries and so create an "enabling international economic environment" for those countries.

Differences over financial resources and the financial mechanism nearly caused the negotiations to collapse. Some members of the G-77 and China demanded commitments to "new and additional" financial resources and creation of a special fund for desertification as the centerpiece of the convention. The OECD Group acted as laggards or a united veto coalition in rejecting provisions for new and additional financing, agreeing only to ensure "adequate" financial resources for anti-desertification programs. The OECD Group felt they bore no responsibility for the problem of desertification worldwide, a position unlike that for the issue of ozone depletion, and were therefore unwilling to incur obligations to increase their financial assistance to affected countries (ENB 1993). The deadlock on a funding mechanism was broken only after the United States played a mediating or "conducting" role and proposed creation of a "global mechanism" under the authority of the Conference of the Parties, to be housed within an existing organization, which would improve monitoring and assessment of existing aid flows and increase coordination among donors. Developing countries remained dissatisfied, but ultimately accepted it as the only compromise acceptable to the donor countries (ENB 1994).

International organizations. While there are many UN agencies and regional organizations involved in combating desertification and drylands degradation (see Chasek and Corell 2002), only a few participated actively in the negotiation of the convention. UNEP played a significant role in helping the negotiations get underway technically, financially and administratively. UNEP, UNDP, through its Office to Combat Desertification and Drought (UNSO, since renamed the UNDP Drylands Development Centre), and the International Fund for Agricultural Development (IFAD) were the main intergovernmental organizations that provided technical support to the secretariat and some of the delegations (Cardy 2001). A number of regional organizations, including the Agence de Cooperation Culturelle et Technique, the Permanent Inter-State Committee for Drought Controlle in the Sahel (CILSS), the Intergovernmental Authority on Drought and Development, the OECD, the Sahara and Sahel Observatory and the Union du Maghreb Arabe also provided technical support to their member states throughout the negotiating process. Occasionally, these organizations intervened on behalf of their member states, but most of the time they helped with coordination, hosted intersessional workshops and produced technical papers. The Intergovernmental Negotiating Committee for Desertification (INCD) Secretariat, led by Arba Diallo, played an activist role in terms of trying to shape the Convention and the design of the future secretariat to meet its own needs. However, unlike Tolba during the Montreal Protocol negotiations, Diallo was unable to play a mediating role between North and South, largely because the developed countries did not trust him (Cardy 2001).

NGOs. NGOs were actively engaged in the UNCCD negotiations. According to Corell (2008: 104), a total of 187 environmental and social NGOs participated in the UNCCD process from January 1993 to June 1994. There was always a core group of about 40 organizations active at the meetings and 30 organizations participated in five or more of the meetings. Of the 30, eleven were based in Africa, two in Asia, six in Europe, three in Latin America and the Caribbean, two in North America and three in Oceania. There were also three "international" NGOs that participated regularly. Unlike in the other cases, Africa was the most represented region: almost one-half of the total participating NGOs were based in Africa. The majority of NGOs attending the UNCCD negotiations represented grassroots interests and many had little to no experience with multilateral negotiations. As a result, the early coordination meetings were unfocused with regard to developing a common strategy and priorities. Some of the more experienced NGOs devoted their time to helping to build capacity in the less experienced NGOs. For example, the Environmental Liaison Center International prepared a "lobby manual" for NGOs involved in the INCD to help maximize influence on the negotiations (Corell 2008: 105).

Unlike in the other two cases, NGOs were given considerable access to the negotiations, due in large part to the precedent set at the Earth Summit. The secretariat even took an active role in supporting NGO participation by recruiting NGOs from developing countries, organizing workshops during the intersessional periods to promote NGO networking and coordination, and providing financial support. Some governments included NGOs on their official delegations to widen the base of decision making and provide a channel for the expertise and know-how of many NGOs. In the eyes of many of the government delegates, NGOs possessed know-how essential for effective treaty implementation and were perceived as the link between the international negotiations and the affected local populations (Corell 2008: 107). This network enabled the UNCCD to be negotiated as a "bottom-up" rather than a "top-down" convention.

NGOs had three goals during the negotiations: (1) encourage the use of a participatory bottom-up approach in the UNCCD implementation; (2) reflect the social and economic consequences of land degradation for populations in affected areas; and (3) ensure provision of "new and additional resources" for dryland management projects in affected developing countries. The resulting treaty contains provisions consistent with many of the NGO goals. Furthermore, NGOs were able to open up new opportunities for participation as they gained the trust and respect of negotiators. Throughout the process NGOs provided written and verbal information at each session and often were consulted by government delegates. They were able to achieve a high level of influence on the negotiations because of three factors: the link between the bottom-up approach and NGO participation in the implementation of the convention; their homogeneous composition and interests, and the fact that NGO participation was encouraged by the negotiators (Corell 2008: 109–111). As a result, NGOs felt a part of the negotiations and expected to be included by governments in the national and local implementation of the convention.

The cohesiveness of the NGOs is a point worth elaborating on. While not all NGOs were from grassroots organizations or from Africa, there was a sense that these interests should have priority. This agreement allowed NGOs to present themselves to the negotiators as a single, coherent bloc, rather than a "plethora of different interest groups" (Corell 2008: 113). Most of the NGO interventions in the plenary and working group sessions were made by one NGO representative speaking on behalf of all of the NGOs attending the INCD. They also collaborated in producing *ECO,* a newsletter that NGOs have published at selected environmental conferences since the UN Conference on the Human Environment in Stockholm in 1972. NGOs used *ECO* to analyze the negotiations from the NGO point of view and inform delegates and other NGOs of their views. NGOs took this networking one step further by forming Le Réseau d'ONG sur la Désertification et la Sécheresse (RIOD), a worldwide network for cooperation among NGOs involved in the implementation of the convention. RIOD was established in June 1994 when the convention was adopted and gained recognition by the Secretariat and governments as an NGO focal point (Corell 2008).

Scientific community. The scientific community potentially had a major role to play in the desertification negotiations, but in the end its influence was minimal. United Nations General Assembly Resolution 47/188, which established the INCD, also called for a

> multidisciplinary panel of experts to provide the necessary expertise in the scientific, technical, legal and other related fields, making full use of the resources and expertise within and available to Governments and/ or organizations of the United Nations system dealing with drought and desertification.
>
> (United Nations General Assembly, 1992)

The resulting 17-member International Panel of Experts on Desertification (IPED) was the central mechanism for scientific input into the negotiations. The experts were appointed by the Executive Secretary of the INCD Secretariat and provided scientific knowledge in the form of presentations at the initial stages of the negotiations, reports, responses to questions from the INCD and assistance to the Secretariat in the preparation of documents. The experts met in Geneva six weeks before each negotiating session and its mandate expired in December 1994, six months after the UNCCD was concluded (Corell 1996: 8). While this is a much more institutionalized structure for scientific input than either the Montreal or Cartagena Protocols, it proved to have little impact.

Corell (1996) examines reasons for the limited impact of the scientific community during the negotiations, including the science of the desertification problem, the lack of expert interest, the politicization of expert advice, and the design of the IPED. She argues that experts who were involved with the negotiating process had little chance to influence the outcome because the IPED came late into the process. By the time the convention was being negotiated, issues such as the definition of desertification were already determined. There was limited time to provide expert reports, which arrived too late in the negotiation process to have significant impact on agenda setting and thus the text of the convention. Some believe that the Panel may have been deliberately designed to be a small group, which would merely serve as scientific legitimization for the negotiations. Moreover, the absence of an already established international network of scientists made it even more difficult for the Panel to have influence over the negotiations.

But while scientific experts were marginalized, NGOs had much more success. Long Martello (2004) argues that understandings of desertification as locally contingent and arising from a complex mix of social, biophysical and economic factors lend support to an INCD and Secretariat who relied little on the IPED and, instead, emphasized traditional and local forms of knowledge and the experience of NGOs in combating desertification and mitigating the effects of drought. This approach to specialized knowledge is also reflected in the convention, which recognizes science and technology as important to desertification policy-making and implementation. But instead of focusing exclusively on "science," the convention emphasizes the broader category of "knowledge," signaling reliance on a wider range of cognitive resources for understanding and ameliorating desertification (Long Martello 2004). This reflects the initial vision of the convention by the INCD Secretariat and many parties as a development assistance convention rather than an environmental one, thus limiting the need for scientific advice.

Business and industry. In contrast with the Montreal and Cartagena Protocols, in the UNCCD there were no business interests to protect the world's drylands, and no industry representatives took part in the negotiations. Business interests were not put at risk by a convention that tackled a problem that was not perceived to be directly caused by industrial activities. Many believed that NGOs in the INCD had greater influence because no business interests were present to divert delegates' attention, provide alternative views, often in opposition to the environment and development NGOs. As has been seen in the other cases, industry participants often compete with NGOs because industry seeks less stringent regulations and NGOs often argue for more restrictive provisions (Corell 2008: 114).

Networks. The UNCCD negotiations did not feature networks as the two previous cases did. The Group of 77 and China is an existing network of developing countries that operated throughout the negotiations. Among state actors, the African Group and the OECD Group could also be considered networks, although, like the G-77 and China, they are more coalitions of like-minded states. While NGOs formed their own network, RIOD, no other formal or informal networks between other actor groups developed during the negotiations. While many NGOs and IGOs supported or enhanced the position of the African states, no new coalitions or networks formed. The minimal role of scientists, industry representatives and developed-country NGOs, gave NGOs from developing countries greater influence in the negotiations. While some developing countries had NGOs on their official delegations, many of the African countries were still wary of working too closely with NGOs, thus impeding further networking.

Reflection on the roles of actors

As these three cases demonstrate, actors and networks play different roles in different treaty negotiations based on the nature of the subject under negotiation as well as the economic interests of the actors involved. As a result, it is difficult to characterize effective networks across treaty negotiations. However, there are some conclusions that can be drawn from these three cases.

1 With regard to state actors, the stronger the influence of pusher states, the higher the chances of an effective negotiated agreement. During the initial Montreal Protocol negotiations, the United States, representing 40 percent of CFC production, advocated strong reductions in the production and consumption of CFCs. Its economic leverage, as well as the fact that it had developed substitutes for some of the ozone depleting substances, strengthened its influence on the negotiations, which eventually resulted in consensus among all participating states, an initial 50 percent reduction of the chemicals and an eventual ban. In the case of the Cartagena Protocol, the strength of both the pusher states (EU members) and the laggards (Miami Group) was nearly equally matched. The Cartagena Protocol would not have been adopted without the skills of Colombian Environment Minister Juan Mayr who was able to facilitate discussion on the key outstanding issues and enable the major coalitions to forge an agreement (Chasek 2001). However, while the Cartagena Protocol was successfully adopted in January 2000 (largely by postponing consideration of divisive issues, including liability) one could argue that it is not an effective agreement because today, over a decade after its adoption and entry into force, no member of the Miami Group is a party to the Protocol.

The UNCCD had a large group of pusher states in the African Group, however, their lack of economic power diminished their influence in the treaty negotiations that were all about development assistance. The holders of the purse strings – the OECD group of countries – controlled the outcome, particularly when it came to issues of financing, the crux of the convention. The comparative weakness of the pusher states resulted in a weaker agreement.

2 When international organizations play an active role, stronger negotiated settlements are more likely. UNEP was responsible for bringing all three issues (ozone depletion, biosafety and desertification) to the international arena in its agenda setting role. Within the negotiations, however, UNEP played different roles. The Montreal Protocol negotiations were convened under the auspices of a strong, activist UNEP that provided technical expertise, secretariat services and mediation. However, in the case of the biosafety and desertification negotiations, while numerous international organizations expressed interest in the process, their roles were limited during the actual negotiations to provision of technical expertise. Not to belittle the importance of technical expertise in the form of workshops, reports and capacity building, which are all crucial during negotiations, none of these organizations pushed the negotiators or played an overt mediating role. The CBD and INCD Secretariats, who had the potential to play a more activist or mediating role, were either unable to do so due to lack of trust (INCD) or elected to play a more facilitative role (CBD). It should be noted, however, that there had been a backlash against UNEP for its activism during the Tolba years, which resulted in a more facilitative role in subsequent administrations.

The active role of international organizations may not always be a positive role, however. While UNEP's active involvement was credited with the successful outcome of the Montreal Protocol and other treaties (including the Basel Convention on the Control of Transboundary Movements of Hazardous Wastes and their Disposal, the Regional Seas Conventions and the CBD), international organizations' activism can also play irrelevant and negative roles. For example, numerous international organizations participate in environmental negotiations as observers yet often do not have any direct influence on the negotiations – many because of limited mandates or because they were not allowed in the room during the crucial part of the negotiations.

In some cases, the results of activism can be more negative. For example, the UNCCD Secretariat organized a high-level segment at the sixth Conference of the Parties in Havana, Cuba, in 2003. The Secretariat wanted to increase media attention and elevate the event to a more authoritative political level, but donor countries showed little enthusiasm. Only 12 heads of state and government attended but no industrialized countries participated. The resulting "Havana Declaration of the Heads of State and Government on the Implementation of the UNCCD" was perceived as a confrontation by the North and drew harsh criticism. The segment may have raised attention but compromised the North–South dynamic in the Conference of the Parties and harmed the reputation of the Secretariat (Bauer 2009b).

3 NGO influence often depends more on their ability to network with and educate state parties than on their ability to participate in the negotiations. In each of these cases, NGOs played active roles during the negotiations, but they had differing results on the outcome. The fewest number of NGOs participated in the negotiation of the Montreal Protocol and had the least amount of access. Yet they were able to conduct successful education campaigns and network with states, which enabled them to have greater influence on the outcome. For example, the Natural Resources Defense Council and the World Resources Institute in the United States helped educate both the public and the US Congress by publishing studies, holding press conferences and funding research. Representatives of US NGOs also traveled to Europe and Japan to stimulate local environmental groups to take a stand on ozone layer protection (Benedick 1991: 28).

While an average of 20 NGOs were present at the biosafety negotiations (Arts and Mack 2003: 26), they also had limited access, especially toward the crucial negotiating sessions at the end of the process. Yet through their networks with like-minded states and scientists, they were able to exert considerable influence, especially on developing country participants. But NGOs had little success in influencing the position of the Miami Group. When the laggards are strong and united (and often supported by business/industry interests), which was also the case in the Montreal Protocol negotiations, NGO influence is limited.

A core group of 40 NGOs participated at the UNCCD negotiations and had guaranteed access and influence on the outcome throughout the process. However, the UNCCD is arguably the weakest of the three. Thus it is sometimes difficult to correlate the ability of NGOs to lobby government negotiators with the strength of the outcome. Most observers would agree that the Montreal Protocol is the most effective of the three treaties, yet environmental NGOs had the least amount of influence on its negotiation.

The impact of NGOs can be directly felt on the Biosafety Protocol, however. Their ability to influence the negotiations was contingent on a combination of lobbying, advocacy, promotion and public pressure, as well as their ability to work in networks within the negotiating process. They had an impact on the following topics: (i) the adoption of the precautionary principle in the Protocol; (ii) the (broadened) scope of the Protocol, including agriculture; (iii) the inclusion of socio-economic considerations with regard to biosafety; and (iv) the reference to the liability issue (in case one government releases LMOs that harm the environment and biodiversity of another party). It should be noted, however, that NGOs generally achieved these results in cooperation with other parties, particularly the pusher states, including some developing countries and some EU members (Arts and Mack 2003: 29; Burgiel 2008). Therefore, it could be hypothesized that NGOs are more influential in negotiating processes when working in cooperation or in networks with pusher states.

In the UNCCD negotiations, NGOs focused primarily on influencing the negotiations and raising awareness in their own local communities. There was never much media attention given to this process and many of the major, large international NGOs did not participate. Among many of the international environmental NGOs, desertification was not seen as a priority environmental issue. As a result, most of the NGOs involved in the negotiations were small, African grassroots organizations that focused more on development than environment, and with little prior negotiating experience. Unlike the other cases, more NGOs who were present at the negotiations were supported by the secretariat and were even part of official delegations, especially in the Latin American countries. Since the NGOs were not seen as threatening, they achieved greater levels of access than NGOs in other negotiations, particularly those that had more serious economic implications.

The NGOs at the UNCCD negotiations also formed their own network, RIOD, to enhance their access, cooperation and influence. RIOD was conceived as a global network of non-governmental and community based organizations in the area of combating desertification. RIOD's mission was to promote and strengthen the participation of civil society in the implementation of the Convention in order to combat desertification and drought at all levels, in particular through national action programs. But once the negotiations of the treaty concluded and the meetings of the Conference of the Parties began, RIOD gradually lost its cohesiveness and was no longer an effective, functioning network.

4 Strong epistemic or scientific communities are likely to generate more effective negotiated settlements if there is scientific consensus and opportunities for scientists and scientific reports to be present in the negotiations. The work of scientists in parallel to the Montreal Protocol negotiations definitely influenced both the decision to negotiate the Protocol as well as the language in the text calling for the establishment of panels of experts to review the control measures (Article 6). The network of scientists in co-sponsored research (UNEP, NASA, NOAA, and the WMO) also contributed to the scientific discussions.

In the biosafety negotiations, there was a division among scientists on the dangers of genetically modified organisms and limited opportunities for them to influence the negotiations. Scientists who were part of NGOs and industry groups were the main purveyors of scientific studies during the negotiations, but the lack of consensus limited both the effectiveness of the epistemic communities and the scientific underpinnings of the Protocol. The desertification negotiations had the structure to allow scientists to participate to influence the negotiations, but the role of the IPED was marginalized and the views of the Convention as more of a development assistance treaty minimized the impact that scientific experts could have. The scientists met in advance of each negotiating session and very few of these "experts" were ever present during the negotiating sessions themselves and the reports of the expert groups were produced too late to influence the outcome. Thus, while there is a strong epistemic community around desertification and drylands degradation, and there are strong networks of scientists in areas such as soil conservation, hydrology, agriculture and ecology, to name a few, they did not have the proper structure to influence the outcome, which is reflected in the minimal role for scientific experts in the treaty itself.

5 The stronger and more united industry positions are, the more effective they are at limiting the scope of negotiated settlements to meet their needs. The business and industry community was divided during the Montreal Protocol negotiations, limiting their impact and paving the way for an eventual compromise on a phase-out schedule for ozone-depleting chemicals. During the Cartagena Protocol negotiations, the business and industry community worked together and even formed a biotechnology industry network to influence the negotiations. As a result of their efforts, as well as their close ties to the Miami Group, who represented their position in the negotiations, the final treaty had no agreed provisions on liability and redress and the advance informed agreement procedure was limited to only those LMOs for direct introduction into the environment. In the UNCCD negotiations, there was no business and industry role whatsoever.

6 Effective networks among different actor-groups can create stronger agreements. While these three cases do not prove anything conclusively, one could argue that when there are networks across actor groups, the resulting agreement is stronger. The Montreal Protocol negotiations demonstrate that the network of environmental NGOs, epistemic communities and pusher states provided each other with enough support to adopt the Montreal Protocol. Many argued that the initial 1987 Protocol was weak, since it didn't call for a complete phase-out of CFCs and halons. However, the subsequent strengthening of the Protocol – enabled in large part by this network – has made it one of the strongest MEAs. The biosafety negotiations showed that there were effective networks of environmental NGOs, epistemic communities, business and industry, and states on both sides of the dispute over LMOs. The pro-biotechnology network and the precautionary network shaped the negotiations and almost led to a stalemate. The resulting agreement, while rejected by the Miami Group, has still provided a structure for addressing the impacts of biotechnology on biodiversity and is stronger because of the role of the precautionary network. The desertification convention, however, did not have networks of different actor-groups. While NGOs did serve on national delegations and have access to the negotiations, they did not form coalitions or networks with states or epistemic communities.

It is also worth noting that international organizations or secretariats are not listed as part of these networks. In these three cases, while international organizations played different roles, they were often more facilitative than activist. Some international organizations actually played the part of epistemic communities in that they provide scientific and technical advice to the negotiations. But others did not and, thus, cannot be considered part of the more activist networks.

Lessons learned going forward

Multilateral environmental negotiations are complex by nature. Different actors, issues, scientific uncertainty, economic implications and the use of consensus decision making all contribute to this complexity. Lessons that can be learned for future negotiations have to take into account the nature of the issue, the potential economic and trade implications of any negotiated outcome, and the diversity of the interests of the actors involved. There is no prescription for a successful outcome to multilateral environmental negotiations. Nor is there any conclusive evidence about the overall impact of different configurations or networks of actors on negotiations. However, a few additional comments can be derived from this study of actors and networks during negotiations.

First, economic interests matter. If states and business and industry groups are concerned that the agreement could have significant impacts on trade (as was the case during the ozone and biosafety negotiations), it takes a strong network of other actors to counterbalance the economic interests with the need for precaution, supported by strong environmental science. While scientists and epistemic communities can provide the science, they often need to network or partner with NGOs, like-minded states, and key international organizations, including secretariats, to bring the issues to the table and lobby successfully for environmentally-sound and precautionary provisions. In the case of the desertification negotiations, economic interests existed but were different. Instead of concern about economic and trade implications for business and industrial interests, affected countries saw the UNCCD as a way to get more economic assistance to combat desertification and mitigate the effects of drought. This limited business and industry interests. Furthermore, many states saw the UNCCD as a lower priority issue as a result.

Second, networks of actors are important. Sometimes, these networks only operate in the negotiating forums as coalitions of convenience when like-minded actors share a similar goal. For these networks to continue through the post-agreement negotiations and implementation phases and demonstrate that they can endure, there needs to be agreement to continue to exchange information and keep the pressure on laggard states and others who may not see the agreement to be in their best economic or political interests. Sometimes, networks, such as RIOD in the UNCCD setting, find that in the absence of ongoing negotiations and the shift to implementation, it is not in their best interest to attend meetings and coordinate activities. The RIOD NGOs found it more cost effective to work on the ground in their own communities. As a result, the network fell apart. However, in other cases, NGOs, like Friends of the Earth and others continued to network on biosafety issues and attempt to counterbalance the interests of the biotechnology industry beyond the adoption of the Cartagena Protocol. Similarly, NGOs and scientists have continued to collaborate and network on ozone-depleting substances for over 25 years.

Finally, different categories of actors in multilateral environmental negotiations cannot be seen as monoliths. Scientists, environmental NGOs, business and industry, states and even international organizations can be divided on how a treaty should be structured and what parties should be required to implement. These positions can even change during the course of negotiations as new scientific evidence emerges, substitutes for chemicals are found, or the definition of what is covered under the treaty evolves over time. As a result, networks evolve. Some may end up being short-term coalitions of convenience, as was the case with RIOD. Others, such as the network working to combat ozone depletion, can continue to work together for decades. When these networks transcend groups and allow non-state actors to network with state actors and have a greater influence on the negotiations (even when kept out of the negotiating room), it is most likely that the network will survive. But for this to happen, the negotiating process must continue. So, perhaps the durability of these networks may actually depend on the longevity of negotiations and the shape of post-agreement negotiating process.

Notes

1   This section is excerpted from Chasek (2001) and Chasek and Wagner (2012).
2   This is not a complete list of attributes. For more details, see Chasek (2001) and Sjöstedt (1993).
3   For detailed analysis of this point, see David Downie, "The Power to Destroy: Understanding Stratospheric Ozone Politics as a Common Pool Resource Problem," in J. Samuel Barkin and George Shambaugh, eds., *Anarchy and the Environment: The International Relations of Common Pool Resources* (Albany, NY: State University of New York Press, 1999), and "An Analysis of the Montreal Protocol on Substances That Deplete the Ozone Layer," staff paper prepared by the Oceans and Environment Program, Office of Technology Assessment, US Congress, December 10, 1987, 9, table 1.
4   The United States, since it is not a party to the Convention on Biological Diversity, was a participating observer to these negotiations.
5   The G-77, which was established in 1964 by 77 developing countries, now has over 130 members, although the original name has been retained because of its historic significance. China, which has the status of associate member, also plays an influential role in the G-77.

References

Arts, B. and Mack, S. (2003) 'Environmental NGOs and the Biosafety Protocol: A Case Study on Political Influence', *European Environment* 13, 19–33.

Bauer, S. (2009a) 'The Ozone Secretariat: The Good Shepherd of Ozone Politics', in Frank Biermann and Bernd Siebenhüner eds., *Managers of Global Change: The Influence of International Environmental Bureaucracies*, Cambridge, MA: MIT Press, 225–244.

Bauer, S. (2009b) 'The Desertification Secretariat: A Castle Made of Sand', in Frank Biermann and Bernd Siebenhüner eds., *Managers of Global Change: The Influence of International Environmental Bureaucracies*, Cambridge, MA: MIT Press, 293–317.

Benedick, R. E. (1991) *Ozone Diplomacy,* Cambridge, MA: Harvard University Press.

Benedick, R. E. (1993) 'Perspectives of a Negotiation Practitioner', in G. Sjöstedt ed., *International Environmental Negotiation*, Newbury Park, CA: Sage Publications, 219–243.

Betsill, M. M. and Corell, E. (2008) 'Analytical Framework: Assessing the Influence of NGO Diplomats', in Michele M. Betsill and Elisabeth Corell eds., *NGO Diplomacy: The Influence of Nongovernmental Organizations in International Environmental Negotiations*, Cambridge: MA: MIT Press, 19–42.

Biermann, F., Siebenhüner, B., Bauer, S., Busch, P.-O., Campe, S., Dingwerth, K., Grothmann, T., Marschinski, R. and Tarradell, M. (2009) 'Studying the Influence of International Bureaucracies: A Conceptual Framework', in F. Biermann and B. Siebenhüner eds., *Managers of Global Change: The Influence of International Environmental Bureaucracies*, Cambridge, MA: MIT Press, 37–74.

Burgiel, S. W. (2008) 'Non-state Actors and the Cartagena Protocol on Biosafety', in Michele M. Betsill and Elisabeth Corell eds., *NGO Diplomacy: The Influence of Nongovernmental Organizations in International Environmental Negotiations*, Cambridge, MA: MIT Press, 67–100.

Cardy, Franklin. (2001) Personal phone interview (18 January).

CBD (Convention on Biological Diversity). (2003) *The Cartagena Protocol on Biosafety: A Record of the Negotiations.* Montreal: Convention on Biological Diversity. Available online at http://www.cbd.int/doc/publications/bs-brochure-03-en.pdf

Chasek, P. (2001) *Earth Negotiations: Analyzing Thirty Years of Environmental Diplomacy*, Tokyo: UNU Press.

Chasek, P. (2007) 'U.S. Policy in the UN Environmental Arena: Powerful Laggard or Constructive Leader', *International Environmental Agreements: Politics, Law and Economics* 7(4), 363–387.

Chasek, P. and Corell, E. (2002) 'Addressing Desertification at the International Level: The Institutional System', in James F. Reynolds and Mark Stafford Smith eds., *Do Humans Create Deserts? The Ecological, Meteorological, and Human Dimensions of Global Desertification*, Berlin: Dahlem University Press.

Chasek, P. and Wagner, L. eds. (2012) *The Roads from Rio: Lessons Learned from Twenty Years of Multilateral Environmental Negotiations*, New York: Resources for the Future Press.

Chasek, P., Downie, D. and Brown, J. W. (2013) *Global Environmental Politics*, 6th edn, Boulder, CO: Westview.

Corell, E. (1996) 'The Failure of Scientific Expertise to Influence the Desertification Negotiations', *WP-96-165* (December), Laxenburg, Austria: IIASA.

Corell, E. (2008) 'NGO Influence on the Negotiations of the Desertification Convention', in M. M. Betsill and E. Corell eds., *NGO Diplomacy: The Influence of Nongovernmental*

Organizations in International Environmental Negotiations, Cambridge, MA: MIT Press, 101–118.

Depledge, J. (2000) 'Rising from the Ashes: the Cartagena Protocol on Biosafety', *Environmental Politics* 9(2), 156–162.

ENB *(Earth Negotiations Bulletin)* (1993) 'Summary of the Second Session of the INC for the Elaboration of an International Convention to Combat Desertification, 13–24 September 1993', *Earth Negotiations Bulletin* 4, no. 22 (September 30).

ENB (1994) 'Summary of the Fifth Session of the INC for the Elaboration of an International Convention to Combat Desertification, 6–17 June 1994', *Earth Negotiations Bulletin* 4, no. 55 (June 20).

Faure, Guy-Olivier and Rubin J. Z. (1993) 'Organizing Concepts and Questions', in Gunnar Sjöstedt ed., *International Environmental Negotiation*, Newbury Park, CA: Sage Publications.

Grundman, R. (1999) 'The Protection of the Ozone Layer'. Case Study for the UN Vision Project on Global Public Policy Networks. Available online at http://www.gppi.net/fileadmin/gppi/Grundmann_Ozone_Layer.pdf

Gupta, A. (2000) 'Governing Trade in Genetically Modified Organisms: The Cartagena Protocol on Biosafety', *Environment* 42(4), 22–33.

Hampson, F. O. (1995) *Multilateral Negotiations: Lessons from Arms Control, Trade and the Environment*, Baltimore, MD: The Johns Hopkins University Press.

Hopmann, P. T. (1996) *The Negotiation Process and the Resolution of International Conflicts*, Columbia, SC: University of South Carolina Press.

Le Prestre, P. (2002) *Governing Global Biodiversity: The Evolution and Implementation of the Convention on Biological Diversity*, Aldershot: Ashgate.

Ling, C. Y. (1998) 'An International Biosafety Protocol: The Fight is Still On', Penang, Malaysia: Third World Network. Available online at http://www.twnside.org.sg/title/fight-cn.htm

Long Martello, M. (2004) 'Expert Advice and Desertification Policy: Past Experience and Current Challenges', *Global Environmental Politics* 4(3), 85–106.

Mee, L. D. (2005) 'The Role of UNEP and UNDP in Multilateral Environmental Agreements', *International Environmental Agreements* 5, 227–263.

Najam, A. (2004) 'The View from the South: Developing Countries in Global Environmental Politics', in Regina S. Axelrod, David L. Downie, and Norman J. Vig, eds., *The Global Environment: Institutions, Law and Policy*, 2nd edn, Washington, DC: Congressional Quarterly Press.

Scott, N. (1985) 'The Evolution of Conference Diplomacy', in L. Dembinski ed., *International Geneva, 1985*, Lausanne: Payot Lausanne.

Siebenhüner, B. (2009) 'The Biodiversity Secretariat: Lean Shark in Troubled Waters', in Frank Biermann and Bernd Siebenhüner eds., *Managers of Global Change: The Influence of International Environmental Bureaucracies*, Cambridge, MA: MIT Press, 264–291.

Sjöstedt, G., Spector, B. I. and Zartman I. W. (1994) 'The Dynamics of Regime-building Negotiations', in Gunnar Sjöstedt, Bertram I. Spector and I. William Zartman eds., *Negotiating International Regimes: Lessons Learned from the United Nations Conference on Environment and Development*, London: Graham and Trotman.

Széll, P. (1993) 'Negotiating on the Ozone Layer', in Gunnar Sjöstedt ed., *International Environmental Negotiation,* Newbury Park, CA: Sage Publications.

Touval, S. (1991) 'Multilateral Negotiation: An Analytic Approach', in J. William Breslin and Jeffrey Z. Rubin eds., *Negotiation Theory and Practice*, Cambridge, MA: The Program on Negotiation at Harvard Law School.

United Nations General Assembly (1992) 'Establishment of An Intergovernmental Negotiating Committee for the Elaboration of An International Convention to Combat Desertification in Those Countries Experiencing Serious Drought and/or Desertification, Particularly in Africa', Resolution 47/188 (22 December).

Young, O. (1993) 'Perspectives on International Organizations', in G. Sjöstedt ed., *International Environmental Negotiation*, Newbury Park, CA: Sage Publications, 244–261.

Zartman, I. W. (1994) 'Two's Company and More's a Crowd: The Complexities of Multilateral Negotiation', in William Zartman ed., *International Multilateral Negotiation*, San Francisco, CA: Jossey-Bass Publishers.

Zartman, I. W. and Berman, M. R. (1982) *The Practical Negotiator*, New Haven, CT: Yale University Press.

4 Actor configurations and compliance tasks in international environmental governance

Olav Schram Stokke

Introduction

What lessons learned about the design of compliance systems in other fields of international environmental governance can be applied to the area of climate change? This chapter argues that best-practice compliance systems can create and expand transnational enforcement networks, reinforce domestic compliance constituencies, and expand the number and categories of actors capable of sounding the non-compliance alarm. Enforcer networks are particularly potent if accompanied by access procedures that allow participation by environmental and industry organizations interested in providing additional compliance information about state or target-group adherence to international commitments. Similarly, domestic compliance constituencies in laggard states are more likely to improve rule adherence if they involve not only environmental agencies and green organizations but also target groups that play by the rules, alongside representatives from sector agencies that recognize that regime-based capacity enhancement may imply material benefits. Also brought out in this chapter is the need to consider individual international regimes within the larger complexes of institutions or governance architectures that affect the issue-area in focus.

Much previous work on compliance systems has focused on the relative merits of the "enforcement school," which emphasizes the deterrence inherent in strong verification capacities and forceful punishment of rule violation (Downs *et al.* 1996; Barrett 2003), and a "management school" that highlights non-adversarial review procedures aimed at identifying and removing impediments to compliance (Chayes and Chayes 1995); for overviews of this debate, see Mitchell (2007) and Raustiala and Slaughter (2002). In contrast, this study rejects the enforcement–management dichotomy and argues that verification, review, and various response actions have complementary roles to play in enhancing compliance. In focus here is how certain combinations of actor involvement support or inhibit specific compliance tasks. Attention to participation patterns in international compliances system also marks, for instance, Victor *et al.* (1998), but this chapter differs from earlier contributions by its sustained attention to the complementary roles of five categories of actors: states, experts sometimes networking into epistemic communities, environmental non-governmental organizations (ENGOs), industry organizations including multinational corporations (MNCs), as well as international organizations (IOs) (see the introductory chapter of this volume).

The next section identifies ways in which these categories of actors can improve compliance performance by supporting or obstructing certain *compliance tasks* of international environmental governance: verification, review, assistance, and sanction. Thereafter I briefly sketch the three governance fields that provide most of the empirical evidence in this chapter: dumping of radioactive waste, vessel-source pollution, and international fisheries. These areas share important characteristics with the climate-change problem. Climate change is a politically maligned problem, in the sense that effective measures to reduce emissions of anthropogenic greenhouse gases must address socially important activities conducted by a wide range of target groups who often have strong incentives for violating regulations (Underdal 2002). Dealing with global warming also requires participation by numerous states that may differ considerably in their willingness or capacity to adopt and implement costly measures. Accordingly, the three policy fields in focus here involve high political malignancy, strong pusher–laggard differentials in regulatory ambition, and great variety among states in problem-solving capacity. They differ significantly over time and across cases as regards the scope of participation by various actor categories in compliance-oriented activities. Such differences are central to the subsequent discussion of best and worst practices in conducting each compliance task, and what actor combinations and institutional features are particularly efficacious. The concluding section summarizes the findings and derives implications for the design of compliance systems and their relationship to broader institutional architectures.

Rule adherence and compliance tasks

Compliance performance refers to the level of adherence to a regime's rules among those bound by it. This concept relates to, but is distinct from, phenomena like regime implementation, enforcement, and effectiveness. Regime implementation refers to the set actions that parties to a regime take within their jurisdiction in response to their international commitments, whether informational, regulatory, or programmatic (see also Chapter 5 of this volume). Such actions may provide important evidence on compliance performance, but they do not constitute it. In turn, enforcement is one of several ways to pursue good compliance performance – by deterring non-compliance, whether by increasing the likelihood that violations will be exposed, or by raising the subsequent sanctions, or both. Enforcement is therefore a contingent rather than a constitutive property of a regime's compliance system. And finally, compliance performance differs considerably from regime effectiveness. A regime can be effective without achieving full compliance among its members, as long as it contributes significantly to solving the problem that motivated states to create the regime (see e.g. Levy *et al.* 1995; Stokke 2012). Conversely, good compliance performance does not imply a causal relationship at all: it only indicates compatibility between the regime and the behavior of states and any target group relevant to state commitments.

These conceptual distinctions are important, because compliance without causality has nothing to tell us about what practices are better or worse. Substantiation of best-practice claims regarding actor configurations in environmental governance must therefore go beyond variation in compliance performance and focus instead on how those configurations *help enhance* rule adherence. This chapter does so by examining certain compliance tasks that international institutions can influence by involving various configurations of actors.

Approaches to compliance

Information on behavior relevant to rule adherence is in focus for two strands of analysis that otherwise disagree on how to improve compliance performance under international regimes: the "enforcement school" and the "management school." The common-property nature of many environmental goods entails that users often face individual incentives to act in ways that are collectively disruptive. While for instance an individual fisher enjoys the full benefit from the catch hauled on board, the costs of that activity in terms of reduced availability of fish for replenishment will be shared by many – including, in the worst of cases, future generations. Some of the costs, in other words, disappear from the actor's cost–benefit calculations; such "externalities" imply problem malignancy and typically generate more of the activity in question than is collectively desirable (Underdal 1987, 2002). One way to overcome this collective-action problem is to shape the incentives of parties by rendering non-compliance more costly, or adherence with international norms more profitable. This logic of consequentiality is emphasized by advocates of the enforcement school, who see compliance information as a crucial means of deterrence that allows states to cross-check the accuracy of national reports and verify whether behavior is in adherence with international commitments, and react to any violation of rules (Downs *et al.* 1996: 393).

As argued within the management school, however, levels of compliance do not typically result from deliberate point-decisions made by states on the basis of expected costs and benefits; rather, they emerge from a complex web of norm-based behavior, bureaucratic routines, and more or less successful attempts to shape target-group behavior (Chayes and Chayes 1995). From this perspective, information about compliance is no less important, but its main role is to clarify impediments to rule adherence and enable the development of adequate, non-adversarial responses, notably the provision of means for assisting laggard states to improve their compliance performance (Victor *et al.*1998b: 19).

In practice, the compliance components of international regimes tend to reflect insights from both the enforcement and the management schools. The remainder of this section examines how various categories of actors can contribute to the four compliance tasks in focus here: verification, review, assistance, and sanctions.

Compliance tasks and actors shaping them

Verification means assessing the completeness and accuracy of compliance-related information and its conformity with pre-established standards for reporting (Loreti *et al.* 2001: 3). The task of review is to evaluate available behavioral information in light of the legal commitments that states have assumed (UNEP 2001). Assistance means enabling or facilitating rule adherence; this can be the appropriate remedy if non-compliance results mostly from lack of capacity to implement international commitments effectively. Sanctions, finally, refers to the imposition of various costs in response to non-adherence.

These compliance tasks can be independently relevant to rule compliance and should not be seen as necessarily arranged in a linear sequence. For instance, a negative compliance review may induce the target of criticism to take rectifying measures even without any subsequent response action by other members of the regime – perhaps due to pressure from domestic ENGOs or lobbying by MNCs with technical solutions for sale. Similarly, a decision within a regime to allocate funds or other forms of assistance to reinforce state capacity to implement international rules does not require any previous rule violation.

The compliance component of an international regime is not alone in driving rule adherence, however. Both the agenda-setting and the negotiated-settlement components (see Chapters 2 and 3) may enhance the compliance pull of international rules, that is, the perception among regime participants that the rules are legitimate (Franck 1990; Raustiala and Slaughter 2002, 541), including by being firmly based in credible and legitimate scientific input (Bodansky 1997; Mitchell *et al.* 2006). Although the significance of those modes of legitimization may vary from case to case, they are relevant to most international environmental institutions, in part because environmental governance typically involves scientific advisory bodies that support the negotiation of settlements. Further, compliance becomes an issue only when states have consented to be bound by specific commitments; such consent is the weightiest among several means for procedural validation of international norms.

Conversely, systems for verification, review, and response can also enhance the normative compliance pull of rules. Take, for instance, the strong compliance capacities inherent in the compulsory jurisdiction of the Dispute Settlement Body of the World Trade Organization (WTO), which indicate the weight that leading states assign to the norm of unrestricted trade. A strong compliance system can also serve to reduce fears among members that others might take advantage of their cooperation, thereby supporting perceptions that the regime yields fair distributional results (Franck 1995).

So, while each of the compliance tasks of verification, review, assistance, and sanction are independently capable of influencing rule adherence, they are likely to reinforce each other, and the causal pathways might involve other governance components as well. With these caveats, we will explore the roles that various configurations of states, expert networks, ENGOs, MNCs, and IOs can play in the conduct of those tasks.

Verification requires access to alternative sources of information for cross-checking national or target-group reports. Systems for compiling such information under international regimes differ in the extent of their centralization, which will be high if the IO plays a salient and active part rather than passively receiving national reports (Hovi 2005). For instance, in the Montreal Protocol regime for combating discharges of ozone-depleting substances, the Secretariat has played a productive role in developing questionnaires aimed at improving compliance-reporting practices among member states (Wettestad 2005: 222). Also non-state actors can be important: in some cases, expert networks provide independent information relevant to the assessment of compliance performance, as the International Council for the Exploration of the Sea (ICES) has done with respect to overfishing on cod in the Northeast Atlantic (Stokke 2012) or as the European Monitoring and Evaluation Program (EMEP) has done under the regime for reducing long-range transboundary air pollution (CLRTAP) in Europe and North America (Wettestad 2007). And as evident in the vessels-source pollution and dumping cases sketched below, civil-society groups such as ENGOs as well as industry organizations like MNCs are frequently allowed to participate as observers in international regimes, and can present information relevant to the compliance question.

Review of whether member states are in compliance with their commitments under international regimes can be conducted by a political decision-making body, or delegated to a specialized body – or simply avoided, as was often the case in the early stages of international environmental governance (Andresen *et al.* 2012). Whereas informal norms may constrain open criticism of the compliance behavior of others, conferences of the parties can provide venues for pusher states to raise such questions, thus enabling a certain dynamics that might improve performance. A general trend in international environmental governance is to create separate IO bodies responsible for such review, at the aggregate or the individual-state level. In this respect, the Implementation Committee set up under the Montreal Protocol served as a model for states operating other environmental regimes, including CLRTAP and the Basel Convention on trade in hazardous waste (Wettestad 2007). Although technical and legal expertise is frequently necessary for evaluating adherence, scientists tend not to play significant roles beyond perhaps encouraging states to adopt stronger compliance measures. Even in sectors where scientists do have privileged access to information about rule compliance, as in fisheries regimes that make use of onboard observers, they are not usually authorized to do so, since such control activities are seen as likely to jeopardize their ability to fulfill their primary function of resource assessment. As shown below, however, there are exceptions to this general rule, for instance in cases where epistemic communities (Haas 1989) can add credibility to the information that forms the basis for review. In contrast, civil-society groups such as ENGOs can and do play important roles in regime-based compliance review. The tasks that TRAFFIC has within the CITES regime, which regulates international trade in endangered species, is a prominent instance of an administrative ENGO at work to enhance international compliance.[1] Such involvement can raise the legitimacy of review procedures (see e.g. Bodansky 1999), but potential downsides of involving ENGOs in international review processes include the unwillingness of some states, or some target groups, to provide information unless they can retain a measure of control on how the data will be used or published. Outside international regimes, partnerships of ENGOs and MNC may set up private certification schemes with third-party review procedures, with the Forest Stewardship Council and the Marine Stewardship Council as two prominent examples (see Chapter 7 of this volume).

As regards *assistance*, important sub-tasks where various actor categories may provide distinctive contributions are funding and technology transfer. Both of these usually require strong interdependence between pusher and laggard states, the engagement of MNCs, and coordination by IOs. Interdependence relationships can generate incentives to provide resources for environmental problem solving abroad and may be extraneous to the issue at hand, including ambitions to improve general political relations with the target state or to strengthen economic integration. One major downside of green aid, aside from the risk of feeding corruption and bad governance unless properly controlled, is that steady flows of external funds and resources may undercut the laggard's preparedness to develop domestic financial muscle in the environmental area, not least in state budgets. With this compliance task, the primary roles of advocacy and administrative ENGOs are, respectively, to provide laggard-state governments or community groups in developing countries with services of various types, and to induce pusher states to provide the necessary funds for capacity-enhancement programs (see e.g. Andresen and Gulbrandsen 2005). Science networks frequently prepare the ground for capacity-enhancement programs by regular or *ad hoc* assessments (e.g. Global Waste Survey, IPCC adaptation chapters) that pinpoint areas in special need of improvement by solutions or technologies already in use elsewhere. The involvement of pusher MNCs is proving highly fruitful in areas like the development and marketing of green technologies. Private-industry participation in a regime's assistance system may also have productive feedback effects on the negotiated-settlement component of governance, by helping to identify standards that reflect available knowledge as to the inconveniences and costs of compliance, and ways to minimize cost without excessively ceding on rule conduciveness (Chayes and Chayes 1995). Moreover, several recent studies suggest that, although direct funding by states to particular projects of their choice will remain a major source, it is important to involve strong IOs with independent financial muscle, such as the Global Environmental Facility (GEF), in order to avoid potential biases from parochial donor interests (see review in Boisson de Chazournes 2007).

Finally, *sanctions* in response to non-compliance can be administered internally or externally to the international regime in question, and may be reputational as well as material. Internal sanctions typically involve suspension of regime privileges, like the right to engage in transactions under the flexibility mechanisms under the Kyoto Protocol of the climate regime (Stokke *et al.* 2005) or eligibility for support from the Multilateral Fund under the Montreal Protocol on ozone. Regime-based sanctions requiring external state implementation are evident in, for instance, the import-ban decisions that members of the International Commission for the Conservation of Atlantic Tunas are to implement on states whose vessels have been found to harvest bluefin tuna or swordfish in violation of rules under that regime (Palmer *et al.* 2006). Advocacy ENGOs like Greenpeace International regularly engage in naming and shaming as well as in documentation of rule violation or problematic aspects of international projects, like those under the Kyoto regime's Clean Development Mechanism (Andresen and Gulbrandsen 2005). Such private shaming is particularly visible if conducted by transnational networks of ENGOs capable of maintaining joint websites, as with the Basel Network's Hall of Shame, which targets states and industry associations criticized for violating the letter or the spirit of international commitments on trade in hazardous substances.

To summarize, states often predominate in the operation of compliance systems under international regimes. However, their continual foot-dragging in providing structures for verification, review, and response has invited engagement by other actors, especially ENGOs and to some extent scientist networks and MNCs. Thus far, we have considered the separate roles that these five actor categories play in enhancing compliance with international environmental commitments. How then do they interact? Here it can be useful to review briefly the variation in compliance performance in the three empirical areas to be dealt with in our best-practice discussion.

Compliance performance in three domains

The three policy areas in focus in this chapter are dumping of radioactive waste, vessel-source pollution, and international fisheries. For each of these I briefly outline the problem in question, the compliance component of the international regime set up to solve the problem, and variation in rule adherence over time and across cases.

Dumping of nuclear waste

The global waste stream is the evil twin of population growth, urbanization and the increasingly intensive use of natural resources; and this stream gets wider every day. Partly for cost reasons, and partly because also land-based disposal may pose severe environmental problems, a significant share of this waste has been dumped or incinerated at sea. A particular cause for worry is radioactive waste. Here I will sketch the international rules constraining the dumping of such material and the system set up to enhance rule compliance.

More than 60 years after the first controlled nuclear fission, no one has come up with a generally accepted solution to the problem of how to deal with the most highly radioactive products – high-level waste and spent nuclear fuel. Globally, the spent fuel produced by the military sector is modest compared to that from the civilian sector, but nuclear waste dumped in violation of international rules is chiefly of military origin. In the 1970s, nuclear dumping provided a politically potent starting point for ENGOs seeking to draw attention also to the dumping of other types of waste under international regulation, such as industrial waste, sewage sludge, and dredged spoils (Stokke 1998).

The basic principle of the regime based on the London Convention of 1972 is that disposal at sea of hazardous waste – defined in terms of toxicity, persistence, and tendency to bioaccumulate in marine organisms – must be forbidden except where all other options are deemed more harmful (Birnie and Boyle 1992: 321). Like many global treaties related to maritime activities, the London Convention is administered by the International Maritime Organization (IMO), a UN specialized agency. Since the entry into force of the London Protocol in 2006, the reverse listing approach has implied that *all* dumping is prohibited unless explicitly permitted by a designated national authority in accordance with international rules (for details, see the Annex).

As to compliance measures, review of rule adherence is based largely on self-reporting, and the IMO staff specifically assigned to work on this Convention are too few to play significant roles in critically assessing implementation practices. On the other hand, considerable transparency is ensured, since Consultative Meetings allow not only relevant international organizations but also a range of business associations and ENGOs to attend as observers. They may make statements, submit documents, and participate freely in plenary and working discussions (Peet 1994), also on compliance matters. At an early stage, some internal structures were put in place to raise the capacities of developing countries to comply, including a trainee program, courses on waste management at the World Maritime University and a series of International Ocean Disposal Symposia (IMO 1991: 97). With time, such capacity enhancement has become more prominent among activities under the London Convention, but various external regimes have proved more influential for the specific compliance problem in focus here – hazardous radioactive wastes.

Around 1990, bits and pieces of information seeped out concerning the hitherto unknown, if not wholly unsuspected, Soviet dumping of radioactive waste in Arctic seas in severe violation of the London Convention. Such dumping had been conducted regularly since the 1960s by the Soviet Northern Fleet as well as the civilian Murmansk Shipping Company, operator of nuclear-powered icebreakers in the Northern Sea Route. Measured at the time of disposal, the total radioactivity dumped into Arctic seas by the Soviet Union is twice as high as that of all previously known dumping (Sjoeblom and Linsley 1994). The most intensely radioactive type of waste comes from nuclear-vessel reactors which still contain spent fuel. In addition, large amounts of low-level liquid waste – like water used in cooling, incineration, or de-activation of radioactive installations – had been disposed of for decades, along with low- to medium-level solid waste in flimsy metal containers highly liable to corrosion.

This repeated and severe non-compliance with international commitments occurred in part because no real verification measures were taken towards the military sector and in part because existing storage and treatment facilities were highly inadequate. Ten years after this dumping scandal exploded, the compliance situation was very different, as we will see below.

Vessel-source pollution

The problem of dealing with vessel-source pollution is a malign one because of the fiercely competitive international freight markets, which provide clear incentives for vessel operators to avoid the costs of preventing or reducing discharges of hazardous substances into the marine environment. Maritime transport is a global industry, as are the international regimes set up to govern it, centered on the IMO. Within this organization, whose membership flags 97 percent of the world's tonnage (Campe 2009: 144), states have negotiated some 50 legally binding treaties and protocols on matters ranging from maritime safety, seafarer competency and training, to marine pollution. In the latter category, especially MARPOL 74/78 on discharges and the OPRC Convention 1990 on oil-spill preparedness and response are relevant to our discussion.[2] Regime deliberations occur within and sometimes outside the five IMO committees and nine sub-committees, with some instruments requiring approval by both the Maritime Safety Committee (MSC) and the Marine Environment Protection Committee (MEPC) (see also the Annex).

While the compliance system of regimes nested in IMO has certain internal components, the more potent parts are external to this organization. Member states are obliged to report on discharge incidents, adequacy of reception facilities, and inspections statistics, but three out of four typically fail to do so (Tan 2006: 275–282). Stubborn resistance among many flag states to mandatory review procedures has been strong and has obstructed the work of the Sub-Committee on Flag State Implementation, tasked with devising ways to encourage flag states to follow up on their commitments under the various treaties. This sub-committee has developed a series of voluntary guidelines, including a Flag-State Assessment Form, supported by substantive criteria and performance indicators, and aimed at facilitating and harmonizing self-evaluation of compliance (La Fayette 2001: 223–225). In 2005, a code on the implementation of mandatory IMO instruments was adopted, directly addressing flag-state obligations, along with a voluntary audit scheme (Ringbom 2011: 367).

The more powerful external compliance components of the global regime for vessel-source pollution evolved gradually, initially triggered by the massive oil spill from the *Amoco Cadiz* accident in 1978 (Tan 2006: 90). Frustrated with the highly variable implementation of existing commitments, especially among flag-of-convenience states, 14 European states drew up the 1982 Paris Memorandum of Understanding (MOU) on port state controls. This instrument, which today has 27 parties, commits states to use their jurisdiction over vessels voluntarily in their ports to collectively raise the frequency and quality of vessel inspection and response action towards sub-standard vessels (Molenaar 2007). The Paris MOU set an example for other maritime regions; today there are nine such regional agreements, covering all of the world's oceans. In addition, several regional seas agreements are important for the implementation of IMO rules, including the Baltic Sea regime that is centered on the Helsinki Commission (Ringbom 2011: 364).

The cases presented in the best- and worst-practice discussion below concern intentional, operational discharges of oil. As Mitchell (1994) has shown, the international regime for dealing with this problem has developed from one based mainly on spatially differentiated discharge standards, specifying certain maximum concentrations of oil that vessels are allowed to discharge, to one that also requires the fitting of certain equipment that greatly reduces the generation of oil slots, and thereby the incentives to violate international discharge standards. The problem of operational oil spillage remains severe, in terms of volume dwarfing the spills associated with maritime accidents (Udell 2011: 270). A 2005 estimate indicated total costs incurred by oil spillage in European waters alone to be around 7.5 billion euros each year (Trieschmann 2010: 214).

The IMO-based regime for intentional oil pollution is highly inclusive of both major industry organizations and transnational environmental groups and important parts of the compliance system are external to the regulatory institution. As with the case of dumping, its compliance performance has varied greatly over time and with respect to the type of regulatory measure.

International fisheries

In the northernmost part of the Northeast Atlantic, two institutions are central for managing the fish stocks that are shared among the coastal states or straddle the adjacent high-seas areas: the bilateral Norwegian–Russian Joint Commission on Fisheries, composed of representatives of the coastal states in the Barents Sea, and the much broader North-East Atlantic Fisheries Commission (NEAFC). The bilateral commission meets annually to adopt and allocate total quotas and other regulations for several shared stocks, which include the world's biggest cod stock, Northeast Arctic cod (Stokke 2012). Also non-coastal states participate in the regime by accepting, in separate bilateral and trilateral agreements, the quotas and technical regulations established by Norway and Russia, in return for gaining access to coastal state waters. Recently the NEAFC, a multilateral organization that manages high-seas stocks in the region, has acquired a role in the system for improving compliance with Northeast Arctic cod regulations (Stokke 2009; see also the Annex).

This regional management system is nested within the global fisheries regime, which means that important parameters are set forth in broader international customary and treaty law. With respect to fisheries management, flag-state jurisdiction has traditionally been central, significantly circumscribed only when harvesters operate in internal waters or in the territorial sea where the coastal state has sovereignty. Various fisheries zones emerged in the postwar period. Since around 1977, coastal states have been entitled to 200-mile exclusive economic zones (EEZs) involving "sovereign rights for the purpose of exploring and exploiting, conserving and managing" the fish stocks and permitting the full range of enforcement activities, including "boarding, inspection, arrest and judicial proceedings."[3] The governance approach inherent in this rights allocation was to minimize the need for strong IOs, leaning instead on coastal-state incentives to manage their national resources sustainably within a spatially expanded jurisdiction.

All the same, the compliance system in focus here has evolved from being largely decentralized, relying heavily on national systems for cross-checking target-group catch reports, to one with significant contributions from international cooperative bodies at bilateral and especially multilateral levels. This multilateralization of the compliance system, centered on the NEAFC Scheme of Control and Enforcement, came in response to a dramatic drop in fisher compliance due to a change in the activity system (Stokke 2009). When, around 2000, Russian vessels began to transship their catches for final delivery in EU member states rather than landing them in one of the coastal states (Hønneland 2006: 80), they undermined the fit between the regime's compliance system and the activities to be monitored. In subsequent years, illegal harvesting of Northeast Arctic cod accounted for 20 to 25 percent of the total catches in some years (ICES 2008). Such levels of quota overfishing jeopardized the stock as well as the legitimacy of regional management measures, and shifted wealth from legal fishers to cheaters while promoting corrupt practices in fish production and distribution in Europe and beyond (Stokke 2009).

Thus, as with the cases of nuclear dumping and intentional oil pollution, considerable ups and downs have marked the compliance performance of the international regime for managing fish stocks in the northernmost part of the Northeast Atlantic. As we will see, among the factors that have caused "ups" is the dynamism of the compliance system – first, through closer networking among relevant enforcement agencies, and then by incorporating compliance capacities based in an institution broader than the one with regulatory competence over the most valuable fisheries.

Diversity and relevance

Overall compliance performance has varied substantially within and among the cases outlined in this section. Those cases have been chosen partly because, like climate change, they present governments with politically demanding or malign problems and wide differences among states in regulatory ambitiousness and capacity for implementation. No less importantly, the great variation these cases display among themselves and over time in their compliance-system *designs*, especially with regard to the configurations of actors involved, makes them well suited for shedding light on best and worst practices.

The stepwise strengthening of the compliance component of the institutions sketched here is representative of international environmental governance, which early on focused more on knowledge building and regulatory advances than on means for improving rule adherence (Andresen 1992). In the shipping, fisheries, and nuclear-waste sectors, stronger compliance measures were achieved after pusher states had exploited the political energy unleashed by severe and spectacular regime failures: disastrous ship accidents, scandalous levels of overfishing, and blatant violation of international dumping rules. More generally, the processes of strengthening the compliance components of international regimes are highly political, and the levels of success reflect the same diversity of drivers and impediments that Chapter 3 examines for the negotiated-settlement component.

Applying the categorization of actors developed in the introductory chapter, in the next section we examine how different configurations of actors engaged in verification, review, assistance and sanctions affect the levels of adherence to international regulations.

Best and worst compliance practices

For each compliance task, this section presents one or more worst- and best-practice cases, pinpointing the factors that can account for variation in overall rule adherence. Best-practice cases involve features that are more advanced than those typically found in international environmental governance and that have proved effective even under malign conditions. In contrast, worst-practice cases fail to contribute significantly to compliance levels and may even disrupt this or other components of the governance system.

Verification: networking, technology, and incentives

Verifying information relevant to compliance involves generating and using information that can allow cross-checking of national reports. As the first set of cases will show, a best-practice verification system supports the creation and expansion of an enforcer network that capitalizes on complementary technologies for collecting information, improves the efficiency of verification activities, and creates individual incentives for reporting on violations.

Vessel-source oil pollution is an area where progress in verification has been particularly rapid in some maritime regions in recent years. This is due in particular to the improved opportunities for integrating traditional sources of information (port-state inspection and aerial surveillance) with satellite-based radars capable of providing national maritime authorities with almost real-time images that combine relatively high resolution and wide coverage, allowing prompt follow-up. Such integration is important because these means for verification have complementary strengths (Trieschmann 2010: 221). Satellite images can identify possible oil spills over wide ranges – but cannot determine their composition or thickness. Moreover, they are vulnerable to false alarms due to look-alike phenomena such as algae blooms or local low-wind areas. Aircraft-borne scanners, microwave radiometers, and laser fluorescence sensors achieve much better resolution; the latter can also determine film thickness and detect oil spills below the surface – but their range is very narrow. Thus, a satellite-based image, typically downloadable after less than 30 minutes, can identify possible rule violations within a wide area, in turn triggering closer examination by aerial or patrol-vessel surveillance (Trieschmann 2010: 223). If integration works well, suspected vessels are likely to face inspection when they enter the next port. Such inspection will involve checks of physical equipment, the crew's operational capability, and a range of compulsory log books, including the oil record, allowing cross-checking of consistency.

An actor configuration conducive to verification involves MNCs ready to exploit business opportunities in environmental-surveillance technology, states with legal competence to conduct vessel inspections, and IOs capable of coordinating reporting and inspection activities. In the best of cases, the IOs in question are complementary in terms of the bureaucratic agencies they involve. For instance, verification activities in the Baltic Sea benefit from the membership of all coastal states in the Paris MOU, involving port authorities within and adjacent to this region, and the regional-seas regime centered on the Helsinki Commission (Helcom), involving a broader set of member-state authorities relevant to environmental protection. Furthermore, with the exception of Russia, all the states of this region are members of the European Union. The Helcom Informal Working Group on Aerial Surveillance is a means for sharing experiences and finding ways to improve oil-pollution surveillance. Helcom parties conduct some 4000 surveillance flights every year, sometimes integrated through a Coordinated Extended Pollution Control Operation (Tahvonen 2010: 237). In 2011, this coordinated operation involved aircraft and patrol vessels from five regional states as well as satellite surveillance provided by the CleanSeaNet Service under the EU-based European Maritime Safety Agency, and lasted for six days (Helsinki Commission 2011). Since all vessels over 300 gross tonnage are obliged under IMO rules to carry an Automatic Identification System (AIS) transponder, backtracking of vessels located near an oil spill can, in conjunction with a regional oil-drift forecast model, help identify one or more likely culprits for subsequent port-state inspection (Tahvonen 2010: 239–240). Thus, an integrated enforcer network like that in the Baltic Sea case combines information generated at the global, regional, and subregional levels, helping to narrow the scope of those suspected of rule violation and allowing more efficient use of the port-state control mechanism.

The most salient contribution that IOs make to verification is to improve the efficiency of state-based efforts. The Paris MOU, for instance, requires that 25 percent of all vessels entering a member's ports are to be inspected. The MOU provides for various response actions, including detainment and in some cases prosecution, if serious violations of IMO rules are exposed. Crucial to the arrangement is a centralized database that provides continuously updated information on what vessels have already been inspected in nearby ports, and with what result. This system allows national port authorities to concentrate on vessels not recently inspected by other states, thereby avoiding duplication of effort, and to target especially those vessels with poor records from previous inspections.

A verification system is further enhanced if it can provide incentives for individuals employed in the industries ultimately targeted by international regulations to come forward with information on non-compliance. In the United States, legislation that implements the MARPOL Convention provides that as much as half of the criminal fines collected from a company convicted of violating those rules can be awarded to such "whistleblowers" (Udell 2010: 279). Such awards can be quite substantial – for instance, in the case of a vessel subsequently found to have engaged in illegal discharges and falsified records, a second engineer was awarded $250,000 for reporting these violations to the US Coast Guard (Udell 2010: 280) – and may help to counteract the social as well as future job-opportunity incentives for remaining silent.

In sum, the verification system for vessel-source oil pollution has emerged from the bad-practice situation prior to the creation of port-state MOUs, to the best-practice status now achieved in certain regional contexts. This improvement has centered on enforcer networks spanning a geographic area that fits the activities regulated and involving state agencies with complementary capacities to generate compliance information. The network is supported by IOs that provide means for coordination and is reinforced by MNC-based advances in surveillance technology and by incentives for individuals within the target groups to report on violations.

Review: network dynamism, access, and the burden of proof

Review here means determining whether behavior is compatible with international commitments or requires some response action. The case of compliance review examined here, rising from worst- to best-practice level, points up the merits of a dynamic enforcer network and the provision of appropriate access for impartial scientists, laggard states, and ENGOs. Even greater potency can be achieved by reversing the burden of proof as to whether target group behavior is compatible with international commitments.

Crucial to the recent success of coastal states in dealing with illegal, unregulated, and unreported (IUU) fishing in the Northeast Atlantic has been the expansion of the institutional boundaries of the compliance system, from a bilateral to a multilateral regime comprising all major market states (many of them laggards in fisheries enforcement). This change was greatly aided by the mobilization of three transnational networks of actors centered on the regional IOs, science, environmental advocacy. Of the two institutional hubs of the Northeast Atlantic fisheries regime, a Permanent Committee on Management and Enforcement under the bilateral Joint Fisheries Commission had been instrumental in building a bilateral enforcer network, subsequently multilateralized through NEAFC. Early review achievements of the Permanent Committee included regular exchanges of information about national fisheries legislation, annual joint seminars involving enforcement personnel, the dispatch of Russian observers to participate in inspections of Russian vessels landing fish in Norwegian ports, and common conversion factors between whole fish and the processed products that enforcement personnel find on board during inspections (Stokke 2012). The depth of this bilateral enforcer network was important for achieving laggard-state acceptance of the later multilateralization of verification and review through NEAFC. Data compiled unilaterally by the pusher state, Norway, through satellite tracking data of fishing and transport-vessel movements to main ports, were combined with assessments of vessel storage capacity that enforcement agencies derived from inspections and vessel registers.

The involvement of science actors in the review task was important because it enhanced the credibility and legitimacy of the compliance information compiled by the pusher state. Large-scale underreporting of catches severely undermines stock-assessment work and is therefore a problem for scientists, not only for managers and for those fishers who play by the rules. In the Northeast

Atlantic, the ICES is the institutional core for a transnational network of leading institutions of marine science. This organization provides management advice to numerous fisheries commissions in the Northeast Atlantic and enjoys a solid reputation for excellence and impartiality (Gullestad 1998), due not least to its peer-review procedures which balance the involvement of researchers from states with economic stakes in the fishery and outside expertise. A special working group tasked by the ICES group to estimate the level of unreported fishing of Northeast Arctic cod in the region upheld the main conclusions from the pusher-state review. Participating in the working group was also the leading Northwest Russian marine science organization, which added legitimacy to the findings.

Other transnational networks became involved in this compliance review process and contributed to a broadening in Russia of the domestic constituency interested in better compliance performance. A fisheries management audit by Russia's Accounts Chamber confirmed substantial unreported fishing by vessels flying the Russian flag, although this audit argued that the magnitude was lower than others had held (Russia 2007). The entry of this new player in Russian fisheries management had been encouraged by its Norwegian counterpart, which had proposed and obtained a parallel audit in both states (Norway 2007). The Russian audit identified numerous weaknesses in the domestic system for responding to rule violations, including fines that were too low to provide real financial disincentives. The Russian Accounts Chamber is directed by a former prime minister, and its entry into Northwest Russian fisheries management added further clout to a growing domestic compliance constituency. That constituency already benefited from rising concern in the federal fisheries bureaucracy that large-scale illegal harvesting and landings abroad were resulting in lower tax revenues and fewer jobs in the Russian processing industry (Jørgensen 2009).

Also transnational ENGO networks were mobilized in this case and maintained pressure on other NEAFC states to accept the amendments necessary for applying the NEAFC Scheme of Control and Enforcement also to fish taken outside the NEAFC regulatory ambit (the high seas). After several years of encouragement by the pusher state, Russia co-sponsored Norway's proposal to amend the scheme to incorporate frozen fish taken inside the regional EEZs, which had provided the basis for scandalously high levels of overfishing (Stokke 2012). Of the other port-state members of NEAFC, whose cooperation was needed to close the verification and review gap, many had been laggards as regards compliance, but their foot-dragging was criticized by transnational ENGOs participating as observers at NEAFC meetings, among them Seas at Risk, the PEW Environmental Group, and the WWF. In short, an expanding coalition of pusher states and ENGOs using information legitimized by a transnational enforcer network and ICES-based epistemic community managed to widen the review system from a bilateral to a multilateral one – which had the effect of further raising its credibility, saliency, and legitimacy.

The multilateral review component based in the NEAFC Scheme of Enforcement and Control is far more inclusive than its bilateral counterpart in terms of the access it provides for ENGOs to present documents and data, but its chief contribution is to reverse the burden of proof concerning whether a state is complying with its international commitments. This it achieves by requiring members to prohibit any NEAFC vessel from landing or transshipping frozen fish in its port unless the flag state of the vessel that caught the fish confirms that the vessel has sufficient quota, has reported the catch and is authorized to fish in the area, and that satellite tracking information data administered by the NEAFC Secretariat corresponds with vessel reports.[4] This innovative flag-state engagement procedure ensures a recurrent external check of not only target-group behavior but also the flag state's implementation of authorization, data recording, and vessel monitoring commitments under global and NEAFC rules. Those who must actively confirm that target-group behavior conforms to international commitments include not only the members of an expanding transnational enforcer network, now involving port authorities and fisheries enforcement agencies in all major market states. Also necessary for a positive finding on the compliance question is confirmation from the IO Secretariat and a wide range of flag-state agencies and private companies involved in a chain of documentation that links flag-state authorization to fish a certain amount of certain species to its landing in a foreign port, frequently following intermediate sales and transshipment to independently operated transport vessels.

Estimates of Russian overfishing of Northeast Arctic cod declined rapidly after the introduction of these broader port-state measures in European states, along with a marked increase in the share of Russian harvests that were landed at home (Stokke 2009). These changes presumably reflect also other developments like the steady rise in purchasing power in Northwest Russia, but they do indicate that expansion of the compliance system has contributed to problem solving.

Similar broadening of the set of actors involved in compliance review has been pursued successfully also in the case of vessel-source pollution. As Mitchell (1994) has shown, the transition from the use of discharge limitations to gradually phased-in equipment standards for new ships virtually removed the non-compliance option – because, to circumvent the new rules, a vessel owner would need partners in crime not only in the shipbuilding industry but also among the classification and insurance MNCs whose services are necessary for entering ship registries, winning freights, and gaining access to ports. The design of the rules thus expanded the number of actors involved in the compliance review, while also ensuring that the compliance review set in already at the vessel-construction stage, before any violation could occur. In the 1970s, the share of the world tanker fleet estimated to be in compliance with existing discharge standards was as low as 50 percent; however, shortly after the entry into force in 1982 of equipment standards that classification societies could implement in their certification procedures, compliance with the new standards was close to full, according to IMO and MOU data (Mitchell *et al.* 1999: 59, 67). Similar observations apply to the subsequent IMO phasing-in rules concerning double hulls. Whereas a mere 9 percent of all crude oil tankers above 10,000 deadweight tonnage had double hulls in 1993, only five years later the proportion was 21 percent, with a projected compliance rate of 81 by 2010 (Tan 2006: 239).

Thus we see that the review system of the Northeast Atlantic fisheries regime has moved from a poor-practice level, with no interaction among national enforcement agencies and scarce political deliberation on compliance questions, to its present best-practice mark. This improvement has resulted from a combination of legitimizing laggard-state and science-network engagement, dynamism in the scope of the transnational enforcer-network, and innovative reversal of the burden of proof regarding rule adherence. Such reversal is achieved by requiring from target groups and member states an unbroken chain of evidence, stamped by a series of independent actors with distinct roles in the production and distribution chain, confirming the behavior as being in line with international commitments.

Assistance: building a broad compliance constituency

To *assist* in compliance means to provide resources that can help states to avoid non-deliberate rule violation. As with review, the best-practice assistance system in focus here – the hazardous-waste dumping regime based on the London Convention, with particular attention to the most politicized substance, nuclear waste – involves compliance performance that rose from scandalously low levels to impressively high ones. From this case we see how access points for ENGOs can help mobilize attention and political energy that is conducive to assistance, especially when linked to an IO-based transnational expert network that can support a broader domestic compliance constituency in the laggard state. It also shows that the institutional boundaries of the assistance system need to be sufficiently dynamic to exploit any external willingness to pay for such assistance, often present when interdependence relationships imply potential donor gains within or adjacent to the issue-area governed.

Whistleblowers within the Russian nuclear complex as well as transnational ENGOs were involved in uncovering the information that unleashed the dumping scandal, in a period when power relationships between the Russian President and the Parliament were in a state of flux, leaving greater leeway for parliamentary committees in an issue-area traditionally marked by secrecy (Stokke 1998). In turn, the scandal triggered willingness to pay for environmental problem solving in Northwest Russia within several IOs and among several neighboring states. While the dumping regime has structures of its own for improving the capacities of its members to fulfill their international commitments, essential parts of its overall assistance system reside in other international institutions; and they made it possible for programs to be implemented to monitor radioactive pollution and to improve Russia's capacity to manage without nuclear dumping. Monitoring obligations concerning dumping sites of nuclear waste had not been taken seriously in the Russian Northwest until the spent-fuel dumping scandal reverberated worldwide around 1990 (Stokke 1998). Encouraged by the Consultative Meeting of the London Convention, the International Atomic Energy Agency established an International Arctic Seas Assessment Programme (Sjoeblom and Linsley 1995). Similarly, under the bilateral Russian–Norwegian Environmental Commission, numerous joint cruises were conducted, also to areas where reactors containing spent fuel had been dumped.

Transnational expert networks centered on several IOs were therefore instrumental in diagnosing the problem and identifying measures for dealing with it. These monitoring activities brought foreign expertise, and with it state-of-the-art technologies and equipment, into Russian implementation activities regarding radioactive waste, financed by Western partners. Such Western willingness to pay for environmental problem solving in Russia was driven partly by vulnerability to nuclear pollution in adjacent marine areas, but mostly by the desire to enmesh this powerful Eastern neighbor in collaborative networks that could reinforce friendly relations in support of general security concerns. Environmental challenges were perceived in part as a window of opportunity to get Russia involved in broader collaboration in the Arctic, where East–West relations had been chilly for decades due to the region's central role in mutual strategic deterrence throughout much of the postwar period (Stokke 2007).

Key to the subsequent improvement in compliance performance was the recruitment of the most relevant segments of Russia's "power agencies" – those responsible for the nuclear and the military sectors – into the domestic compliance constituency. That was possible thanks to the Western funds and expertise made available for developing and implementing programs aimed at enhancing Russian capacities to treat and store various categories of nuclear waste, and to transport waste out of the region. The largest source of funding for such projects has been the US Cooperative Threat Reduction program, linked to international agreements on strategic arms reduction (on background and early experiences, see Shields and Potter 1997). Activities under the dumping regime have been important for nuclear waste deriving from civilian reactors as well as military installations of lesser strategic concern. Responding to criticism of a 1993 release of low-level liquid waste, the Russian environmental minister put the incident down to irresponsibility on the part of the Navy and the nuclear industry, but hastened to add that Western technology and financial resources would speed up the process of acquiring the ability to do without such dumping (IMO Doc. LC 16/14, Annex 6). In response, an international Technical Advisory Assistance Team was set up to develop projects on treatment and storage facilities. Japan and Russia soon signed an agreement on constructing a treatment facility in the Far East for low-level liquid waste. Further, Norway and Russia agreed on a two-year assessment program to deal with nuclear-waste challenges in a reprocessing plant near Chelyabinsk in the Urals. Representatives of a dozen Russian ministries and other agencies responsible for dealing with radioactive waste participated in meetings under the International Atomic Energy Agency on nuclear waste management (Stokke 2000). Among the long-term programs deriving from this flurry of activities we may note the Arctic Military Environmental Cooperation, involving the defense ministries of Russia, Norway, the United States, and the UK, which has funded and overseen a series of nuclear-safety projects in Northwest Russia, especially targeting treatment and storage facilities as well as containers suitable for transporting waste out of the region for reprocessing or longer-term storage (Ortman 2009). In 2002, the Group of Eight leaders created the G8 Global Partnership against the Spread of Weapons and Materials of Mass Destruction to help coordinate and implement relevant projects (Thornton 2002). Russia is not known to have dumped high-level radioactive material after the dumping scandal broke, and it joined the London Convention ban on low-level waste in 2005 (IMO 2005).

The case of Arctic nuclear dumping, then, has involved creating, from scratch, an international compliance-assistance system for dealing with a highly politicized, sensitive problem. Best practice in this respect is to generate outside willingness to fund environmental projects, which frequently requires substantial interdependence relationships between donor and recipient countries, thus highlighting the interaction of global regimes with regional institutions. Transnational ENGOs with connections to whistleblowers can help prepare the ground for assistance activities. Crucial to success is the involvement of not only environmental agencies and interested ENGOs but also experts and decision makers in more powerful government agencies as well as leading target groups, in order to achieve a domestic compliance constituency with sufficient political and financial clout.

Sanctions: internal means, externally compatible

A *sanctions* component of a compliance system requires the ability to impose significant costs, reputational or material, on those who violate their international commitments. Evidence from the cases reviewed in this chapter indicates that key institutional requirements are liberal access procedures for ENGOs, to allow shaming activities less constrained (if at all) by diplomatic etiquette, suspendable treaty rights, and means of triggering external enforcement by states or MNCs without undermining the enforcer's commitments under other regimes, notably those relating to international trade.

Reputational sanctions in the form of naming and shaming have become increasingly common in international environmental governance, and are prevalent also in the dumping case drawn upon in this chapter, although hardly at cutting-edge levels. For example, harsh criticism from several states and ENGOs attending the Consultative Meeting of the London Convention following Russia's 1993 dumping operation of low-level liquid radioactive waste in the Sea of Japan induced Russia to drop its plans for a second operation and to pledge to cease such operations completely within a few years (Stokke 1998).

Closer to best-practice here is the dynamic "targeting" mechanism under the regional port-state control agreements aimed at boosting the incentives to adhere to IMO rules. Since 1993, the MOU Secretariat has published a targeting factor for each vessel, based on frequency of inspection and detainment (Tan 2006: 91). A high factor increases the likelihood of inspection and thus, if the vessel is sub-standard, the risk of costly detainment, repairs, or retrofitting. This information is made publicly available, thereby exposing the vessel operators to ship brokers, insurers, and charterers worldwide, reducing their competitiveness. This is a dynamic targeting mechanism that now also provides information on a vessel's classification society and, where appropriate, the charterer (Tan 2006: 92), thus spreading the reputational cost among a broader set of MNCs able to influence compliance standards in the industry.

Even more cutting-edge sanction practices are evident in a set of trade-related measures under the multilateral fisheries case, the NEAFC Scheme of Control and Enforcement. Those measures impose material sanctions in addition to reputational ones, provide due-process safeguards to those targeted for sanctions, and avoid violation of international free-trade rules. In addition to the means described above for suspending the landing rights of member-state flagged vessels unable to document that their cargoes have been taken in compliance with national and international fisheries rules, the NEAFC has developed a vessel-list approach that applies also to non-parties (Stokke 2009). On its Observation List are non-party flagged vessels that have been sighted fishing in a given region and have not established that the catches they want to land originate from regulated harvesting. Such preliminary listing entails denial of landing, transshipment and access to services in member-state ports or by vessels flying the flag of a NEAFC member. A subsidiary body meets annually to review the NEAFC Observation List in light of any flag-state explanation or other relevant information, and to recommend to the Commission whether a vessel should be removed from the list or transferred to the Confirmed List, which implies even heavier sanctions. Contracting parties to NEAFC are to deny port entry, fishing rights, and the granting of their flag to vessels on the Confirmed List. Moreover, their companies and nationals shall not be allowed to charter such vessels or import fish from them, and are encouraged to avoid their produce also at later stages in the distribution chain. The vessel lists are in the public domain and facilitate the mobilization of ENGOs, MNCs (including fishing companies that play by the rules), as well as processors and service providers that have strong brand names or that take on corporate environmental responsibility for other reasons. The backbone of this material-sanction system is a state-level enforcer network reinforced by provisions and services from the regional IO as well as MNCs operating in the production and distribution chain.

These material sanctions would not qualify the system for best-practice status had they not been adapted to fit the "environmental window" of the WTO, defined first in GATT's Article XX. Subject to the chapeau requirement that trade restrictions "are not applied in a manner which would constitute a means of arbitrary or unjustifiable discrimination ... or a disguised restriction on international trade," such measures may be compatible with the global trade regime if they are "necessary to protect human, animal or plant life or health" or "relating to the conservation of exhaustible natural resources if such measures are made effective in conjunction with restrictions on domestic production and consumption." Subsequent decisions by dispute settlement bodies have clarified these compatibility criteria (Stokke 2004). A first test is that the state wishing to apply sanctions must have exhausted less restrictive measures, passed in the case of NEAFC due to the many non-trade measures in the compliance portfolio as well as the absence of more trade-restrictive measures applied by other international fisheries commissions, especially in the tuna trade. Such more restrictive measures include "white lists," whereby only explicitly named vessels are allowed to land or transship their catches, and import bans on states whose vessels have been found to be in non-compliance (Palmer *et al.* 2006). The second and third compatibility tests are that any discrimination has been minimized and that requirements for avoiding the trade restriction do not excessively interfere with the sovereignty of the target state. Those tests too have been passed in the case of the NEAFC, since non-parties can avoid trade measures by applying for "co-operating non-Contracting Party" status available to those who agree to play by the same rules as NEAFC parties do, and since the system incorporates key features of a globally endorsed FAO Model Scheme on Port State Measures (Stokke 2009).

Thus we see that a strong enforcer network is fundamental to a best-practice sanction system. Such a network must have the competence to suspend regime privileges, and will be strengthened by access procedures that give prominence to transnational expert networks and engage outspoken ENGOs as well as MNCs interested in driving swindlers out of the market or protecting their international reputation among service providers or customers. Since external sanctions typically involve trade measures, a relatively strong IO component is also important – for the greater cost-efficiency it provides with respect to compiling information about non-compliers, and because a multilateral basis improves the grounds for arguing that trade sanctions are compatible with international trade rules.

Conclusions

Best-practice compliance systems serve to create and expand transnational enforcement networks, reinforce domestic compliance constituencies, and expand the number and categories of actors capable of sounding the non-compliance alarm.

This chapter has brought out the significance of transnational enforcer networks involving the main governmental agencies in pusher as well as laggard states and engaging in verification, review, and response activities. Enforcer networks are particularly potent if the compliance system also provides access and facilitates participation by other categories of actors, primarily transnational networks of ENGOs and MNCs that can provide additional information about state or target-group adherence to international commitments. Some sanction measures under international regimes oblige business organizations, including MNCs, to avoid commercial transactions with companies found to engage in activities that are incompatible with international rules.

Another finding concerns the benefits of building a strong domestic compliance constituency in each significant laggard state, involving not only environmental agencies and advocacy or insider ENGOs but also some of the major target groups as well as the governmental agencies that project the greatest power within the issue-area addressed by the regime. Important instruments here are the regime's structures for mobilizing assistance, whether by internal resources or by triggering program activities under other institutions. Industry groups may also have reasons of their own for contributing to review procedures, capacity-enhancement projects, or sanctions against violators – the reasons may range from an interest in a level playing ground and driving cheaters out the competition, to the prospects of lucrative contracts for selling cutting-edge green technology.

Finally, this chapter has shown the merits of operating individual international regimes with continuous attention to the larger complexes of institutions that affect the activities in focus. The ability of transnational enforcer networks to deliver effectively on verification, review, and response depends on institutional dynamism, often in the form of expanding the boundaries of the compliance system to mobilize the jurisdiction of non-parties to the regime. Such interplay management, aimed at triggering action under another regime, is also important for the ability of pusher states to raise the funds necessary for assisting laggards in meeting their international obligations.

Notes

1 On various categories of NGOs, see the Introduction in this book.
2 MARPOL 73/78 = International Convention for the Prevention of Pollution from Ships 1983 as Modified by the Protocol of 1978 Relating Thereto; OPRC = International Convention on Oil Pollution Preparedness, Response and Co-operation.
3 Law of the Sea Convention, Arts. 56 (sovereign rights in the exclusive economic zone) and 73, para. 1 (enforcement). Available at http://www.un.org/Depts/los/index.htm.
4 NEAFC Scheme of Control and Enforcement (adopted 2006, with subsequent amendments), Chapter V (Port State Control of foreign fishing vessels), especially Articles 22 (prior notice), 23 (authorization to land or transship), and 20 (scope); text of the scheme is available at (www.neafc.org).

References

Andresen, S. (1992) 'International Verification in Practice: A Brief Account of Experiences from Relevant International Cooperative Measures', in Erik Lykke, ed., *Achieving Environmental Goals: The Concept and Practice of Environmental Performance Review*, London: Belhaven Press, 101–118.

Andresen, S. and Gulbrandsen, L. H. (2005) 'The Role of Green NGOs in Promoting Climate Compliance', in O. S. Stokke, J. Hovi and G. Ulfstein, eds., *Implementing the Climate Regime: International Compliance*, London: Earthscan, 169–186.

Andresen, S., Boasson, E. L. & Hønneland, G., eds., (2012) *International Environmental Agreements: An Introduction*. London: Routledge.

Andresen, S., Skodvin, T., Underdal, A. and Wettestad, J. (2000) *Science and Politics in International Environmental Regimes,* Manchester: Manchester University Press.

Barrett, S. (2003) *Environment and Statecraft: The Strategy of Environmental Treaty-Making*, Oxford: Oxford University Press.

Biermann, F. (2008) 'Earth System Governance: A Research Agenda', in Oran R. Young, Leslie A. King and Heike Schroeder, eds., *Institutions and Environmental Change: Principal Findings, Applications, and Research Frontiers*, Cambridge, MA: MIT Press, 277–301.

Birnie, P. and Boyle, A. E. (1992) *International Law and the Environment*, Oxford: Clarendon Press.

Bodansky, D. (1999) 'The Legitimacy of International Governance: A Coming Challenge for International Environmental Law?', *American Journal of International Law* 93, 596–624.

Boisson de Chazournes, L. (2007) 'Technical and Financial Assistance', in D. Bodansky, J. Brunnée and E. Hey, eds., *The Oxford Handbook of International Environmental Law*, Oxford: Oxford University Press, 947–973.

Campe, S. (2009) 'The Secretariat of the International Maritime Organization: A Tanker for Tankers', in Frank Biermann and Bernd Siebenhüner, eds., *Managers of Global Change: The Influence of Environmental Bureaucracies*, Cambridge, MA: MIT Press.

Chayes, A. and Chayes, A. H. (1995) *The New Sovereignty: Compliance with Treaties in International Regulatory Regimes,* Cambridge, MA: Harvard University Press.

Downs, G. W., Rocke, D. M. and Barsoom, P. N. (1996) 'Is the Good News about Compliance Good News about Cooperation?', *International Organization* 50, 379–406.

Franck, T. M. (1990) *The Power of Legitimacy Among Nations,* New York: Oxford University Press.

Franck, T. M. (1995) *Fairness in International Law and Institutions,* Oxford: Clarendon Press.

Gullestad, P. (1998) 'The Scope for Research in Practical Fishery Management', *Fisheries Research* 37, 251–258.

Haas, P. M. (1989) 'Do Regimes Matter? Epistemic Communities and Mediterranean Pollution Control', *International Organization* 43, 377–405.

Helsinki Commission. (2011) 'Another Clean Year in the Baltic: Little Oil Found in Aerial Surveillance Operation', *Press Release* 3 September 2011. http://www.helcom.fi/press_office/news_helcom/en_GB/SuperCEPCO_2011/ (retrieved 15 September 2011).

Hønneland, G. (2006) *Kvotekamp og kyststatssolidaritet: Norsk-russisk fiskeriforvaltning gjennom 30 år,* Bergen: Fagbokforlaget.

Hovi, J. (2005) 'The Pros and Cons of External Enforcement', in O. S. Stokke, J. Hovi and G. Ulfstein, eds., *Implementing the Climate Regime: International Compliance,* London: Earthscan, 129–146.

ICES (2008) Report of the ICES Advisory Committee on Fisheries Management, Advisory Committee on the Marine Environment and Advisory Committee on Ecosystems, 2006. ICES Advice 2008, Book 3.

IMO (International Maritime Organization). (1991) *The London Dumping Convention: The First Decade and Beyond,* London: IMO.

IMO (International Maritime Organization). (2005) 'Russian Federation Accepts Ban on Dumping of Radioactive Wastes Under 1972 London Convention', *IMO Briefing* 26/2005.

JCF (Joint Commission on Fisheries). (1995) 'Protokoll fra den 24. sesjon i Den blandede norsk–russiske fiskerikommisjon', on file with the author and available from the Norwegian Ministry of Fisheries and Coastal Affairs.

JCF (Joint Commission on Fisheries). (1996) 'Protokoll fra den 25. sesjon i Den blandede norsk–russiske fiskerikommisjon', on file with the author and available from the Norwegian Ministry of Fisheries and Coastal Affairs.

Jørgensen, Anne-Kristin. (2009) 'Recent Developments in the Russian Fisheries Sector', in E. W. Rowe, ed., *Russia and the North,* Ottawa: University of Ottawa Press, 87–106.

Kahler, M. (2000) 'Conclusions: The Causes and Consequences of Legalization', *International Organization* 53, 661–683.

La Fayette, L. A. de. (2001) 'The Marine Environmental Protection Committee: The Conjunction of the Law of the Sea and International Environmental Law', *The International Journal of Marine and Coastal Law* 16, 155–238.

Levy, M. A., Young, O. R. and Zürn, M. (1995) 'The Study of International Regimes', *European Journal of International Relations* 1(3): 267–330.

Loreti, C. P., Foster, S. A. and Obbagy, J. E. (2001) *An Overview of Greenhouse Gas Emissions Verification Issues,* Arlington, VA: Pew Center on Global Climate Change.

Mitchell, R. B. (1994) *Intentional Oil Pollution at Sea: Environmental Policy and Treaty Compliance,* Cambridge, MA: MIT Press.

Mitchell, R. B. (2007) 'Compliance Theory: Compliance, Effectiveness, and Behaviour Change in International Environmental Law', in D. Bodansky, J. Brunnée and E. Hey, eds., *The Oxford Handbook of International Environmental Law,* Oxford: Oxford University Press, 893–921.

Mitchell, R. B., Clark, W. C. and Cash, D. W. (2006) 'Information and Influence', in R. B. Mitchell, William C. Clark, David W. Cash and Nancy M. Dickson, eds., *Global Environmental Assessments: Information and Influence,* Cambridge, MA: MIT Press, 307–338.

Mitchell, R., McConnell, M. L., Roginko, A. and Barrett, A. (1999) 'International Vessel-Source Oil Pollution', in O. R. Young, ed., *The Effectiveness of International Environmental Regimes: Causal Connections and Behavioral Mechanisms,* Cambridge, MA: MIT Press, 33–90.

Molenaar, E. J. (2007) 'Port State Jurisdiction: Towards Comprehensive, Mandatory and Global Coverage', *Ocean Development & International Law* 38, 225–257.

Norway, Directorate of Fisheries. (2007) *Russisk fiske av torsk og hyse 2006: Statusrapport,* Bergen: Directorate of Fisheries.

Oberthür, S. and Stokke, O. S., eds. (2011) *Managing Institutional Complexity: Regime Interplay and Global Environmental Change,* Cambridge, MA: MIT Press.

Ortman, C. (2009) *Radioactive Waste Impacts Mitigated by the Arctic Military Environmental Cooperation Program: Lessons in International Cooperation,* Dissertation, University of Cambridge, Churchill College.

Palmer, A., Chaytor B. and Werksman, J. (2006) 'Interactions Between the World Trade Organization and International Environmental Regimes', in S. Oberthür and T. Gehring, eds., *Institutional Interaction in Global Environmental Governance: Synergy and Conflict among International and EU Policies,* Cambridge, MA: MIT Press,181–204.

Peet, G. (1994) 'The Role of (Environmental) Non-Governmental Organizations at the Marine Environmental Protection Committee (MEPC) of the International Maritime Organization (IMO), and at the London Dumping Convention (LDC)', *Ocean and Coastal Management* 22, 3–18.

Raustiala, K. and Slaughter, Anne-Marie. (2002) 'International Law, International Relations, and Compliance', in W. Carlsnaes, T. Risse and B. A. Simmons, eds., *Handbook of International Relations,* Thousand Oaks, CA: Sage, 538–558.

Ringbom, H. (2011) 'Regulatory Layers in Shipping', in D. Vidas and P. J. Schei, eds., *The World Ocean in Globalization,* Leiden: Martinus Nijhoff, 345–370.

Russia, Accounts Chamber (2007) Rapport om resultatene av ekspertanalysen 'Effektiviteten av utnyttelsen av kvoter på akvatiske biologiske ressurser tildelt for 2004–2005 til Den russiske føderasjon og Kongeriket Norge i samsvar med Den blandede russisk–norske fiskerikommisjonens bestemmelser. Published (in Norwegian) in Norway OAG 2007. Riksrevisjonens undersøkelse av forvaltningen og kontrollen av fiskeressursene i Barentshavet og Norskehavet – en parallell revisjon mellom norsk og russisk riksrevisjon, 203–238. Oslo: Office of the Auditor General, Doc. 3:2.

Shields, J. M. and Potter, W. C., eds. (1997) *Dismantling the Cold War: The U.S. and NIS Perspectives on the Nunn–Lugar Cooperative Threat Reduction Program,* Cambridge, MA: MIT Press.

Sjoeblom, Kirsti-Liisa and Linsley, G. (1994) 'Sea Disposal of Radioactive Wastes: The London Convention 1972', *IAEA Bulletin* 36(2), 12–16.

Sjoeblom, Kirsti-Liisa and Linsley, G. (1995) 'The International Arctic Seas Assessment Project: Progress Report', *IAEA Bulletin* 37(2), 25–30.

Stokke, O. S. (1998) 'Nuclear Dumping in Arctic Seas: Russian Implementation of the London Convention', in D. G. Victor, K. Raustiala and E. B. Skolnikoff, eds., *The Implementation and Effectiveness of International Environmental Commitments: Theory and Practice,* Cambridge, MA: MIT Press, 475–517.

Stokke, O. S. (2000) 'Sub-regional Cooperation and Protection of the Arctic Marine Environment: Ehe Barents Sea', in D. Vidas, ed., *Protecting the Polar Marine*

Environment: Law and Policy for Pollution Prevention, 124–148, Cambridge: Cambridge University Press.

Stokke, O. S. (2004) 'Trade Measures and Climate Compliance: Interplay Between WTO and the Marrakesh Accords', *International Environmental Agreements* 4, 339–357.

Stokke, O. S. (2007) 'Examining the Consequences of Arctic Institutions', in O. S. Stokke and G. Hønneland, eds., *International Cooperation and Arctic Governance: Regime Effectiveness and Northern Region Building*, London: Routledge, 12–26.

Stokke, O. S. (2009) 'Trade Measures and the Combat of IUU Fishing: Institutional Interplay and Effective Governance', in the Northeast Atlantic, *Marine Policy* 33, 339–349.

Stokke, O. S. (2012) *Disaggregating International Regimes: A New Approach to Evaluation and Comparison*, Cambridge, MA: MIT Press.

Stokke, O. S., Hovi, J. and Ulfstein, G., eds., (2005) *Implementing the Climate Regime: International Compliance*, London: Earthscan.

Tahvonen, K. (2010) 'Monitoring Oil Pollution from Ships: Experiences from the Northern Baltic Basin', in D. Vidas, ed., *Law, Technology and Science for Oceans in Globalization: IUU Fishing, Oil Pollution, Bioprospecting, Outer Continental Shelf*, Leiden: Martinus Nijhoff, 231–244.

Tan, A. Kee-Jin. (2006) *Vessel-Source Marine Pollution: The Law and Politics of International Regulation*, Cambridge: Cambridge University Press.

Thornton, C. L. (2002) 'The G8 Global Partnership against the Spread of Weapons and Materials of Mass Destruction', *The Non-Proliferation Review* 9(3), 135–152.

Trieschmann, O. (2010) 'Illegal Oil Spills from Ships: Monitoring by Remote Sensing', in D. Vidas, ed., *Law, Technology and Science for Oceans in Globalization: IUU Fishing, Oil Pollution, Bioprospecting, Outer Continental Shelf*, Leiden: Martinus Nijhoff, 213–230.

Udell, R. A. (2010) 'United States Criminal Enforcement of Deliberate Vessel Pollution: A Document-Based Approach to MARPOL', in D. Vidas, ed., *Law, Technology and Science for Oceans in Globalization: IUU Fishing, Oil Pollution, Bioprospecting, Outer Continental Shelf*, Leiden: Martinus Nijhoff, 291–305.

Underdal, A. (1987) 'International Cooperation: Transforming "Needs" into "Deeds"', *Journal of Peace Research* 24, 167–183.

Underdal, A. (2002) 'One Question, Two Answers', in E. L. Miles, A. Underdal, S. Andresen, J. Wettestad, J. B. Skjærseth and E. M. Carlin, eds., *Environmental Regime Effectiveness: Confronting Theory with Evidence*, Cambridge, MA: MIT Press, 3–45.

UNEP (2001) *Guidelines on Compliance with and Enforcement of Multilateral Environmental Agreements*, Nairobi: UNEP.

Victor, D. G., Raustiala, K. and Skolnikoff, E. B., eds., (1998) *The Implementation and Effectiveness of International Environmental Commitments: Theory and Practice*. Cambridge, MA: MIT Press.

Wettestad, J. (2005) 'Enhancing Climate Compliance: What are the Lessons to Learn from Environmental Regimes and the EU?', in O. S. Stokke, J. Hovi and G. Ulfstein, eds., *Implementing the Climate Regime: International Compliance*, London: Earthscan, 209–232.

Wettestad, J. (2007) 'Monitoring and Verification', in D. Bodansky, J. Brunnée and E. Hey, eds., *The Oxford Handbook of International Environmental Law*, Oxford: Oxford University Press, 974–994.

5 The mismatch of implementation networks in international environmental regimes

Lessons from different agreements

José Antônio Puppim de Oliveira

Introduction

Implementation is about when the governance hits the ground to make an effect. The scholars and practitioners in public policy, particularly environmental policy, have been tardy in incorporating implementation in their analyses. The literature on international environmental governance is even more behind in the implementation analyses (Victor *et al.* 1998). There is a scarcity of serious academic attention to international environmental policy implementation, though scholars have heard so much about how important it is.

Many people still view international environmental policymaking as a matter of negotiating and signing international environmental agreements, and creating international agencies and secretariats. However, reality has taught a different story. International environmental policies, programs, and projects often fail to be implemented or exert unexpected impacts. Because scholars have often viewed implementation as secondary to policymaking, the literature, particularly in political sciences, often focuses on legislative and administrative processes: how issues arrive on the agenda, how international laws are approved, and how international bodies are created. It is assumed that implementation would follow the decisions or agreements. The top-down approach still prevails, even though there is a growing literature on MEA effectiveness (Haas *et al.* 1993; Miles 2002), which is relevant to understand implementation.

It is not always that implementation follows agreements. National and subnational governments are in general ahead of international regimes in the governance of environmental issues. Moreover, many actions at the local level start without direct "top-down" agreement influence. For example, in climate change, many sub-national governments implement policies that solve international environmental issues before countries sign them (e.g., city policies to tackle climate change in the EEUU). There are a myriad of networks of local actors at different levels implementing policies that are still being discussed at international level.

The understanding of policy implementation is key to creating effective international environmental regimes. Many of the diplomats in the negotiations of environmental agreements have little idea about how implementation would take place or is taking place in their own countries. So, they may decide on something that is not implementable or with little effectiveness to catalyze what is happening already on the ground. This mismatch between the international governance system and understanding the national and sub-national action creates ineffective agreements and regimes with regard to implementation (Pinto and Puppim 2008). There is sometimes a "decoupling" between the networks working on the ground and those coming from the top. My main argument is that effective implementation happens when networks at the top (international or high government level) match those at the bottom.

Moreover, those implementation networks at the bottom differ a lot in terms of actors and their arrangements according to the place and issue. On the top international level, the networks also are very different depending on the issue, even in the same regime. For example, MNCs in the CBD are interested in Access and Benefit Sharing (ABS) and biotech regulation, and less in local city plans of action or desert biodiversity.

The aim of this chapter is to understand the networks of implementation in several regimes at different levels (from international to national to local, and in different topics of the regime) mainly in three agreements: the Convention on Biological Diversity (CBD), the United Nations Convention to Combat Desertification (UNCCD), and the regime to control Ozone Depleting Substances (ODS); as well as insights from other bilateral and multilateral agreements and national and local policy regimes. Besides secondary information, this research was based on several cases the author was involved in, as well as interviews with more than ten experts working directly in the regimes addressed. Because implementation outcomes are not the same in different areas or countries, we will have good and bad cases in the same regime. There is a rich myriad of objects to study and get important lessons on implementation of international environmental regimes.

Implementation of international environmental agreements

Implementation of international environmental regimes refers to their effects on the ground in order to achieve the necessary changes to foster the objectives of the agreements. Implementation has a critical component at the international level, where political pressure and resources may come to influence the stakeholders make changes necessary to achieve the goals of the agreement.. However, perhaps the most important forces to determine the effectiveness of international regimes depend on the decisions at the national and sub-national levels, both in the governments as well as in the civil society.

Environmental policies in general, in developing countries in particular, face several implementation challenges (Puppim de Oliveira 2002, 2008). In many parts of the world, environmental issues are not a priority in the domestic political agenda. Even when an environmental concern is in the political agenda, policies may lack funding or administrative and legal support to be implemented. Governments may be poor enough to allocate resources for the implementation, or the issue can even be a source of heated debate, becoming an "unwanted" issue for funding or regulation in the political agenda, such as the climate change debate in the USA in 2011 and 2012. When resources are available, implementation actors may lack the technical or organizational capacity to develop implementation actions. This is common particularly in developing countries. Finally, parts of the local actors, such as governments and groups in the local population, may not participate in the implementation process or may oppose the implementation as it may go against their interests or values (Puppim de Oliveira 2005).

The literature in domestic policy studies has been tardy in recognizing the importance of implementation studies (Pressman and Wildavsky 1973) and has struggled to define implementation in a conceptual robust manner (Rein and Rabinovitz 1977; Sabatier 1986). The literature on international regimes has also been slow in incorporating analyses of implementation, though more studies have come to light in the 1990s (Victor *et al.* 1998), particularly the conceptual part. There is also an important literature on MEA effectiveness that is relevant to the work on implementation (Haas *et al.* 1998; Miles 2002). One of the reasons is that any analyses of implementation require agreements and regimes to be functioning for a certain time, and many regimes are relatively new. Another reason is the emphasis of the literature on analyses relevant for international studies in political science, which are more interested in the political aspects of the agreements at international level, even when it analyses implementation.

Until 1970s, implementation was assumed to be an automatic follow-up from political statements or legislations (Pressman and Wildavsky 1973) and the implementation process could be completely controlled in a centralized manner from the top (Mazmanian and Sabatier 1983; Van Meter and Van Horn 1975). Nevertheless, understanding implementation has shown to be a difficult endeavor as it involves a complex chain of events related and not related to the particular policy being analyzed. External factors and conditions can be determinant of the results of a policy target, but it is difficult to separate the effects from the agreements and other factors. For example, the success of the international regime to control Ozone Depleting Substances (ODS) in many countries is attributed largely to the economic interest of the ODS-producing companies to move to a new generation of substances. International agreements may have been important, but their implementation was heavily influenced by the interests of those large companies.

Moreover, it is also complex to separate the effects of international regimes on domestic policies from domestic drivers. In another example in the ODS control, many domestic policies to regulate ODS, such as those in the USA, Sweden and Norway, were in place in 1970s, well before the international regime started to be developed (UNEP 1995).

Finally, there is a myriad of on-going sub-national and non-governmental initiatives to tackle environmental problems of international relevance, even when the particular national government is not part of an international regime. In the United States, a non-ratifying party of the Kyoto Protocol, 170 cities and 29 states had plans related to climate change in 2008 (Wheeler 2008) and others are involved in the implementation of the CBD at sub-national level.

Regarding the link between governance and combination of actors, the involvement of the so-called "development-oriented" agents besides environmental actors are crucial for the implementation processes. In general, the former actors have the resources (human and financial) and the knowledge to reach the needed results, and the latter are important to set the agenda and push and evaluate the results. For example, the case of protected areas in the state of Bahia in Brazil, development-oriented agencies (like tourism and urban development) were responsible for the establishment of the protected area, but environmentalists and the environmental agency had a major role in overlooking the process through a committee with powers to assess projects and stop development. The direct involvement of a development agency helped to bring resources to the implementation of protected area policy as development agencies have many more resources, but their actions were under control of environmental actors (Puppim de Oliveira 2008).

Understanding the local political economy and how it plays out with the international component is a key to understand how they can be effective to drive changes on the ground. There is a multitude of policy processes going on at the national and sub-national level, both in the environmental sector and outside it (for example, in the energy or agriculture sectors), that are relevant to a particular international regime. Many of those processes are not related to a specific international regime, but can be influential to determine the effectiveness of its implementation. Coupling the international regime with those domestic processes, as well as with other international regimes and initiatives, can be determinant of the results achieved on the ground. How to create governance mechanisms to match these processes can definitively affect the effectiveness of the international regime.

Testing the hypotheses: factors that influence implementation

Based on the three regimes described above, some factors that may influence implementation were analyzed in order to understand the implementation effectiveness of international environmental regimes. Those factors are related to the hypotheses set in the introduction of the book (HBPi and HWPi are the hypotheses on best practices or hypotheses on worst practices described in the part on implementation in the Introduction). In this section, I examine under what conditions and circumstances certain activities by important actors or combinations of actors may be effective to deliver results. The discussions will lead to some general lessons later in this chapter.

Capacity building by international organizations (IOs) or more developed countries

HBP 1. Vigorous capacity building by IOs or developed states is likely to render more effective implementation in developing countries.

Capacity building can be important to have effective and efficient implementation of international agreements. In many agreements, capacity building comes from international organizations or more developed countries, which generally hold the expertise, interests and resources to deliver capacity building activities. However, strong capacity building is not sufficient, and sometimes not even necessary to achieve the goals of implementation in many cases.

First, capacity depends on the implementing institutional environment: to whom, when and how the capacity building efforts will take place. In many settings, effective implementation involves a series of actions by different institutional actors, sometimes at different levels, within and outside the government, including business and NGOs. For example, the actions to phase out the production of ODS in China were centralized at the national level by the environmental agency initially. The agency became the ozone focal point and gained capacity to develop and manage projects to control the ODS, as it did not have much experience in project management in the past. The agency was responsible for managing all the resources canalized from the Multilateral Fund for the Protection of the Ozone Layer (MF) (Zhao and Ortolano 2003). However, implementation lagged behind because local governments had little information and involvement in the early stages, even though they are key to control the certain substances for industrial production in many local economic activities. Moreover, central government was too far away from the main sources of information about where the ODS were. As local environmental protection bureaus started to receive information and training to deal with ODS, implementation began to move smoothly, as they had much more information and control over the local industries and many of them were even controlled by Chinese local governments. This is a case of best practices, where decentralization of activities allowed the capacity building to happen with the best knowledge of local needs.

Second, organizations that are provided with capacity building should have the right enabling institutional environment to put into practice the capacity gained. Lack of funding and enabling autonomy can incur stalled implementation even when strong capacity building is available. The relative success of the control of ODS is largely due to the exclusive funding the MF provides to enable implementation, which is limited in instances of other agreements. Countries were also required to set deadlines and targets to have access to the MF. Thus, many countries passed legislation to control ODS at national level, which supplemented the actions catalyzed by the projects financed by the MF, setting the right environment for implementation to take place. However, in many developing countries, such as Brazil, there was not a well-established capacity to recover the existing ODS already in use, as those actions should be taken by small firms, such as car mechanics or refrigerator repair shops, which did not have the skills or equipment for recycling or proper disposal of the ODS. In this case, the lack of capital to expand many small-scale refrigerant gas recyclers hinders the capacity to recover all the refrigerant gases in use, including ODS (Puppim de Oliveira 2011b). The government may have the resources and certain capacity at governmental level, but the private sector, in this case small repair shops, did not have the capacity or training, or the incentives, to implement the policy at the local level.

On the other hand, the establishment and proper management of protected areas, one of the goals of the Convention on Biological Diversity (CBD), has lacked funding in developing countries even though some countries have good human resources capacity, such as some African countries, which have been acquired with support from developed countries or large international conservation NGOs, such as the WWF. However, even though the total amount is not high, there is little effort to mobilize a stable source of funding from developed countries for the management of the protected areas in the medium and long term (Bruner *et al.* 2004).

Capacity building can also come from other actors in the policy arena, besides IOs and developed states. For example, many NGOs are involved in capacity building for strengthening the actions related to the UNCCD, as the developed states are reluctant to be engaged in the agreement process. Some of the achievements in controlling desertification came from the efforts from NGOs allied to local actors. For example, Resource Projects Samburu, a Kenyan NGO, has collaborated with working the National Coordination Committee on Desertification (NCCD), the national entity to coordinate NGO working on combating desertification. The NGO helps the pastoral people of the Samburu District to contribute to the local plan to combat desertification, building maps and supporting the implementation with labor and local knowledge (Kasusya 1998). Other developing countries as capacity builders can be another alternative, especially when the agreement does not involve a more developed country or international organization. However, there is still considerable overlap and lack of information sharing between international organizations and other actors, which affect effectiveness of capacity building and the availability of information for decisions. There are some examples of good practice in Peru where the focal points of both UNCCD and the International Tropical Timber Organization (ITTO) together with support from ITTO carried out an evaluation of the impact of forest fires on the country's ecosystems and designed a contingent plan to combat desertification along the Piura River (Chasek 2011).

The efforts in capacity building and financial aid should also focus on maintaining the system in the long term, as all efforts can be wasted if the capacity building and resources are withdrawn, such as in some African countries. For example, in the case of Namibia, the efforts of the National Action Programs under the UNCCD were likely to be discontinued since funding by the German technical cooperation agency (GTZ) was withdrawn at the beginning of this century (Poulsen and Lo 2006).

Administrative capacity and implementation outcomes

HBP 2. States with strong administrative capacity are likely to implement more effectively than weaker states.

HWP 1. Weak administrative capacity (of those who implement) renders low implementation.

Administrative capacity is a determining factor to explain implementation of environmental policies in many cases, particularly when the implementation involves regulatory measures. Enforcement of regulations depends heavily on the administrative capacity of the state and resources, and this capacity varies largely among the states and even issues. Developed countries tend to have a larger administrative capacity and resources to implement environmental policies than developing countries (Puppim de Oliveira 2008).

For example, there are several challenges in the implementation of the access and benefit sharing (ABS) regimes under the Convention on Biological Diversity (CBD) in African countries. Implementation has been too centralized in the hands of the central government with little participation of sub-national governments, and there is a lack of mechanisms to allow effective participation of local communities and to follow up the agreements (Prip *et al.* 2010). The ODS control in developing countries also took a while to catch up because of lack of capacity, and not only because of the period of grace they were given. Brazil was said to be slow in the implementation of the Montreal Protocol because of the lack of national infrastructure, education and training at the beginning of the 1990s. For example, contact points at the beginning of the 1990s were not available for those looking for resources from MF that delayed the implementation of the agreement (Machado 1993).

However, depending on the kind of international regime, and its national dynamics, administrative capacity may not reveal the whole picture of implementation and explain variations (Puppim de Oliveira 2011a). As far as regimes that do not require national legislation or enforcement from the state are concerned, administrative capacity may not be important enough to lead to implementation, such as the regimes that require just volunteer participation. In an area of forest, which lacks a strong international regime, for example, there have been many voluntary regimes for forest preservation linked to biodiversity regimes where local communities commit to protect the forest, sometimes compensated by payments of ecosystem services. The case of Costa Rica is emblematic, as the country has developed a relatively well functioning system of payment for ecosystem services (PES) in forests since the 1990s, with some positive results, without a large administrative capacity, and this also brings down administrative costs (Pagiola 2008). There was new legislation passed (Forest Law No.7575, enacted in 1996), but one of the reasons for the success of the effectiveness of the PES was to use existing capacity by earlier existing programs dealing with landowner and forest management. This is a good example of how networks at the top can be coupled with existing networks at the bottom.

The local environmental and political conditions are also a factor that administrative capacity may be limited to determine more effective implementation of international agreements. Even governments with weak capacity can be effective in moving global agendas locally when favorable conditions are in place. For example, one of the factors to assess the progress of the implementation of national biodiversity strategies and action plans (NBSAPs) of the CBD is the percentage of the territory under protected areas. Countries with apparently low administrative capacity, like Bhutan, Algeria and Belize, have some of the largest percentages of their territories as protected areas in the world, comprising approximately 39 percent, 36 percent and 26 percent of their total land surface respectively. Those numbers are much greater than the percentages of many European countries, such as Belgium or Spain, which have stronger administrative capacity. The protected area system in Bhutan is also "one of the most comprehensive in the world not only in terms of area coverage but also in terms of the balance and contiguity in distribution across the country" (Pirp *et al.* 2010).

Areas allocated to be environmentally protected may depend a lot on the availability of land in good environmental conditions, local property rights conditions (such as land under state control, for example), the political commitment of governments to set aside land for environmental protection, and the local institutional conditions that may lead to allocation of funding for protected areas (Puppim de Oliveira 2002, 2008). For example, the effectiveness of the participation of local actors in the enforcement of protected areas in the state of Bahia in Brazil was proportionally related to how early those actors got involved in the process. In an analysis of the implementation effort in several protected areas, more participation of local governmental and non-governmental organizations in the implementation and support of higher-level governmental organizations in the enforcement of the protected area guidelines came from cases where those actors were involved in the early process of management plan and other decisions (Puppim de Oliveira 2005).

In some cases, the commitment of the government to the MEAs can lead to strong efforts to build capacity to a more effective implementation at the local level, even though the problem may have been on the agenda for a large period of time. Iran, which has a large area affected by desertification, changed the relevance of combating desertification at the national level, after the country committed to UNCCD. The preparation of the National Action Programme (NAP) led to several positive changes to combat desertification there, including a set of legislative measures that, for example, allocated funding to the provinces most affected by desertification and created managerial capacity to implement and report actions related to desertification (Amiraslani and Dragovich 2010). Technical capacity in research has improved significantly to inform implementing organizations. During the last 30 years the Iranian government has promoted research activities to improve measures to desertification. Several Iranian universities now offer postgraduate courses on desertification and there are a number of well-developed research organizations involved in the topic, such as the Research Institute of Forests and Rangelands affiliated to the Ministry of Agriculture. These organizations generate information and prepare personnel to help to implement measures to combat desertification. Research capacity and measures to combat desertification existed already, but the international regime affected the way resources were allocated and the speed and degree the capacity was created. Thus, the effectiveness of implementation depends on how the actions coming from the top match those coming from the bottom or already in existence.

Therefore, states with strong administrative capacity may be able to advance implementation when conditions permit as they are able to mobilize resources (technical and human, and generally funding) more effectively than states with weak capacity. Nevertheless, the institutional factors may be an explanatory variable (i.e. an enabling or obstructing factor to implementation). Moreover, the capacity may help in certain aspects where it matters. For example, countries with strong administrative capacity may not be able to create protected areas but they can administer and enforce rules effectively in the existing protected areas.

The role of businesses

> *HBP 3.* Implementation of multilateral commitments by states and business will be stronger if they were included in negotiations. However, such involvement may have an effect on shaping the nature of the commitments which they are implementing, by design or through mere outputs.

> *HWP 3.* If relevant stakeholders are not included in policy making and negotiations, implementation is likely to be low.

> *HWP 4.* The higher the political and economic stakes involved, the implementation is likely to be lower.

Companies know better than almost anyone else how and what can and cannot be done in their own production processes to achieve certain environmental outcomes. However, they can be powerful actors in the international and national policy arenas to shape international agreements and national legislation for their own interest, besides lobbying and financing studies that show evidence supporting their own position. In the case of the ODS control, CFC-producing companies, which were skeptical at the beginning, became very active in responding to legislators and trying to deny the relationship between CFCs and the ozone hole at the beginning. They were also active in trying to influence discussions in the Montreal Protocol (MP). However, when science was clear, they started to cooperate and today they are active in influencing the implementation to phase out the CFCs, such as the case of the American company DuPont. The ozone depleting potential (ODP) of all controlled ODS decreased more than 93 percent between 1986 and 2004 (UNEP 2005) with strong participation of the private sector. Even though some countries started regulating some ODS before the international agreements, many countries made significant changes in some industrial and commercial sectors as the result of the implementation of the agreement. Thus, even with little effect in shaping the outcome of the agreement in the negotiation process (but involved in the process), the companies were engaged in the implementation later on.

Implementation of multilateral agreements is linked to the negotiation processes, but how these links evolve and shape both negotiation and implementation are still unclear. Actors affected by the agreement have interest in shaping the negotiation outcomes, but they can also provide valuable information to the negotiation process. Moreover, they could be more willing to cooperate if they participate in the decision process or perceive they will be affected somehow by the decisions. For example, businesses have little interest in the UNCCD as they are little affected by the decisions on desertification in poor countries, which have a relatively low effectiveness in implementation. Thus, the stakes involved do not necessarily need to be high to have low implementation.

Companies can also influence agreements to make them weaker, so implementation will not regulate their business directly. Businesses are actively participating in shaping international regimes and their implementation depends on the business's interests, or countries defending their businesses, in moving the agenda ahead, and generally they lobby heavily against any form of international regulation which is not voluntary. For example, American pharmaceutical companies, agribusinesses and other biotech-dependent companies have been fiercely involved in the negotiations on biodiversity, particularly those related to Genetically Modified Organisms or GMOs (Cartagena Protocol) or sharing of benefits of genetic resources (Nagoya Protocol). The position of those companies is one of the main reasons why the United States has not ratified the CBD, though the country continues to participate in the discussions. This has hindered the implementation of the agreements, as the United States is one of the key players in the area of biotechnology.

A heavier business regulation at international level would hardly gain approval from the business communities or the parties, and its enforcement as a law would be prohibitively expensive in many cases. However, businesses can be an influential force in shaping both negotiations and implementation, and even desirable, but business input in the negotiation process should be mediated to have the right balance between getting the right information for shaping the negotiations to have more effective implementation, and avoiding the process of being captured by business interests.

Influence of NGOs and media

HBP 4. Shaming and blaming by NGOs, amplified by media (business) may ensure greater effectiveness.

HWP 2. Net discounted losers (MNCs) without countervailing forces (i.e. NGOs, IOs and science) will lead to low implementation.

The role of NGOs has been essential in moving the environmental agenda at all levels over the decades, from global to local actions. The shaming and blaming was the first strategy environmental NGOs used to raise the awareness and press for strict environmental regulations at the national level, particularly to curb environmental pollution in the industrialized countries. They were also key to moving the international environmental agenda. Many advocating NGOs aimed to have a more collaborative role with business and governments by implementing projects, but some still keep shaming and blaming as part of their actions. How NGOs act (inside or outside the formal processes) and the intensity of their actions are key to influencing negotiation processes (Fisher 2004). However, the relationship between implementation effectiveness and shaming-and-blaming actions is not straightforward, as the dynamics of implementation may play out at the national or local level where NGOs may not be active or even exist.

Many of the shaming-and-blaming actions actually obtained wide political support from the public and positive coverage from the media, helping to press the companies and governments to act. In the case of ODS control, media coverage and NGO pressure was key in forcing the US Congress to fund more research and call the companies to explain their actions and make commitments. The NGOs organized a few protests and reports on ODS and counter-lobbied the efforts of the companies to influence legislators. The media also provided good coverage of the scientific findings of the impacts of ODS on the ozone layer and the NGOs' protests influenced many legislators, particularly those that were undecided about whether or how to legislate ODS. Later on, the legislation to control ODS in the US was enacted, even before the Vienna Convention, helping to reduce ODS significantly prematurely as US production and consumption encompassed a large part of the world production. Later on, this led to the US ratification of the Montreal Protocol, and even to be one of the "pushers" of the negotiation process (Benedick 1998).

Lack of strong agreement that may lead to losses in companies (MNCs) will have low implementation without countervailing forces. The local market structure and political economy also influences implementation. In countries where there is more open competition in the local market, economically and technically viable solutions can win quickly without much NGO, scientific or media intervention. The local political economy was important to determine the pace of many conversions in the aerosol sector. Markets for propellants were highly closed in 1980s, as this was an industry of easy entrance and countries tried to protect their own industry. In some countries, there were oligopolies that had interests in preventing the conversions from CFCs to Hydrocarbon Aerosol Propellants (HAPs). In others, the market alone was most responsible for the changes. For example, in Guatemala where NGOs, media and scientific influence is not particularly strong, when a few fillers of an economically feasible alternative entered the small market and when a filler started to produce the first hydrocarbon propellant (HAPs), their price differential led the competitors, which still used CFCs, to rapidly move to HAPs to avoid loss of market share or cease trading (UNEP 1995).

On the other hand, shaming and blaming can be divisive and stall implementation or the flow of funding. The UNCCD has been very open to the participation of NGOs both in international policy making and implementation, but it shows a slow implementation and a clear division in the parties between developed and developing countries. Developed countries were reluctant to recognize desertification as a global issue and critical of the decentralized manner for the implementation of the convention. NGOs with the support of some developing countries criticized heavily the role of developed countries in the UNCCD, creating tension between developing countries, which needed funding for their programmes, and developed countries, which were the main source of funding. In the COP-06 in Havana, Cuba, in 2003 this blame-and-shame by NGOs fueled the divisions in the high-level session when more polemical leaders, such as Cuba's

Fidel Castro, criticized openly the role of leaders of rich countries in the process, which led to the boycott in the presence of high-level representatives of rich countries (donors) in the COP, reflecting also in the funding for implementation (Bauer, 2008). Nevertheless, since 2003 the tensions have been reduced (and the incidents in COP-06 forgotten) and UNCCD has had some success recently in framing desertification as a global problem with support from rich and poor countries and thus including the implementation actions of the convention in the financing portfolio of the Global Environmental Facility (GEF), generating funding for implementation of actions related to UNCCD. In August 2010, the UN also declared the beginning of the United Nations Decade for Deserts and the Fight Against Desertification, bringing more attention to the issue.

Scientific reporting for shaping implementation

HBP 5. Scientific reporting can build or reinforce state implementation.

Scientific reports have been an important force to spur political interest in environmental issues and move policy implementation. They provide legitimacy for policymakers to take action on policy implementation through the allocation of funding for more research or projects, or for enacting legislation.

One good example of how a scientific report shaped a whole discussion on the issue is the process of controlling ODS. The science was used to guide policy making and implementation, even with strong opposition from large corporations. For example, DuPont reacted very aggressively when chemists Frank S. Rowland and Mario Molina admitted that CFCs could be causing the destruction of the stratospheric ozone layer, which led them to be awarded a Nobel Prize in 1995. DuPont was one of the inventors of CFCs and had a large share of the CFC market. The company campaigned intensively and suggested the studies on CFCs and ozone depletion were fraudulent. DuPont founded the Alliance for Responsible CFC Policy to inform businesses and refute scientific evidence from academia.[1] However, after more studies were produced and surmounting pressure from NGOs and the American Congress, the company started to cooperate and use alternatives that were economically and financially viable. Thus, scientific reporting reinforced with pressure from NGOs and political legitimation can change the attitude opposing MNCs. Political and scientific legitimation together is key to changing public perceptions, business attitudes, and behaviors.

On the other hand, some agreements have weak scientific input in the discussions, such as the case of desertification. The UNCCD emerged with a strong link to the scientific community during the 1977 United Nations Conference on Desertification (UNCOD). UNEP had grandiose plans to bring scientific knowledge to show the impacts of desertification on the population and propose mitigation measures for tackling land degradation (Rhodes 1991). However, after the formalization of the regime at the international level with the establishment of the UNCCD, the links between science and policy became weaker along the years, as scientific input was given "officially" by the very politicized Committee on Science and Technology (CST), which consists mainly of government officials, rather than independent scientists, and they only meet for a very short time during the COPs. Thus, scientific input was seen as politicized, losing influence in the process (Bauer 2009).

Most of the international agreements have a technical body, but they tend to be very politicized, and sometimes the members are government officials and not independent scientists. Their reports have a more political role to mediate different technical views on certain issues, which frequently reflect the positions of parties, rather than producing scientific information for policymakers. The Intergovernmental Panel on Climate Change (IPCC) has been an exception so far. Because it has a certain degree of independence (even though its members are appointed by parties), its role has been crucial in attracting media and political attention to the climate change debate. Other conventions are moving towards models similar to IPCC. The CBD has its Subsidiary Body on Scientific, Technical and Technological Advice (SBSTTA), which is "to provide the Conference of the Parties (COP) and, as appropriate, its other subsidiary bodies, with timely advice relating to the implementation of the Convention" (CBD 2011). It also produces periodically the GBO (Global Biodiversity Outlook) and other studies. However, the United Nations recently created the Intergovernmental Platform on Biodiversity and Ecosystem Services (IPBES), which will be a more independent body aimed to producing more independent scientific assessments for policymaking to strengthen the science input in the biodiversity related to international negotiations. The credible reports and their media coverage, like the IPCC or Millennium Ecosystem Assessment (MA), besides boosting international implementation mechanisms (such as GEF or MF), influence implementation at national and sub-national level, as the topics gain the attention of domestic politicians and local NGOs bringing resources for implementation.

Lessons on networks for implementation

The discussion and tests of the hypotheses can teach many lessons to implementation of international environmental regimes, which are discussed below.

Disconnection between negotiations and implementation at the international level

Networks that influence implementation can be very different from those that influence negotiations in certain regimes. At the international level, implementation actions tend to be disconnected from the main negotiations. Negotiations tend to happen under the coordination of a small body, such as a secretariat or a bilateral commission, but are entirely controlled by the parties. Secretariats can have more or less power to guide the negotiations, and the parties have an even power in shaping the process. However, when regimes get to funding issues, generally the decisions change to a different forum or organization, where generally the donors have much more control, even when the secretariat is reliable and efficient. For example, in the Global Environmental Facility (GEF), which supports the implementation of projects related to biodiversity, climate change, ODS, POPs, international water and desertification, has a different kind of governance than the international negotiation regimes, and the implementation is done through different organizations. This mismatch between negotiations and implementation of decisions can cause ineffectiveness as implementers are more accountable to those that fund than from those who take decisions in the negotiations. In the Montreal Protocol, one of the best practices, negotiations are under the small secretariat based in Nairobi, but the implementation at the international level are more influenced by the Multilateral Fund for the Protection of the Ozone Layer (MF) based in Montreal, where donors have more power than in the negotiations, but both bodies still reflect the negotiations and the parties of the same treaty. In other more complex structures, like the GEF with several agreements and agencies (UNEP, World Bank, UNDP, etc.) involved, there is a difficult connection between negotiation processes and parties and funding agencies and their recipients (Pinto and Puppim de Oliveira 2008).

Mismatch between international negotiators and national and sub-national implementers

There is often a mismatch between the negotiators and the implementers in the same country. In many countries, negotiations are often led by diplomats, who have international experience and generally have the right skills for performing well in international negotiations, but sometimes lack knowledge about the implementation system at home, as they may have little familiarity with the technical part or how the public bureaucracy or actors networks function at home. After the agreement, the implementation remained in the hands of the technical personnel of the countries, which sometimes do not have the resources to implement the agreement in the way it was shaped. For example, the ODS regime was initially left in the hands of national government in China, but the capacity to implement it was at the local level, which had information and control over the sources of ODS. The implementation just became more effective when those local actors were involved in the process (Zhao and Ortolano 2003).

Actors in networks at the international level do not always have the same values, power and interests as the networks of the same actors at national or local level. For example, the companies that participate in the international negotiations are generally large MNCs, but often small and medium Enterprises (SMEs) are more important to have an effective implementation at the local level in many cases, particularly in developing countries that lack large firms. For example, in the case of ODS, large companies like DuPont have resources and access to policymakers and international negotiations, but a small Brazilian firm that recycles refrigerant gases cannot attend the negotiations and has little access to the negotiators, though the company could play an important role in the implementation locally and regionally. The interests of the two firms are quite different. While large producers of refrigerant gases want to sell more new gases, and have little interest in recycling, the small firm wanted more incentives and tougher regulation to promote recycling of gases (this asymmetry continues in the climate negotiations, as the new less-depleting refrigerant gases cause climate change). This case is an example of bad practice, where those "less prominent" actors, such SMEs, are often unaware of the international discussions and implementation efforts and lack the capacity to make the necessary changes to address the issues. For example, in the case of ODS control, the effective implementation in developing countries depends on a large number of small shops dealing with maintenance of refrigerators and cars. Thus, there is a disparity in the flow of information and interest represented at the international level and those at the local level. An example of good practice is the Global Partnership on Cities and Biodiversity linked to CBD implementation. The partnership formed by international organizations and local authorities creates tools and is the voice of the sub-national governments in the implementation of the CBD (Puppim *et al*. 2011). As a result of the partnership efforts, the decision X/22 recognizing the importance of involving sub-national governments and local authorities in the implementation of the CBD was revealed during CBD COP-10 in Nagoya.

Local actors have different priorities for policy actions than the objectives of many international agreements and their implementation (Pinto and Puppim de Oliveira 2008). The mismatch can be large in the environmental area. For example, local governments, businesses and population in many parts of the Amazon depend on the timber industry to collect economic benefits from the forest in the short-term, but they are rarely involved or informed about international negotiations whose implementation depends on their changes in behavior. The preservation of the biodiversity has a much larger and diffuse impact, but the locals are just marginally benefiting from those in the long term. Some alternative solutions to bridge this gap have been built. The REDD+ or similar programs at the sub-national level can be one alternative to institutionalizing some of the missing links between local and international actors. There are some initiatives by sub-national governments in the Amazon. One example of good practice is the initiative of the Brazilian state of Amazonas that created the Amazonas Sustainable Foundations (FAS) to tap domestic and international sources to pay for ecosystem services for local communities living in preserved areas. This program is called Bolsa Floresta and is similar to an existing program to paying families to keep children at school. Established with an initial funding of R$40 million (US$20 million), half from the state government and half from a private Brazilian bank, 90 percent of the foundation's resources come from private voluntary donations. In August 2012, the program benefited more than 32,000 families who helped to preserve the forest (FAS 2012). The need to balance the local interest in the global agenda is key to getting support for implementation at the local level and bridge the global-local gap.

Economic and technical characteristics of the solution influence implementation

The implementation of environmental policies depends on the technical complexity of finding solutions. Environmental agreements can speed up technical changes, by bringing political and market pressures and financial resources to develop alternatives. Those alternatives are more easily implemented in countries with larger technical capacity and financial and economic incentives to finance the technical changes. Moreover, small issues that can be tackled by relatively small changes in larger economic systems are more likely to be implemented. For example, when the problem of the ozone hole linked to CFCs arose in the 1970s, CFC producing and consuming companies and countries were under pressure to find substitutes. CFCs appeared in the 1930s and were widely used in the industrial and commercial sectors. The aerosol sector accounted for 60 percent of all CFC usage in the mid-1970s. The sector was key to the implementation of national and international policies to control ODS because it was the only sector which had an economically-viable known technical solution, the Hydrocarbon Aerosol Propellants (HAPs), which was used in 80 percent of the total conversions from CFCs to alternative propellants (UNEP 1995). Even before the findings of Molina and Rowland (1974), HAPs had already been substituting CFCs since the 1950s, as the latter were expensive and could cause some of the technical problems when used for certain products and in certain conditions. Nevertheless, HAPs had still some drawbacks as they could not be used in certain products, were not available in certain cases and could cause accidents in some filling pumps. However, the technology for substituting CFCs in aerosols was available and could be a really safe substitute when properly implemented. Thus, even before the MP, countries started forcing the conversions through national legislatures (UNEP 1995), such as the United States and Sweden.

Reducing the distance between knowledge and policy is crucial, as this gap is still large in many international regimes. Most of the agreements have the technical bodies or committees but they tend to be inadequate for the challenges to be addressed, or heavily influenced by politics by the parties, such as the Subsidiary Body on Scientific, Technical and Technological Advice (SBSTTA) of the CBD. Initiatives like the IPCC, which have a certain independence and large capacity due to the large number of contributors, can help to bridge the distance between the international policymakers and the possible problems to be addressed and solutions that can be pursued.

The local political economy and technical capacity of countries determine the pace and costs of implementation

Implementation in developing countries also depends on the local political economy and the local technical capacity to carry out technical changes. Countries with better technical capacity and more sophisticated industry can more easily adapt to changes coming from international agreements through small incentives or funding.

For example, in the ODS case, the conversion of the aerosol sector was not a problem for developed countries with a highly sophisticated and capitalized chemical industry. However, many developing countries[2] had a long way to go to convert the CFC usage in the aerosol sector, as they needed capital, but also technical capacity. HAPs were less expensive than CFCs in almost all cases, but countries needed to have quality HAPs available for the kind of products they manufactured, the technology to convert both the product formulation and safe filling, and capital to make the conversions. Thus some developing countries, such as Mexico, Brazil, Argentina and the Philippines, could convert their aerosol sector at a relatively fast pace because they already had experience with HAPs in 1980s. Others, such as China, India, Indonesia and Tunisia, took more time to adapt their industries, as they did not have good quality HAPs or the technology to fill aerosols safely. The Mexican case was driven by a propellant company established at the beginning of the 1970s that produced the HAPs, one of the alternatives for CFCs. Gradually over time, the company disseminated the HAP-filling technology to its domestic aerosol fillers as part of its strategy. The fillers moved from CFCs to HAPs as capital for financing the change became available. Thus the technological and financial capacity of the private industry in the country determined the pace of change, even when the solution was economically viable for a long time.

The effectiveness of the implementation of international environmental agreements is also largely dependent on the local political situation. The emergence of a political demand at higher level can change the balance of political and economic forces at the local level, which can facilitate or hinder the implementation. For example, the effective implementation in the case of the agreement to regulate the threat of transboundary pollution from a Brazilian coal-fired power plant between Uruguay and Brazil was the result of the dynamics of the local environmental politics in the State of Rio Grande do Sul in Brazil, where the plant was located. For long time, the state environmental agency wanted to regulate the level of pollution in the plant, as local authorities, farmers and civil society groups were complaining about the impacts. However, the state environmental agency was weak politically and its actions against the company were blocked. Moreover, the company was under state control, which made enforcement by their own state government difficult (the case of the "fox taking care of the chicken coop"). When the demands from Uruguay came, there was a change in dynamics, and the pro-environmental groups in government and civil society were able to make the company to comply with local regulations (Rotulo Decuadra and Puppim de Oliveira 2008). Thus, like the example above, higher level political backing can be an influential factor in the local balance of economic and political power, when local organizations or networks can become more powerful forces or legitimately pursue their actions or public interests at the local level equivalent to higher level public interest.

Conclusions

The implementation of international environmental agreements implies results and advancements in the specific environmental situation at the national level. To comply with the agreements, parties have to transform the international commitments into policy, programs, regulations and projects. In order to be more effective, the implementation of those agreements has to pursue the objectives of the specific agreements, but also couple with the existing international initiatives and regimes and particularly to the situation at the national level in terms of existing policies and institutions already working in areas related to the environmental issue at the stake. Many international regimes are not effectively tuned in to what is happening in the countries which take part in the discussions. The representatives of the countries are the only source of information about the situation in the country, and sometimes they have limited in-depth knowledge of the situation at the different levels and sectors in the country. This chapter analyzes the implementation at different levels and sectors to draw some general lessons.

First, international regimes have limited capacity to promote rapid widespread changes in several countries and sectors at the same time. Funding generally is limited for the amount of changes necessary in all parties. Funding sources tend to focus their funding on actions in developing countries, but nevertheless resources are very limited. Moreover, the limited international funding sources are generally dispersed through several multilateral and bilateral agencies, international bodies and NGOs with little coordination. Domestic funding from the public and private sectors need to make a large contribution to the amount needed for the changes. Coordination of the available funding and implementation mechanism are key to the effectiveness of implementation. Additionally, funding should be aligned with both the agreement and the country's needs. As described above as an example of best practice, the case of the Multilateral Fund to control ODS illustrates the need for the participation of the same donors and beneficiaries with close coordination of the implementation arm (the fund) and the negotiations process.

Second, domestic policies for tackling the same environmental issues targeted by the international agreements generally exist in many countries prior to the ratification of specific environmental agreements and their implementation. For example, the regulations to control ODS existed in the United States and Europe much earlier than the international agreements (UNEP 1995). When the Vienna Convention or the Montreal Protocol came to existence the emissions from some domestic sectors were already falling. In the CBD, countries have been protecting their biodiversity for different reasons for centuries, and natural parks and reserves existed in almost every country including developing countries when the convention came into force. Desertification has been a policy issue in many countries. In Iran, for example, because of the large extent of drylands and increasing pressure on them, actions to combat desertification in the country existed for several decades before the UNCCD (Amiraslani and Dragovich 2010). Thus, when the international agreement comes into force, its implementation will depend on the situation of the national and sub-national governments already in place, and good implementation depends on the alignment of policies from the agreement with those at the national level but also at the local level. The example of the Global Partnership on Cities and Biodiversity and the CBD process mentioned earlier can be good practice that can be followed by other agreements. The official inclusion of sub-national governments as part of the implementation of the agreements can help boost implementation at the local level and assist in coordinating local and higher level (national and sub-national) processes.

Third, implementation of environmental agreements adds one more component to the local political economy. They can be important to change political and market forces to promote the objectives of the agreement. Agreements can bring international projects or economic incentives to force the necessary changes locally. In many cases, the objectives of the agreement and its implementation are not completely allied to the local interests. Those antagonistic interests tend to adapt to comply with the new situation, sometimes even benefiting from it, or they can try to reject the changes targeted by the implementation actions. For example, the international political interest of conserving biodiversity in the CBD and the local political and economic interests in the Amazon are quite different, creating a mismatch between efforts of implementation at the international level and reality of interests and results at the local level. There is a need for understanding the local political economy and creating mechanisms of flexibility to adapt global interests to the local needs in the short and medium term.

Notes

1 Now called The Alliance for Responsible Atmospheric Policy, www.arap.org
2 Montreal Protocol defines countries in Article 5 as those with a per capita consumption of ODS less than 300 grams per year.

References

Abbott, K., Keohane, R.O., Moravcsik, A., Slaughter, A. and Snidal, D. (2000) 'The concept of legalization', *International Organization* 54(3), 401–419.

Amiraslani, F. and Deirdre, D. (2010) 'Cross-sectoral and participatory approaches to combating desertification: The Iranian experience', *Natural Resources Forum* 34(2),140–154.

Bauer, S. (2008) 'Bureaucratic authority and the implementation of international treaties', in J. Joachim, B. Reinalda and B. Verbeek, eds., *International Organizations and Implementation: Enforces, Managers, Authorities?* New York: Routledge, 62–74.

Bauer, S. (2009) 'The ozone secretariat: the good shepherd of ozone politics', in Frank Biermann and Bernd Siebenhüner, eds., *Managers of Global Change: The Influence of International Environmental Bureaucracies*, Cambridge: MIT Press, 225–244.

Benedick, R.E. (1998) *Ozone Diplomacy. New Directions in Safeguarding the Planet*, Cambridge, MA: Harvard University Press.

Bruner, A.G., Gullison, R.E. and Balmford, A. (2004) 'Financial costs and shortfalls of managing and expanding protected-area systems in developing countries', *BioScience* 54, 1119–1126.

CBD (Convention on Biological Diversity) (2010) 'Local authorities', available at: http://www.cbd.int/authorities accessed on 22 December 2010.

CBD (Convention on Biological Diversity) (2011) 'Subsidiary body on scientific, technical and technological advice', available at: http://www.cbd.int/sbstta/, accessed on 17 February 2011.

Chasek, P., Essahli, W., Akhtar-Schuster, M., Stringer, L.C. and Thomas, R. (2011) 'Integrated land degradation monitoring and assessment: horizontal knowledge management at the national and international levels', *Land Degradation & Development* 2(2), 272–284.

FAS (Fundação Amazonas Sustentável) (2012), available at: www.fas-amazonas.org, accessed on 5 September 2012.

Fisher, D.R. (2004) 'Civil society protest and participation: civic engagement within the multilateral governance regime', in N. Kanie and P. M. Haas, eds., *Emerging Forces in Environmental Governance*, Tokyo: United Nations University Press.

Gareau, B.J. (2010) 'A critical review of the successful CFC phase-out versus the delayed methyl bromide phase-out in the Montreal Protocol', *International and Environmental and Agreements: Politics, and Law and Economics* 10(3), 209–231.

Haas, P.M.K., Robert, O., Levy, M.A., eds. (1993) *Institutions for the Earth: Sources of Effective International Environmental Protection*, Global Environmental Accords Series, Cambridge, MAMIT Press.

Hanf, K. and Underdal, A. (1998). 'Domesticating international commitments: linking national and international decision-making', in A. Underdal, ed., *The Politics of International Environmental Management*, Dordrecht: Kluwer.

Hossay, P. (2006) *Unsustainable*, London, Zed Books.

Kasusya, P. (1998) 'Combating desertification in northern Kenya (Samburu) through community action: a community case experience', *Journal of Arid Environments* 39, 325–329.

Machado, C.S.M. (1993) 'Reducing emissions of ozone-depleting substances in Brazil', *Global Environmental Change* 4(3), 350–356.

Mazmanian, D.A. and Sabatier, P.A. (1983) *Implementation and Public Policy*, Chicago, IL: Scott Foresman.

MF (Multilateral Fund for the Implementation of the Montreal Protocol) (2011), available at: www.multilateralfund.org, accessed on 15 February 2011.

Miles, E.L. (2002) *Environmental Regime Effectiveness: Confronting Theory with Evidence*, Cambridge, MA: MIT Press.

Molina, M. (2007) 'Climate change – learning from the stratospheric ozone challenge', in H.J. Schellnhuber, N. Tern, M. Molina, V. Huber and S. Kadner, *The Global Sustainability: A Nobel Cause*, Cambridge: Cambridge University Press, 155–165.

Molina, M. and Rowland, F.S. (1974) 'Stratospheric sink for chlorofluoromethanes: chlorine atom-catalysed destruction of ozone', *Nature* 249, 810–812.

NASA (National Aeronautics and Space Administration) (2011), available at: ozonewatch. gsfc.nasa.gov/meteorology/annual_data.html, accessed on 9 February 2011.

Norman, C., DeCanio, S. and Fan, L. (2008) 'The Montreal Protocol at 20: ongoing opportunities for integration with climate protection', *Global Environmental Change* 18(2), 330–340.

Pagiola, S. (2008) 'Payments for environmental services in Costa Rica', *Ecological Economics* 65(4), 663–674.

Pinto, R.R. and Puppim de Oliveira, J.A. (2008) 'Implementation challenges in protecting the global environmental commons: the case of climate change policies in Brazil', *Public Administration and Development* 28(5), 340–350.

Poulsen, L. and Lo, M. (2006) 'Promoting good governance through the implementation of the UNCCD', in P.M. Johnson, K. Mayrand and M. Paquin, eds., *Governing Global Desertification: Linking Environmental Degradation, Poverty and Participation*, Aldershot: Ashgate, 109–130.

Pressman, J.L. and Wildavsky, A. (1973) *Implementation*, Berkeley, CA: University of California Press.

Prip, C., Gross, T., Johnston, S. and Vierros, M. (2010) *Biodiversity Planning: An Assessment of National Biodiversity Strategies and Action Plans*, Yokohama: United Nations University Institute of Advanced Studies.

Puppim de Oliveira, J.A. (2002) 'Implementing environmental policies in developing countries through decentralization: the case of protected areas in Bahia, Brazil', *World Development* 30(10), 1713–1736.

Puppim de Oliveira, J.A. (2005) 'Enforcing protected area guidelines in Brazil: what explains participation in the implementation process?', *Journal of Planning Education and Research* 24(4), 420–436.

Puppim de Oliveira, J.A. (2008) *Implementation of Environmental Policies in Developing Countries*, Albany, NY: SUNY Press.

Puppim de Oliveira, J.A. (2009) 'The implementation of climate change related policies at the subnational level: an analysis of three countries', *Habitat International* 33(3), 253–259.

Puppim de Oliveira, J.A. (2011a) 'Why an air pollution achiever lags on climate policy? The case of local policy implementation in Mie, Japan', *Environment & Planning A* 43, 1894–1909.

Puppim de Oliveira, J.A. (2011b) 'Bridging the gap between small firms and investors to promote investments for green innovation in developing countries: two cases in Brazil', *International Journal Technological Learning, Innovation and Development* 4(4), 259–276.

Puppim de Oliveira, J.A., Balaban, O., Doll, C.N.H., Moreno-Penaranda, R., Gasparatos, A., Iossifova, D. and Suwa, A. (2011) 'Cities, biodiversity and governance: perspectives and governance challenges for the convention on biological diversity at the city level', *Biological Conservation* 144(5): 1302–1313.

Rein, M. and Rabinovitz, F.F. (1977) 'Implementation: a theoretical perspective', Working Paper No. 43, Cambridge, MA: Joint Center for Urban Studies of MIT and Harvard University.

Rhodes, S.L. (1991) 'Rethinking desertification – what do we know and what have we learned', *World Development* 19(9), 1137–1143.

Rotulo Decuadra, D.E. and Puppim de Oliveira, J.A. (2008) 'Learning from the implementation of international environmental agreements between developing countries only: the case Brazil-Uruguay over the acid rain from UTPM Termo Power Plant', *International and Environmental and Agreements: Politics, and Law and Economics* 8(4), 389–408.

Sabatier, P.A. (1986) 'Top-down and bottom-up approaches to implementation research: a critical analysis and a suggested synthesis', *Journal of Public Policy* 6(1), 21–48.

UNEP (1995) 'Aerosol sector conversion in action', manuscript from OzoneAction Clearinghouse, March.

UNEP (2005) *Production and Consumption of Ozone Depleting Substances under the Montreal Protocol 1986–2004*, Nairobi: UNEP.

US EPA (United States Environmental Protection Agency) (2011), available at: http://www.epa.gov/ozone/awards/, accessed on 2 February 2011.

Van Meter, D. and Van Horn, C.E. (1975) 'The policy implementation process', *Administration and Society* 6(4), 445–488.

Victor, D.G, Raustiala, K. and Skolnikoff, E.B., eds., (1998) *The Implementation and Effectiveness of International Environmental Commitments*, Cambridge, MA: MIT Press.

Wheeler, S.M. (2008) 'State and municipal climate change plans: the first generation', *Journal of the American Planning Association* 74(4), 481–496.

Zhao, J. and Ortolano, L. (2003) 'The Chinese government's role in implementing multilateral environmental agreements: the case of the Montreal Protocol', *The China Quarterly* 175, 708–725.

6 Resilience and biodiversity governance

The processes of actor configurations which support and limit resilience

Casey Stevens

Introduction

How do environmental governance arrangements persist in the face of political divisions and adapt to changing environmental conditions? Many areas of international environmental politics are beset with severe political intractability, environmental problems that are rapidly degrading in nonlinear fashion, and the persistent problems of collective action and effective rule design. Within these struggles, many have been unable to make authoritative collective decisions or have found those collective decisions largely locked-in despite changes in information. Some environmental governance arrangements, however, have been resilient under these pressures and maintained the credibility of the authority of the decisions and the capacity to adapt to changing environmental conditions. Resilient governance has been a goal specifically emphasized in the Global Environmental Outlook 4 and the Millennium Ecosystem Assessment among others.

This chapter finds that an interrelationship between moderately exclusive selection of parties to the governance arrangement and some shared normative frame by those parties are key generative processes for fostering resilient governance. This argument has particular weight on the issue of actor configurations in that different particular array can either promote these mechanisms or hinder them. The inclusion of contributors to the problem, NGO channeling into specific tasks, and thick networks with actors sharing basic beliefs are found to be key to the configurations in order for resilient environmental governance.

Biodiversity governance arrangements serve as illustrative examples because of the variety of actor configurations across different governance arrangements. Coupling of scientific communities, nongovernmental organizations, local communities, international organizations, various state actors, and increasingly multinational corporation and private sector actors means that biodiversity governance is a ripe field for studying the implications of actor configurations. This diversity of actors is not an unintended outcome in biodiversity governances, but a result of its particular history encouraging participation from a variety of actors; indeed, the First Law of Biodiversity Governance is attention to the matching of actor configurations with the scope and scale of particular problems (Soberon and Sarukhan 2010).

This chapter focuses specifically on the configurations in UNESCO's *Man and the Biosphere* (MAB) project, the Convention on International Trade in Endangered Species (CITES) with the illustrative case of management of the African elephant, and the work in the Convention on Biological Diversity (CBD). These three cases highlight very different actor configurations and outcomes on resilience. While not exhaustive of different actor configurations, the two cases of resilient governance, MAB and CITES, and the limiting case of the CBD do highlight the importance of actor configurations on resilient governance. The study aims for the case studies to operate as contrasts of contexts (Skocpol and Somers 1980), highlighting specific mechanisms and their interrelationship with one another and the supportive or limiting role played by the actor configurations (for a fuller explanation of the strengths and weaknesses of this approach, see Falleti and Lynch 2009).

The first section will discuss the concept of resilience with particular emphasis on the intertwined concepts of persistence and adaptability as key for thinking about resilience. The next section will discuss relevant mechanisms identified in literature on network governance and how these are expected to lead from actor configurations to resilient outcomes. Brief focuses on MAB, CITES, and CBD will highlight actor configurations, network dynamics, and resilience outcomes. Following the case studies, the chapter will conclude with a section exploring the possible generalizability and articulation of specific best and worst practices to be learned from these cases.

Studying resilience

Resilient governance can be broadly defined as "the governance institution persisting over time and being able to accurately respond to new challenges" (Introduction, this volume). As articulated in the introduction, resilience has two different dimensions: persistence and adaptability to changing problems. In the context of international environmental governance, it can be understood as adaptive management across national borders. Rather than creating static rules for governing a problem or developing new institutions and rules for each reassessment of the problem, resilience is primarily about governance arrangements maintaining their ability to make authoritative decisions regarding changed understandings of environmental conditions (Young 2010).

Persistence is primarily about the credibility of the governance arrangement to members (and potential members) and thus goes beyond its functional existence. Functional existence is an inadequate operationalization of persistence because extensive transition costs (Tullock 1975) may make actors averse to reinvest costs in new governance arrangements without necessarily providing the arrangement with the ability to implement agreements among members. Genschel explains that

> institutions cause large initial set-up costs. Actors have to learn rules, codes, and conventions. They have to develop particular skills, competencies, and tools, establish specialized personal contacts, and sometimes they even have to set

up extra physical infrastructures. All these assets take time, money and effort to build up ... They represent a durable form of capital. However, this capital tends to be institution-specific to some degree. It cannot easily be transferred.

(Genschel 1997)

Credibility provides a more appropriate operationalization of persistence of governance in multilateral environmental agreements.

As highlighted in the introduction, this credibility or authoritative rule making is largely based on the ability to get continued compliance from the members. As such it may most clearly be related to what Barnett and Finemore term *delegated authority* (Barnett and Finnemore 2005) or Suchman's *pragmatic legitimacy* (Suchman 1995). As opposed then to expertise-based legitimacy or moral-based legitimacy, credibility is supported by the belief in other actors complying with the agreement. Work on international alliances has found that persistence of arrangements relies heavily on expected compliance by other actors (Walt 1997; Wallander 2000; see also, Leeds and Savun 2007). Forces like political intractability, weak guidance or leadership, rigid rules, and the ability of other states to implement rules have been highlighted as limiting factors on the ability for international environmental agreements' authoritative rule making capacity (Kutting 2000; Young *et al.* 2008).

Coupled with persistence is the need for adaptability in the rules, based upon new understandings, to deal more effectively with the problem. The instructive case of the Northern Pacific fur seal efforts is most instructive in this regard, as the inability to update requirements eventually resulted in the collapse of the regime (Young 2010). Not simply evaluation and updating, adaptive governance involves social learning by the members of the governance arrangement on developing and evaluating new approaches to the problem (Lee 1993). Folke *et al.* explain that "Because the self-organizing properties of complex ecosystems and associated management systems seem to cause uncertainty to grow over time, understanding should be continuously updated and adjusted, and each management action viewed as an opportunity to further learn how to adapt to changing circumstances" (Folke *et al.* 2005). Adaptive capacity is largely based upon the epistemic legitimacy of governance arrangements and their ability to both refine understandings about the problem and communicate this from experts to other decision-makers (Pahl-Wostl 2009).

Work on socio-ecological system governance has generally emphasized that effective adaptive governance largely focuses on the "rules-in-use" in the governance arrangement (Ostrom 2005, 2010). Particularly salient are those rules which encourage and foster social learning, experimental policy-making, and network communication about results and understandings (Anderies *et al.* 2006; Crona and Bodin 2006; Folke 2006; Olsson *et al.* 2006; Walker *et al.* 2006; Walker and Salt 2006). The epistemic legitimacy then is generally supported, as the capacity for the governance arrangement to actually deal with the problem is seen to be increasing.

The persistence and adaptive capacity of governance arrangements then revolves around the intertwined and interacting belief in compliance with rules by other actors and belief in the ability of the governance arrangement to address the problem effectively. As stated in the introduction: "for governance arrangements to be resilient they must be perceived to be legitimate to the major actors involved in performing the governance components." Lack of key actors (or signals by those actors that they will not comply with certain decisions), suspicion of politically-tainted scientific advice, lack of policy capacity of the governance arrangement, and networks that do not provide new ideas or are based around a few key chokepoints (or gatekeepers) are all reasonable expectations for limiting forces on resilience.

This general position finds salience in explaining the lack of resilience in many other environmental governance arrangements. International forestry governance for example has seen the persistence of the International Tropic Timber Organization (ITTO) be severely limited when the World Wildlife Fund removed their advisers from national delegations and functionally decreased the involvement by some major actors (Humphreys 2004). Lack of a clear scientific community has reduced the capacity for any rules established to be ratcheted up to becoming significant (Werland 2009). Nesting of the United Nations Forum on Forests and the ITTO in UN ECOSOC and UNCTAD respectively, has been constraining in that neither of these bodies could provide particular competencies or tools to be used in rule adaptation (Humphreys 2003; Persson 2005). The persistence and adaptive capacity of the organizations is severely hampered by its lack of both pragmatic and epistemic legitimacy.

Studying resilience as a governance outcome is problematic in that there are some key conceptual and measurement problems regarding resilient governance. Initially, the problem is that resilience is often not an outcome that can be empirically separated from other processes. A governance arrangement may appear persistent simply as a result of political fortune. The ability of governance arrangements to make authoritative decisions may be the result of a lack of political disagreement on a particular issue rather than the credibility of the actors involved. Similarly, resilience, as conceptualized here, is a latent condition rather than something constantly being demonstrated in governance arrangements (Gunderson 2000). These measurement problems are addressed with a triangulation of efforts: case selection, assessments of progress on rule-making, and statements by rule-makers in official documents. The cases highlighted as the core part of this chapter all have been beset by both political intractability and the need to update their rules based upon increasing scientific understandings. Qualitative analysis of the progress on rule-making and statements in official documents of the three arrangements will illuminate resilience and brittleness in the arrangements.

Organization of case studies

Biodiversity governance arrangements generally deal with a host of different problems ranging from single species conservation to entire ecosystem and landscape maintenance (Franklin 1993). At the international level, these configurations have included all of the major different types of actors involved in international environmental politics. Closer examination of the resilience results in UNESCO's MAB, CITES, and the CBD are instructive of the impacts of these configurations.

As the study aims at highlighting context and mechanisms, each case will be divided into three different sections. First, the actor configuration of the specific governance arrangement will be detailed. Where possible, the distinctions provided in the introduction (for example, between laggard and pusher states) will be highlighted as well. This will be broad and will largely be discussing the active actor configurations in the arrangement over the years 2000–2010 if not otherwise specified.

Second, each case will highlight the mechanisms of selection of membership within the organizations. The selection of parties in governance arrangement is relevant in highlighting the credibility and, in some instances, the adaptability of the arrangement. The possible mechanisms of selection, as developed by Archon Fung, ranging from exclusive to extremely open are: Expert Administrators, Elected Representatives, Professional Stakeholders, Lay Stakeholders, Random Selection, Open Targeting, Open Self-Selection, Diffuse, Public Sphere (Fung 2006). This is not the point to fully extrapolate these particular mechanisms, but merely to highlight that there are tradeoffs with the authoritative decision making in each one and that inclusion does not necessarily correlate with legitimacy.

In addition, the mechanisms of networked governance or the mechanisms of linking different parts of the governance arrangement to one another will be highlighted in each case. There are generally five different types of networked governance mechanisms, arranged from thin network mechanisms to thick network mechanisms: Restricted Access to Exchanges, Collective Sanctions, General Reciprocity, Reputation, and Macroculture (or shared understandings) (Jones, Hesterly *et al.* 1997; Das and Teng 2002). These five mechanisms may be coupled with one another and with other mechanisms, and are not mutually exclusive. Identifying network mechanisms is important for this study in that they help understand how different actor configurations actually impact the resilience of the arrangement.

Finally, the resilience of each governance arrangement will be assessed. For ease of specifications, each will be assessed on both persistence and adaptive capacity as highlighted above and in the introduction to the volume. This aids in identifying the specific impact of certain practices on the overall resilience or brittleness of the arrangement. As resilience is a changing condition of governance arrangements as capacity and capabilities shift, these shifts will be generally identified in the discussion of the cases.

Man and biosphere (MAB) project

Actor configuration

States and activist NGOS are extremely active throughout the negotiations and meetings of the agreement. Other international organizations maintain a consistent presence in many of the forums. And in recent meetings, multinational corporations, often represented with industry associations, and local groups, both local governments and indigenous peoples' organizations, have become increasingly active.

Founded in 1971, MAB largely operated as a fairly loose network of biosphere reserves with a focus primarily on conservation of unique and important ecosystems for scientific study. Even at this early point, however, the core scientific network was fairly thick sharing understandings of the emerging field of ecology. The governance arrangement and its World Network on Biosphere Reserves teamed up scientists with local conservation efforts. The core scientists involved in MAB served as key gatekeepers to the governance arrangement. For example, in the 1990s, internal assessments of the organization resulted in findings that not enough biosphere managers and conservation bureaucrats were included in discussions about the World Network on Biosphere Reserves (ICC-MAB 1992). Efforts were then made to deepen the network to include these additional actors in the governance arrangement.

This core network was of key significance during times of stress within the governance arrangement. The most significant period was between 1985 (Minsk Conference) and the 1995 Seville meeting. The period from the founding of the organization up to Minsk had included rapid growth of sites in the World Network of Biosphere Reserves; however, many of these were already existing sites which changed little of management as a result of their inclusion and were largely limited to Western Europe and North America. The period following Minsk saw a dramatic fall in the number of new biosphere reserves from a number of different factors. Funding for the agreement was severely constrained as a result of defection by the United States and the United Kingdom from UNESCO, the organization nesting MAB. The World Network also was constrained by a lack of communication between members and little development on sharing experiences across members. Lack of clear processes to integrate development into the program limited its ability to expand to new areas in Latin America, Africa and Asia (Ishwaran *et al.* 2008).

The scientific community was largely able to continue their efforts through this time and to significantly increase the governance approach in the Seville meeting. Even though the United States and the United Kingdom had withdrawn from UNESCO, MAB-affiliated scientists and projects in these countries continued through this time. In addition, the community began expanding to new constituencies by largely integrating sustainable development and a range of social scientists and managers (more significantly) into the governance arrangement (Batisse 1997). This is most dramatically articulated in the 1995 Seville strategy which aims: first, to integrate sustainable development into the biosphere reserve strategies and goals and, second, to develop explicit criteria for inclusion of sites in the network and periodic review of biosphere reserves along these criteria (Price *et al.* 2010).

The strengthening of the governance requirements affiliated with inclusion of the network have caused some limitations from some major actors. This has been most dramatically seen in the withdrawal of individual sites from the World Network of Biosphere Reserves in Norway, Sweden, Australia and the United Kingdom (Price *et al.* 2010). In addition, there has been some substantial questioning of the importance of the governance arrangement by policymakers in Western Europe and the United States. For example, the Nordic Council of Ministers, Nature and Outdoor Recreation Group argued that "the Biosphere Reserve concept does not at the moment, contribute anything new to already ongoing activities in the framework of, for instance, the establishment and management of traditional reserves, Local Agenda 21 and international monitoring systems" (Statement by the Nordic Council of Ministers Nature and Outdoor Recreation Group, quoted in Hokkanen 2001). Similarly, at the 2010 International Coordinating Committee (ICC) meeting of the MAB, they identified 114 biosphere reserves of the 300 pre-Seville biosphere reserves which had failed to submit required periodic reviews demonstrating their compliance with the economic enrichment provision (ICC-MAB 2010). Of those sites, the vast majority are from the United States (47 or 41 percent) which has failed to perform any periodic review of any biosphere reserves. This issue may quickly come to a head as the ICC has begun suggesting it will delist any sites which have not submitted periodic review, and the United States has largely stopped attending ICC meetings.

The major actors are primarily scientific communities, but there is some inclusion of major states (including substantial laggards early on in the program), NGOs (mainly administrative and national) and also limited involvement of either international organizations or multinational corporations.

Mechanisms

The selection mechanism for inclusion to the major governance-making areas of the MAB (largely the International Conferences on Biosphere Reserves, advisory committees, and exchange of information through the World Network of Biosphere Reserves and less so the ICC) is largely professional stakeholders. Actors are included to the extent that they share the general understandings of the scientific network. This can include local conservation managers, state delegations, NGOs and international organizations; however, the largely technical nature of the conference and the focus on the overall purpose of MAB limits their inclusion. Thus, NGO membership in the organization is largely those with shared epistemologies to the core of the MAB like the International Council for Science (ICSU), the International Union of Biological Sciences (IUBS), the World Conservation Union (IUCN), and the Scientific Committee on Problems of the Environment (SCOPE). National-level MAB groups are also important in directing decisions and fostering the growth of the organization, and largely determine the work of delegations.

As such, a selection process, reputation and macroculture appear to be significant modes of coordinating the network. Shared understandings and reputation to the rest of the network provide some positive impacts on the governance arrangement in that they link together disparate actors across time. Interestingly, these mechanisms seem to serve to foster creative and experimental policy making. The International Conferences and network management activities actively highlight original inclusion efforts and attempts to develop ideas on sustainable development (Ishwaran *et al.* 2008). In addition, the recent development of the Michel Batisse award in the organization has largely encouraged original management schemes of particular problems. A further illustrative example is the efforts over the past years to include urban areas as possible biosphere reserves. Although challenging much of the pre-1995 conception of biosphere reserves, scientists relying upon the shared understandings that have developed in the community and encouraged original positions have begun pushing for the possible inclusion of urban areas in the network.

Resilience

During the post-Minsk period, the organization has limited persistence and the adaptability was largely constrained. The lack of expansion of new sites during this time is a strong indicator of a lack of persistence in the arrangement (see Table 6.1). In addition the capacity of the arrangement was severely questioned by important actors. In 1995, IUCN summarized that "no built-in way of evaluating performance and no standardized measure with which to evaluate the economic, social, and ecological progress was made. Consequently, it [was] difficult to identify what constitutes 'successful' implementation throughout the Network as a whole" (IUCN quoted in Price *et al.* 2010). Meeting reports in the early 1990s were largely concerned with the role of the organization in a different institutional world, with an emphasis on sustainable development and an international organization (the CBD) dedicated to biodiversity issues.

However, with the adjustments in Seville and the continued thick network of scientists, the governance arrangement has developed substantial persistence and adaptive capacity. The Seville Strategy and the Madrid Action Plan have transformed the biosphere reserves from a loose, unmonitored, network of biosphere reserves into a key governance project for biodiversity protection (Price *et al.* 2010). The ramping up of new biosphere reserves in the post-Seville period, the wider geographical distribution, and the more stringent requirements on sites are all signs of strong persistence and adaptability.

Table 6.1 Number of biosphere reserves under the MAB program created during the periods, by region

	First period 1976–1984 Inception–Minsk	Second period 1985–1995 Minsk–Seville	Third period 1996–2007 post-Seville	Fourth period 2008–2010 post-Madrid
Africa	27	3	17	4
Middle East and North Africa	20	3	10	3
Asia and Pacific	33	10	40	11
Europe and North America	128	46	75	10
Latin America and the Caribbean	28	22	44	7
Total	236	84	187	35

Source: Ishrwahan and Persic 2008 and ICC-MAB reports for 2008, 2009, and 2010

This change in situation is largely the result of the gradual ratcheting up as the original constituency expanded to include new constituencies. The science-dominated agenda was not able to ignore wider political concerns; however, it was able to persist through the political storms and gradually expand its constituencies to include new actors giving support to significantly expanded governance efforts.

The Convention on International Trade of Endangered Species (CITES)

CITES has a host of different governance efforts and programs regarding different trade restrictions and reporting requirements. One of the most important of these efforts for understanding resilience is the governance of the African elephant. This struggle has been beset by extreme political differences and developing understanding of the state of the species with pleas for updating governance. In addition, the struggle had wider implications on CITES as it resulted in the removal of a Secretary General of CITES by UNEP, a protracted struggle between CITES and UNEP that followed, threatened withdrawal from the treaty by key range states, and an overhaul of the listing procedures of the organization as a whole. The governance of African elephants is thus selected as a focus in order to highlight actor configurations and their impacts on resilience.

Actor configuration

Currently, the actor configuration for governance of the African elephant is a mix between the range states (some of which are laggards and others are pushers for strong protection), CITES and representative of its administrative bodies, and administrative NGOs coupled with scientific study of elephant habitats and range. As there has not been much legal trade in ivory since the ban in 1989, there are few multinational corporations with access, and none are actively included in the efforts.

This configuration is quite a departure from the earlier periods of the African elephant governance efforts which were dominated by political NGOs. Many commentators have pointed to NGO pressure as the fundamental cause of the initial move of African elephants as a species from Appendix II (quota-based trade allowed) to Appendix I (trade ban) (Sands and Bedecarre 1990; Princen 1994). NGO pressure on states had largely pushed for the listing decision for African elephants. Moving far beyond pressure on the states, NGO pressure influenced all parts of the CITES governance structure. At the 1989 COP in Lausanne, during the ivory discussions, the Secretariat passed a legal interpretation of the ruling which would have created an exception for preexisting stockpiles of ivory, but the World Wildlife Fund immediately responded with an independent legal interpretation which would have not created such an exception. The United States and other important parties supported the WWF interpretation and it became the primary legal interpretation of the decision (Sands and Bedecarre 1990).

The polarization reached a high point when NGO pressure on UNEP caused that organization to replace the secretary general of CITES who had supported a managed trading scheme rather than an outright ban on ivory (Sand 1997; Andresen 2001, 2002). Eugene Lapointe was removed from his position in 1990 and CITES was left without a Secretariat for two years while UNEP directly managed the organization. Although there were charges of malfeasance against Lapointe, the result was that the relationship between UNEP and the CITES secretariat position was clearly detailed in an agreement signed in 1992 between the two institutions.

Science bodies of the organization were similarly used by the World Wildlife Fund, Greenpeace and others for their specific goals in opposing any managed species use. Most importantly, there appeared to be a division between activist NGOs and administrative NGOs during this time. This is demonstrated by the joint effort by IUCN and some of the range states to push for a "beneficial use" exception if trade could be shown to promote conservation and health of the species while activist NGOs (such as the International Fund for Animal Welfare) pushed for the continuation of the ban (Sand 1997; Santiapillai 2009).

The legitimacy crisis of CITES during the debate about the ivory ban and following it led to a general feeling by parties that the institution was becoming increasingly polarized. This polarization was making itself manifest in decisions which were based on political arguments rather than clear criteria and which increasingly took an all or nothing approach. Following a pattern to be followed in future listing procedures, the CITES Secretariat put together a committee of biologists to establish clear conditions for listing species in different Annexes to the agreement. The guidelines which were developed by the *ad hoc* group of scientists were unanimously adopted at the 1994 COP in Fort Lauderdale.

The result was an institutional environment which gradually developed a highly modulated structure with specific tasks played in different forums coupled with general coordination from the secretary general. The result is that today, as Gehring and Ruffing explain:

> The scientific assessment stage establishes a veritable discourse on the merits of a listing proposal. Its triadic structure and its integration into the larger listing procedure deprive the member states, and other stakeholders, of their bargaining power and commit them to the commonly accepted listing criteria. As a result, a protected niche for the exchange of arguments emerges.
>
> (Gehring and Ruffing 2008)

The listing procedure itself has an actor configuration emphasizing specific roles played by a variety of actors including using IUCN's Red List as a key indicator of endangered species (the Red List itself has shifted from the charismatic species to more adequately reflect the scientific data and focus on other species), the establishment of some permanent and *ad hoc* committees, the use of TRAFFIC as an enforcement monitoring system and, most importantly, predefined rules of procedure and criteria for the decisions.

This modulated and task-oriented structure has been extensively used in the governance of African elephant populations. CITES has created Monitor the

Illegal Killing of Elephants (MIKE); the Elephant Trade Information System (ETIS) and IUCN coupled these efforts with its African Elephant Specialist Group. These groups have roles and tasks largely established by the Conference of Parties and the CITES ones are almost always guided by the Secretary General of the organization; however, their work has been largely accepted by all parties, and recommendations have been key at both COP13 and COP15 for final decision making. Inclusion of actors then is configured by extensive support from the secretariat, from scientists, administrative NGOs, all range states, and other states as key funders for efforts in the range states (both the EU and the United States have been key funders for the MIKE system).

Mechanisms

The selection mechanism of CITES now seems to be a combination of professional stakeholders, expert administrators (the CITES secretary-general staff), and lay stakeholders. Administrative NGOs, conservation authorities in the countries, representatives of the CITES secretary general staff and other experts have played key roles in the MIKE process. Activist NGOs have largely participated at the level of the Conference of Parties commenting on the information and recommendations made to CITES. There is little self-selection of membership and the modulated structure does seem to require continual effort by members.

More significantly, the network governance mechanism most relevant is restricted access. Jones *et al.* emphasize that restricted access can be important in network governance in that it fosters the development of communication protocols and shared routines for all the actors involved. Since the reforms in the mid-1990s, the interactions in the different modules of CITES have begun to increasingly delve into specifics and complying with requirements rather than deviating to other issues (Gehring and Ruffing 2008). This is not simply in the committees of CITES but has influenced the COP, the various programs like MIKE and EMIT, the supporting administrative NGOs like TRAFFIC, and even the engagement of activist NGOs with the organization. The discussion now is increasingly about judging species listings based upon pre-determined criteria and this has been done by all actors. The condition giving rise to restricted access may be the deployment of outside assessments and other reflective mechanisms (Siebenhuner 2008). Reflective mechanisms coming from the outside of the agreement may foster such restricted access, as the task of evaluation becomes modularly controlled, others might follow.

Within governance practices and discussions themselves, reputation seems to be a primary mechanism for them attempting to justify their decisions based upon trusted evidence and the established criteria. Although there are still some substantive disagreements, for example about the valuation of a ton of ivory on the black market (Santiapillai 2009), the shared focuses may even be forming a monoculture in CITES.

Resilience

Some of the persistence of CITES is largely based upon its easy opt-out provisions; however, what is significant is that this opt-out by states has been significantly decreasing over time. After the 1989 ban on trade in produce of African elephants, South Africa and other key range states opted out of the provision. Since the mid-1990s though, even when the COP votes to restrict trade there has been no opting out by the range states of the requirements. With flexibility in regulations for some states adopted in 1997 and 2000 (those states where elephant stocks were deemed not be threatened) and with allowance of one-time sales in the 2000s, these states have continued to push for limited ivory sales rather than opt out of the decision. These flexibility measures have been controversial to many activist NGOs; however, there is evidence they have not impacted the illegal poaching of ivory significantly and the procedures of CITES were quite rigorous even in allowing the flexibility (Gillson and Lindsay 2003; Stiles 2004; Wasser *et al.* 2010). The result is that both the authority of the governance arrangement in keeping parties involved even when decisions go against their wishes and the adoption of flexible measures when supported by their evidentiary system demonstrates increasing resilience of the arrangement.

Convention on Biological Diversity as a limiting case

Actor configuration

The CBD includes every type of actor through the process of decision-making and governance. State actors are fairly active throughout, activist NGOs are extremely active, scientists participate in many forums, multinational corporations have increasingly sent industry associations and some corporations themselves participate, other international organizational connections are ubiquitous, and a host of other actors like indigenous peoples and local governments also participate widely and have been integrated into the governance structure. The size of actors included in the actual Conference of Parties meetings is quite substantial. The 2009 COP9 meeting, for example, included 500 NGOs, industry organizations, and international organizations in attendance in addition to the state parties. COP10 was even larger and included more and more actors. Although at key moments state actors do withdraw and negotiate bilaterally or in small groups, for example with the 2010 Nagoya Protocol (Tsioumani 2010), the norm seems to be inclusion of multiple actors at various different levels.

This wide array of actors though is not causing the formation of any sustained network of actors participating in governance arrangement. Participation is largely geography dependent and few actors are engaged in sustained participation across the governance arrangement. For example, looking at the attendance of nonstate actors' participation in COP meetings of the Cartagena Protocol (2002-COP1, 2004-COP2, 2006-COP3, 2008-COP4, 2010-COP5), some of the meetings that can be expected to have the most consistent networks engaged in deliberations, demonstrates that of the 429 total nonstate actors which participated in the

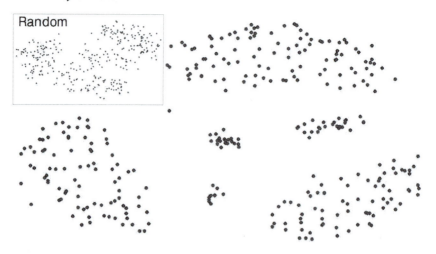

Figure 6.1 Network clusters of Nonstate Actors in Participation at COP3, COP4, and COP5 of the Cartagena Protocol of the CBD (compared to random network form). Created using UCINET software (Borgatti *et al.* 2002)

meetings, only 96 (22 percent) participated in more than one meeting and only 11 (2.5 percent) attended all five meetings. The network is extremely thin and lacks any coherent, repetitive membership. Figure 6.1 presents the network graph of these connections for COP3–COP5 and emphasizes precisely this disparate culture. Although the attendance at COP meetings is partially geographically determined, so that Malaysian NGOs attend the Kuala Lumpur meeting, the number of participants is relatively stable across meetings. If overall attendance stays at about the same level, but there is extensive turnover in parties, this is significant evidence of a weak network of actors involved in a governance agreement.

Coupled with the weak and disparate connections between actors involved, the arrangement also does not channel the influence of the actors. Instead, struggles and disagreements pervade much of the organization and most forums are impacted by a variety of actors with different agendas and goals. This is most clear with the Subsidiary Body on Scientific, Technical and Technological Advice (SBSSTA), which, in the words of Koetz *et al.*

> remains trapped between trying to be a body of scientific nature as originally conceptualised, and depreciating the more political nature it has developed in reality, and which at least officially it is not permitted to have. SBSSTA 13, where an over-emphasis on procedural considerations has led to deadlocks and to much of the text of the recommendations transmitted to CoP9 being bracketed (i.e. not agreed on), is an example of the consequences of such situations, and left many concerned about the Convention's functioning in general.
>
> (Koetz *et al.* 2008)

The political polarization of the SBSSTA resulted in a situation where many actors abandoned pursuing the creation of a science body within the CBD at all and instead participated in the creation of the Intergovernmental Platform on Biodiversity and Ecosystem Services (IPBES). Although it is possible that the creation of IPBES will help the resilience of the CBD, the negotiations for the formation of IPBES in January 2013 showed many of the same divisions which had developed in the SBSSTA.

The actor configuration of the CBD is largely a result of the negotiating environment in which it was formed. The negotiating environment in the formation and early years of the CBD was primarily defined by pushing on conservation issues by the Nordic states and Western Europe, and pushing on equitable benefit sharing by developing countries with the United States being the major laggard on both aspects (Rosendal 2000). The resulting situation, with developing countries having a larger share of the resources, is that an inclusive treaty was established with participation as the primary benefit for actors to remain involved. Inclusion of NGOs and civil society participants was thus a key part of the actor configuration because of the divergent pushing needed and may have been used as an attempt to try and get additional members joining. Further, in the mid-1990s, the CBD became an alternative forum to push access and equity issues for anti-globalization NGOs who had found the WTO and other organizations unaccommodating. Thus, for instance, as a response to the CBD-established expert panel, a variety of NGOs linked and created their own expert panel which included a host of anti-neoliberal thinkers and activists such as Vandana Shiva, Brian Goodwin, and Gurdial Singh Nijar, which then contributed seriously in following negotiations (Kleinman and Kinchy 2007). This actor configuration is further exemplified by the two protocols that the CBD has agreed to in 20 years: both the Cartagena Protocol on Biosafety and access and benefit sharing in the Nagoya Protocol are issues which are largely prioritized by NGO communities and of little interest to the major laggard in the system, the United States (Arts and Mack 2002). Both agreements were negotiated with significant involvement by NGOs and accommodated multiple issues resulting in narrowly tailored, noncomprehensive protocols.

The most notable lack of the actor configuration is that of some of the major states and major contributing industries when specific guidelines are established. Although the only notable absent non-member to the CBD is the United States, which has had an impact on restraining the persistence of the organization (Faizi 2004), there is more serious lack of agreement from most of the major genetically modified agricultural producing and exporting states in the Cartagena Protocol. Although some genetically modified agricultural companies do participate in the Cartagena process, many do not. Although the Nagoya Protocol is still relatively new (it had just opened for signature at the time of writing), lack of agreement by Europe and the United States will seriously constrain the functioning of the Protocol.

Mechanisms

The selection mechanism for the CBD is largely self-selection, although on key issues there is some targeted recruitment. Willing actors with time and commitment have general access to much of the CBD governance structure. A large impact of this is geographically determined by the site of the meeting with local organizations often turning out in large numbers at the conference. Some of those organizations and groups with resources or strong interest in the discussion may follow the organization, but generally involvement seems to be based more on proximity than interest. Recruited membership does happen from chairs of major meetings in the region, country, and city to generate a large local contingent of participation. Outside this targeting, however, there seems to be little targeted recruiting or more exclusive selection mechanisms in operation.

The network governance mechanism in operation is general reciprocity of recognition. The actors generally allow wide inclusion and the governance system attempts to work through such an inclusive system. As noted above, this wide recognition and open agreement was largely a part of the organization as a result of the two different pushers. Wide recognition, transparency, and open agreement by all involved is highly supported from many actors. For example, the closed door negotiations among few parties that led to the Nagoya Protocol text was criticized by many with one delegate declaring that "Behind-the-scenes deals cannot be the standard for negotiating such important issues" (Earth Negotiations Bulletin 2010). Although other actors were largely kept out of the final formal Nagoya Protocol negotiations, many had been involved in the process leading to the final negotiations, and NGO, multinational, and scientific advice had been sought throughout the process.

This is all exemplified in the creation of contact groups at CBD high-level meetings where the conference groups state and some nonstate actors get together to discuss and develop final issues for votes. The selection is largely based upon those parties who have shown an interest in the issue, and the mutual recognition of actors translates across into contact groups. Particularly at technical meetings, multinational corporations and NGOs can take over much of the agenda and shape the meetings. These contact groups then are closely connected to working groups where NGOs and MNCs have significant presence in the organizations.

Resilience

The CBD is low on both persistence and in terms of its adaptability. The core agenda of the CBD has received little attention and no solid agreement on actual requirements by state parties to begin reducing the loss of biodiversity. Instead, agreements are largely about other issues important to the CBD agenda, but which have been particularly highlighted by NGO communities: once again, biosafety and access and benefit sharing. Lack of major, important actors in these agreements seriously further tempers the persistence of the organization. Adaptability is similarly restrained within the organization, particularly on the core agenda.

Table 6.2 Resilience comparison of Man and Biosphere, CITES, and CBD

	Selection mechanisms	*Networked governance mechanisms*	*Resilience*
MAB	Professional stakeholders	Reputation and Macroculture	Post-1995 strong persistence and adaptability
CITES	Professional stakeholders, expert administrators and some lay stakeholders	Restricted access (on the micro level, reputation is a key governance mechanism)	Post-1994 strong persistence and adaptability
CBD	Open self-selection with some targeted selection	General reciprocity of recognition	No notable persistence and adaptability

However, even outside the core agenda, there is little updating of policy and instead focus is largely on technical aspects of implementing the agreement. The CBD then is currently exhibiting low resilience and neither has major contributors invested in the collective decision making nor is actively improving its adaptive capacity.

Summary of case studies

MAB and CITES generally developed from eras of limited resilience into persistent and adaptive governance arrangements, while the CBD has not developed these dynamics. Before moving to the conclusion, this brief section will evaluate the actor configurations and how they seemed to provide resilient configurations.

The inclusion of major contributors to the governance constellation proved particularly important to limiting the faith that actors would put in the organizations. While MAB was beset by political wrangling in its nesting organization (UNESCO), the willingness of other parties to invest in the governance arrangement dropped. While countries were opting-out of CITES decisions, the persistence of its efforts were generally restrained. As both of these cases were able to bring major contributors to the problems into the governance arrangement, the resilience increased dramatically. The lack of U.S. involvement in the CBD and the lack of any major involvement by major MNCs or genetically modified organism producing countries in Cartagena is constraining on the CBD's ability to get the capacity for authoritative rule making.

The role of science is particularly relevant in all three cases and particularly the maintenance of a distinct realm for experts maintained by international organizations. The secretary general of CITES illuminates this instructively and the lack of a distinct and protected science realm is constraining upon the CBD. In addition, the fostering of the epistemic community in a protected space within a strong international organization seems to be important in the cases of CITES and MAB; in contrast, in any possibility of supporting an epistemic community, the CBD is constrained by the politicization of the science body and the very weak networks that exist within the organization. MAB offers an example of the governance institutions being largely controlled by an epistemic community of ecologists. The interesting configuration here is that there is little tie to a single strong international organization and the scientists, in fact, made up for the weak international organization at key points. However, the linkages of scientists with other international science programs, such as SCOPE, create important linkages of international organizations supporting the epistemic community from a variety of angles.

Nongovernmental organization involvement can aid or hinder resilience largely based upon the selection mechanism in the governance arrangement. The management of NGO activity in MAB and their modular assignment in CITES since 1994 have both been key to the resilience of these organizations. CITES pre-1994 was an instructive case of activist NGOs weakening the authoritative rule-making ability of the governance arrangement, similar to what we see now in the CBD. Administrative NGOs are very important to the actors' belief in the capacity of organizations to address the problems; and, when provided specific tasks, these NGOs are quite supportive of resilience. Activist NGOs, in contrast, when provided with access to state parties and IOs tend to push for static solutions that may reduce the capability of the governance arrangement to maintain its authority.

The exploration of mechanisms may provide guidance to other possible and actual actor configurations and their impact on resilience. Generally, these cases highlight that exclusive selection mechanisms may feed resilience, but this should not be taken as infinitely true. This may seem counterintuitive as exclusive selection mechanisms may trade off with wide legitimacy of the decisions and information. Instead, of such a uni-dimensional view of legitimacy, the larger context of interrelated mechanisms in play provides a more thorough conception (Fung 2006). From these cases, it seems that coupling these exclusive selection mechanisms with network governance mechanisms common in thick networks may provide an optimal steadiness regarding legitimacy and exclusivity. Those mechanisms which are more likely to operate in thick network (such as reputation and macroculture) should provide exclusive selection with wider impact than the specific community. MAB's extension into sustainable development and the modular structure in CITES are good examples of this particular coupling. When open selection procedures are coupled with thin network governance mechanisms then these conditions will limit the legitimacy of the rules outside of a narrow network of actors, as the case of the CBD demonstrates. Actor configurations provide key means of generating or limiting these mechanisms, and the particular array of actors was found in these cases to be very important for resilience outcomes.

One final note in summary of the cases is the interaction of the key mechanisms of focus in this chapter with other mechanisms, particularly the policy ratchet effect (Huber and Stephens 2001) and reflective mechanisms (Siebenhuner 2008). The ratchet effect involves expanding a constituency with benefits delivered to new groups. At the level of international governance, exclusive mechanisms of selection may foster this by allowing gradual inclusion of new actors and locking them into the governance arrangement with focused benefits. In MAB, this involved inclusion of new actors in the World Network of Biosphere Reserves with some cooperative situations, funding, and increasingly benefits from ecotourism and other managed uses. Reflective mechanisms of assessments may contribute to specific selection and governance mechanisms which feed resilience. Removing evaluation from the political wrangling of the arrangements may be important as it was in CITES for spurring other features of the governance arrangement to be removed from the political wrangling. However, this does not seem to hold absolutely, but depends upon the outcome of the assessment.

Resilient governance

In a governance terrain where actors are fairly unconstrained to shop around for preferable forums, where science can easily become a political battleground, and where few governance projects start off with strong institutions and dedicated constituencies, all of which are particularly salient problems in international biodiversity governance, how can some governance arrangements be resilient? This chapter argues that the processes that bring actors together in governance are crucial in understanding when resilience is possible and where other outcomes, such as arrested development or collapse, are more likely. Focused selection mechanisms, rather than open selection mechanisms, seem crucial to lending credibility to the authoritative rule-making of the governance arrangement. Similarly, shared normative contexts between members seems to allow adaptation to be a smoother process.

The findings here then are neither supporting the transformational model, favoring open forums and gradual transformation of large number of actors, nor a political economy model, where concerns with free riding and enforcement prove constraining to most agreements (Downs 2000). The approach to resilience in this chapter emphasizes that the actor configurations are crucial in understanding the processes that may cause free riding to be a concern among actors or that may result in constructivist transformation of those actors. The process of inclusion and what processes hold networks together are of crucial importance when understanding resilience.

Some middle-level findings form tractable lessons from the cases explored in biodiversity governance. Further analysis can lend credence to these points, but at this juncture it is fruitful to conclude by making them as explicit as possible.

1   *Functional division of labor for types of actors can prevent the spread of internal polarization throughout the governance arrangement.* The Type II partnerships envisioned in Johannesburg all promoted partnerships that seemed to include multiple actors in many of the governance stages (Andonova and Levy 2003/2004). This may not actually feed resilience as modularity and clear divisions of labor may be more important to form resilient organizations. However, MAB and CITES demonstrate that such divisions of labor should be mutually agreed divisions and not prevent actors from the possibility of accessing the governance arrangement.

a. *Administrative NGOs can feed resilience if their methods for data collection are transparent and the information is scale and time appropriate.* This is most clearly the case with TRAFFIC in CITES which monitors illegal trade in endangered species. The data is clear and provides excellent data for policymakers. The Monitoring of Illegal Killing of Elephants (MIKE) system, in contrast, has some limitations in the scope of the information. Administrative NGO activities though can be key to the resilience because it removes scientific arguments from the actual organization entirely.

b. *Conversely, resilience could be weakened if the governance arrangement does not restrain the activities of NGOs.* Unrestrained NGO activity can result in a spread of active politicization of issues and prevent the organization from adequately responding to this. This is what happened in CBD, but also in CITES.

c. *Organizational secretariats can play key roles in connecting and moving information and ideas through the modules.* The CITES secretariat has begun to embody the role of facilitator of usable knowledge from the scientific bodies to the political bodies. This was not accomplished without significant trial and error, but the Fort Lauderdale guidelines show how secretariats are able to move information through different modules in a productive manner.

2 *Coherent, sustained single-actor groups can provide stabilizing forces for external disturbances.* When the United States and United Kingdom withdrew from UNESCO, the core of scientists maintained their connections and helped support MAB's activities. This can arise in any actor configuration, but this core needs a thick network connected with actors outside the single group. The initial work on epistemic communities, for example, found that the linkages into government for the epistemic community were important (Haas 1990). Similarly, the thick connections from MIKE in CITES to the rest of the organization proved important in largely stabilizing the ivory debates.

3 *The main contributors to the problems must be meaningfully included in the governance process in order to allow responses to internal problems.* Without the largest contributor to the problem included, confidence in the arrangement decreases and autonomous decision making and adaptive capacity are reduced. Although the opposite effect seems to occur in the CBD, where "the CBD's popularity stems in part from the United States' initial refusal to sign it" (Raustiala and Victor 1997), the inability of the CBD to adapt serious obligations since seems to confirm the limiting factor of not including major contributors to the problem. In addition, with the opt-out provisions of CITES, internal disagreements can often maintain years of side-payments, coalitional politics, and involve other modules of the governance arrangement in the internal problems.

References

Anderies, J., Walker, B. and Kinzig, A. P. (2006) 'Fifteen Weddings and a Funeral: Case Studies and Resilience-based Management', *Ecology and Society* 11(1).

Andonova, L. B. and Levy, M. A. (2003/2004) 'Francising Global Governance: Making Sense of the Johannesburg Type II Partnerships', *Yearbook of International Co-Operation on Environment and Development* 19–32.

Andresen, S. (2001–2002) 'Global Environmental Governance: UN Fragmentation and Co-Ordination', *Yearbook of International Co-Operation on Environment and Development* 18–26.

Arts, B. and Mack, S. (2002) 'Environmental NGOs and the Biosafety Protocol: A Case Study of Political Influence', *European Environment* 13, 19–33.

Barnett, M. and Finnemore, M. (2005) 'The Power of Liberal International Organizations', in M. Barnett and R. Duvall, *Power in Global Governance*, New York: Cambridge University Press, 161–184.

Batisse, M. (1997) 'Biosphere Reserves: A Challenge for Biodiversity Conservation and Regional Development', *Environment* 39(5), 7–33.

Borgatti, S. P., Everett, M. G. and Freeman, L. C. (2002) *Ucinet for Windows: Software for Social Network Analysis*, Cambridge, MA: Analytic Technologies.

Crona, B. and Bodin, O. (2006) 'What You Know Is Who You Know? Communication Patterns Among Resource Users as a Prerequisite for Co-Management', *Ecology and Society* 11(2), 7–30.

Das, T. K. and Teng, B. S. (2002) 'Alliance Constellations: A Social Exchange Perspective', *Academy of Management Review* 27(3), 445–456.

Downs, G. W. (2000) 'Constructing Effective Environmental Regimes', *Annual Review of Political Science* 3, 25–42.

Earth Negotiations Bulletin (2010) 'Summary of the Tenth Conference of the Parties to the Convention on Biological Diversity', *The International Institute for Sustainable Development* 9(544).

Faizi, S. (2004) 'CBD: The Unmaking of a Treaty', *Current Science* 86(11), 1471–1474.

Falleti, T. G. and Lynch, J. F. (2009) 'Context and Causal Mechanisms in Political Analysis', *Comparative Political Studies* 42(9), 1143–1166.

Folke, C. (2006) 'Resilience: The Emergence of A Perspective for Social-ecological Systems Analyses', *Global Environmental Change* 16, 253–267.

Folke, C., Hahn, T., Olsson, P. and Norberg, J. (2005) 'Adaptive Governance of Social-Ecological Systems', *Annual Review of Environment and Resources* 30, 441–473.

Franklin, J. F. (1993) 'Preserving Biodiversity: Species, Ecosystems, or Landscapes', *Ecological Applications* 3(2), 202–205.

Fung, A. (2006) 'Varieties of Participation in Complex Governance', *Public Administration Review* 66–75.

Gehring, T. and Ruffing, E. (2008) 'When Arguments Prevail over Power: The CITES Procedure for the Listing of Endangered Species', *Global Environmental Politics* 8(2), 123–148.

Genschel, P. (1997) 'The Dynamics of Inertia: Instituional Persistencce and Change in Telecommunications in Health Care', *Governance* 10(1), 43–66.

Gillson, L. and Lindsay, K. (2003) 'Ivory and Ecology – Changing Perspectives on Elephant Management and The International Trade in Ivory', *Environmental Science & Policy* 6, 411–419.

Gunderson, L. H. (2000) 'Ecological Resilience – In Theory and Application', *Annual Review of Ecology and Systematics* 31, 425–439.

Haas, P. M. (1990) *Saving the Mediterranean: The Politics of International Environmental Cooperation*, New York: Columbia University Press.

Hokkanen, T. (2001) 'Linking Biosphere Reserves with Decision Making in the Nordic Countries', in *Seville+5: International Meeting of Experts*, UNESCO: Paris, 159.

Huber, E. and Stephens, J. D. (2001) *Development and Crisis of the Welfare State: Parties and Policies in Global Markets*, Chicago: University of Chicago Press.

Humphreys, D. (2003) 'The United Nations Forum on Forests: Anatomy of a Stalled International Process', *Global Environmental Change* 13, 319–323.

Humphreys, D. (2004) 'Redefining the Issues: NGO Influence on International Forest Negotiations', *Global Environmental Politics* 4(2), 51–74.

ICC-MAB (1992) Twelfth Session: Report from the Man and the Biosphere (MAB) ICSU/ SCOPE Evaluation Committee. Paris, UNESCO. SC-93/CONF.215/INF.2.

ICC-MAB (2010) Twenty-Second Session, Final Report. Paris, UNESCO. SC-10/ Conf.201/21.

Ishwaran, N., Persic, A. and Tri, N. H. (2008) 'Concept and Practice: The Case of UNESCO Biosphere Reserves', *International Journal of Environment and Sustainable Development* 7(2), 118–131.

Jones, C., Hesterly, W. S. and Borgatti, S. P. (1997) 'A General Theory of Network Governance: Exchange Conditions and Social Mechanisms', *Academy of Management Review* 22(4).

Kleinman, D. L. and Kinchy, A. J. (2007) 'Against the Neoliberal Steamroller? The Biosafety Protocol and the Social Regulation of Agricultural Biotechnologies', *Agriculture and Human Values* 24(2), 195–206.

Koetz, T., Bridgewater, P., van den Hove, S. and Siebenhuner B. (2008) 'The Role of the Subsidiary Body on Scientific, Technical and Technological Advice to the Convention on Biological Diversity as a Science-Policy Interface', *Environmental Science & Policy* 11, 505–516.

Kutting, G. (2000) *Environment, Society, and International Relations: Towards More Effective International Environmental Agreements*, New York: Routledge.

Lee, K. N. (1993) *Compass and Gyroscope: Integrating Science and Politics for The Environment*, Washington, DC: Island Press.

Leeds, B. A. and Savun, B. (2007) 'Terminating Alliances: Why do States Abrogate Agreements?', *The Journal of Politics* 69(4), 1118–1132.

Olsson, P., Gunderson, L. H., Carpenter, S. R., Ryan, P., Lebel, L., Folke, C. and Holling, C. S. (2006) 'Shooting the Rapids: Navigating Transitions to Adaptive Governance of the Social-Ecological Systems', *Ecology and Society* 11(1).

Ostrom, E. (2005) *Understanding Institutional Diversity*, Princeton, NJ: Princeton University Press.

Ostrom, E. (2010) 'Beyond Markets and States: Polycentric Governance of Complex Economic Systems', *American Economic Review* 100: 641–672.

Pahl-Wostl, C. (2009) 'A Conceptual Framework for Analyzing Adaptive Capacity and Multi-level Learning Processes in Resource Governance Regimes', *Global Environmental Change* 19: 354–365.

Persson, R. (2005). 'Where is the United Nations Forum on Forests Going?', *International Forestry Review* 7(4): 348–357.

Price, M. F., Park, J. J. and Bouamrane, M. (2010) 'Reporting Progress on Internationally Designated Sites: The Periodic Review of Biosphere Reserves', *Environmental Science & Policy* 13: 549–557.

Princen, T. (1994) 'The Ivory Trade Ban: NGOs and International Conservation', in T. Princen and M. Finger, *Environmental NGOs in World Politics: Linking the Local and the Global*, New York: Routledge, 121–159.

Raustiala, K. andVictor, D. G. (1997) 'Biodiversity since Rio: The Future of the Convention on Biological Diversity', *Environment* 38(4), 17–43.

Rosendal, G. K. (2000) *The Convention on Biological Diversity and Developing Countries*, Dordrecht: Kluwer Academic.

Sand, P. H. (1997) 'Whither CITES? The Evolution of a Treaty Regime in the Borderland of Trade and Environment', *European Journal of International Law* 8(1), 29–58.

Sands, P. J. and Bedecarre, A. P. (1990) 'Convention of International Trade in Endangered Species: The Role of Public Interest Non-Governmental Organization in Ensuring the Effective Enforcement of the Ivory Trade Ban', *Boston College Environmental Affairs Law Review* 17(4), 799–822.

Santiapillai, C. (2009) 'African Elephants: Surviving by The Skin of Their Teeth', *Current Science* 97(7), 995–997.

Siebenhuner, B. (2008) 'Learning in International Organization in Global Environmental Governance', *Global Environmental Politics* 8(4), 92–116.

Skocpol, T. and Somers, M. (1980) 'The Uses of Comparative History in Macrosocial Inquiry', *Comparative Studies in Sociology and History* 22(2), 174–197.

Soberon, J. M. and Sarukhan, J. K. (2010) 'A New Mechanism for Science-Policy Transfer and Biodiversity Governance', *Environmental Conservation* 36(4), 265–267.

Stiles, D. (2004) 'The Ivory Trade and Elephant Conservation', *Environmental Conservation* 31(4), 309–321.

Suchman, M. C. (1995) 'Managing Legitimacy: Strategic and Institutional Approaches', *Academy of Management Review* 20(3), 571–610.

Tsioumani, E. (2010) 'Access and Benefit Sharing: The Nagoya Protocol', *Environmental Policy and Law* 40(6), 288–292.

Tullock, G. (1975) 'The Transitional Gains Trap', *The Bell Journal of Economics* 6(2), 671–678.

Walker, B. and Salt, D. (2006) *Resilience Thinking: Sustaining Ecosystems and People in a Changing World*, Washington, DC: Island Press.

Walker, B., Anderies, J. M., Kinzig, A. P. and Ryan, P., (2006) 'Exploring Resilience in Social-Ecological Systems through Comparative Studies and Theory Development: Introduction to the Special Issue', *Ecology and Society* 11(1).

Wallander, C. A. (2000) 'Institutional Assets and Adaptability: NATO after the Cold War', *International Organization* 54(4), 705–735.

Walt, S. M. (1997) 'Why Alliances Endure or Collapse', *Survival* 39(1), 156–179.

Wasser, S., Poole, J., Lee, P., Lindsay, K., Dobson, A., Hart, J., Douglas-Hamilton, I., Wittemeyer, G., Granli, P., Morgan, B., Gunn, J., Alberts, S., Beyers, R., Chiyo, P., Croze, H., Estes, R., Gobush, K., Joram, P., Kokoti, A., Kingdon, J., King, L., Macdonald, D., Moss, C., Mutayoba, B., Njumbi, S., Omondi P. and Nowak, K. (2010) 'Elephants, Ivory, and Trade', *Science* 327, 1331–1333.

Werland, S. (2009) 'Global Forest Governance – Bringing Forestry Science (Back) In', *Forest Policy and Economics* 11, 446–451.

Young, O. R. (2010) *Institutional Dynamics: Emergent Patterns in International Environmental Governance*, Cambridge, MA: MIT Press.

Young, O. R., King, L. A. and Schroeder, H. (2008) *Institutions and Environmental Change: Principal Findings, Applications, and Research Frontiers*, Cambridge, MA: MIT Press.

7 Governance components in private regulation

Implications for legitimacy, authority and effectiveness

Graeme Auld, Benjamin Cashore and Stefan Renckens

Introduction

For over two generations now public policy and international relations (IR) scholars have been attempting to describe and understand the increasing role that non-governmental organizations (NGOs) and civil society have played in not only advocating for public policies through agenda setting and issue framing, but actively participating in rule-making, enforcement, and evaluation. Identified as a shift from "government" to "governance" (Rosenau and Czempiel 1992), these changes have occurred through a range of processes, including "public–private" partnerships in which governance components are shared, but also through arenas in which NGOs act as governing authorities (Auld *et al.* 2008).

The purpose of this chapter is to shed light on a unique partnership within these broad trends: multi-stakeholder certification initiatives. These initiatives develop and implement policies by turning not to intergovernmental agreements or domestic sovereign governments for ultimate authority, but instead to incentives from customers that request goods and services produced in compliance with pre-established environmental and social standards. Referred to by some as "non-state market driven" (NSMD) global governance (Cashore 2002; Cashore *et al.* 2004; Bernstein and Cashore 2007) these initiatives confront two tasks. First, similar to governments and intergovernmental processes, they follow a cycle from agenda setting/issue framing through to enforcement and evaluation, what the introductory chapter terms governance components. Second, unlike governmental efforts, they must attempt to *achieve*, rather than *maintain*, authority and legitimacy to govern. Hence, while they turn to the marketplace to create compliance incentives and gain governing authority, seemingly adopting "business friendly" approaches often championed as alternatives to regulation, their standards and approaches are highly regulatory – i.e., they identify specific rules and practices to which firms must adhere. As a result, any effort to understand the short- and long-term effectiveness of these initiatives must examine the processes by which authority and legitimacy are intertwined with decisions made throughout its policy cycle.

While much emphasis has been placed on conceptualizing authority and legitimacy (Bernstein and Cashore 2007; Cashore 2002), and identifying a complex set of factors that might explain the emergence of these initiatives (Bartley 2007; Cashore *et al.* 2004; Pattberg 2007), our chapter focuses on better understanding how the structure of NSMD *policy networks* affects decisions made at different stages of an NSMD system's policy cycle (i.e., governance components). What is important for our chapter, and in contrast to the influence of traditional public policy networks, is that the exclusion or absence of some actors in the network membership will not only influence agenda setting and issue framing within the network. Decisions at these stages of the policy cycle that are seen as downplaying the interests of excluded members, can lead to the emergence of competing NSMD systems, in which excluded actors become dominant members of the networks affecting the new NSMD system. These dynamics, in turn, affect and shape regulatory decisions at the negotiated settlement (i.e., decision making) stage in each NSMD system over the scope and prescriptiveness of the standards against which firms are certified, as each network acts as a governance arena for the development of rules.

In the remainder of this chapter, we proceed as follows. First, we locate NSMD systems within the broader context of the shift from government to governance, and highlight how networks feature in explaining their emergent properties and policy cycles. Second, we review two features that are crucial for understanding how network structure influences the various governance components within NSMD systems: a market's supply chain structure; and relations among actors that make and shape policy decisions in NSMD systems. Third, we analyze the role of these network features in influencing NSMD systems' governance components. We use four key NSMD systems to illustrate and assess the argument: the Forest Stewardship Council (FSC), the Marine Stewardship Council (MSC), Fairtrade International (FLO), and e-Stewards. We then reflect on these findings for broader questions of legitimacy and authority, which has been largely under-theorized.[1]

From government to governance and the characterization of multi-stakeholder NSMD governance systems

Until the 1990s, policy scientists placed much of their attention on the institutions of *government*: scholars were curious about how sovereign states developed domestic policies or agreed to support international institutions. Recognition since this time that societal steering is not always derived from state-directed government efforts has led scholars to expand their focus to "governance" institutions in general. Several factors explain this change, including the emergence of multi-stakeholder policy networks (Rhodes 1997), transnational coalitions (Keck and Sikkink 1998; Knill and Lehmkuhl 2002), public–private partnerships (Börzel and Risse 2005), the emergence of "new public management" approaches in which private actors often implement public policy objectives (Salaman 2002), and developing country-focused transnational private conservation networks (Balboa 2009). All of these sit alongside traditional government institutions (Glück *et al.* 2005). While useful to demark broad trends, research assessing the causes of the emergence of these networks is difficult because so many different processes and dynamics are conflated underneath them (Auld *et al.* 2008).

A range of scholars within IR, comparative politics, and public policy seeking to understand the implications of this burgeoning private regulatory field have conceptualized them as "transnational new governance" (Abbott and Snidal 2009), "civil regulation" (Vogel 2008), "transnational steering mechanisms" (Rosenau 1995), and "private authority" (Cutler *et al.* 1999). To promote more causal research, we focus on one unique form: non-state market driven (NSMD) global governance (Cashore 2002; Cashore *et al.* 2004; Bernstein and Cashore 2007). These initiatives have five key features that, taken together, give them significant potential for developing purposeful and authoritative global governance.

The most critical feature is that governments do not create or require adherence to the rules. The sovereign authority that governments possess to develop rules and to which society more or less adheres does *not* apply. No one can be incarcerated or fined for failing to comply. This characteristic is particularly important as it distinguishes NSMD governance from many other forms of governance where states are the central actor in the network. Here, the state remains important for various reasons, such as providing a general legal framework (see, Cashore 2002), but its role in the governance process will be different as the private standard-setting process does not draw on the state's authority directly. Second, NSMD governance systems govern the "social domain" (Ruggie 2004) – requiring profit-maximizing firms to undertake costly reforms that they otherwise would not pursue. This focus on regulating externalities distinguishes NSMD systems from other arenas of private authority, such as coordination over essential components of electrical systems and similar technical standards (the original reason for the creation of the International Electrotechnical Commission and then the International Organization for Standardization), in which the rationale for support – in this case efficiency – emerges immediately from the certification itself (Büthe and Mattli 2011; Büthe 2010). This also distinguishes NSMD systems from environmental management system (EMS) approaches in which firms are certified for developing internal procedures, but which develop *no* prescriptions about on-the-ground behavior (Clapp 1998; Delmas 2002).

Three additional characteristics are central to the analytic aims of this chapter. First, NSMD governance systems constitute governing arenas in which adaptation, inclusion, and learning occurs over time and across stakeholders. However, as we examine below, the precise way in which this inclusion works requires more careful attention, particularly the nature of interactions among stakeholders and the power dynamics that result. Second, these systems have independent verification procedures designed to ensure that the regulated operator actually meets the stated standards. Verification is important because it provides the validation necessary for a certification program to achieve legitimacy as certified products are then demanded and consumed along the market's supply chain. This distinguishes NSMD systems from many forms of corporate social responsibility with limited or no outside monitoring (Gunningham *et al.* 1998). Third, authority is granted through the market's supply chain. To increase economic incentives, environmental organizations may act through boycotts and other direct action initiatives to convince large retailers to adopt purchasing policies favoring NSMD

Table 7.1 Key features of NSMD governance

Role of the state	State does not use its sovereign authority to directly require adherence to rules
Institutionalized governance mechanism	Procedures in place designed to create adaptation, inclusion, and learning over time across a wide range of stakeholders
The social domain	Development of prescriptive rules governing environmental and social problems to which firms must adhere
Enforcement	Compliance must be verified
Role of the market	Support emanates from producers and consumers along the supply chain who evaluate the costs and benefits of joining

Source: Adapted from Cashore (2002), Cashore *et al.* (2004), and Bernstein and Cashore (2007)

certification systems. Hence, the market's supply chain is the institutional arena in which evaluations over support occur.

These final characteristics direct our attention to the networks of actors involved in the development and operation of these initiatives – those actors with the potential to make or break the success of any given NSMD program in the short and longer term. One particular feature in this respect is that the origins of NSMD initiatives are frequently affected by the character of the public policy networks at the local, national, and international levels. Elliott (2000, 2001), for instance, conceptualized certification as a fast track mechanism designed to circumvent blocked international and domestic forest policy governance processes. Likewise, Cashore's (2002) and Cashore *et al.*'s (2004) examination of the forest sector identified that, initially, different policy networks support separate conceptions of forest certification. Conception 1 programs were initiated by environmental and social activists frustrated with their inability to influence domestic and international regulatory processes that they felt were "captured" by business interests. They sought to create multi-stakeholder initiatives that were more democratic, open, and transparent than the domestic public policy networks and intergovernmental efforts.[2] Certification programs such as the FSC drew on corporatist approaches to policymaking by creating a particular type of tripartite governance system, which structurally balances the voting power of three blocs – environmental interests, social interests (including indigenous and community-rights NGOs), and business/economic interests, while government was excluded from formal decision-making. The program's global standard was prescriptive and wide-ranging, addressing a host of natural resource management challenges, including biodiversity, local water pollution, and wildlife protection, as well as community rights and worker protection (Meidinger 2003).

Conception 2 programs, by contrast, were initiated by industry actors that sought to maintain their position in shaping and influencing domestic environmental and resource management. They championed a discretionary approach to certification and a narrower coverage of policy concerns. In forestry, this conception was institutionalized in a set of programs in Canada, the United States, Sweden, Germany, Finland, and elsewhere in Europe, many of which were organized initially under the umbrella of the Pan-European Forest Certification (PEFC) system. (The PEFC has since expanded its geographical scope and changed its name to the Programme for the Endorsement of Forest Certification.)

Considerable attention has been paid to the interaction between these two conceptions of forest certification. Overdevest's (2010, 2005) work details how competitive benchmarking exercises, which compare the certification standards of different programs, have facilitated convergence among the standards, though significant differences remain (McDermott *et al.* 2008). Bartley and Smith (2007) and Dingwerth and Pattberg (2009) broaden this analysis to look at the interactions among many private governance programs with an emerging "organizational field." Here relationships within a larger network shape the evolution of individual programs via isomorphic pressures (see also, Fransen 2010).

For analytic traction, we focus largely on conception 1 initiatives, but reflect on what this means for competition with conception 2 programs in the section on legitimacy, authority and effectiveness.[3] This is an important focus since NSMD systems vary in form. In the following sections, we will examine the formalized approaches for making policy choices, identifying which organizations are involved as policy participants (i.e., they have a formal vote over policy) and as policy advocates (i.e., they lobby for policy choices, but have no vote), as well as the importance of the structure of a market's supply chain and the regulatory targets that are chosen. We will explore each of these features' influence over the agenda setting, issue framing, and other governance components of NSMD systems, and assess their effects on questions of authority, legitimacy and effectiveness.

Private governance networks and the markets they regulate

Supply chains and regulatory targets

From early analyses of NSMD systems, scholars have been sensitive to the structure of a market's supply chain as a consideration shaping the manner in which these systems emerge, develop and gain potential authority (Roberts 2003; Auld 2009; Cashore *et al.* 2004; Gulbrandsen 2005). Across programs, there is important variability in the facets of a market's supply chain that are regulated, and where in the supply chain the regulated targets are situated. While these features ultimately matter for the enforcement of standards, the means by which this occurs, as we discuss below, differ in ways that affect how NSMD governance obtains and maintains legitimacy and authority.

For our cases, we identify and discuss two differences in the structure of markets in which NSMD systems have emerged. First, there is the geographical location of the regulatory targets. In some instances, for example with tropical commodities, the production mainly takes place in the global south while consumption is predominantly located in the global north. In other cases, such as with fisheries, consumption and production overlap geographically to a much greater extent. We will return to this geographical dimension while analyzing the compliance and implementation component of NSMD systems. Second, programs choose different regulatory targets along a given market's supply chain. Though often supported by NGO targeting of critical buyers as a means of enforcement, this pressure is separate from the requirements set by the programs for distributors, traders or primary/ secondary processors that want to buy or sell products certified by the program. In the discussion below, we identify the following three considerations: is the locus of certification upstream or downstream; are tracking requirements only imposed on regulatory targets or also imposed on others in the supply chain; and, are there any requirements other than tracking imposed upon a product's supply chain?

Considering the regulatory target and supply chain requirements as interconnected features, three general patterns emerge among our cases (Table 7.2). First, there are programs where the regulated targets are primary producers and only tracking requirements are imposed on downstream participants in the program. One example is the MSC. The program regulates the management of capture fisheries. It has a standard comprising three principles, addressing: sustainability of the targeted stock; integrity of habitat and the aquatic system; and operations and planning systems for the fishery's activities (Marine Stewardship Council 2010b). A separate standard sets requirements for tracking certified products from the fishing operation to the final consumer. Instead of imposing social or environmental requirements, this standard is limited to technical requirements for ensuring, *inter alia*, the physical separation of certified and uncertified seafood, percentage flavoring limits, and adherence with labeling rules (Marine Stewardship Council 2010a).

The second pattern occurs with programs where the regulatory targets deal with the final stages of a linear supply chain, such as disposal and recycling, and where no extra demands are placed on other segments of the supply chain.

Table 7.2 Regulatory focus and requirements of NSMD networks

Features of regulation and regulatory targets	Programs			
	FSC	*MSC*	*FLO*	*e-Stewards*
Beginning of value chain (producer/manager)	Yes	Yes	Yes	No
End of value chain (recycler/ disposer)	No*	No	No	Yes
Tracking requirements for firms who buy and sell certified products? (middle of value chain)	Yes	Yes	Yes	No
Environmental or social rules for firms who buy and sell certified products? (middle of value chain)	No	No	Yes	No

Note: * The exception is for the FSC's recycled paper label, in which case the disposal/recycling end of the supply chain is the target of the program's tracking rules

The e-Stewards certification program, for example, targets recyclers, refurbishers, asset managers, refiners, and redeployment companies dealing with discarded electronic equipment (Basel Action Network 2009). Tracking requirements for the certified companies apply downstream to the clients of these companies, but without extra demands imposed on those clients. These tracking requirements involve keeping information on all incoming and outgoing materials and waste, in order to control where outgoing materials end up, be it with end processors or as reuse material. As a way of engaging actors that are located upstream in the supply chain, the e-Stewards program also allows companies, non-profits and government institutions to become "e-Stewards Enterprises." These organizations sign a licensing agreement with which they indicate that they will primarily deal with e-Stewards certified recyclers when disposing of their old electronic equipment. The main requirement is that annual information on used recyclers has to be disclosed. Like the certified recyclers, these organizations can use the e-Stewards logo to indicate their engagement (e-Stewards 2011).

In the final pattern, the program imposes social or environmental requirements on the regulatory target and buyers, traders, retailers and others along the supply chain that go beyond tracking. These requirements are separate from the targeting pressure that may be exerted on buyers (such as retailers) to support a program in the sense of exclusively buying certified products. Instead, they are requirements that are meant to advance one or more of a program's social and environmental goals. Fair trade certification and labeling overseen by FLO is probably the most quintessential example. The program has requirements at the producer level, which set out conditions which producers must meet to participate in the program. Similar to the first category of programs, here as well there are requirements for tracking the certified good from farm to retail shelf. However, there are additional requirements imposed on these companies, including requirements to provide pre-financing to the producers and paying higher prices for their products (Auld 2010b).

These distinctions are important as they indicate that the evaluations of regulatory targets across sectors are likely to vary. First, there are settings where building support for a program will itself be a collective good. Cashore *et al.* (2007) refer in this respect to the "chicken and egg" conundrum of building market support: lack of demand for certification will result in lack of supply, while lack of supply means that demand will be difficult to nurture. The more complicated or long a supply chain, and the larger the requirements imposed on the different stages of the supply chain, the more challenging this conundrum will become as many players will need to simultaneously engage in the process for supply and demand to connect. Second, the locus of certification efforts – at the production or the recycling stage of the supply chain – appears to matter for how likely a direct incentive will emerge for products to be designed with less harmful contents. In the case of electronics recycling, the targeted environmental improvements are not geared towards the production process or the product itself, but to the recycling of products. Electronics recycling certification programs as such do not provide direct incentives for producers to make the devices more environmentally friendly. They only intend to make the recycling process less harmful.

Agency and governance structures

Beyond examining the influence of the market's supply chain, an analysis of NSMD networks also needs to pay attention to the actual actors involved in making and influencing policy choices. Drawing on policy work that sees a network as an independent variable, we use two distinctions developed by scholars examining public policy networks (cf. Atkinson and Coleman 1989; Coleman and Skogstad 1990): (1) What are the formalized approaches for making policy choices? That is, do they reflect "pluralist," "clientelist," or "corporatist," and top-down or bottom-up approaches? (2) Which organizations tend to be involved as policy participants or as policy advocates?

These questions help us unpack differences among NSMD systems. The FSC, as noted before, follows a "tripartite" or "corporatist" approach to policy making in which economic, social and environmental actors each share one third of the votes at the global level (see also Tollefson *et al.* 2008). Each chamber is also divided equally among organizations from the global south and north. While this appears to indicate a "top-down" approach, the FSC's General Assembly sets the overall direction, but specific rules are developed through "bottom-up" national or subnational processes, themselves mirroring to varying degrees, but also modifying, the tripartite structure. While this corporatist approach describes formalized policy making, the broader network is much more diffuse. Most members of the network have either chosen not to participate in formal decisions (especially businesses) or are forbidden to do so (such as government actors as regulators). Hence, in practice a relatively narrow set of players decides the policies, which affect whether, when, and how the vast majority of "policy advocates" maintain affiliation in the network.

The MSC arguably emerged as a "clientelist" network. Without attaching a pejorative meaning to the concept, we use the term "clientelist" to refer to networks which are linked to (the interests of) specific individual organizations. The MSC initially had strong ties to its two founders: the World Wide Fund for Nature (WWF) and Unilever. These ties were soon severed, but the program has still retained a more centralized governance structure, which envisions the role of stakeholders as more policy advocates than participants that provide technical advice and information (Auld and Gulbrandsen 2010). It has a Technical Advisory Board and a Stakeholder Council that exist to inform the decisions of the Board of Trustees, but it lacks the decentralized processes for deliberating standards development that the FSC adopted. Hence, although it has moved away from its clientelist origins, it remains less open to the network of "policy advocates" that exists around it, which comprises various fisheries-focused organizations pursuing their own activities on fisheries management issues (see also Tollefson *et al.* 2008; Auld 2009).

FLO emerged out of a "bottom-up" process that sought to coordinate existing national labeling initiatives that had spread across Europe and beyond after the Max Havelaar initiative formed in the Netherlands in the late 1980s. These national labeling initiatives comprised the key policy participants in the network, making the arrangement a kind of "pressure pluralist" network, in the sense of many dispersed groups attempting to influence the collective outcome. Each national initiative retained some autonomy, but remained reliant on policy advocates in their own national markets. For instance, in the UK, the Fairtrade Foundation had close ties to Oxfam, CAFOD, Christian AID, and Traidcraft, whereas Transfair USA had ties to the Ford Foundation, Equal Exchange, and Global Exchange (Auld 2009). More recently, FLO has exerted greater control over the national initiatives and has opened membership to producer associations, reflecting a shift to include an important "policy advocate" into the position of a more direct "policy participant" (Auld 2010a). However, as of September 2011, the US national fairtrade labeling initiative announced it will end its FLO membership and take its own approach, a decision reflecting the longstanding challenges FLO has had to coordinate as a network (Auld 2009).

The e-Stewards program emerged as a "clientelist" initiative, in the sense that it was – and so far remains – heavily linked to one specific organization, i.e., the Basel Action Network (BAN). After its initial involvement in a US Environmental Protection Agency (EPA) facilitated multi-stakeholder forum (which would result in a competing certification standard, called Responsible Recycling (R2) practices), BAN developed the e-Stewards standard with input from a select group of industry players (Renckens 2013). A few months after the official release of the program in 2010, a Leadership Council was established, which will provide technical assistance, policy expertise, and assist in marketing and promotional efforts (Basel Action Network 2010). A select group of representatives from recyclers, collectors, enterprises, NGOs, and local government make up the Leadership Council. Hence, as is the case with the MSC, the input of other policy actors, both as participant and as advocate, is rather limited so far.

Assessing governance components of NSMD systems

Given the above described supply chain and agency dynamics, what are the similarities and differences across NSMD governance systems when analyzing the governance components identified in the introductory chapter of this volume? There are many different policy decisions that could be traced in this regard. In this section we focus on just one critical consideration: the level at which standards are set to address a given problem.

Agenda setting and issue framing

As mentioned in the introduction of this chapter, the analysis of agenda setting and issue framing when applied in the context of NSMD governance systems is different from the agenda-setting chapter of this volume. When analyzing multilateral agreements and public policy networks, one generally looks at the influence of networks on the agenda setting process in a different forum than the network itself. In the case of NSMD systems, however, processes of agenda setting and issue framing also influence the formation of these networks, which then, *as networks*, engage in decision making, since the network itself is the governance arena for the development of rules.

Two key considerations require attention then in this governance component. The first is determining which actors, from business to environmental or social NGOs, are involved as policy participants or advocates in the NSMD network. As indicated above, empirical analysis shows that NSMD programs generally form on the basis of common interests of what Vogel (1995) has called "Baptist-bootlegger" coalitions, in which economic and environmental/social interests align around a common goal of establishing differentiation in the market by means of product characteristics. The second and related issue concerns the degree to which actors in these networks then share a common and unified understanding of the problem requiring attention. Any given policy problem can have many competing understandings (Stone 1989). This matters for NSMD systems for three reasons. First, from the perspective of these systems as organizations, a multiplicity of demands may allow more wiggle room for the program in how it strategizes to advance its mandate (Oliver 1991). Second, this has implications for how we think about the role of NGOs in the evolution of NSMD systems as a governance arena. Third, it may also shape the relationship and shifting alliances between NGOs and businesses along a supply chain, where different partnerships and coalitions form due to common interests in advancing some shared concern. Hence, for thinking about the direction NSMD programs will travel, unpacking the networks matters.

Across the sectors, there are very few instances where a single common understanding of the problem exists, which is partly a reflection of very different worldviews about the nature of and solutions to global problems (Clapp and Dauvergne 2005). The disagreements come in two principal forms. First, there are differences in how *environmental problems themselves* are understood. In natural resource management sectors a key debate centers on whether improving management practices is sufficient or whether the focus should be on outright protection of critical resources, ensuring they are never directly used for commercial or industrial purposes. There are also debates between those promoting reduced consumption versus environmentally friendly consumption. The former has been a central and longstanding concern within the forest sector, with certain NGOs strongly advocating for forest protection in general and in specific areas where logging plans exist. It has since become a consideration for fisheries. After negotiations for the Earth Summit and the Convention on Biological Diversity in 1992, attention to marine protection rose. The World Bank, the International Union for Conservation of Nature (IUCN), and the Great Barrier Reef Marine Park Authority of Australia, for instance, released a report on global marine protection that identified 155 areas where new protection or better management of existing protection was highly recommended (Kenworthy 1995). Hence, debates about appropriate forest or fisheries management are both often pitted against arguments for habitat protection via terrestrial and marine parks.

A second policy issue concerns the *problem definitions over social considerations*, such as the rights and needs of local communities, and *their relationship to the environmental considerations* delineated above. For instance, rules that lead to a reduction in the amount of wood an operation can harvest in a year can reduce job opportunities and incomes for local communities. Similarly, demands for extensive data to scientifically validate the appropriate management of a resource can create barriers for smaller and poorly resourced communities or operators. In the case of electronic waste recycling – a problem that gained attention due to the unveiling of often illegal trade in hazardous electronic waste to countries in the global south – an important debate has been whether the problem should be defined as an environmental and health problem, or as one of economic efficiency and materials recovery. The main divide cannot just be depicted as one between environmental NGOs and industry, as within industry as well there is a divide between those favoring an environmental and economic justice interpretation and those emphasizing gains from trade and the development of recycling opportunities in developing countries.

In NSMD agenda setting and issue framing processes, these tensions matter for a wide range of decisions. However, they are particularly significant for how decisions about standards reach the agenda for consideration by the programs and how the above trade-offs are framed. With the MSC, for instance, Unilever and WWF had different reasons for wanting to form a seafood certification program. Unilever had reputation and supply sustainability and stability concerns. WWF had broad concerns about ocean ecosystem integrity. The MSC, thus, emerged to serve their respective and different needs. However, this early partnership and the common needs it embodied, as we discuss below, framed the issue of sustainable fisheries in a particular manner that largely excluded the social considerations just noted and focused on certifying fisheries that demonstrates they were on a trajectory towards environmental sustainability.

Negotiated settlement

The influence of the involvement of specific actors and the degree to which they share problem definitions plays out within NSMD systems in the decisions about the standards these programs set. Are standards set at such a high level that they become de facto "gold standards" to which few firms are able to adhere and which provide a model for policy making? Or are the standards set at a relatively low level that focuses on weeding out the worst players, rather than focusing on the top? We turn to how these questions were answered in discussing the decisions our case study programs made, taking into account that decisions are not static and standards are evolving over time.

The FSC, reflecting its original network structure, and especially strong influence of environmental NGOs as policy participants, focused on either "eco-forestry" or "top level" standards higher than even the strongest public policy regulations (Lawson and Cashore 2001; Cashore and Lawson 2003; Cashore *et al.* 2004). However, over time there was increasing recognition that policies should be modified to gain the support of business and hence build market share (McDermott *et al.* 2009).

For the community of fair trade labeling initiatives and now FLO, the requirement to pay a premium to participant producers has long differentiated the program from other initiatives, which leave price determinations to the market (Daviron and Ponte 2005). Unlike the forestry case, agreement has not emerged that this standard or others of the program should be relaxed. Rather, reflecting the shift of producers from policy advocate to participant, and responding to broader pressure from the fair trade community, FLO announced an increase in the price premium in 2007 (Bacon 2010).

For the MSC, the standard was designed to move participants towards sustainability over time and not necessarily to recognize only those operations that were already sustainable (May *et al.* 2003). Many policy advocates have criticized the program for this approach, particularly due to controversies over certain fisheries where NGOs were actively campaigning against the fishery leading up to or during a fishery's certification efforts (see Highleyman *et al.* 2004). And while other things about the program have been modified over the course of its development – such as the assessment methodology and procedures – the overall standards have remained the same (Auld and Gulbrandsen 2010).

In the case of the e-Stewards program the decision was made to set the bar high. This resulted from the specific network of actors that developed the program, who agreed on banning the exports of hazardous electronic waste from OECD to non-OECD countries. This stance differentiates the program from its main competitor program – R2 – which is dominated by industry interests that define the problem more in terms of efficiency and materials recovery. As the e-Stewards program was only recently established (April 2010) the standard has not been changed yet. It is not expected that this will happen soon either. Based on the *raison d'être* of its main initiator (i.e., BAN), the program considers its aim is to implement the definitions of hazardous wastes as set by the 1989 Basel Convention on the Control of Transboundary Movements of Hazardous Wastes and their Disposal, and a 1995 amendment to the Convention that bans the trade in hazardous wastes from OECD to non-OECD countries, but which has still not entered into force (Renckens 2013).

Compliance/implementation

As mentioned earlier, one of the characteristics that distinguish NSMD governance from other corporate social responsibility initiatives is that all NSMD systems involve third party assessments against the program's standards, which is a result of the way the network of actors have conceived the programs they developed. However, the manner in which third party assessment is conducted and the incentives for doing so vary.

The FSC does not conduct certification services but accredits separate organizations to certify forest managers according to its standards. The initial accreditation was done by a FSC Accreditation Business Unit. Since 2006, it has been handled by an independent business, Accreditation Services International (ASI). Accredited certifiers are responsible for assessing adherence with both

FSC forest management standards and tracking requirements for chain-of-custody operators. The MSC takes a very similar approach, also using accreditation, and has even begun using ASI for accreditation. A main difference between the programs is, however, that the MSC uses the certification process to define local interpretations of the program's global standard whereas the FSC only allows certifiers to do so in the absence of an FSC-approved national standard (Meidinger 2006; Auld and Gulbrandsen 2010).

FLO and e-Stewards use a different approach. FLO began with an in-house certification committee, but since 2003, this service has been handed over to FLO-Cert, which is an organization solely dedicated to providing certification services for the program (Auld 2009). The e-Stewards program defers to the ANSI-ASQ National Accreditation Board (ANAB) for this function, which is a body that accredits across a broad range of issues and has membership within the International Accreditation Forum (IAF) (e-Stewards 2010). This is different from FSC and MSC in that the ANAB is a body to which the state has delegated authority as part of a broader set of institutions governing global technical standards and the certification services used to verify compliance with them. ASI, on the other hand, is a body set up separately by the FSC, and hence this establishes a different division between which actors are policy participants and policy advocates for this governance component of the MSC and FSC versus the e-Stewards program.

Turning to implementation, the voluntary nature of NSMD systems combined with different existing practices, rules, and capacities across regions, countries, and even operators within a country, mean that there are challenges with uneven and unbalanced uptake. Although there is considerable variation within countries in terms of the capacities of operators to participate in voluntary certification programs, the trends in uptake to this point highlight that operators from developing countries face greater barriers to participation. Several studies refer to the high direct costs of auditing and certification as the main impediments to the uptake of NSMD governance systems in the global south (Ebeling and Yasué 2009; Morris and Dunne 2004; Ponte 2008; Thornber*et al.* 1999; Vandergeest 2007). Verification or auditing of compliance can be an expensive proposition. It involves field visits by expert officials, significant paper work, and follow up to ensure practices continue.

The policy environment in which a regulatory target operates also influences uptake. Those operators that must perform to a high level to adhere to the law will find participating in certification, all else equal, a degree easier than operators practicing in environments where laws are weak, or exist but are not enforced. Furthermore, the presence of stronger institutions (e.g., relating to land tenure security or secure access to fishing quotas) also increases certification's potential. For instance, Ebeling and Yasue (2009) compared forest certification in Bolivia and Ecuador to find that stronger government enforcement of forestry regulations, compatibility of domestic forestry laws with certification requirements, and tax benefits to certified producers increase the likelihood of companies seeking certification. There are also barriers associated with limited technical knowledge about product qualities, limited connection to market channels, particularly vis-à-vis accessing international markets, limited marketing expertise, and poor infrastructure, which can inhibit smooth tracking of certified products and impose extra costs (Pattberg 2006; Cashore *et al.* 2006; Morris and Dunne 2004). Besides access to the consumer market in the global north, Melo and Wolf (2007) identify that access to what they call "non-local resources" also determines which firms might achieve certification in the global south. These non-local resources include access to financial capital, and technology and knowledge to develop certified production.[4] Finally, the programs may also be less well-resourced to certify in these parts of the world. A lack of accredited auditors in the global south can lead to costly delays in the certification process, whereas competition between multiple auditors is expected to reduce costs (Morris and Dunne 2004; Ponte 2008).

A key concern with this uneven uptake is that certification might become a non-tariff trade barrier (Delzeit and Holm-Müller 2009; Pattberg 2006). If retailers in the north, for example, will only sell certified products, and if fewer of these products come from countries of the global south or least developed countries in the case of tropical commodities, such as coffee, then this could be seen as an unfair trade barrier preventing poorer producers from accessing these markets. Although it remains to be seen how NSMD programs would fare if a claim was taken to the World Trade Organization (Bernstein and Hannah 2008), it remains a concern that certification will actually make it harder for producers in certain countries to access global markets (Fuchs *et al.* 2009).

To deal with these challenges and to enhance fairness, programs have done a number of things to make them more compatible with conditions in particular countries and overcome the challenges operators in these countries face. Many programs have ways of making a set of global principles and criteria appropriately tailored to the social, political and ecological conditions of a region. The FSC does this both by delegating standard-setting work to national initiatives or, when these standards are not yet in place, letting accredited auditors develop generic standards for a region. The MSC gives the auditor control over the localization process. Programs have also developed initiatives tailored to ease access for regulatory targets that may face high barriers to entry. The MSC has its Developing World Programme, an initiative designed to get more stakeholders from developing countries involved in and aware of the MSC, and ensures the MSC standard remains relevant to these fisheries (Marine Stewardship Council 2007, 2008). The FSC developed initiatives such as group certification, resource management certification and the Small and Low Intensity Managed Forests program, all of which make it easier for small operators to become FSC certified. Policy participants and advocates within the NSMD networks have also undertaken their own activities to overcome this challenge. There have been considerable attempts by foundations and development assistance agencies to provide funds to increase participation in certain countries, including supporting step-wise processes or covering certification costs for operators that would otherwise struggle to participate (GEF 2006; Klooster 2006).

A final consideration for implementation and compliance turns to the nature of the incentives the marketplace offers to operators that choose to certify. A first consideration is consumer knowledge, for which there exists wide variation. Fair trade represents one extreme. Surveys in many European countries indicate consumers have reasonably widespread awareness of fair trade initiatives. A 2004 study, for instance, found 63 percent of respondents in Luxembourg, 50 percent of UK respondents, 44 percent of Irish respondents, and 37 percent of Swedish respondents indicating knowing the Fairtrade label (Krier 2005). Knowledge of other NSMD systems, while changing, is generally lower, although concerted efforts to build awareness in certain markets has improved this (e.g., the FSC in the Netherlands) (Auld *et al.* 2008). Second, actual market rewards also vary. The character of the supply chain and the regulatory target appear to have affected how these incentives have developed. Certain high value, exotic hardwoods fetch sizable premiums in the European market (Espach 2006; Kollert and Lagan 2007; Nebel *et al.* 2005); however, on the whole, premiums have been inconsistent for standard commodity paper and wood products, even if operators see certification as important for gaining or maintaining access to markets. Research on fair trade indicates that the higher price requirements translate into premiums along the supply chain; however, these initiatives are the exception among NSMD systems. Finally, and related, we see differences between those programs which have an on-product label directed at engaging consumers and those that do not. The e-Stewards program, for example, does have a logo that certified firms can use on their website, yet given the locus of the regulatory target and the type of activity that is certified (i.e., a recycling process, and not the production process of a product) there is no on-product label. Many other NSMD programs, on the other hand, do have such an on-product label that consumers can identify. This can be important for the future development of an NSMD program when consumers become a key driver of uptake, a point we turn to below.

Implications for authority, legitimacy and effectiveness

The above review of the various governance components is critical for understanding authority, legitimacy and effectiveness. There may be, for instance, an inverse relationship initially between high standards, which tend to result from networks that are not business captured, and the ability to build widespread support necessary for the amelioration of certain problems.

Initially (i.e., at "Time 1"), those promoting certification programs as a means to promote regulatory compliance face a dilemma: they either create programs with high standards that few companies are able to meet, or they create programs with relatively low standards that many are able to meet. In both cases, in the absence of significant changes in market demand (which are almost always incremental in nature owing to the chicken and egg conundrum mentioned above), impacts on compliance and behavior will be relatively low (Table 7.3).

Three propositions result.

Table 7.3 The dilemma of high and low certification requirements

	Requirements	
	High	*Low*
Level of firm support	Low	High
Impacts on sustainability	Low	Low

Source: Cashore *et al.* (2007)

H1: Those firms or managers *already practicing closest to the standards* are likely to be among the first to join.

H2: Where standards are deemed too high but the idea of certification is supported, *alternative programs may emerge* that offer lower standards or a more "business friendly" policy environment.

H3: Direct impacts "on the ground" at earlier stages of evolution are more likely to occur around relatively focused/delimited problems than those that require complete market penetration for any meaningful resolution.

These propositions pose fundamental challenges to certification assessments and evaluations that are not sensitive to both historical and future temporal changes in supply and demand. In those cases where firms, facing relatively high regulations, have a self-interest in certifying because they are already practicing close to the standards, an effectiveness study focusing on behavioral changes might conclude that certification has little impact (or might inadvertently exaggerate changes by selectively choosing positive correlations). However, an evaluator aware that initial choices might kick start a supply and demand "chicken and egg" process providing firms that did not join at Time 1 an economic reason for joining at Time 2, would need to theorize carefully about future impacts. Similarly, a focus on consumer "willingness to pay" (Anderson and Hansen 2004; Aguilar and Vlosky 2007; Budak *et al.* 2006; Krystallis and Chryssohoidis 2005) arguably misses the most important question by failing to theorize about possible triggers of consumer transformation, a question which surveys alone are often ill-equipped to explore.

How might we draw on the assessment above to reflect on the evolutionary potential of NSMD programs and the impacts on authority, legitimacy and effectiveness? While the historical dynamics to date reveal existing potential and challenges, most scholars and practitioners agree that the greatest potential of certification lies in how strategists might intervene, and institutions might evolve, to become more authoritative and durable features of global environmental governance. To develop such a perspective, Bernstein and Cashore (2007) focus their attention on how the "Time 1" dynamics noted above might cover those firms who have yet to join owing to the costs of compliance. Moving in this direction, they argue, means addressing the dilemma in Table 7.3 because in the absence of increased market incentives, a certification program will have to lower its standards to gain broader support (Cashore *et al.* 2007). This dilemma can, and has, contributed to the proliferation of competing programs that are often more "business friendly" networks (conception 2 programs, mentioned above), or emphasize "brown" over "green/social" stakeholder processes, which dramatically shapes problem definition and which differ from conception 1 programs on the basis of the strictness of their standards.

Standards development and the role of third party verification will be contingent on understanding where in the evolutionary pathway these processes happen to be situated. Early on too many standards and too much oversight may reduce network support, but too little may render them ineffective. However, once networks achieve wide scale support, standards and auditing can be increased in a way that rewards, rather than punishes regulatory targets. In these cases the approaches taken would need to provide exemplary problem-focused standards and procedures.

Conclusion

Our review reveals that the governance components of agenda-setting and issue-framing negotiated settlement, and compliance and implementation are affected by differences in the market supply chains regulated by NSMD systems and the different structures of NSMD policy networks. We focused on four lead NSMD initiatives. We identified a connection between the early clientelist structure of the MSC network and the focus and stringency of its standards. Many policy advocates have criticized the program's approach to certifying fisheries operators which are on their way to sustainability, rather than only awarding those with a proven track record of sustainable practices. The FSC, by contrast, with a broader network, organized as a tripartite system of interest-based chambers, has established broad and stringent standards. FLO merged a community of national fair trade labeling initiatives, which became the key policy participants in a pressure pluralist network. This network has partly been responsible for reducing the influence of producers which have long been seeking a stronger voice in the organization, particularly to push for greater premiums. The e-Stewards program, finally, has similar origins to the MSC, yet has set relatively high standards, due to the key influence of its main initiator and its focus on setting standards aimed to implement the definitions of hazardous wastes as set by the Basel Convention and a still-unimplemented 1995 amendment to the Convention banning the trade in hazardous wastes from OECD to non-OECD countries.

The distinctions drawn allow us to consider better how business-dominated and NGO-dominated networks draw on the "multi-stakeholder" approach to further different aims. For instance, conception 2 initiatives often mirror previous "business-government" captured networks that give little attention to other interests. Instead, these programs tend to give more weight to those stakeholders promoting economic goals, including labor unions or faculty from schools supporting sectors such as forestry or mining. They limit, on the other hand, the role of organizations that give weight to environmental and social objectives. In such cases, conception 2 programs can *expand*, rather than contract, the number of organizations involved as policy participants. Similarly, conception 1 programs expand the set of policy participants, but in a way that includes different actors. The FSC, for example, does not limit the number of organizations, but instead assigns them to three chambers – environmental, economic and social – with the same weight in voting. This approach gives the FSC network a "corporatist" approach to policy development, even though beneath this tripartite model are a host of other organizations which act as policy advocates, some of which may even be participants in the policy deliberations of conception 2 programs.

A final key insight from the above exploration is that effects can change over time. Because the end point of the evolution of private governance systems is not necessarily a multilateral intergovernmental agreement – though it might become synergistically coupled with such an institution (Auld *et al.* 2009) – the other chapters' analyses of and conclusions regarding the various governance components might not fit well with an analysis of private regulatory systems. For instance, a "skewed" agenda-setting stage resulting from NGO dominance may mean NSMD programs play a different role than a program addressing an agenda set by a broad set of actors. Indeed, if the aim of private regulation is to serve as a model for government efforts, we need to think about NSMD systems differently than for situations where a complementary intergovernmental process does not exist or where one is unlikely to emerge.

This chapter makes clear the importance of a dynamic perspective for understanding the strategies necessary to steer NSMD governance systems. The dual goals of policy development and the need to achieve, rather than maintain, authority, pose a much more complicated set of factors with which to generate overall conclusions. This added complexity, however, makes the generation of clear prescriptions that emphasize strategic choices with the potential to yield widely shared notions of the appropriate structure, inclusiveness and powers of private governance networks one of the most important arenas of analysis for scholars and practitioners of NSMD networks.

Notes

1 For exceptions see Lawson and Cashore (2001), Cashore and Lawson (2003), Auld (2009), and Tollesfon, Gale and Haley (2008).
2 We must emphasize that any heuristic is necessarily an "ideal type" that does not capture fully the range of nuanced differences across programs and within programs over time. Instead, the "ideal type" becomes a way of understanding these changes – enabling, rather than constraining, scholarship on a highly dynamic institutional and policy environment.
3 We treat emergence of NSMD systems then as largely given. Focusing on emergence would mean analyzing how other policy networks in the organizational field affect the NSMD network, and this would interfere with our initial goals of analyzing the relationship between one particular type of program (i.e., NSMD programs) in its many varieties and the identified governance components.
4 They readily acknowledge, however, that such north–south linkages can create potential dependency relations as well (see also, Nigh 1997; Mendez 2008).

References

Abbott, K. W. and Snidal, D. (2009) 'Strengthening International Regulation Through Transnational New Governance: Overcoming the Orchestration Deficit', *Vanderbilt Journal of Transnational Law* 42 (2), 501–578.

Aguilar, F. X. and Vlosky, R. P. (2007) 'Consumer Willingness to Pay Price Premiums for Environmentally Certified Wood Products in the U.S.', *Forest Policy and Economics* 9 (8), 1100–1112.

Anderson, R. C. and Hansen, E. N. (2004) 'Determining Consumer Preferences for Ecolabeled Forest Products', *Journal of Forestry* 102 (4), 28–32.

Atkinson, M. and Coleman, W. D. (1989) 'Strong States and Weak States: Sectoral Policy Networks in Advanced Capitalist Economies', *British Journal of Political Science* 19, 47–67.

Auld, G. (2009) 'Reversal of Fortune: How Early Choices Can Alter the Logic of Market-based Authority', Doctoral Dissertation, School of Forestry and Environmental Studies, Yale University, New Haven, CT.

——. (2010a) 'Assessing Certification as Governance: Effects and Broader Consequences for Coffee', *Journal of Environment and Development* 19 (2), 215–241.

——. (2010b). 'Certification as Governance: Current Impact and Future Prospects', in Meera Warrier, ed., *The Politics of Fair Trade*, London: Routledge.

Auld, G. and Gulbrandsen, L. H. (2010) 'Transparency in Nonstate Certification: Consequences for Accountability and Legitimacy', *Global Environmental Politics* 10 (3), 97–119.

Auld, G., Bernstein, S. and Cashore, B. (2008) 'The New Corporate Social Responsibility', *Annual Review of Environment and Resources* 33 (1), 413–435.

Auld, G., Gulbrandsen, L. H. and McDermott, C. (2008) 'Certification Schemes and the Impact on Forests and Forestry', *Annual Review of Environment and Resources* 33 (1), 187–211.

Bacon, C. M. (2010) 'Who Decides What is Fair in Fair Trade? The Agri-environmental Governance of Standards, Access, and Price', *Journal of Peasant Studies* 37 (1), 111–147.

Balboa, C. (2009) 'When Nongovernmental Organizations Govern: Accountability in Private Conservation Networks', Graduate School of Arts and Social Sciences, Yale University, New Haven, CT.

Bartley, T. (2007) 'Institutional Emergence in An Era of Globalization: The Rise of Transnational Private Regulation of Labor and Environmental Conditions', *American Journal of Sociology* 113 (2), 297–351.

Bartley, T. and Smith, S. (2007) The Evolution of Transnational Fields of Governance: A Network Analytic Approach', Bloomington, IN: Department of Sociology, Indiana University.

Basel Action Network (2009) 'Performance Requirements Excerpted from the e-Stewards Standard for Responsible Recycling and Reuse of Electronic Equipment', Version 1.0. Seattle: Basel Action Network.

——. (2010) 'Diverse New Advisory Body to Guide Responsible e-Recycling', Electronic Newsletter.

Bernstein, S. and Cashore, B. (2007) 'Can Non-State Global Governance be Legitimate? An Analytical Framework', *Regulation & Governance* 1 (4), 347–371.

Bernstein, S. and Hannah, E. (2008) 'Non-state Global Standard Setting and The WTO: Legitimacy and The Need for Regulatory Space', *Journal of International Economic Law* 11 (3),575–608.

Börzel, T. A. and Risse, T. (2005) 'Public–Private Partnerships: Effective and Legitimate Tools of Transnational Governance?', in E. Grand and L. Pauly, eds., *Complex Sovereignty: On the Reconstitution of Political Authority in the 21st Century*, Toronto, Buffalo, London: University of Toronto Press.

Budak, F., Budak, D. B., Kacira, O. O. and Yavuz, M. C.. (2006) 'Consumer Willingness to Pay for Organic Sea Bass in Turkey', *Israeli Journal of Aquaculture-Bamidgeh* 58 (2), 116–123.

Büthe, T. (2010) 'Engineering Uncontestedness? The Institutional Development of the International Electrotechnical Commission (IEC) as a Private Regulator', *Business and Politics* 12 (3), Article 4.

Büthe, T. and Mattli, W. (2011) *New Global Rulers: the Privatization of Regulation in the World Economy*, Princeton, NJ: Princeton University Press.

Cashore, B. (2002) 'Legitimacy and The Privatization of Environmental Governance: How Non-state Market-driven (NSMD) Governance Systems Gain Rule-making Authority', *Governance – an International Journal of Policy and Administration* 15 (4), 503–529.

Cashore, B., Auld, G., Bernstein, S. and McDermott, C. (2007) 'Can Non-state Governance "Ratchet Up" Global Environmental Standards? Lessons from the Forest Sector', *Review of European Community and International Environmental Law* 16 (2), 158–172.

Cashore, B., Auld, G. and Newsom, D. (2004) *Governing Through Markets: Forest Certification and the Emergence of Non-State Authority*, New Haven, CT: Yale University Press.

Cashore, B., Gale, F., Meidinger, E. and Newsom, D. (2006) 'Forest Certification in Developing and Transitioning Countries', *Environment* 48 (9), 6–25.

Cashore, B. and Lawson, H. (2003) 'Private Policy Networks and Sustainable Forestry Policy: Comparing Forest Certification Experiences in the US Northeast and the Canadian Maritimes', *Canadian-American Public Policy* 53.

Clapp, J. (1998) 'The Privatization of Global Environmental Governance: ISO 14000 and the Developing World', *Environmental Governance* 4 (3), 295–316.

Clapp, J. and Dauvergne, P. (2005) *Paths to a Green World: The Political Economy of the Global Environment*, Cambridge, MA: MIT Press.

Coleman, W. D. and Skogstad, G., eds. (1990) *Policy Communities and Public Policy in Canada: A Structural Approach*, Mississauga, ON: Copp Clark Pitman Ltd.

Cutler, A. C., Haufler, V. and Porter, T., eds. (1999) *Private Authority and International Affairs*, Albany, NY: State University of New York Press.

Daviron, B. and Ponte, S. (2005) *The Coffee Paradox: Global Markets, Commodity Trade and the Elusive Promise of Development*, London and New York: Zed Books Ltd in association with CTA Wageningen.

Delmas, M. (2002) 'The Diffusion of Environmental Management Standards in Europe and in the United States: An Institutional Perspective', *Policy Sciences* 35, 91–119.

Delzeit, R. and Holm-Müller, K. (2009) 'Steps to Discern Sustainability Criteria for a Certification Scheme of Bioethanol in Brazil: Approach and Difficulties', *Energy* 34 (5), 662–668.

Dingwerth, K. and Pattberg, P. (2009) 'World Politics and Organizational Fields: The Case of Transnational Sustainability Governance', *European Journal of International Relations* 15 (4),707–743.

Ebeling, J. and Yasué, M. (2009) 'The Effectiveness of Market-Based Conservation in the Tropics: Forest Certification in Ecuador and Bolivia', *Journal of Environmental Management* 90 (2), 1145–1153.

Elliott, C. (2000) *Forest Certification: A Policy Network Perspective*, Centre for International Forestry Research (CIFOR). [Place of publication missing]

Elliott, C. and Schlaepfer, R. (2001) 'The Advocacy Coalition Framework: Appliction to the Policy Process for the Development of Forest Certification in Sweden', *Journal of European Public Policy* 8 (4), 642–661.

Espach, R. (2006) 'When Is Sustainable Forestry sustainable? The Forest Stewardship Council in Argentina and Brazil', *Global Environmental Politics* 6 (2), 55–84.

e-Stewards. *Accreditation* (2010 [cited March 21, 2011]). Available from http://e-stewards.org/certification-overview/accreditation/.

——. Current e-Stewards Enterprises (2011). Available from http://e-stewards.org/recycle-responsibly/enterprises/current-e-stewards-enterprises/.

Fransen, L. (2010) 'Minding Their Own Business? Firms and Activists in the Making of Private Labour Regulations', PhD Dissertation, University of Amsterdam, Amsterdam.

Fuchs, D., Kalfagianni, A. and Arentsen, M. (2009) 'Retail Power, Private Standards, and Sustainability in the Global Food System', in Jennifer Clapp and Doris Fuchs, eds., *Corporate Power in Global Agrifood Governance*, Cambridge, MA: MIT Press.

GEF (2006) 'Biodiversity Conservation in Coffee: Transforming Productive Practices in the Coffee Sector by Increasing Market Demand for Certified Sustainable Coffee,' UNDP-GEF – A partnership funded by GEF and implemented by UNDP 2006. Accessed January 20 2010. http://www.undp.org/gef/portfolio/writeups/bd/sust_coffee.html.

Glück, P., Rayner, J. and Cashore, B. (2005) 'Changes in the Governance of Forest Resources', in Gerardo Mery, Rene Alfaro, Markku Kanninen and Maxim Labovikov, eds., *Forests in the Global Balance – Changing Paradigms*, Helsinki: IUFRO World Series.

Gulbrandsen, L. H. (2005) 'Explaining Different Approaches to Voluntary Standards: A Study of Forest Certification Choices in Norway and Sweden', *Journal of Environmental Policy and Planning* 7 (1), 43–59.

Gunningham, N., Grabosky, P. N. and Sinclair, D., eds. (1998) *Smart Regulation: Designing Environmental Policy*, *Oxford Socio-legal Studies*, Oxford and New York: Clarendon Press and Oxford University Press.

Highleyman, S., Mathews Amos, A. and Cauley, H. (2004) 'An Independent Assessment of the Marine Stewardship Council', Draft Report Prepared for Homeland Foundation, Oak Foundation, and The Pew Charitable Trusts. Sandy River Plt., ME: Wildhavens Consulting.

Keck, M. E. and Sikkink, K. (1998) *Activists Beyond Borders: Advocacy Networks in International Politics*, Ithaca, NY and London: Cornell University Press.

Kenworthy, T. (2008) *Marine Protection Sites Proposed: World Bank, Conservation Groups Offer Ambitious Preservation Plan*, The Washington Post, June 24 1995 [cited August 13 2008]. Available from http://www.lexisnexis.com/.

Klooster, D. (2006) 'Environmental Certification of Forests in Mexico: the Political Ecology of a Non-governmental Market Intervention', *Annals of the Association of American Geographers* 96 (3), 541–565.

Knill, C. and Lehmkuhl, D. (2002) 'Private Actors and the State: Internationalization and Changing Patterns of Governance', *Governance: An International Journal of Policy, Administration, and Institutions* 15 (1), 41– 63.

Kollert, W. and Lagan, P. (2007) 'Do Certified Tropical Logs Fetch a Market Premium? A Comparative Price Analysis from Sabah, Malaysia', *Forest Policy and Economics* 9 (7), 862–868.

Krier, Jean-Marie (2006) *Fair Trade in Europe 2005: Facts and Figures on Fair Trade in 25 European Countries* [Online report]. Fair Trade Advocacy Office, December

2005 [cited March 13 2006]. Available from http://www.worldshops.org/news/new/FairTradeinEurope2005.pdf.

Krystallis, A. and Chryssohoidis, G. (2005) 'Consumers' Willingness to Pay for Organic Food – Factors that Affect It and Variation per Organic Product Type', *British Food Journal* 107 (4–5), 320–343.

Lawson, J. and Cashore, B. (2001) 'Firm Choices on Sustainable Forestry Forest Certification: The Case of JD Irving, Ltd', in B. Cashore, L. Teeter and D. Zhang, eds., *Forest Policy for Private Forestry*, Wallingford; UK: CABI Publishing.

Marine Stewardship Council. (2007) 'Developing World Fisheries Embark on Journey to MSC Eco-label', Marine Stewardship Council, November 29 2007. Accessed May 13 2010. http://www.msc.org/newsroom/news/developing-world-fisheries-embark-on-journey-to ?fromsearch=1&newsquery=developing+world+program&year=&month=&isnewssear ch=1.

——. (2008) *Annual Report 2007/2008*, London: Marine Stewardship Council.

——. (2010) *MSC Chain of Custody Standard* (Version 2.1) [Standards document]. Marine Stewardship Council, May 1 2010a [cited May 12 2010]. Available from http://www.msc.org/documents/scheme-documents/msc-standards/MSC_Chain_of_Custody_Standard.doc/view.

——. (2010) *MSC Fishery Standard: Principles and Criteria for Sustainable Fishing* (Version 1.1), Marine Stewardship Council, May 1 2010b [cited May 22 2010]. Available from http://www.msc.org/documents/scheme-documents/msc-standards/MSC_environmental_standard_for_sustainable_fishing.pdf.

May, B., Leadbitter, D., Sutton, M. and Weber, M. (2003) 'The Marine Stewardship Council (MSC): Background, Rationale and Challenges', in Bruce Phillips, Trevor Ward and Chet Chaffee, eds., *Eco-Labelling in Fisheries: What Is It All About?*, Oxford: Blackwell.

McDermott, C. L., Cashore, B. and Kanowski, P. (2009) 'Setting the Bar: An International Comparison of Public and Private Forest Policy Specifications and Implications for Explaining Policy Trends', *Journal of Integrative Environmental Sciences* 6 (3), 217–237.

McDermott, C. L., Noah, E. and Cashore, B. (2008) 'Differences that "Matter"? A Framework for Comparing Environmental Certification Standards and Government Policies', *Journal of Environmental Policy and Planning* 10 (1), 47–70.

Meidinger, E. E. (2003) 'Environmental Law for Global Civil Society: the Forest Certification Prototype', in Errol Meidinger, Christopher Elliott and Gerhard Oesten, eds., *Social and Political Dimensions of Forest Certification*, Remagen-Oberwinter: Forstbuch.

——. (2006) 'The Administrative Law of Global Private–Public Regulation: The Case of Forestry', *European Journal of International Law* 17 (1), 47–87.

Melo, C. and Wolf, S. (2007) 'Ecocertification of Ecuadorian Bananas: Prospects for Progressive North–South Linkages', *Studies in Comparative International Development* 42 (3/4), 256–278.

Mendez, V. E. (2008) 'Farmers' Livelihoods and Biodiversity Conservation in a Coffee Landscape of El Salvador', in Christopher M. Bacon, V. Ernesto Mendez, Stephen R. Gliessman, David Goodman and Jonathan A. Fox, eds., *Confronting the Coffee Crisis: Fair Trade, Sustainable Livelihoods and Ecosystems in Mexico and Central America*, Cambridge, MA: MIT Press.

Morris, M. and Dunne, N. (2004) 'Driving Environmental Certification: Its Impact on the Furniture and Timber Products Value Chain in South Africa', *Geoforum* 35 (2): 251–266.

Nebel, G., Quevedo, L., Jacobsen, J. B. and Helles, F. (2005) 'Development and Economic Significance of Forest Certification: The Case of FSC in Bolivia', *Forest Policy and Economics* 7 (2), 175–186.

Nigh, R. (1997) 'Organic Agriculture and Globalization: A Maya Associative Corporation in Chiapas, Mexico', *Human Organization* 56 (4), 427.

Oliver, C. (1991) 'Strategic Responses to Institutional Processes', *Academy of Management Review* 16 (1), 145–179.

Overdevest, C. (2005) 'Treadmill Politics, Information Politics and Public Policy: Toward a Political Economy of Information', *Organization & Environment* 18 (1), 72–90.

———. (2010) 'Comparing Forest Certification Schemes: The Case of Ratcheting Standards in the Forest Sector', *Socio-Economic Review* 8 (1), 47–76.

Pattberg, P. (2006) 'Private Governance and the South: Lessons from Global Forest Politics', *Third World Quarterly* 27 (4), 579–593.

Pattberg, P. (2007) *Private Institutions and Global Governance. The New Politics of Environmental Sustainability*, Cheltenham/Northampton, MA: Edward Elgar Publishing.

Ponte, S. (2008) 'Greener than Thou: The Political Economy of Fish Ecolabeling and its Local Manifestations in South Africa', *World Development* 36 (1), 159–175.

Renckens, S. (2013) 'The Basel Convention, US Politics, and the Emergence of Non-State E-waste Recycling Certification', *International Environmental Agreements* DOI: 10.1007/s10784-013-9220-7.

Rhodes, R. A. W. (1997) *Understanding Governance: Policy Networks, Governance, Reflexivity, and Accountability*, Buckingham: Open University Press.

Roberts, S. (2003) 'Supply Chain Specific? Understanding the Patchy Success of Ethical Sourcing Initiatives', *Journal of Business Ethics* 44 (2), 159–170.

Rosenau, J. N. (1995) 'Governance in the Twenty-first Century', *Global Governance* 1 (1), 13–43.

Rosenau, J. N. and Czempiel, E-O. (1992) *Governance without Government: Order and Change in World Politics*, Cambridge: Cambridge University Press.

Ruggie, J. G. (2004) 'Reconstituting the Global Public Domain – Issues, Actors, and Practices', *European Journal of International Relations* 10 (4), 499–531.

Salaman, L. M. (2002) 'Introduction', *The Tools of Government: A Guide to the New Governance*, New York: Oxford University Press.

Stone, D. (1989) 'Causal Stories and the Formation of Policy Agendas', *Political Science Quarterly* 104, 281–300.

Thornber, K., Plouvier, D. and Bass, S. (1999) 'Certification: Barriers to Benefits. A Discussion of Equity Implications', in *A Forest Certification Advisory Group Briefing Paper*.

Tollefson, C., Gale, F. and Haley, D. (2008) *Setting the Standard: Certification, Governance and The Forest Stewardship Council*, Vancouver: UBC Press.

Vandergeest, P. (2007) 'Certification and Communities: Alternatives for Regulating the Environmental and Social Impacts of Shrimp Farming', *World Development* 35 (7), 1152–1171.

Vogel, D. (1995) *Trading Up. Consumer and Environmental Regulation in a Global Economy, Cambridge*, MA: Harvard University Press.

———. (2008) 'Private Global Business Regulation', *Annual Review of Political Science* 11 (1), 261–282.

8 Actor configurations in the climate regime

The states call the shots

Steinar Andresen, Norichika Kanie and Peter M. Haas

Introduction

The efforts of the international community to deal with the challenge of climate change have received over the last two decades the most attention of any environmental problems by policy-makers, the media and the public. The main reason so much political energy has been invested in dealing with this problem is that it is *not* only an environmental problem. It goes to the core of everyday life in all corners of the world and touches upon key issues as economic growth, energy use as well as trade issues. This makes climate change a very malign issue as developing countries give most priority to economic growth to move out of poverty, and developed countries are reluctant to change their comfortable but energy-consuming lifestyles. Short-term national, political and economic interests have been key decision premises during the negotiations of a climate regime, not long-term concern for the planet and future generations. This has, however, not prevented massive and creative efforts by various non-state actors like cities, municipalities, environmental non-governmental organizations (NGOs) and international organizations as well as some large multi-national corporations (MNCs) to deal with the issue, often through various forms of partnerships. Still, so far they have not been enough to curb the trend of rising emissions. The bottom line in a problem-solving perspective is therefore that while emissions of Greenhouse Gasses (GHGs) need to be significantly reduced, they are still rising sharply. Are there ways in which this negative trend can be changed, for example by introducing new actor configurations promoting good governance as suggested in this volume?

So far the United Nations (UN) has provided the main international venue to deal with climate change. Intuitively this makes sense as climate change is a truly global problem and all states need to be included, essential not the least from a legitimacy point of view. However the UN encompasses a number of diplomatic bottlenecks based on its inclusive and state-centric nature. Due to the lack of progress along the UN track many policy-makers and academics argue that supplements or alternatives are needed. They argue that the problem needs to be dealt with through various types of *regime complexes* as climate change is not only an environmental problem, other international institutions need to be involved (Keohane and Victor 2011). More recently such complexes have emerged and many argue that the climate change governance systems are increasingly polycentric (Ostrom 2010; Cole 2011). In a similar vein they argue the UN process is too state centric; a more transnational approach is needed (Abbott 2013). To some extent our approach on actor configurations belongs to this last school of thought, although it is realized that states have a key role to play. Another line of argument is that it is more effective to deal with the issue in more exclusive "clubs" among major economies (and emitters) than the unruly 190 + Conference of Parties (COPs) (Victor 2011). One of the latest fads is that we need a technological "quick fix" to deal with the problem, and for example geo engineering has been discussed as one possible solution (Bodansky 2011).

As the UN track is the dominant one we will go through the various components in the making of the climate regime, agenda setting, negotiations, compliance and implementation. What are the merits and shortcomings of the approaches chosen and could more have been achieved with a different approach, including the combination of actor configurations outlined in the current project? The achievements and potential of various partnerships and other more exclusive approaches will be discussed towards the end. Considering the long time-frame and the complexity of the issue, only some of the main features of the process will be discussed.

Several streams of initial agenda setting

We conceive agenda setting on climate change in a sequential way until the start of negotiations within the International Negotiating Committee (INC) in 1991. Systematic scientific research started in the 1950s on the earth's climate system. During the next 20 years this was seen as an exclusive scientific issue. US scientists were dominating but several transnational scientific networks emerged in the 1960s. In the 1970s the political relevance of the issue was highlighted by the United Nations Environmental Programme (UNEP). World Meteorological Organizations (WMO), UNEP and International Council for Science (ICSU) played key roles in organizing a series of workshops in the 1980s. At a 1985 meeting, scientists acting in their personal capacities stated that "in the first half of the next century a rise of global mean temperatures would occur which is greater than any in man's history" (Agrawala 1998: 608). In the period immediately after this conference climate change was rapidly emerging on the international political agenda. UNEP's Executive Director Tolba played an important role in this process. The mood of policy activism was strengthened at the 1988 World Conference on the Changing Atmosphere in Toronto, Canada. This was not an inter-governmental conference but a forceful combination of activist scientists, activist politicians and environmental NGOs (Andresen and Agrawala 2002; Haas and McCabe 2001). It called for the industrialized countries to cut their carbon dioxide (CO_2) emissions by 20 percent by 2005. This target and time-tables approach was an example of learning from the ozone regime. This approach was accepted by the large majority of states as the guideline for the most fair and effective way to deal with the issue in the subsequent process (Andresen and Boasson 2012).

Apart from the activist scientists the three mentioned international organizations (IOs) played key roles in this early agenda-setting phase. According to Agrawala (1998: 608): "The fourth and final player, the United States was in a unique position." The United States had by far the most cumulative expertise in climate change research and a number of climate assessments had been carried out. Parallel to the non-state "activist" agenda ending up with the Toronto meeting, another process ended up in the Intergovernmental Panel on Climate Change (IPCC) with the United States in the driver's seat. Due to strong differences of opinion among key US actors a compromise was reached in 1986 to suggest an international intergovernmental scientific mechanism. Key US policymakers did not expect any scientific agreement, thereby reducing pressure for policy action (Antholis and Talbott 2010). The US viewpoint was communicated to the WMO, and in 1987 it decided to set up such a mechanism together with UNEP.

Since the latter stage of agenda setting, three basic international cleavages emerged, "virtually unchanged today" (Bodansky and Rajamani 2012: 6): a division between developed states on ambition and regulatory approach; a division between developing and developed countries; and a division within the developing countries. The first conflict line was most prominent in the agenda-setting stage. Numerous international political conferences were arranged. They turned into what has been labeled a "green beauty contest" between some of the OECD nations to adopt the most ambitious national emissions reduction targets with little or no attention to the economic costs involved (Andresen and Butenschøn 2001). An important background factor was the strong public attention towards the environment caused by external events like the ozone hole and the Chernobyl disaster. The two major players were the United States and the EU. The EU was a strong champion of the target and time-table approach and also wanted commitments to be *legally binding*, strongly supported by the environmental community. In stark contrast was the position by the United States, arguing for a bottom-up policy based on national interests and priorities, strongly influenced by business and industry. By the end of the agenda-setting stage the United States was seen as the laggard while the EU was hailed as the pusher and leader by environmentalists and other activists (Andresen and Agrawala 2002).

The developed countries accepted the positions that they needed to take the lead on the issue but there was disagreement on the organization of the negotiation process. The developed countries wanted the process to be organized under WMO and UNEP, modeled after the organization of the IPCC, while the developing countries argued that it should be directly under the auspices of the UN General Assembly, resenting the more narrowly technical domain of the two IOs (Bodansky and Rajamani 2012). They would be better represented by an inclusive UN approach and thereby stressing that this was also a development issue.

While developing countries agreed on the broad principles, there were deep-seated political conflicts between the Alliance of Small Island States (AOSIS) and the oil-producing nations in Organizations of Petroleum Exporting Countries

(OPEC). A third pole stressed their right to development and poverty eradication and wanted no infringement on their sovereignty. This faction was spearheaded by China, India and Brazil, three of the four members of the BASIC alliance, to be set up almost two decades later (Bodansky and Rajamani 2012).

In short, the early agenda-setting stage was dominated by scientists but key international organizations were also quick to enter the scene. Activists of various kinds were very important in shaping the subsequent ambition, frame and approach, particularly activist scientists, while the United States was very important in shaping the IPCC. Other states became increasingly important in the later stages and major conflict lines remained virtually unchanged over the next 25 years.

A snapshot of the process of negotiations: from quite dynamic to very slow

It did not take much more than a year for the INC to finish negotiation over a Climate Convention, a typical framework convention without much regulatory bite, but a necessary first step. At the first COP the parties agreed to strengthen Annex 1 commitments and "The Berlin Mandate turned the principle of special treatment for developing countries into an outright exemption from binding targets" (Antholis and Talbott 2010: 30). In contrast to the Convention, the Kyoto Protocol was a legally binding target and time-table approach strengthening and specifying emission cuts for developed (Annex I) countries. It is commonly referred to as a "top-down" approach as the goals are negotiated internationally, but states have significant leeway regarding how the goals shall be met (Bodansky and Rajamani 2012). Considering the complexity of the issue and the high number of actors involved, it was quite a remarkable achievement to make a framework convention in a year and a half and add a Protocol fleshing out specific obligations as well as adding new and innovative flexible mechanisms during a two-year period.

However, the process may not have been as dynamic as hoped. The Protocol was full of "invisible brackets" and it took four years before the parties agreed on a watered-down Protocol through the adoption of the Marrakech Accords (Hovi *et al.* 2003). The decision of the US Bush administration not to ratify the Kyoto Protocol also substantially delayed entry into force. Another four years went by before the Protocol entered into force in 2005. The Earth Negotiation Bulletin (ENB) quote from 2003 is symptomatic: "there was undoubtedly a sense of treading the same waters, if not pedaling backwards on a range of other issues" (ENB, Vol. 12 No 231:17). Looming large over the whole process was the issue of commitments once Kyoto expired in 2012, but progress was extremely modest. Symptomatically, it was decided to have a seminar on the issue in 2005 (ENB Volume 12 No. 260: 15). Since 2005 the question whether the existing "two-track" regime should be continued with specific legally binding commitments only for developed countries. Many saw the adoption of the Bali Action Plan in 2007 as a major break-through as all parties for the first time agreed to conduct formal negotiations on a new regime. The negotiations, however, were still to be conducted under two separate tracks indicating that major developing countries were not ready to undertake international commitments. Industrialized countries remained fixated on mitigation, while developing countries were also increasingly concerned with adaptation. Following different tracks for each agenda made it extremely difficult to reach a grand bargain or even to make tactical trade-offs.

COP 15 in Copenhagen in December 2009 did not end up as the milestone it was supposed to be. It has been described as "the mountain that gave birth to a mouse" (Andresen and Boasson 2012: 58). The final document was not a formally adopted UN document and it seemingly represented the farewell to the top-down legally binding approach. The accord was a "bottom-up" "pledge-and-review" approach. The "pledge" part implied that the parties themselves set their own emissions reduction targets for 2020. The result is a set of widely diverging emissions reduction targets difficult to compare and with strong differences in terms of the levels of ambitions. The distinction between developed and developing countries was upheld as the former should set economy wide targets while developing countries should adopt "nationally appropriate mitigation actions" (NAMAs) to slow their emissions. Measure, Report and Verify (MRV) the emissions are the bottom line for monitoring and reviewing the process, but only developing countries receiving assistance were exposed to international review. The Accord in principle recognizes the scientific view that the increase in global temperatures should not exceed 2 degrees Celsius from pre-industrial levels. The parties also agreed to raise funds of $30 billion from 2010–2012 and an additional $100 billion per year by 2020 to help developing countries cut their emissions.

The basic principles in the Accord were accepted and refined by all parties in November 2010 and formally adopted into the UN regime by the Cancun Agreement. While Copenhagen was seen as a failure by most observers, many regarded Cancun as quite successful. As the substance was essentially the same this is surprising, but the explanation is simple. Cancun was a success in terms of process as all were included in the decision-making process, in contrast to the closed-door diplomacy in Copenhagen (Andresen and Boasson 2012). The most important decision that came out of COP 17 in Durban in 2011 was the launching of yet another *ad hoc* process, the Ad Hoc Working Group on the Durban Platform (ADP) to negotiate a post-2020 climate agreement by 2015. The Durban Platform calls for a protocol, or a legal instrument, or an agreed outcome with legal force under the Convention and applicable to all parties. According to one source: "This lack of clarity will likely lead to some rather creative interpretations of the three 'legal' options" (IISD Report December 2011:2). Why was it necessary to launch a new process and why not continue under the 2007 Bali Action Plan as a basis for a new regime as was intended? The reason was that the developed countries interpreted this plan as creating a firewall between developing countries' *commitments* and developed countries' *actions*. They therefore insisted on a new process "with a clean slate on differentiations" (Bodansky and Rajamani 2012: 14). For the first time there is no reference to common but differentiated responsibilities in the document although the equity issue is referred to. COP 18 in Doha 2012 provided no clarification on the post-2020 regime. Apart from some haggling over finance, most energy was used on the content of the second commitment period of the Kyoto Protocol and the usual last-minute compromise was reached. It is important that *some* countries still have legally binding commitments but Kyoto 2 has turned into an EU + mini regime. In sum, the process has moved backwards recently, judged by the percentage of emissions exposed to direct international regulations, but the "firewall" between developed and developing countries may be about to fall.

Compliance and implementation: not enough to reduce emissions

The reporting requirements under the Protocol are quite comprehensive and they have been considerably expanded over time, and the use of independent Expert Review Teams is more intrusive than in most environmental regimes. Reporting requirements for non-Annex 1 countries have been much weaker but have been tightened somewhat more recently. The Global Environmental Fund (GEF) has played a key role in facilitating reporting both in terms of assistance and financing. Still, insufficient and old data is a severe problem and in a recent article in *Nature* it has been suggested that China may be under-reporting its emissions by as much as 1.4 billion tons a year, roughly the same as Japan's overall emissions (*The Economist* 2012: 60).

The compliance system of the Kyoto Protocol may look strong on paper but is rather weak in practice. It consists of a Compliance Committee composed of a Facilitative Branch and an Enforcement Branch. The Enforcement Branch has three specific tasks: first, consider parties' reporting requirements; second, eligibility for participating in the flexible mechanisms; and third, whether the emission targets have been met. In the case of non-compliance for each ton of emissions by which the party has exceeded its target in the first commitment period, 1.3 tons will be deducted in the next commitment period and the party will also be suspended from selling emission units.

So far the Enforcement Branch has only dealt with four countries, all relating to monitoring and reporting requirements, and compliance with emission targets will not be raised until 2015 (Oberthur and Lefeber 2010). The Facilitative Branch is responsible for potential non-compliance with its emission target, but to date the Facilitative Branch has not used this measure. The weak compliance system is illustrated by the case of Canada. Before it left the Protocol it publicly declared that it did not intend to meet its emission target. Still, "It is highly doubtful whether the Protocol would be capable of inducing compliance on the part of states that do not intend to adopt additional policies or measures to return to and stay on course" (Torney and Fujiwara 2010: 5). Moreover, although the emission limitations have a legally binding character, the compliance mechanism is non-binding in its consequences (Halvorsen and Hovi, 2006). This begs the question of the real significance of legally binding commitments, a key issue during the negotiations.

Seemingly there does not appear to be a need for a strong compliance system for the Kyoto Protocol as the development of emission figures indicates that non-compliance is not a problem. The latest official figures from the Subsidiary Body for Implementation (16 November 2012) from 1990 to 2010 show total aggregate emissions excluding land use and forestry (LULUCF) has been reduced by 8.9 percent among the 42 Kyoto parties. The main reason emissions are down, however, is the strong reductions in the Economies in Transition (EIT) countries, some 40 percent, but this is *not* related to the climate regime but economic restructuring and economic downturn after the fall of the Iron Curtain. For the rest of the Annex 1 countries emissions have increased by some 5 percent.

The emissions trading system laid down in the Kyoto Protocol has never been put to use, but it may have inspired trading regime in for example Australia, California, Tokyo and not the least the EU. The EU is the most important Annex 1 Party in terms of emissions as well as political clout and the EU is on track to meeting its 8 percent reduction goal, although all members will not necessarily meet their individual target indicating that the EU is not only ready to "talk the talk" but also "walk the walk." The EU emissions trading scheme, the ETS, was no doubt triggered by the Kyoto Protocol, but due to the recent international stalemate the development of this system has been driven more by the Commission and pusher states that the climate regime. It has undoubtedly led to emission reductions but due to low carbon price and excess quotas distributed the system has not been as effective as expected. Factors unrelated to climate policies are also important in explaining GHG reductions; the EU front-runner policy has also been reduced as others do not follow suit, as well as the effects of the economic recession (Skjærseth, 2013). Other key countries like Japan, facing problems with domestic reduction, will probably meet their target through extensive use of the Clean Development Mechanism (CDM).

In contrast to the various trading schemes established, the CDM flows directly from the Kyoto Protocol. The use of this mechanism has increased considerably over time, although there was opposition initially from both developing and 'progressive' developed countries. The aim of the CDM is to provide low-cost emission reductions to the Annex 1 parties while at the same time contributing to sustainable development in developing countries hosting the projects. When assessing the CDM it is important to remember that it was never intended to reduce GHG emissions, as emissions reductions made by CDM projects in developing countries are used to compensate for emissions not being made in Annex 1 countries. Through recent comprehensive studies of the CDM it has been concluded that the goal achievement of the CDM has been very low. The CDM is successful in terms of the large number of projects initiated but the score in terms of cost-effectiveness as well as sustainable development is quite low. The conclusion in terms of problem-solving effectiveness is even more depressing: "The direct effect of the CDM is hence probably an increase rather than decrease of global emissions" (Lund 2013: 42). In short, the CDM has not been an example of a successful public–private partnership. From a fairness perspective it is also a problem that advanced developing countries like China get most projects while the least developed countries hardly get any.

The only key party outside the Protocol during the whole period of its existence has been the United States. During the Bush administration voluntary approaches and initiatives at local and state levels characterized the process (Selin and VanDeveer 2007). Still, a study in 2007 concluded:

> Indeed, when one compares trends in per capita emissions, it is striking that the only country to see decline other than the three "windfall countries" (Russia, UK and Germany) is the US which has been vilified for its decision not to ratify the Kyoto Protocol.
>
> (Harrison and Sundstrom 2007:13)

This illustrates emissions may well be reduced also for non-Kyoto partners. More importantly it illustrates the weakness of the simple aggregate UNFCCC emission data, not paying attention to crucial factors like economic development and population growth. This weakness is also amply illustrated in the United States more recently. Based only on emissions figures – and not its causes – the traditional "climate villain" the United States now stands forth as a "climate hero" due to its steep emissions reductions more recently (Aftenposten 2013). True, this is in part the result of measures introduced by the Environmental Protection Agency (EPA), but it is primarily a result of the explosion in the extraction of shale gas – with no links to climate policies – but strongly reducing the use of coal. Thereby the United States may reach its goal of a 17 percent reduction (base year 2005) by 2020, reflecting the random exercise of setting numerical targets when control over key parameters is very limited, as the US goal was based on a quota trading system that never materialized.

As some 85 percent of the emissions come from non-Kyoto partners, the Protocol is getting increasingly irrelevant. According to recent reports from the International Energy Agency (IEA) and UNEP, in 2011 global emissions increased by 3.2 percent (Wynn 2012). There was a slight decrease in the Organization for Economic Cooperation and Development (OECD) region, but this is more than offset by more than 6 percent increase in developing countries. China and India were responsible for the brunt of the emissions increase, some 9 percent increase. These countries have no "hard" international obligations and China and India were explicit that their adopted targets were domestic targets and not internationally binding. Considering the modest significance of a legally binding target, this does not necessarily make much of a difference. When these goals are stated and under international scrutiny most countries will care about their reputational costs and try to reach their targets. However these targets are usually relatively modest, making them fairly easy to meet. This does not mean that, for example, the world's largest emitter China neglects the problem. It has been thoroughly documented that a number of measures have been introduced to reduce its emissions (Stensdal 2012). The problem is that this is not enough to prevent a continued strong rise in emissions in China as well as elsewhere in the developing world.

Although emissions are rising, there are efforts to reduce it. One issue that has received considerable attention recently is UN REDD +, in an attempt to reduce deforestation, an effective and quick measure to reduce CO_2 emissions. There are 46 partner countries in the South but so far only four donating countries, and total contributions are slightly above US$100 million. To our knowledge little or nothing is known of the practical effects in terms of emissions reductions of these efforts. Although developing countries complain of lacking finance from the developed countries, and probably rightly so, still climate is one of two priority areas for the GEF (Rosendal and Andresen 2011). Developing countries have received support for the idea that other funding mechanisms than the GEF is needed and over time many funds have been established, but their financial muscles have been weak (Bodansky and Rajamani 2012). The main exception is the effort to raise US$20 billion promised at COP 15 as it is reported that this goal has almost been reached. Much time has also been spent on negotiating a Green Climate Fund, but so far it is more like a bathtub without water.

In short, the compliance system is very weak in practice and implementation efforts fail to offset steadily increasing emissions although considerable efforts are made at various governance levels. Also, the rise and fall of emissions are often related more to economic development than domestic or international climate policies.

Explaining the development: the significance of actor configurations

Agenda setting: the key role of activists

In line with the analysis of the chapter on agenda setting, states may play important roles as the IPCC might not have been established or it might not have had an intergovernmental nature had it not been for the United States. There may be both positive and negative aspects of the intergovernmental nature of the IPCC. According to the chairman of the INC, Jean Ripert, its intergovernmental nature was necessary to *educate the negotiators and was the key to the signing of the Climate Convention in 1992* (Agrawala 1998). And as we saw in the agenda-setting chapter in this volume, keeping a link between scientific networks, or epistemic communities, and negotiation is an important aspect for best-practice agenda setting. The potential downside is equally well known; the political influence over science, especially as the assessment summaries are politically negotiated, may undermine its scientific credibility (Haas 2004). Would an independent scientific body have more influence and pave the way for a more effective regime? Given the overall neglect of scientific advice we doubt that this would be the case unless strong IOs had played a stronger role. The key is the ability of an IO to work with scientific networks, while also coordinating the link between the agenda-setting and negotiation process. Agenda setting proved very important for the subsequent process of negotiations. The main conflict lines were established and they have been extremely stable up to this day. Moreover, seemingly *the* best way to deal with the problem was agreed upon by most actors, to a large extent driven by activists of various kinds. We do not think they overestimated the dangers of the problem, but they underestimated the complexity of the issue. Simply copying the stratospheric ozone approach may have been tempting, but not necessarily the best way to handle climate change as it was much more complex than the ozone model.

The ambitious approach was no doubt also driven by a proactive public triggered by external events, and this important factor was neglected in our earlier assumptions. Our categorization of actors was also too simple. For example, scientists are no homogenous category; some are activists, others are more cautious, and they may play quite different roles. Finally, at the time it certainly seemed fair that the rich countries should take the lead, but this created a static division that no longer applies – but it has been exceedingly difficult to get rid of.

Negotiations: the predominance of states

The main explanation for slow progress is captured by the state-centered nature of the negotiations and the pusher–laggard dimension is crucial. As laggards were much more powerful this led to a slow pace and deadlock. The key players are the United States, the EU and G-77/China. While the United States and the EU were long the dominant players, G-77 has also been influential by arguing primary responsibility of developed countries. Their influence has probably been enhanced due to their ability to get the UN as the appropriate all-inclusive negotiation forum. More recently, reflecting new geopolitical realities, the BASIC countries have become increasingly important, particularly China. The concept of G-2 has also surfaced, the label of the two most important players, the United States and China. By traditional standards the United States and the G-77/China have been the laggards while the EU and AOSIS have been the pushers. During most of these 20 years the laggards have been much stronger than the pushers, providing the most important explanation for the painstakingly slow process. As we shall have more to say about this later, such a pusher–laggard dichotomy is not as clear-cut a political device as portrayed in Chapter 1. First we give a brief overview of how these key actors have influenced the process.

Due to US opposition the Climate Convention ended without a legally binding target. Internal EU strife was the most important reason for the lack of EU influence. The period from 1995–1997 represents the only dynamic period in the history of the climate regime because the United States and the EU agreed on a top-down LBA target and time-table approach. This was strongly supported by the G-77/China as long as it did not apply to them. The Protocol was a genuine compromise as the United States got their institutions (the flexible mechanisms), the EU got their numbers and the developing countries avoided commitments. The problem was that the venue for the negotiations was not the only place decisions were taken – illustrated by the fierce opposition to a Kyoto-like approach in the US Senate, not the least due to fierce lobbying from affected US industries (Agrawala and Andresen 1999). Due to internal US opposition the Protocol never became the milestone many believed it to be at the time, and the United States did its utmost to water down the Protocol during the next COPs while the EU attempted to preserve its environmental integrity. When the United States left the Protocol track in 2001, the "Gang of Four" (Australia, Canada, Japan and Russia) upheld the previous US opposition and won through with most of their demands. However, had it not been for the EU the Protocol would probably have been dead (Hovi *et al.* 2003).

During the Clinton administration the United States had tried to push the emerging economies to take on commitments. This changed with the Bush-administration (2001–2008). As the United States as well as the G-77/China did not want to take on commitments, a *de facto* alliance between them emerged as both actors refused even to discuss the issue of future commitments. There was considerable optimism with Obama as US President from 2009 as he had made climate change a key focus of his Presidential campaign (Skodvin and Andresen 2009). Still, when facing domestic realities, including the financial crisis, his ambitions waned. The United States was a key architect behind the bottom-up approach and was able to get the EU accept this as a means of trying to get emerging economies on board. The most important veto-player at this conjunction was, however, not the United States but China, stripping the Accord of all goals apart from the two-degree goal. With the EU sidelined, the final deal was made by the United States and the BASIC countries. The North–South divide regarding commitments is now the dominant one, providing the main explanation for the recent stalemate.

Is it reasonable to label developing countries and particularly the emerging economies as laggards because they have been so reluctant to take on commitments? In a problem-solving perspective the answer is yes as this has legitimized the continued increase of emissions from the South. From an equity perspective the answer is no if we consider historic emissions. In this perspective developed countries and particularly the United States has the most responsibility for causing this problem. However legitimate, if this perspective is used as a guideline for inaction by the developing countries, the problem will never be solved as the present world is very different compared to when the Convention was adopted. Now more than 50 of the non-Annex I countries have higher per capita emissions than the poorest Kyoto partners (Bodansky and Rajamani 2012). Per capita emissions in South Africa are now higher than in Europe, China's per capita emissions are almost on par with Sweden, and Brazil's per capita emissions are higher than Norwegian emissions (Aftenposten 2013). In short, the climate regime hammered out in the 1990s was reasonable at the time, but not in 2013. That is, the static North–South divide is a major deficiency of the climate regime. Based on these new realities it is understandable that the developed countries attempt to remove this "firewall." Again, categorization of actors is not as simple as we had thought. They are also dynamic and change over time. A new and more adaptive system needs to be made, for example when a certain per capita emission level is reached, commitments need to kick in (Greenspan and Ziegler 2012). The interests of the poorest nations must be considered, while emerging economies must realize their obligations – unless they want to be seen as laggards and blockers to a more effective regime.

As noted, those in favor of the top-down legally binding approach have been seen as pushers, dating back to the framing of the issue in the agenda setting, while opponents have been seen as laggards. Considering the recent development towards a bottom-up approach and the modest practical effects of LBA, is this division necessarily so clear cut? Interestingly, already during the INC process in 1991, Japan, supported by the United States, suggested a pledge and review approach but the idea was met with scorn from the EU as well as the environmental community and it went nowhere (Bodansky 1993; Hattori 1999). Could it be that if this seemingly less ambitious approach had been adopted some 20 years ago, it would have been easier to involve emerging economies and the United States? We will never get an answer to this, but we do know that the "politically correct" approach has not been effective at international level and that it will probably not be part of the 2020 regime. Still, the bottom-up approach as it has been materialized so far is not very promising as the pledges are too weak to address the problem effectively. Be that as it may, considering the complexity of the issue the pusher–laggard divide may be too simple both as an analytical concept as well as a political label in this context. This is amply illustrated by considering the many non-climate policy-related drivers explaining GHG emissions. Also, what seems to be a typical laggard approach at one point in time may be hailed as a pusher approach at another point in time. When the flexible mechanisms were introduced by the United States they were seen by the EU as a way to avoid domestic emissions reductions. When quota trading was introduced some years later by the EU it was seen as an example of progressive EU climate policy (Skodvin and Andresen 2006). Regardless of labels, the main reason for slow progress is the failure of the large majority of states to deal effectively with the issue.

The lack of political will and ability among key players is the most important reason for the lack of progress, but what has been the effect of choosing the all-inclusive UN approach? A first observation is that there is a strong mismatch between time and resources invested and the results achieved. The number of meetings and participants have increased strongly over time. Participation had more than doubled from the adoption of the Kyoto Protocol (9,850) to the "milestone" COP in Copenhagen in 2009 (276,540). Moreover, while there were two official preparatory meetings before COP 3 in 1997, this had doubled in 2009 when the negotiators were sitting together for more than two months. Add to this that there was no negotiating text when the high-level segment arrived and that the final text was hammered out behind closed doors by a handful of powerful state leaders. To put it bluntly, this is an example of ineffective multilateral UN diplomacy. We cannot say that this specific approach has been the reason for the modest achievements made. But we can conclude that although more time, manpower and money have been invested, fewer results have been attained.

Negotiations, compliance and implementation: the role of non-state actors

To simplify, the gist of the argument in the current project is that there needs to be strong presence and involvement by non-state actors like NGOs, IOs and scientists while the role of MNCs should not be too dominating. First, what about the role of IOs playing a very important role in early agenda setting? Their role during negotiations has been very modest. UNEP was very important in establishing the climate regime, but has been more or less de-coupled from the process after the start of negotiations. One reason may be that certain states were reluctant to involve UNEP as they feared a strong UNEP, based on experiences from the ozone regime (Agrawala 1998). The United Nations Framework Convention on Climate Change (UNFCCC) Secretariat has shown little interest and willingness in the ambition of UNEP to coordinate various activities of Multilateral Environmental Agreements (MEAs), claiming it is essentially a waste of time (Andresen and Rosendal 2009). This may be due to the large size of the UNFCCC Secretariat, the biggest MEA Secretariat, indicating that they have sufficient resources and see no additional need for UNEP.

Although the Climate Secretariat by comparative standards is large, it has not exerted much autonomous influence during the process of negotiations and its role has primarily been one of facilitation. It has not been an "activist" secretariat like the desertification secretariat (Bauer 2009). It has been an important hub of information for the regime, but a review of the studies on the climate regime negotiations suggests that it has not shaped political outcomes (Depledge 2007; Bush 2009). Why has the secretariat been so cautious? The main reason is the very malign nature of the climate issue. The very high political stakes "have impaired the climate secretariat's potential to influence and confined it to its role as technocratic bureaucracy" (Bush 2009: 252).

Environmental NGOs, IOs and scientists were all very important, particularly in the early phase of agenda setting, but they lost most of their direct influence when negotiations started. Due to the high political and economic stakes, which were only realistically realized after the Kyoto Conference by most actors (Kanie 2003), governments wanted full control over the process. To measure influence is fraught with methodological difficulties (Betsill and Corell 2008). But in this case it is straightforward to provide a crude measure of the lack of influence of scientists and environmental NGOs due to the huge discrepancy between their position and negotiation outcomes. The IPCC has become increasingly alarmist and certain that emissions are man-made and has strongly stressed the need for dramatic reductions. This message has been endorsed by the environmental community but neither group has been listened to by negotiator; but there are some nuances in the picture. The strong support of environmental NGOs for the legally-binding agreed (LBA) target and time-table approach may have had some effect for this approach to be dominating for so long. Whether this is "good" is as noted, not self-evident. When environmental NGOs have alliances with powerful states, influence may be enhanced but the problem of causality also looms large in such cases (Gulbransen and Andresen 2004). Domestic environmental NGO lobbying may have been somewhat more effective, particularly in the EU, while business influence has been stronger in the United States (Vig and Faure 2004). At the international level one of the rare instances of direct environmental NGO influence is their role played in assisting and creating understanding for the AOSIS countries. Still, the overall picture in terms of their direct influence of scientists as well as environmental NGOs is very modest.

The more indirect influence from these actors, bypassing the process of negotiation, however, should not be underestimated. Over the past 20 years the perceptions of the climate change problem has changed beyond recognition, especially in the Western world, but one can also see advertisements for a climate-friendly green economy on the subways in Beijing, unthinkable some years ago (Stensdal 2012). Climate change is no longer seen as a complex, vague and unreal scientific proposition. Climate variations and weather events are now commonly interpreted as effects of climate change. Both scientists and the environmental community have probably contributed more to these new widely-held perceptions and actions than the sterile climate negotiations. They can become quite influential particularly when these non-state actors work together, and are also "assisted" by external events.

Between 2005–2008, climate change attracted unprecedented interest in the media and the public at large. This was a period characterized by strong economic growth, and the assumed effects of climate change were effectively visualized in the media and the green community through melting glaciers, polar bears looking for ice, and tropical storms and natural disasters like Hurricane Katrina. Such visualization – in contrast to more slowly emerging and invisible environmental threats – often facilitates scientific influence (Underdal 1989). The prestige of the IPCC also received a boost when it was awarded the Nobel Peace Prize (together with Al Gore) in 2007. The combination of positive economic development, effective NGO lobbying, visualization of the problem and a strong consensual scientific message have probably contributed to a lot of the climate measures and activities, initiated at various governance levels. It may also have contributed somewhat to the relative success of the COP13 in Bali. However, the vulnerability of this "coalition" was demonstrated when the economic crisis hit the world economy during the fall of 2008. The public sentiment shifted dramatically and the recovery of the economy was the name of the game, not climate change. Opinion polls showed declining interest in the issue, probably reinforced by the decreased legitimacy of the IPCC through "climate-gate." In short, the development of the economy and public opinion are important drivers in explaining the development of climate policies, an aspect neglected in our perspective.

Regardless of variations in the economy and public opinion, a strong and enduring momentum has been created outside the formal negotiations to deal with climate change. It may be that a global norm to combat climate change has emerged. At least rising emissions do not equal inaction on the ground. All kinds of actors – and actor configurations – participate in these initiatives: cities, local authorities, emissions trading schemes at various levels, international organizations, environmental NGOs, various grass-roots organizations, important sectors of the business community as well as research organizations (Cole 2011; Abbott 2013). In some of these processes the UNFCCC Secretariat plays an important coordinating role. One only needs to look at the incredible number of side events at the climate COPs, exhibiting vigor, energy and innovation – in stark contrast to the sterile and slow process of negotiations. However most of them have sprung up outside the framework of the negotiation process. These actors certainly contribute to "good governance" and most of them are probably doing an excellent job. We doubt that there are any other environmental issue areas with such activity and creativity. Thus, in order to get a more comprehensive overview of what is happening within this issue area and as the most interesting actions take place outside the UN negotiations, one needs to cast the net wider than what was done in the Introduction in terms of relevant actors.

Non-state actors like environmental NGOs, scientists and IOs have had limited direct influence on the process of negotiations, but together with a number of other non-state actors they have been important in spurring a wide range of activities outside the process of negotiations. Throughout, the role of the economy as well as public opinion has been important for the course of actions.

Mending the UN regime? Supplementary approaches and "quick fixes"

The discussion on improving the UN process has focused on various design principles as well as drawing lessons from non-environmental regimes like weapons and trade regimes (UNEP/WRI 2011; Greenspan and Ziegler 2012). A number of interesting and highly relevant points are discussed such as the need to build mutual trust through reporting and verification: the significance of the legal approach should not be overrated; ratification means very different things to different countries; although a treaty is not ratified, it may still be followed in practice; the need to simplify the process through outsourcing of some issues to other regimes; "variable geometry" (differences in commitments) and "graduation" (capacities change over time). Our main problem with these as well as other interesting suggestions is that they are not discussed in terms of *political feasibility* (Biermann *et al.* 2010). That is, we believe quite a few of the negotiators are aware of these problems – as well as the potential remedies – but they cannot be implemented as one or more key parties object to them. In that sense to look at supplementary approaches is more interesting as they exist in practice, many in the form of various types of partnerships.

For a long time the UN climate regime was the "only game in town," but over the last few years a number of other relevant institutions have been established or seen as relevant for climate change. Some cast the net very wide and Abbott has identified 69 relevant institutions while others zoom in on some of the most obvious candidates (Abbott 2012; Keohane and Victor 2011). We can only discuss a few of these. The most important candidate for a long time was the Asia Pacific Partnership on Clean Development and Climate (APP) established in 2006 with the United States and Australia as the founding fathers. The composition of APP was highly interesting as other large emitters were involved: China, Japan, Canada, South Korea and India. Officially APP was set up as a supplement to the UN regime, but it has been documented that its founding fathers saw it more as a potential alternative (McGee 2010). Its architecture was also almost diametrically opposed to the UN regime. Apart from its exclusive nature there were no binding commitments, a bottom-up approach, and it was based on the philosophy that environmental quality improves with economic growth. In contrast to the economy-wide approach of the Kyoto Protocol, the APP represented a sectoral approach where partners collaborated closely with business and industry on eight specific sectors. The environmental NGO community strongly resented the APP and most discussion was concentrated on whether this was a threat to the UNFCCC or not (McGee 2010). The added value of APP remains questionable. There was no mechanism to evaluate GHG emissions reduction in APP, and many of the activities are based on business-as-usual cooperation within the sectors. Limited activities were addressed on technology development and transfer, which were supposed to have been their primary target (Kanie *et al.* 2013).

In 2011 it was decided to close it down. With new and more pro-UN administrations in both the United States and Australia the political momentum seems to have disappeared. However, three of the eight task forces continued under a new partnership, the Global Superior Energy Performance Partnership (GSEP) with a stronger focus on environmental performance, and the aim is to expand participation to a global scale (Fujiwara 2012). It was a result of an initiative of the Clean Energy Ministerial Meeting in 2010 and has been accepted as a task group under the International Partnership for Energy Efficiency Cooperation (IPEEC). This partnership accounts for 75 percent of global GDP and the EU is also a member. This initiative has not been very visible and it is unknown what has come out of it.

Another US initiative under the Bush administration was the establishment of the Major Economies Meeting in 2007, representing an informal discussion forum for the world's largest economies – and emitters – responsible for some 80 percent of total emissions. This initiative was *de facto* endorsed by the Obama administration through the establishment of the Major Economies Forum (MEF) in 2009. Obama has been pushing this initiative quite actively as he stresses the need to have supplements to the UN process. Both the IPEEC and the MEF have focused on development of clean technologies. Other more exclusive forums like the G-8, the G-20 as well as the World Economic Forum (WEF) have a somewhat different focus aiming to create an informal mechanism for dialogue with different stakeholders (Kim and Chung 2012). Such more limited forums could also be important in gradually breaking down the sterile barrier between Annex I and non-Annex I plaguing the UN process as the countries in the G-20 meet on a more equal footing. Regarding the G-20 it has also been argued that it has been quite important in terms of securing finance at COP 15, engaging with business as well as working towards reducing energy subsidies (Kim and Chung 2012). The 2°C goal was also first discussed at a G-8 meeting. Although the potential of such forums should not be underestimated, so far they have been better at setting ambitious goals rather than implementing them (Barbier 2010).

Another more exclusive approach is the Climate and Clean Air Coalition (CCAC), launched in February 2012 by UNEP and six countries, including the United States and Canada, both very active in promoting this initiative. The goal is to reduce the emission of black carbon, or soot. Recent research has shown that this is a much bigger contributor to climate change than previously thought. It is now regarded the second most important source of global warming. What makes it particularly interesting is the fact that it is very short lived, compared to CO_2, giving reductions an immediate effect. Emissions – as well as health problems – following from black carbon are primarily a problem in developing countries and largely result from dirty stoves. Thus, if realized, this can be a win–win cost-effective approach and membership has expanded rapidly, with almost 30 countries from both developed and developing world. However finance has been modest so far. The initiative has been met with some skepticism from the green community as it has been spear-headed by the United States and Canada which do not have a proactive climate policy at home, focusing instead on developing countries' emissions. It is also notable than none of the BASIC countries have yet joined the club.

As noted, a number of other partnerships with varying focus and participation have been established and some of them have been rather extensively analyzed (Greene 2013; Abbott 2013). However these analyses tend to take a "process-perspective," giving an account of these vibrant and creative activities without focusing on whether this leads to reduced emissions. We agree that: "The real test is whether these other forums are achieving their core purpose of reducing GHG emissions" (Greenspan and Ziegler 2012). But as this question is rarely addressed we do not know whether this is the case. But we know that bottom-line, global emissions are rising. Therefore, however creative many of these partnerships may be, like the UN regime they are powerless to stop the rising emissions.

Another more fundamental but also controversial "quick fix" is geo-engineering. Geo-engineering refers to the deliberate and large-scale intervention of the Earth climate system to moderate global warming. There are two main approaches. One is the carbon dioxide removal techniques addressing the root causes of climate change by removing the gases from the atmosphere. The other is the solar radiation approach attempting to offset the effects of greenhouse gases by causing the earth to absorb less solar radiation. These techniques have usually been suggested as supplements to adaptation and mitigation, not as a substitute. Still, geo-engineering represents the only possible technique to reduce temperatures in the short term. However, so far only computer modeling is conducted and no large-scale project has been carried out. Needless to say the technique is highly controversial and the IPPCC in its last report concluded that this option remained largely unproven (Bodansky 2011).

Conclusion: good governance, bad governance or mission impossible?

There is no environmental problem that has been attacked with so much political, economic and institutional vigor at all governance levels as the climate change problem. By far, the most important forum has been the UNFCCC negotiations in which all nations of the world have been heavily involved for more than 20 years of increasingly intense negotiations. As expected, non-state actors played key roles at the agenda-setting stage and activists of various kinds were instrumental in framing how to deal with the issue. This approach was endorsed by most state actors and the environmental community as the most effective and ambitious approach. Although these activists and subsequently states did not underestimate the seriousness of the problem, they underestimated the complexity, and it is uncertain whether the target and time-table approach was the superior approach. The United States played a key role in setting up the IPCC and in deciding its intergovernmental nature. Whether this governance approach is good or bad is also a contested issue. Overall, agenda setting proved to be very important for the subsequent negotiations as the main conflict lines were established and have remained virtually unchanged until today, a major reason for the lack of progress.

The process of negotiations was initially quite dynamic, primarily as the traditional antagonists, the United States and the EU, agreed on LBA in the COPs leading up to the adoption of the Kyoto Protocol. Although states have invested significantly more time and resources in the UN process, over the last decade progress has been very limited as political will on the part of major actors has been lacking. Pusher–laggard dynamics proved more problematic than expected, not the least as other factors than climate politics is crucial in determining the level of emissions. Also, it is not self-evident that the LBA has been the most effective approach and what has been judged a laggard approach at one time has later been regarded as a pusher approach. Also, while emerging economies may be seen as laggards in a problem-solving perspective this is not the case in an equity perspective, stressing the significance of historic emissions. Still, unless both industrialized and major developing countries agree to take on much tougher measures the problem will never be solved and the simple North-South "firewall" needs to be removed. Owing to the high political stakes involved, the process has been extremely state centric, and environmental NGOs, IOs and scientists have had very limited direct effect on the process of negotiations. It may well be that more could have been achieved if these actors had more influence, but that has not been politically feasible. Still, the indirect influence of these actors in triggering action at other levels by bypassing the negotiators should not be underestimated. It may be that a global norm to combat climate change is emerging which, at the least, would provide an important backdrop for movement in improving all components of climate change governance.

The compliance system of the climate regime is virtually non-existent for the large majority of members and it has not really been put up for test with the Kyoto Protocol. Most Kyoto partners have complied with their commitments, but non-related climate drivers like economic development, population increase (or decrease) and changing energy mix often make a huge difference. Illustrating this point, the United States, a non-Kyoto partner, is among the countries with the steepest emissions reductions over the last few years. Therefore, a much more refined system for measuring the development of emissions is needed. Variations in public opinion may also make a difference for action on the ground, a perspective not reflected on our analytical perspective.

A number of institutions, often various types of partnerships, have been established to deal with the issue outside the UN regime. Many analysts have praised these initiatives as an important contribution to a multi-level or polycentric approach needed to bypass the state-centric sterile UN negotiations. This may well be the case, but we know little or nothing about what all these initiatives have caused in terms of what should be their goal: emissions reductions. As the bottom line is steadily increasing emissions, we know that neither the UN nor other approaches have so far been able to reverse this trend. Based on existing projections for economic growth, population growth and energy mix, exceeding the 2°-goal of the Copenhagen Accord seems unavoidable. In order to make significant progress we need international pressures to rapidly accelerate technological change. This issue is more extensively discussed in the concluding chapter where we present some more "visionary" ideas on how to approach the climate issue.

References

Abbott, K. (2012) 'The transitional regime complex for climate change', *Environment and Planning Government and Policy*, 30, 571–590.

Abbott, K. (2013) 'Constructing a transnational climate change regime: Bypassing and managing states', *Social Science Research Network (SSRN)*, February 9.

Aftenposten, January 16, 2013, 'That is why the U.S. turns into a climate hero (in Norwegian)'.

Agrawala, S. (1998) 'Context and early origins of the intergovernmental panel on climate change', *Climatic Change*, 39 (4), 605–620.

Agrawala, S. and Andresen, S. (1999) 'Indispensability and indefensibility? The United States in the climate treaty negotiations', *Global Governance: A Review of Multilateralism and International Organizations,* 5 (4), 457–482.

Aldy, J. E. and Stavins, R. N., eds. (2007) *Architectures for Agreement*, Cambridge: Cambridge University Press.

Andresen, S. and Agrawala, S. (2002) 'Leaders, pushers and laggards in the making of the climate regime', *Global Environmental Change*, 12 (1), 41–51.

Andresen, S. and Butenschøn, S. (2001) 'Norwegian climate policy: From pusher to laggard?', *International Environmental Agreements: Politics, Law and Economics,* Volume 1 No. 3, 337–356.

Andresen, S. and Rosendal, K. (2009) 'The role of the United Nations Environment Programme in the coordination of multilateral environmental agreements', in Biermann, Frank, Bernd Siebenhuner and Anna Schreyogg, eds., *International Organizations in Global Environmental Governance,* London: Routledge, 133–151.

Antholis, W. and Talbott, S. (2010) *Fast Forward: Ethics and Politics in the Age of Global Warming*, Brookings Focus Book.

Barbier, E. B. (2010) 'A global green recovery, the G20 and international STO cooperation in clean energy', *STI Policy Review,* 1 (3), 1–15.

Bauer, S. (2009) 'The desertification secretariat: a castle made of sand', in Biermann, Frank and Bernd Siebenhuner, eds., *Managers of Global Change: The Influence of Environmental Bureaucracies,* Cambridge: MA: MIT Press.

Betsill, M. and Corell, E., eds. (2008) *NGO Diplomacy The Influence of Nongovernmental Organizations in International Environmental Negotiations*, Cambridge: MA: MIT Press.

Biermann, F. and Pattberg, P. *et al.*, eds. (2010) *Global Climate Change Governance Beyond 2012: Architecture, Agency and Adaptation*, Cambridge: Cambridge University Press.

Bodansky, D. (1993) 'The United Nations framework convention on climate change: A commentary', *Yale Journal of International Law,* 18, 451–558.

Bodansky, D. (2011) 'Governing climate engineering: scenarios for analysis', Discussion Paper 2011-47, Harvard Project on Climate Agreements.

Bodansky, D. and Rajamani, L. (2012) 'The evolution and governance architecture of the climate change regime', October 28, *Social Science Research Network (SSRN).*

Bulkeley, H. and Schroeder, H. (2011) 'Beyond state/non-state divides: Global cities and the governing of climate change', *European Journal of International Relations,*18 (4),741–764.

Bush, P.-O. (2009) 'The climate secretariat: Making a living in a straitjacket', in Biermann, Frank and Bernd Siebenhuner, eds., *Managers of Global Change The Influence of Environmental Bureaucracies,* Cambridge, MA: MIT Press, 245–265.

Cole, D. H. (2011) 'From global to polycentric climate governance', *EUI Working Papers (RSCAS 2011/30),* Robert Schuman Center for Advanced Studies, European University Institute.

Council, I. (2010) Climate Change Assessments: Review of the Process and Procedures of the IPCC.

Depledge, J. (2007) 'A special relationship: Chairpersons and the Secretariat in the climate change negotiations', *Global Environmental Politics,* 7 (1), 45–68.

ENB, Earth Negotiating Bulletin (ENB) Volume 12 No. 231.

ENB, Earth Negotiating Bulletin (ENB) Volume 12 No. 260.

Fujiwara, N. (2012) 'Sector-specific activities as the driving force towards a low-carbon economy from the Asia-Pacific partnership to a global partnership', *Center for European Policy Briefs (CEPS) Policy Brief,* No. 262, January 2012.

Greene, J. (2013) 'Order out of chaos: Public and private rules for managing carbon', *Global Environmental Politics,* 13 (2), 1–25.

Greenspan, B. R. and Ziegler, M. *et al.* (2012) *Building International Climate Cooperation Lessons from the Weapons and Trade Regimes for Achieving International Climate Goals,* Washington, DC: World Resources Institute.

Gulbrandsen, L. and Andresen, S. (2004) 'NGO influence in the implementation of the Kyoto Protocol: Compliance, flexibility mechanisms and sinks', *Global Environmental Politics,* 4 (4), 54–75.

Haas, P. M. (2004) 'When does power listen to truth? A constructivist approach to the policy process', *Journal of European Public Policy,* 11 (4), 569–592.

Halvorsen, A. and Hovi, J. (2006) 'The nature, origin and impact of legally binding consequences: The case of the climate regime', *International Environmental Agreements,* 6 (2), 157–171.

Harrison, K. and Sundstrom, L. M. (2007) 'The comparative politics of climate change', *Global Environmental Politics,* 7 (4), 1–19.

Hattori, T. (1999) 'The road to the Kyoto Conference: An assessment of the Japanese two-dimensional negotiation', *International Negotiation,* 4 (2), 167–195.

Hoffmann, M. J. (2011) *Climate Governance at the Crossroads,* Oxford: Oxford University Press.

Hovi, J., Skodvin, T. and Andersen, S. (2003) 'The persistence of the Kyoto Protocol: Why other Annex 1 countries move without the United States', *Global Environmental Politics,* 3 (4), 1–24.

International Institute for Sustainable Development (IISD) Report, December 2011.

Kanie, N. (2003) 'Leadership in multilateral negotiation and domestic policy: The Netherlands at the Kyoto Protocol negotiation', *International Negotiation,* 8, 339–365.

Kanie, N., Suzuki, M. and Iguchi, M. (2013) 'Fragmentation of international low-carbon technology governance: An assessment in terms of barriers to technology development', *Global Environmental Research*, 17, (1).

Keohane, R. and Victor, D. (2011) 'The regime complex for climate change', *Perspectives on Politics,* March, 9 (7), 7–23.

Kim, J. A. and Chung, S-Y. (2012) 'The role of the G20 in governing the climate change regime', *International Environmental Agreements: Politics, Law and Economics*, published online May 12.

Lee, T. (2013) 'Global cities and transnational climate change networks', *Global Environmental Politics*, 13 (1), 108–127.

Lund, E. (2013) 'Hybrid governance in practice. Public and private actors in the Kyoto Protocol's clean development mechanism', Ph.D. Thesis, Lund University, Sweden.

McGee, J. (2010) 'The Asia Pacific partnership and contestation for the future of the international climate regime', Ph.D. Thesis, Graduate School of the Environment, Macquarie University, Sydney, Australia.

Oberthur, S. and Lefeber, R. (2010) 'Holding countries to account: The Kyoto Protocol's compliance system revised after four years' experience', *Climate Law*, 1 (1), 133–158.

Ostrom E. (2010) 'Polycentric systems for coping with collective action and global environmental change', *Global Environmental Change*, 20, 550–557.

Rosendal, K. and Andresen, S. (2011) 'Institutional design for improved forest governance through REDD: Lessons from the Global Environmental Facility', *Ecological Economics*, 70 (11), 1918–1925.

Selin, H. and VanDeveer, S. (2007) 'Political science and predictions: What is next for US climate change policy?', *Review of Policy Research,* 24, (1), 1–27.

Skjærseth, J. B. (2013) *The EU Climate and Energy Package: Causes, Content and Consequences*, Report 2, Oslo: Fridtjof Nansen Institute.

Skodvin, T. and Andresen, S. (2006) 'Leadership revisited', *Global Environmental Politics*, 6 (3), 13–27.

Skodvin, T. and Andresen, S. (2009) 'An agenda for change in US climate policies? Presidential ambitions and Congressional powers', *International Environmental Agreements: Politics, Law and Economics*, 9, 263–280.

Stensdal, I. (2012) 'China's climate change policy 1988–2011: From zero to hero?' *FNI Report*, 10, The Fridtjof Nansen Institute.

Torney, D. and Fujiwara, N. (2010) 'National commitments, compliance and the future of the Kyoto Protocol', *Center for European Policy Studies (CEPS) Policy Brief*, No.226/ November.

Underdal, A. (1989) 'The politics of science in international resource management: A summary', in Andresen, Steinar and Willy Østreng, eds., *International Resource Management,* London and New York: Belhaven Press, 253–269.

UNEP and World Resources Institute (2011) 'Building the climate change regime survey and analysis of approaches', Working Paper.

Victor, D. (2011) *Global Warming Gridlock Creating More Effective Strategies for Protecting the Planet*, Cambridge: Cambridge University Press.

Vig, N. J. and Faure, M. G., eds. (2004) *Green Giants Environmental Policies of the United States and the European Union*, Cambridge: MA: MIT Press.

Wynn, P. (2012) 'Global greenhouse gas emissions continue to rise', *The Christian Science Monitor,* July 20.

9 Conclusion

Lessons from pluralistic green governance

Norichika Kanie, Peter M. Haas and Steinar Andresen

It has been 40 years since the first United Nations conference on the environment (United Nations Conference on Human Environment, UNCHE) was held in Stockholm in 1972. Issues at the time were mostly about coordinating responses to many local environmental problems, such as air pollution, water pollution and waste management, which had emerged as a result of rapid economic growth in many industrialized countries. Forty years later, science has presented a variety of environmental problems that were not politically recognized by many in 1972. We have witnessed in recent years environmental phenomena unprecedented in frequency and magnitude of events. Causes and effects of many of these problems are global in nature, crossing well beyond man-made national borders, although many "traditional" environmental problems remain in existence or have become worsened. To aggravate the situation, many of these problems are likely to cause abrupt and irreversible changes that may make it impossible to maintain the Earth's life-support system in healthy shape (Rockström *et al.* 2009).

These changing characteristics of collective problems mean that actions to tackle them should change as well (Biermann *et al.* 2012a, 2012b; Kanie *et al.* 2012). Global environmental problems can no longer be dealt with independently of coupled and causally connected issues. Despite these transformative challenges, institutions dealing with the environment or issues of sustainability (to put it in a broader context) remain based on state-oriented designs and processes of international relations established in the past century. Some environmental policy events in recent years, such as the Copenhagen Climate Change Conference (COP 15), the Commission on Sustainable Development's nineteenth session, and Rio Plus 20 – all of which failed to produce satisfactory outcomes – are examples of the stalemate the world is facing. Sovereign states no longer tackle the new challenges solely by themselves as international relations since the 1970s have increasingly been conducted through interactions amongst state and various types of non-state actors. We need to better recognize a post-national-sovereignty order that mirrors the current dynamics of international relations.

A key feature of such post-sovereign governance is the emergent division of labor amongst actors involved in environmental governance (Meyer 1997; Andresen *et al.* 2000; Miles *et al.* 2002; Kanie and Haas 2004; Busch *et al.* 2005; Pauly and Grande 2005; Haas 2007) that comprises global green pluralism. The research presented in this book identifies some of the best, and worst to some extent, practices in terms of configuration of actors in the various governance components. Some examples confirm the hypotheses as put forward in Chapter 1, which are largely drawn from the extensive secondary literature on international environmental governance and considerations of the motivations and resources of each actor group, while others reject the hypotheses and present new findings based on in-depth case studies.

The next section summarizes the findings of the chapters, cast in terms of different governance components. This will be followed by our observations on the key findings from this research project with particular focus on linkages between components, network and configuration of actor groups, and legitimacy. Finally we make a challenge to apply our findings into climate change as a "test case" before concluding.

Insights about actor configuration in governance components

Our approach to case studies

The overlapping cases across components confirm our initial hunch that the array of actors varies between components, even for the same regime. In particular the actual actors within these analytic clusters vary widely. For example, while a small number of major IOs recur frequently across issues and regimes – most notably UNEP – the NGOs, epistemic communities and private firms are much more selective. Most of these non-state actors may be active in one component of a particular regime, but they are not necessarily present in all of the same components for each regime, or present across regimes. There is no coherence to multi-actor governance. Environmental governance with an actor-based focus remains highly differentiated. While there is an emergent set of pressures from growing non-state involvement in international environmental politics, its effect remains very specialized. This is not to say that it is insignificant; it contributes to improved governance of many environmental problems, including epistemic communities in agenda setting, ENGOs in negotiation, and IOs in implementation and compliance.

The cases studies span a variety of different environmental challenges. For example, the three case studies in Chapter 3, namely the Vienna Convention for the Protection of the Ozone Layer, the Convention on Biological Diversity and its Cartagena Protocol on Biosafety, and the United Nations Convention to Combat Desertification (UNCCD), represent the ubiquitous common features of virtually all trans-boundary and global environmental threats. They require international collective action by states concerned about distributive issues, reciprocity, and effectiveness. In addition all are related to broad international management problems such as chemicals management, biodiversity, technology and trade, as well as land management and economic development. They are all global in scale, although UNCCD is considered by many as a case of scale mismatch.

The cases selected are those that the chapter authors regarded as most salient for addressing the questions about the actors engaged in performing the components they studied. The cases in Chapter 3 are very different in character from those chosen in other chapters. For example, the EU plays a distinctive role in Chapter 2, which deals only with cases on regional agreements (LRTAP and the Baltic), while such a distinctive role of the EU is absent in the other cases and components. Chapter 4 derives lessons from global and regional scales of international governance. Reflecting the global nature of international shipping, the IMO has near-universal membership whereas the Fisheries case highlights the interplay of two regional institutions, the Russo-Norwegian Joint Fisheries Commission and the broader NEAFC. Similarly, the compliance lessons derived from the Nuclear-dumping case brings out the division of labor that has evolved between global institutions like the IAEA and the IMO-based dumping regime and several regional bodies, including the G8, capable of generating funds and technologies for capacity-building purposes. These different cases are selected as they are considered to represent best, or worst, practices in each governance component in view of actor configurations.

The degree of malignancy of the issues varies at the international and national level. Internationally some of the most contentious and difficult have been Desertification and Biodiversity, whereas Ozone is widely regarded as one of the great triumphs of multilateral environmental diplomacy. At the regional level Desertification is particularly malignant (if desertification is properly viewed as a regional scale challenge). However, general regional cooperation is usually more benign, simply because there are fewer actors involved. Cooperation is easier if it takes place in the richer OECD region where the differences in will and ability between the actors are less pronounced than within global regimes. Over time European cooperative efforts have become quite effective due to the political and economic efforts and effects of the EU integration, and the political context in Europe becomes less malign with the end of the Cold War. Climate change, as discussed earlier, is probably one of the most malign issues facing decision makers, making insights and learning from lessons regarding good governance practices from other regimes and components particularly important. However, in order to discuss the relevance of these insights, we always have to control for problem structure. That is, unfortunately, the successful features from benign issue areas cannot simply be copied in more malign issue areas like climate change.

In line with previous research, however, we see that the "malign–benign" dichotomy is not written in stone (Miles *et al.* 2002). Good performance of the regime components helped to shift problems which appeared malign at the state level of analysis to be more benign problems. Agenda setting in LRTAP helped change state preferences about negotiated settlements, and led to more effective controls over sulphur dioxide through the application of the critical loads idea (Haas and McCabe 2001; VanDeveer 2004; Ishii 2011; VanDeveer in this volume). Changing the international institutional context and elevating the level of political participation to the Ministerial level in the North Sea and Baltic regions also helped overcome deadlock in negotiations.

Our findings suggest that problem structure can be altered when configuration of actors is effectively in place.

Agenda setting

Agenda setting here is seen as a set of complex processes that are embedded in larger, ongoing social and political institutions and dynamics, rather than a one-off event. Desirable agenda setting is a process that confidently identifies and updates problems for collective governance that are real and can be tractably addressed. We have witnessed this process occurring over a period of 30 or 40 years in the case studies, and even longer in other environmental regimes, such as pesticide use in developing countries, or climate change. Agenda setting typically precedes negotiations, with the focus on framing of the issue. Subsequently, agenda setting continues in parallel with negotiation and – for long-term regimes – compliance and implementation, which also feeds back into agenda setting. Therefore, issues like compliance and implementation, and thus funding and equity, can become agenda items in themselves.

Contrary to our hypotheses about agenda setting, states have played a greater role than expected. We expected good agenda setting to come from the combination of science NGOs, media and international organizations (IOs), but Chapter 2 pointed out that leading states played a major role. States have important roles in maintaining environmental policy networks during the continuous agenda-setting process, and often IOs help coordinate these networks. VanDeveer also points to the importance of a high-level approach in agenda setting, evident in the Baltic region and particularly important in the 1980s and the 1990s because of lack of effort by bureaucrats, mired in collective action problems which impeded taking bold actions. He suggests that shaping state institutions and actors is the most important leverage point for shaping the international agenda over the years, although the causal relations have not yet been entirely clarified.

There is a need to differentiate the role of states. We know that leading states and laggard states play different roles in negotiation. This distinction should also be recognized in agenda setting. States are not the unitary category of actors they were – maybe a bit naively – assumed to be in Chapter 1. Whereas lead states in these cases, the Nordic states and Germany, and more recently the European Union (EU), play a crucial role in agenda setting throughout both processes, the laggard states (in this case, the Soviet Union/Russia), play no role whatsoever. Laggard states may be more important in preventing effective implementation of ambitious goals set forth in the agenda setting, which in turn affects agenda setting for the next stage.

States with strong scientific capacity played an active role in setting the international agenda on environmental issues which they have identified as being salient to them. But questions remain: do strong domestic institutions lead to leadership, or is it that the leading states have decided to invest in building effective institutions at the domestic level? For instance, once enforcement capacities have been improved, do the countries become more vigorous leaders in rule making? Further work is necessary to answer these questions.

Furthermore, this insight leads us to pay attention to yet another important state-based institution but one that goes beyond the nation state system – the key role of the EU in agenda setting. Successful agenda setting of the LRTAP is linked to the increasingly important role of the EU in international environmental policy. The EU is particularly important as many members to the LRTAP Convention are also members of the EU. The EU appears to function as a device to scale-up a state-level initiative by the leading states to mobilize international processes. That is, when successfully mobilizing international decision-making, the EU can function as a power device for a member state to international process (Kanie 2003). The EU was equally important for agenda setting in the Baltic. As the integration of Central and Eastern European countries into the EU coincides with the agenda-setting process of the Baltic, the newly integrated countries had to satisfy the EU policy standards and regulations; EU goals in the HELCOM action plan are simultaneously pursued. Because countries in the Baltic region did not have advanced and comprehensive environmental policy comparable to the European Union, EU policies helped to raise the level of their policies. This is an example of interests which are not directly environmental, such as European integration in this case, propelling environmental policy.

Although the EU has been important in agenda setting in these cases, we should be careful about generalizing these lessons. For both cases the setting is regional and mainly European, probably the most advanced region in the environmental arena in the world today. Attention should therefore be paid to the particular political culture of Europe. A simultaneous integration process with regime development is one thing, but the unique features of Europe are another, such as its culture of networks, or a tendency to utilize regulation and a target-based approach to policies (Kohler-Koch 1995; Peterson 1995; Ansell 2000; Marks, Hooghe *et al.* 1996; Hooghe and Marks 2001; Marks and Hooghe 2004; Sabel and Zeitlin 2010). In terms of actor configuration, however, in principle important roles that a regional organization could play may still be applied to other regions. Regional organization may externally provide added value for leading states by providing additional power, while internally it facilitates the upgrading of policy standards throughout the member states. In practice, however, no other regional organizations so far have the political and economic clout possessed by the EU.

Networks play an important role throughout the agenda-setting process, and increase in importance over time. The LRTAP has a stable, narrow network with a scientific and technical orientation, and therefore may be considered by some to lack as much legitimacy. Apart from the established scientific bodies in the regime, the International Institute for Applied Systems Analysis (IIASA) and the Organization for Economic Co-operation and Development (OECD) are key actors. They provide models and cost estimates that are directly used in policies adopted. Importantly, representatives of lead states are also included in the network, keeping the inter-governmental process in the loop and securing the representatives informed. Business and industry are not explicitly included in the network, but they had interactions with the process through the Secretariat and working groups on best available technologies (Haas and McCabe 2001).

In contrast, the Baltic had significantly more actors included in very broad networks. Such broad networks are instrumental in bringing in a broader and more holistic approach, and increase legitimacy. However, as it is so broad, the agenda-setting function directly linked to the regime-building process is hard to pin down exactly. Although initially there was a strong link to HELCOM, it is hard to identify causal relations between the networks and agenda setting over time.

Although Chapter 2 did not investigate poor agenda-setting practices in detail, drawing on insights from other chapters, the agenda setting for UNCCD is rather controversial. At first glance, it could be considered a case of bad agenda setting as the problem was cast on a global scale where it has subsequently failed to attract the attention of the major international actors and did not lead to negotiated outcomes that were implemented (Stringer 2008). In our language the agenda was inaccurate and not tractable. Whereas the salient stakeholders and actors affected by desertification were regional – African – the issues was conceptually misspecified as a global problem. However, this could be construed as clever agenda-setting, as it shed light on the land degradation issue, which is otherwise overlooked by the international community, at the expense of attracting funding support from the international community.

Negotiation

States are the key players in international multilateral negotiations. Chapter 3 confirmed that their role was crucial for successfully negotiated settlements. Our hypothesis on the relations between "pusher" states and good agreement is strongly confirmed. If the pusher states are strong, the chances of reaching a successful agreement are higher and if the laggard states are strong, the chances of reaching a successful agreement are low. If negotiated settlements are reached in such cases they are likely to be mere hollow shells. In the much studied case of ozone, a strong pusher state (the United States) played a key role in forging the agreement, resulting in an effective regime. Indeed, agreement was also reached in the UNCCD and Cartagena Protocol, but the pusher state was exceedingly weak in the former case, while the pusher and laggards were equally strong in the latter, resulting in less-successful settlements. The findings in Chapter 3 as well as prior analysis have demonstrated that pusher states in combination with epistemic communities provide treaties which reflect substantive scientific consensus and are more environmentally effective, for such instances as stratospheric ozone and LRTAP, than those negotiated without scientific participation (Haas 2007; Andresen 2000; Miles *et al.* 2001; Underdal 2002).

Other actors may play important roles in negotiations as well. For example, international organization (IO) may have an important role to create a linkage between the network of scientific actors and negotiation process as in the case of ozone, which contributed to successful settlements. Contrary to this is the case of UNCCD, where strong scientific networks existed in various related issue areas and there was also a strong epistemic community around desertification and dry land degradation, but there was a mismatch between these communities and issues discussed in negotiation. No international organization intervened to create an effective linkage between the network of scientists and the multilateral negotiation process. Actually, the Secretariat did create a scientific expert panel, but there were some players who saw this as a development cooperation treaty and not an environmental treaty, and downplayed science.

This observation resonates well with our hypothesis that "strong international organizations and epistemic communities are likely to generate effective negotiated settlements." When IOs play an active role, stronger negotiated settlements are more likely. Similarly, strong epistemic communities are also likely to generate stronger negotiated settlements, but on condition that there is scientific consensus and opportunities for scientists to make an input to the negotiations. In the biosafety issue there is strong science, but disagreement is also strong with no "neutral" scientific basis and scientists tend to work either with business or environmental actors, which was leading to a weak agreement.

The stronger and more united industry positions are, the more effective they are at influencing the scope of negotiated settlements. In the case of Ozone, business and industry groups were split at the beginning. However, over time they found common ground to accept stronger regulations following anticipated new markets from CFC substitutes. Similarly, when key industrial players are opposed to strong regulations like in the Cartagena Protocol, key states refrain from participation, strongly reducing the value of the agreement.

Chasek argues that the agreements are more successful when there are networks across actor groups. There was a strong and uniform network over time in the case of ozone, which was one probable reason for the successful agreement. In the Cartagena Protocol's case, there were two opposing networks reflecting the two opposing blocks in negotiation. The result was an agreement that was neither very effective nor universal.[1] There were no discernible networks across actor groups in the UNCCD and the agreement was exceedingly weak.

The influence of NGOs often depended more on their ability to network or to cooperate with state parties than on their ability to participate in the negotiations. It is often believed by researchers, practitioners and policy analysts that the more open the access to negotiations for NGOs, the more successful the negotiated settlement, as NGOs are considered to be the true champions of the environment. Interestingly, the cases do not support this assumption, as they had least access when the Montreal Protocol was negotiated and most access to the UNCCD. In the end, participation is about the legitimacy of the process rather than about the success of the negotiation, and NGO participation is often contested among states. Even when the distance in interests and positions between the NGOs and key states is large, NGOs' network with some weaker states still functioned as a counterbalance to laggards. NGOs are also included in some states' delegations, while not included in those of other states (Green 2008; Kanie 2013). The degree of NGO participation may have more impact on vertical linkage in governance rather than the effectiveness of negotiated settlements. The UNCCD illustrates this well. There was fairly open access for local actors, but the level of ambition and effectiveness is low. In the ozone regime, they played an important role in lobbying/networking at the domestic level.

Compliance

Chapter 4 focuses on four compliance tasks – verification, review, assistance and sanctions. Most of the hypotheses presented in the introduction are corroborated in Stokke's chapter. Partnerships between multinational corporations (MNCs) and NGOs can lead to effective enforcement and compliance, including partnerships on the ground between productive sectors and NGOs. This is the case in the sanctions part of a compliance system where environmental NGOs (ENGOs) and MNCs that are interested in driving swindlers out of the market or protecting their international reputation work together. And this supports another hypothesis about MNCs: the MNCs that anticipate net discounted benefits will comply and contribute to better compliance performance among others. It is also confirmed that capacity building, an important activity in the assistance task, facilitating rule adherence and supporting transnational expert networks centered on IOs, can improve compliance among the laggard states.

Importantly, the chapter demonstrates that best practice compliance systems can create and expand transnational enforcement networks, reinforce domestic compliance constituencies, and expand the number and categories of actors capable of sounding the non-compliance alarm. Information is key to all the compliance tasks, and it is effectively managed when a database is centralized and provides continuously updated information on verification activities and associated findings. Stokke points out that integrating a network of enforcement agencies that taps traditional sources of information (such as physical inspection and aerial surveillance) and one with access to new technologies with broader spatial range (such as a satellite observation system) results in more efficient use of costly inspection capacities and better compliance performance. For this, an actor configuration involving MNCs developing and marketing new technologies, nation states with authoritative inspection competence and an IO(s) with the capacity to coordinate verification, review and enforcement activities proved to be important.

A good compliance system expands the transnational enforcer network, through either rule design or the deliberate management of interplay between relevant international institutions (Oberthür and Stokke 2011). Good compliance performance can emerge from well-designed rules that allow expanding the number of actors involved in the compliance review. An example of this is the transition from the use of discharge limitations to gradually phased-in equipment standards for new ships. Such a phased-in equipment rule can make circumventing compliance almost impossible, because circumvention requires a vessel owner working with partners in crime not only in the shipbuilding industry, but also in classification and insurance MNCs, as their services are necessary for entering ship registries, winning freight contracts, and gaining access to ports. Conversely, there are also cases where expanding the number of actors involved in a compliance task can improve the fit between a compliance system and the regulated activities. In the fisheries case, an expanding coalition of pusher states and ENGOs using information legitimized by a transnational enforcer network and epistemic community helped to expand the boundaries of the review system from bilateral to multilateral levels. The new, multilateral compliance system raised the credibility, saliency and legitimacy of the review and also minimized the tension between the trade-restrictive port state control sanctions and international trade rules.

As Stokke points out, the assistance part of a compliance system can prove instrumental for expanding the "compliance constituency" – i.e., those with material or turf-based stakes in a good compliance performance – beyond the traditionally "green" actor set of pusher states, environmental agencies and interested ENGOs. The ultimate targets of international environmental regulations in a laggard state tend to be well positioned in domestic political and bureaucratic networks, so overcoming incentives for non-compliance can be challenging. As evident in the nuclear-waste case, international institutions can provide financial or technological means for motivating positive engagement by target groups as well as those national agencies that project the greatest power in the relevant issue area. The underlying willingness to pay for environmental projects in a foreign country may require a substantial interdependent relationship between the donor and the recipient country. Such interdependence is often greater in regional contexts than globally, which again points to the general significance of a conducive interplay between international institutions at different levels of governance.

Implementation

Implementation is about the domestic enforcement of national policies and laws. Implementation does not always take place following international agreements, and may also occur in advance of internationally negotiated commitments. National and subnational governments in lead states with companies that see it in their interests to solve the relevant problems usually have the best record when it comes to implementation. Climate change, which will be addressed later, is a primary example of this. Although global regime building is stagnant, lead actors like the EU and many local and city-level initiatives implement various climate measures. Air pollution is another, but in this case their primary interest may lie in local health impact rather than trans-boundary pollution.

Still, in most cases implementation follows negotiation and international agreement. Connectedness between an international negotiation process and implementation is, therefore, a key for best practice implementation. Implementation of multilateral commitments tends to be more effective if key stakeholders are included in the process of negotiations. This is confirmed in Chapter 5. Specifically, implementation will be smoother if there is an overlap, or a network, between those who negotiate and those who implement. Those actors include IOs, lead states and agencies within a state, private actors, but also local governments, as implementation often moves smoothly when local governments, which are close to implementation targets, receive information and are involved from the early stages.

The importance of international negotiations and implementation is also confirmed on the UNCCD by Chapter 3. Although it was not a successful regime in terms of making a negotiated settlement, involvement of many local ENGOs in the negotiation process made implementation of the regime more effective, despite the weak negotiated settlement.

The disconnection between negotiation and implementation becomes particularly severe when it comes to funding issues, because implementers are accountable to those that provide funding. GEF is a typical example and it is influential in implementation of projects particularly related to biodiversity and climate change, but to some extent also to POPs (The Stockholm Convention on Persistent Organic Pollutants), international water and desertification. The GEF with its close links to the World Bank is structured very differently from environmental regimes and communication between the respective COPs (Conference of the Parties) and the GEF is often difficult and may thereby hamper effective implementation (Rosendal and Andresen 2011). Therefore, funding negotiation, which is deeply related to implementation, should reflect the decision-making dynamics of the regime negotiation. A better model is found in the Montreal Protocol, where donors are influential in funding implementation through the Multilateral Fund for the Protection of the Ozone Layer, securing a closer coordination between negotiations and funding/implementation. Conversely, the dynamics of the negotiations on funding and donor-recipient relations should be well reflected in the regime negotiation. Lack of participation by the same donors and beneficiaries with no coordination with the negotiations process often result in ineffective implementation. This finding echoes the point made in Chapter 4, underlining the importance of engagement of non-environmental funders in the environmental issues. Linking and networking the environmental community with key funding agencies is essential.

In line with our assumptions, and as has been well documented elsewhere, implementation practice is generally very different between developed states and developing states, as well as between states with stronger capacity and weak capacity (Machado Carvalho 1993; Puppim de Oliveira 2008; Pripp *et al.* 2010). In general, countries with better technical capacity and more sophisticated industry can more easily live up to international commitments. In the ozone regime, the conversion of the aerosol sector was relatively easy for developed countries with highly sophisticated and capitalized chemical industry. But many developing countries, with less capital and technical capacity than in the industrialized states, took much longer time to convert from CFC usage in the aerosol sector. The Montreal Ozone Fund and the grace period for developing countries' compliance with CFC cuts reflects this political reality of developing countries' interests as well as the widely shared understanding of the policy need to provide enhanced capacity for LDC compliance.

Institutional support for LDC implementation applies only in regimes which require national legislation and widespread enforcement. For voluntary or more aspirational regimes founded on soft law, such as in forest preservation, a mobilized network of industry, NGOs and scientists on the ground can promote implementation. The case of Costa Rica, as provided in Chapter 5, shows that local communities networked with national officials and developed a well-functioning system of payment for ecosystem services. Findings from development studies indicate that top-down efforts from international aid agencies that do not engage with local groups on the ground are ineffective at implementation (Puppim de Oliveira 2005).

We assumed that vigorous capacity building by IOs or developed states is likely to render more effective implementation in developing countries, but that capacity building has to target the "right" actor, not necessarily referring to a state agency. In fact, Puppim de Oliveira shows that capacity building for national officials is not enough, and that capacity building in best practices needs to include local governments and small firms in the formal and informal sector, which actually do the implementation at the ground level. Implementation of the ozone regime in China has shown the importance of involving local governments. In contrast, in the case of Brazil, the lack of capacity building at the level of small repair shops to recycle or properly dispose of ozone depleting substances hindered effective implementation.

Shaming and blaming by NGOs does not always work. Oliveira finds instances in UNCCD where NGOs with the support of some developing countries attacked the position of developed countries on the account that they did not recognize desertification as a global issue and decentralized implementation of the convention. Such NGO activity resulted in low funding provisions, hampering implementation especially in the developing countries needing funding for effective implementation. That is, different mechanisms may be at work in developed and developing countries contributing to nuance in our hypotheses.

Scientific reporting backed up with pressure from ENGOs and political movement in a key state can change the attitude of laggard MNCs, as witnessed in the case of ozone. Also, domestic economic opportunities created by implementation or the prospect of implementation may lead firms who were otherwise anticipating net discounted losses from environmental governance to support implementation efforts.

Resilience

Resilience has come to be considered an important governance component in recent years, although less attention has so far been paid to it than to other governance components. Resilience entails maintaining a dynamic balance between social changes, governance, and environmental conditions. As regimes mature, in order to remain effective and relevant they must adapt to political changes within them and to environmental conditions outside them. Effective governance entails a reflective mechanism, as those responsible for governance continually adjust the governance mechanisms to changing social, economic and political conditions as well as the direct environmental conditions that are the substantive focus of the governance efforts. As environmental governance increasingly has to face new and sometimes unpredicted challenges posed by natural and social systems and their interactions, more attention has been paid to the need for resilience in recent years. Resilience entails not only a dynamic agenda-setting process but also coupled flexibility in adjusting other governance components to a changing policy environment. Chapter 6 on resilience corroborated two important hypotheses. First, it supported that major contributors (states and MNCs) to the problem need to be a part of the governance arrangements, directly or indirectly, in order for the arrangements to be resilient. CBD is the clearest example of this: where lack of a main actor shapes the resilient dynamics, it prevents comprehensive adaptation of rules and causes broad, shallow networks over other networks. CITES shows how the United States and Europe as pushers together can be important. They joined and pushed together on a number of ivory decisions. In addition, range states (potential laggards) were split over Gabon's burning its ivory stock; other range states supporting conservation; others, managed trade; and others, full trade. The result is that range states are divided and pushers are largely united.

Second, unrestrained NGO activities will weaken resilience, as it results in a spread of strong politicization of issues and prevents the institution from adequately solving the issue at hand. Broader inclusion works best when it operates polycentrically at the national level, complemented by multi-scalar (but not hierarchical) networks between the international system and the national decision-making space. The World Network of Biosphere Reserves in MAB, for instance, fostered resilience significantly through a polycentric arrangement with local biosphere reserve managers and stakeholders, national MAB councils, the international coordinating council, and outside scientific advice interacting in focused tasks while connected to elaborate network connections to other levels of actors on focused tasks. Caribbean conservation arrangements are more resilient when the scientific, NGO and corporate stakeholder configurations operate within a country as well as with counterparts outside the country in international organizations, the national government (state), and foreign aid agencies. Stevens cautions that a broader network operates to offset the potential control of governance by powerful private actors, such as real estate developers in his cases of conservation management.

MAB and CITES have been resilient, with participation from all actor groups. The CBD is not resilient, in large part because no effective means of coordination is in place to mediate NGO influences, and without the involvement of the United States there is little interest in clarifying the coordinating space. As Chasek shows in Chapter 3 with the Cartagena protocol (and which is largely repeated in the Nagoya protocol), NGOs were given free rein to influence negotiations.

Groups where members recognize one another's legitimacy can foster resilience. This is clearest in MAB where the group of scientists who shared a focus and empirical needs supported the organization during the 1980s and reformed the organization. In addition, the MIKE program in CITES unites actors around a coherent discussion of guidelines. On the contrary, CBD and early CITES suffered from legitimacy problems, and did not foster resilience. In the CBD one dynamic is opposition to what is perceived as the United States' illegitimacy, because of its opposition. In its early years CITES was less resilient before 1994 and had difficulty in adopting decisions, as actors had not yet formulated common goals and were suspicious of one another's intentions. Stevens argued that the focused selection mechanism for actors, rather than an open selection mechanism, renders credibility to the arrangement, and that "coupling these exclusive selection mechanisms with network governance mechanisms common in thick networks may provide an optimal steadiness regarding legitimacy and exclusivity." CBD suggests that a broad network that is shaped by factors other than legitimacy or governance goals will be detrimental to legitimacy and resilience. MAB and CITES currently indicate how thick networks of actors with lots of interaction with one another can be important. Resilient networks have benefits for persistence, in part because of regular information flows, in part because of trust and institutionalized legitimacy for the stakeholders.

Partnerships: a special kind of actor configuration

The most outstanding characteristic of private partnerships, or non-state market driven (NSMD) global governance, as termed by Auld *et al.*, is the non-state-centric nature of the arrangement. This and other types of partnerships often provide a complementary mechanism to a regime (such as e-Stewards) to fill the gap when intergovernmental cooperation failed or was not undertaken. The promise of NSMDs is to influence global supply chains and thereby directly influence economic activities to change the course of action. The NSMDs described in Chapter 7 vary across a number of analytic divisions: the network configurations are organized by different political schemas (corporatist, pluralist and clientelist); and the actual rules vary by product or process; and by whether they are extremely demanding, universally achievable with meaningful effects, or merely least common denominator green washing.

The configuration of actors is vital for understanding the form and effectiveness of these NMSDs. The actual analysis goes well beyond the crude formulation of the best practice hypothesis for networked partnerships. Firms tended to support more demanding guidelines when they are already close to those levels. Hence, the firm "leaders" for NSMDs tended to be actors that, for other reasons, were already close to the standards. Industrial players who either fear losing autonomy through such partnerships and/or view standards as imposing additional requirements, may be viewed as "laggards" in that they will either support no NSMD at all, or will join more "business friendly alternatives." Implementation occurs best when there is participation from firms and NGOs throughout the supply chain, entailing many different types of firms (the ultimate seller, buyers, traders, retailers) spread geographically along the supply chain. As the authors note, such efforts work best when there are informed and affluent consumers in the final market. Thus such schemes work better for retail goods (including fish and forest products) than for intermediate goods used by industry.

While NGO oversight was important for inducing and rewarding compliance by firms, more important seemingly was the nature of the commitments themselves.

In contrast to the influence of traditional public policy networks, the exclusion or absence of some actors in the network membership will not only influence agenda setting and issue framing within the network. Decisions at these governance components that are seen as downplaying the interests of excluded members can lead to the emergence of competing NSMD systems, in which excluded actors become dominant members of the networks affecting the new NSMD system. These dynamics, in turn, affect and shape regulatory decisions at the negotiated settlement (i.e. decision making) stage in each NSMD system over the scope and prescriptiveness of the standards against which firms are certified, as each network acts as a governance arena for the development of rules. This implies that there might be an inverse relationship initially between high standards, which tend to result from networks that are not business captured, and the ability to build widespread support necessary for the amelioration of certain problems. This does not only influence legitimacy evaluations of these programs, but also research that takes a one-time snapshot approach instead of an evolutionary perspective on institution building.

Dynamics of actor configuration

Few dynamic effects were found between actor groups active in different governance configurations, or between configurations themselves, be they in the same regime or across regimes. For example, networks organized for agenda setting in ozone had little influence over other components for ozone, or for network dynamics in other regimes. Table 9.1 reviews the array of actor groupings involved in the components and cases. Also, most regimes developed in isolation from one another. Regime complexes are unintended consequences of evolving environmental governance.

While patterns of actor involvement correspond to variations in the performance of particular governance components, most actor groupings and governance configurations remain decoupled from one another. These observations may be an artifact of the research design for this project, as the data in this book are aggregated at the scale of actor groupings – so few instances of specific actors are discussed, beyond the United States, the EU or UNEP. For instance, the particular epistemic communities are different in each case.

The overlapping cases across components confirm our initial hunch that the array of actors varies between regime components, even for the same regime. While configurations of actor groups do correlate well with the performance of various governance components, the actual makeup of these groups in terms of specific actors varies widely. Which NGO or epistemic community or firm is involved in a particular component for one particular regime does not mean that it will be involved either in other components, or necessarily in other issues areas as well. UNEP is the most commonly occurring IO, which is a strong reason for why UNEP's presence with other actors yields agendas with a primarily environmental focus. Other IOs would be more likely to impart a focus consistent with their missions. Thus the EU is likely to impart an agenda or frame promoting

Table 9.1 Observed actor group involvement in different governance components

	State	IO	Science	NGO	MNC
Agenda setting	×	×	×		
LRTAP	×	×	×		
HELCOM	×	×			
Negotiation	×	×	×	×	
Ozone	×	×	×	×	×
CBD	×	×	× (divided)	×	×
UNCCD	×	×		×	
Compliance	×	×	×	×	×
MARPOL	×	×			×
Fisheries	×	×	×	×	×
Nuclear Waste	×	×		×	×
Implementation	×	×	× (weak)		×
Ozone	×	×	×	×	×
CBD	×	×	×		
UNCCD	×			×	
Resilience	×	×	×	×	×
MAB		×	×		
CITES	×	×	×	× (73–mid-90s)	
CBD	×	×	×	× (mid-90s)	×

more goals than would UNEP, whereas the World Bank and UNDP focus on development agendas and the WTO stresses trade liberalization, at times at the expense of environmental goals. This is why some chapters addressed the need for involving financial actors, be it an IO or ministry, in environmental compliance and enforcement. Without their involvement environmental outcomes are likely to remain modest.

Environmental governance with an actor-based focus is highly differentiated. The now extensive case-study literature seems to support this notion that few individual actors recur in multiple regimes or components (Betsill and Corell 2008; Biermann *et al.* 2012a, b; Chasek *et al.* 2010).

Linkages between components

Now we turn to the linkages between governance components. There are two kinds of linkages to consider: the linkage on the same component but different regimes, and the one between components in the same regime. Our question is: what is the effect of actor configurations on shaping these linkages?

With regard to the linkage between the same component in different regimes, there is the case of the interplay between the North Sea and the Baltic in the preceding chapters. This linkage was strengthened mainly through the EU in agenda setting and implementation, and there was positive learning between them. There are various ways to make the link, but the function of ministerial conferences is emphasized as an important device for successful agenda setting, as they bring together many different issues, and such a high-level political forum brings about a good opportunity for interested countries in promoting another regime. The fisheries cases demonstrate how pusher states in one regime can band together to expand the compliance system of another and broader regime to reinstate a good fit between the relevant institutional complexes when the activities under regulation have expanded spatially. The EU also standardizes regional and national environmental policies across issue areas, as it provides pressure to apply the same kind of methodologies for reducing emissions, and thereby linkage in terms of policy approach may also occur (Sbragia 1996; Oberthur and Pallemaerts 2010; Kluvankova-Oravska and Chobotova 2012). Learning, innovation and spillover operate as the salient social mechanisms of change from the array of actors involved within the EU aegis (Jordan *et al.* 2003; Adger and Jordan 2009).

Although the current research does not shed light on the linkages from one component to another in the same regime, there are suggestive glimmerings in parts of these chapters. We saw the linkage between compliance/implementation and negotiation, compliance/implementation and agenda setting, agenda setting and negotiation, as well as between resilience and agenda setting. The chapters suggested that an important key connecting agenda setting and negotiation process is the ability of an IO to work with scientific network. An independent scientific body would have influence over negotiation while avoiding the political influence over science, particularly in such a case as IPCC in which the assessment summaries are politically negotiated, when a strong IO plays a strong role. With regard to the linkage made from compliance/implementation to negotiation, there are instances of an "implementation turn" during the 2000s, as many actors came to include implementation design concerns on the agenda of existing and new regimes. This instance of substantive feedback between components is driven by the experiences of many actors – NGOs, states and IOs – involved in implementing regimes over time.

Networks and configurations of actor groups

Looking through the findings of the chapters, we realize that no single actor exercises influence independent of other actors. In other words, in the issue area of the environment, where many sub-issues are linked with each other and maybe other issues such as economic and social issues are interconnected by its nature, governance can be a creation of the synergistic or conflictive joint behavior of actors, be it by a single actor or by a network of actors. Untangling actor configuration and examining the cause of best governance practices composed of synergistic actor relations is an important task of this concluding chapter.

Table 9.2 Organization of actor groupings

Case	Organization of network	Key groups	Contribution to performance of component
Baltic agenda setting	Expansive network	NGOs, MNCs, IO secretariat	High
LRTAP agenda setting and negotiation	Technocratic network	Scientists, states, IO secretariat, MNCs (through IO)	High
Ozone agenda setting, negotiation and compliance	Advocacy coalitions and network of IO and science	Scientists, MNCs, states, IO secretariat	High
Biosafety agenda setting and negotiation	Advocacy coalitions of conflicting networks	NGOs, scientists, states, IO secretariat	High (negative)
UNCCD negotiation	Advocacy coalition of NGOs and states	NGOs and states	Low
Fisheries compliance	Expanding multi-level technocratic network	States, IO, scientists, some NGOs	Low, then high
Ship pollution compliance	Expanding multi-level technocratic network	IO, states, MNCs	Low, then high
Nuclear waste-dumping compliance	Expanding multi-level network	IO, states, NGOs, MNCs	Low, then high
CITES, MAB resilience	Multi-level network	Scientists, states, NGOs, MNCs	High

Most of the chapters investigate the configurations of actors, but have little to say about the glue that holds the configurations together, or the structure of the networks. We know little still about key actors who may serve as hubs amongst the broader spokes of networked relations. Analytically we can talk about the actor groups involved in each case. Table 9.2 provides examples of how the actor groups are organized in a number of cases.

Networked groups operated in a number of cases as indicated above. In these instances actor groups interacted with one another on a regular basis over time. Members shared common goals of addressing a particular environmental threat, and realized a division of labor based on differential capabilities from which each and all stood to gain from exchange. This was often information, but at times (such as with partnerships and in the Baltic) it rested on the legitimacy that actors acquired from participating in the governance operation.

These networks were technocratically based in some instances, such as the regularized connections between scientists and IOs in LRTAP and stratospheric ozone. In others the networks were more expansive, drawn from broader actor groupings who were more interested in policy outcomes, mobilizing concern, and attracting financial resources. One limit to non-technocratic networks, such as in the Baltic, is the need for NGOs to temper their critique and public scrutiny and public advocacy activities in order to maintain a working relationship with MNCs within the network. No evidence is available about any compensatory restraint exercised by companies. Thus the adversarial gains of linking NGOs with firms may be muted by virtue of the need by NGOs to retain their legitimacy through their participation.

Even in other arrangements the actors were organized into groups based on self-interested convenience, such as Sabatier's advocacy coalitions. In these instances groups came together occasionally, but lacked the ongoing network and community, and resilience.

Information is often a key resource which actors value and share within the network. Asymmetries in information possession encourage actors to operate together. VanDeveer shows that the density of actors in the Baltic and in LRTAP constitute a network of actors who regularly interact over time and share common goals. Stevens indicates how a vertical and horizontal network contributes to resilient governance through the rapid flow of information in a variety of conservation governance schemes, including MAB. In compliance, Stokke offers a functional argument for why actors should remain committed to a network because of the collective benefits which accrue from information sharing and from the conversion of that information to implementation. Conversely, the arrangement of actors within Cashore's partnerships appear much closer to more transitory advocacy coalitions, where NGOs and companies each remain voluntarily within the configuration so long as they deem their interests satisfied by the certificates.

In these cases, networked configurations seem to contribute to stronger and more resilient governance than do more short-term configurations of convenience.

Legitimacy

Legitimacy is a key factor for the integrity of each component as well as for the integrity of the configuration of actors. All actors voluntarily participate in these networks. Whether actors choose to continue to participate, in the absence of compulsion, rests on their impression of the legitimacy of their shared project and the extent to which they view the participation of other actor groups as legitimate. Whether states are swayed by the influence of configurations of actors depends on the legitimacy of the network.

While few chapters looked explicitly at legitimacy, in particular it contributed to resilience and the social authority of NMSDs. Interestingly, actors had different notions of legitimacy in each case. In the resiliency cases involving nature conservation, actors valued information about verification which would enable each to better pursue its own conservation goals. In the NMSDs, legitimacy depended upon collective market-based outcomes which would affect demand for members' products, or the direct environmental consequences of the schemes in the eyes of NGOs. In CBD the involvement of the United States delegitimated negotiating dynamics, because of the US position and reputation in biodiversity as a spoiler. The legitimacy of networks in the eyes of their participants also rests on the transparency of information-gathering procedures.

When actors believe that the other actors' involvement is legitimate, and that the institutional arrangements themselves are legitimate, then resilience is likely to be achieved. There are few accounts in this volume where actors dispute others' involvement. The legitimacy of private partnerships is a bit more of a concern, given the often adversarial relationships between NGOs and MNCs, and the fact that many of the labels and certification schemes are not well understood by consumers, so that they are unable to distinguish between schemes with stronger and weaker commitments and effectiveness, thus contributing to a broader lack of legitimacy by a skeptical public (Bernstein and Cashore 2008; Cashore 2002).

Escaping gridlock on climate governance

We now turn to applying the lessons from pluralistic green governance in the past to one of the biggest challenges of environmental governance we are facing in the twenty-first century – climate change. As addressed in the previous chapter, the problem with climate change is that the problem is politically daunting, and has been addressed in international institutions in which the diplomatic efforts are not up to the task. Governments are reluctant to pursue effective initiatives, so that the magnitude of the threat continues to get worse. Few countries have not met their limited Kyoto goals, and projections of emissions indicate a clear likelihood of exceeding 450 ppm by mid-century. Despite UNFCC and Kyoto, GHG emissions continued to grow rapidly from 2000–2010, and it appears extremely difficult to reduce emissions by 2020 down the path that corresponds to achieving the "2 degree" target (UNEP 2011).

In this section we seek to apply lessons from our project to generate insights about actor configurations to address this problem. We do not address policy or institutional questions, believing rather that policy and institutional choices follow from the political influence of influential transboundary coalitions.[2]

To a large extent the reason that the problem is seemingly intractable is that diplomats have been following approaches based on institutions and contexts in which the configurations of actors favor negligible outcomes, or even worst practices in our formulation. The existing problem is that the configurations of actors inhibit meaningful governance. The challenge is to build transnational constituency to induce broader change – diplomatic and technological.

The IPCC is the only game in town. Despite expressing clear consensus about the urgency of addressing anthropogenic climate change, the four IPCC reports cannot be said to have significantly influenced the treaty negotiations beyond keeping the issue on the agenda. Nor have they elevated political concern amongst elites or the mass public, although there exists some regional variance. It would be hard to imagine that the negotiated outcomes would be any slower, less demanding, or less effective on affecting the pace of global warming in the absence of the IPCC reports. The IPCC suffers from legitimacy problems, because of a few lapses in accuracy of its estimates, and because of concerns about political influence over the IPCC process, leading to potential bias or lapses in impartiality (Haas 2004; InterAcademy Council 2010). To a large extent the IPCC's inability to significantly affect the international negotiating process is due to the perceived narrow relationship between governments and the IPCC scientific community. The IPCC's influence could be extended if the independence of the scientists could be promoted. Major authors could be appointed by the UN Secretary General, based on nominations from international scientific unions of national academies of science. The breadth of the agenda-setting coalition could also be expanded with the involvement of NGO authors, and by setting the geographic scale of the reports at the national and sub-national level, so that more stakeholders are directly engaged by the information. The secretariats of the UNFCCC and SBSTA could work with IPCC scientists to better integrate the scientific studies into verifying compliance with the next legal treaty.

In the absence of meaningful rules, the political task is to build a viable international constituency or network behind energy-efficient and clean energy technologies through collaborative government support for R&D and diffusion, combined with partnerships that span a variety of sectors. Pew estimates a $2.3 trillion market for cleaner energy (Pew Charitable Trust 2010). Widened public–private technological partnerships can help broaden this coalition as well as accelerate the commercialization of real technological solutions that can be more easily embraced through international negotiations. The Emerging Climate Technology Center and Network (CTCN[3]), together with the OECD, IEA, and IRENA, offer possible institutional venues, as well as such independent efforts as the successor of the Asia-Pacific partnership and the like. Implementing these new technologies on the ground will require working closely with local stakeholders (Kanie *et al.* 2013). Coordinated networks between cities offer an opportunity for building sub-national coalitions amongst science, NGOs, civil authorities and the private sector (Bulkeley and Schroeder 2012; Hoffmann 2011). Such efforts could contribute to rule making and more rapid enforcement of negotiated rules, or even the adoption of common rules and practices in advance of internationally negotiated common rules.

Civil Society and private sector industries that could help form natural coalitions – but which are presently too small and isolated to exercise much influence over collective political deliberations on climate change – include environmental NGOs, the insurance industry (particularly reinsurance), venture capitalists, the construction industry, manufacturers of monitoring equipment (including smart meters for households), the renewables industry, and the manufacturing sector. Large firms such as Westinghouse and Siemens are likely to gain from producing all forms of energy technology. Engagement of these actors makes the regime resilient, but they should be configured in such a way that the lessons from best practices will be applied.

Conclusion

The different categories of actors in multilateral environmental governance are not monolithic. We have learned from the collection of case studies in this volume and other related findings that the configuration and combination of actors influences the success or failure of environmental governance components. In this volume we did not try to provide a comprehensive analysis of these issues, but to raise the importance of the issues and to make a first step toward identifying the best actor combination in different components of governance.

To summarize the findings in chapters, a few general observations can be made. First, IOs have an important role in managing scientific network and linking them with inter-governmental or governmental processes, be it agenda setting or negotiation. Second, states are still important for successful governance, also in terms of network of actors. In other words, involving states in a network is a key for best practices. It should be noted that the state is not a unitary category throughout components. An alternative to governance with states is market-based partnerships. Third, appropriate actor configuration is indispensable for the best practice. Unrestricted participation of NGOs results in negative consequences, but their partnership with business and industry has good implications. These actor configurations also serve as a foundation for resilient governance.

Governance in the twenty-first century – in what is being referred to as the "anthropocene" era with environmental issues at the forefront – requires different types of governance from the twentieth century. We know that in many instances traditional international relations centering on the nation state no longer function well. This century will need to see a restructuring of governance to address environmental and sustainability issues while simultaneously addressing economic and social issues.

An important political question is to what extent can and will states allow authority to diffuse internationally from the state to non-state actors. Is this widely documented diffusion of authority subject to control by nation states or is it a consequence of the new array of issues on the international agenda and the technological developments which allow non-state actors to exercise meaningful influence internationally? Future empirical studies could shed light on the questions of how ENGOs and epistemic communities work together. When will ENGOs prevail over epistemic communities? When will epistemic communities prevail over ENGOs? Such empirically grounded work should also provide insights into the broad questions of how do states choose which IOs to utilize for negotiating accords? We have found islands of governance in a complex sea of problems, but few examples yet of coupled governance that is able to effectively capture coupled problems. Hopes for institutional homology between governance and the complexity of the environmental systems being governed remains elusive. Yet as the memory of the Cold War fades as a structuring element to international relations, growing awareness of the anthropocene and of complex global environmental threats may lead to a new and broader appreciation of how to fashion new governance arrangements that are appropriate to the need to capture not only the connections between environmental threats, but also the links between environmental issues and other issues on the international agenda.

The key is how to configure the actors involved in the activities functioning in governance, and to utilize the network of actors. Public policy should be oriented to do so. We hope this volume serves as a stepping stone on that path.

Notes

1 Nonetheless, without business and industry networked with the states "the position of the Miami Group might have been less stringent" (Chapter 3, p.69).
2 For efforts to address the climate change deadlock through policy and institutional designs see Aldy and Stavins (2007); Biermann, Pattberg *et al.* (2010).
3 http://unfccc.int/ttclear/jsp/CTCN.jsp

References

Adger, W. N. and Jordan, A., eds. (2009) *Governing Sustainability*, Cambidge: Cambridge University Press.

Andresen, S., Skodvin, T., Underdal, A. and Wettestad, J. (2000) *Science and Politics in International Environmental Regimes*, Manchester: Manchester University Press.

Ansell, C. (2000) 'The Networked Polity: Regional Development in Western Europe Governance', *An International Journal of Policy and Administration*, 13 (3), 303–333.

Betsill, M. M. and Corell, E., eds. (2008) *NGO Diplomacy: The Influence of Nongovernmental Organizations in International Environmental Negotiations*, Cambridge, MA: MIT Press.

Bernstein, S. and Cashore, B. (2008) 'The Two-Level Logic of Non-State Market Driven Governance', in Volker Rittberger, Martin Nettesheim and Carmen Huckel, eds., *Changing Patterns of Authority in the Global Political Economy: Volume II: New Actors and Forms of Regulation*, New York: Palgrave Macmillan.

Biermann, F., Abbott, K., Andresen, S., Bäckstrand, K., Bernstein, S., Betsill, M. M., Bulkeley, H., Cashore, B., Clapp, J., Folke, C., Gupta, A., Gupta, J., Haas, P. M., Jordan, A., Kanie, N., Kluvánková-Oravská, T., Lebel, L., Liverman, D., Meadowcroft, J., Mitchell, R. B., Newell, P., Oberthür, S., Olsson, L., Pattberg, P., Sánchez-Rodríguez, R., Schroeder, H., Underdal, A., Camargo Vieira, S., Vogel, C., Young, O. R., Brock, A. and Zondervan, R. (2012a) 'Transforming Governance and Institutions for Global Sustainability: Key Insights from the Earth System Governance Project', *Current Opinion in Environmental Sustainability*, 4, 51–60.

Biermann, F., Abbott, K., Andresen, S., Bäckstrand, K., Bernstein, S., Betsill, M. M., Bulkeley, H., Cashore, B., Clapp, J., Folke, C., Gupta, A., Gupta, J., Haas, P. M., Jordan, A., Kanie, N., Kluvánková-Oravská, T., Lebel, L., Liverman, D., Meadowcroft, J., Mitchell, R. B., Newell, P., Oberthür, S., Olsson, L., Pattberg, P., Sánchez-Rodríguez, R., Schroeder, H., Underdal, A., Camargo Vieira, S., Vogel, C., Young, O. R., Brock, A. and Zondervan, R. (2012b) 'Navigating the Anthropocene: Improving Earth System Governance', *Science*, 335 (6074), 1306–1307.

Bulkeley, H. and Schroeder, H. (2012) 'Beyond State/Non-State Divides: Global Cities and the Governing of Climate Change', *European Journal of International Relations*, 18 (4), 743–766.

Busch, P.-O., Jorgens, H. and Tews, K. (2005) 'The Global Diffusion of Regulatory Instruments: The Making of a New International Environmental Regime', *The Annals of the American Academy of Political and Social Science*, 598, 146–167.

Cashore, B. (2002) 'Legitimacy and the Privatization of Environmental Governance', *Governance,* 15 (4), 503–529.

Chasek, P., Downie, D. and Brown, J. W. (2010) *Global Environmental Politics* 5th edn, Boulder, CO: Westview Press.

Green, J. F. (2008) 'Private Authority in Global Environmental Politics: Delegation to Non-state Actors in Multilateral Environmental Treaties', conference paper, *American Political Science Association Annual Meeting*.

Haas, P. (2004) 'Addressing the Global Governance Deficit', *Global Environmental Politics,* 11 (4), 1–19.

Haas, P. M. (2007) 'Epistemic Communities', in D. Bodansky, J. Brunnee and E. Hey, *The Oxford Handbook of International Environmental Law,* New York: Oxford University Press, 791–806.

Haas, P. M. and McCabe, D. (2001) 'Amplifiers or Dampeners: International Institutions and Social Learning in The Management of Global Environmental Risks', in *Learning to Manage Global Environmental Risks, Vol. 1,* Cambridge, MA: MIT Press, 323–348.

Hooghe, L. and Marks, G. (2001) *Multilevel Governance and European Integration,* Boulder, CO: Rowman & Littlefield Publishers.

InterAcademy Council (2010) Climate Change Assessments: Review of the Process and Procedures of the IPCC, IAS Secretariat, Amsterdam.

Ishii, A. (2011) 'Scientists Learn Not Only Science but Also Diplomacy: Learning Processes in the European Transboundary Air Pollution Regime', in Rolf Lidskog and Goran Sundqvist, eds., *Governing the Air: The Dynamics of Science, Policy and Citizen Interation,* Cambridge, MA: MIT Press, 163–194.

Jordan, A., Wurzel, R. K. W. and Zito, A. R. (2003) '"New" Instruments of Environmental Governance: Patterns and Pathways of Change', *Environmental Politics,* 12 (1), 1–24.

Kanie N. (2003) 'Leadership in Multilateral Negotiation and Domestic Policy: The Netherlands at the Kyoto Protocol Negotiation', *International Negotiation,* 8 (2), 339–365.

Kanie, N., Betsill, M. M., Zondervan, R., Biermann, F. and Young, O. R. (2012) 'A Charter Moment: Restructuring Governance for Sustainability', *Public and Administration and Development,* 32, 292–304.

Kanie, N. and Haas, P. M., eds. (2004) *Emerging Forces in Environmental Governance,* Tokyo: UNU Press.

Kanie, N., Suzuki, M. and Iguchi, M. (2013) 'Fragmentation of International Low-carbon Technology Governance: An Assessment in Terms of Barriers to Technology Development', *Global Environmental Research,* 17 (1), 61–70.

Kanie, N. (2013) 'NGO Participation in the Global Climate Change Decision-making Process: A Key for Facilitating Climate Talks', in G. Sjostedt and A.M. Penetrante, eds., *Climate Change Negotiations: A Guide to Resolving Disputes and Facilitating Multilateral Cooperation,* London: Routledge, 169–187.

Kluvankova-Oravska, T. and Chobotova, V. (2012) 'Regional Governance Arrangements', in F. Biermann and P. Pattberg, eds., *Global Environmental Governance Reconsidered,* Cambridge, MA: MIT Press, 219–235.

Kohler-Koch, B. (1995) 'The Strength of Weakness: The Transformation of Governance in the EU', in Sverker Gustavsson and Leif Lewin, eds., *The Future of the Nation-State,* London: Routledge, 93–117.

Machado Carvalho, S. M. (1993) 'Reducing Emissions of Ozone-depleting Substances in Brazil', *Global Environmental Change,* 4 (3), 350–356.

Marks, G. and Hooghe, L. (2004) 'Contrasting Visions of Multi-level Governance', in I. Bache and M. Flinders, *Multi-level Governance,* Oxford: Oxford University Press, 15–30.

Marks, G., Hooghe, L. and Blank, K. (1996) 'European Integration from the 1980s: State-Centric v. Multi-level Governance', *Journal of Common Market Studies,* 34 (3), 342–378.

Meyer, J. W. (1997) 'The Structuring of a World Environmental Regime', *International Organization,* 51 (4), 623–651

Miles, E. L., Underdal, A., Andresen, S., Wettestad, J. and Carlin, E. (2001) *Environmental Regime Effectiveness: Confronting Theory with Evidence*, Cambridge, MA: MIT Press.

Oberthür, S. and Pallemaerts, M., eds. (2010) *The New Climate Policies of the European Union: Internal Legislation and Climate Diplomacy*, Brussels: VUB Press

Oberthür, S. and Stokke, O. S., eds. (2011) *Managing Institutional Complexity: Regime Interplay and Global Environmental Change*, Cambridge MA: MIT Press.

Peterson, John (1995) 'Decision-making in the European Union: Towards a Framework for Analysis', *Journal of European Public Policy*, 2 (1), 69–93.

Pew Charitable Trust (2010) 'Global Clean Power: A $2.3 Trillion Opportunity', online, available from http://www.pewtrusts.org/our_work_report_detail.aspx?id=62357 (accessed 31 March 2013).

Prip, C., Gross, T., Johnston, S. and Vierros, M. (2010) *Biodiversity Planning: An Assessment of National Biodiversity Strategies and Action Plans,* Yokohama: United Nations University Institute of Advanced Studies.

Puppim de Oliveira, J. A. (2005) 'Enforcing Protected Area Guidelines in Brazil: What Explains Participation in the Implementation Process?', *Journal of Planning Education and Research,* 24 (4), 420–436.

Puppim de Oliveira, J. A. (2008) *Implementation of Environmental Policies in Developing Countries*, Albany, NY: SUNY Press.

Rockström, J. *et al.* (2009) 'A Safe Operating Space for Humanity', *Nature,* 461, 472–475.

Rosendal, K. and Andresen, S. (2011) 'Institutional design for improved forest governance through REDD: Lessons from the Global Environmental Facility', *Ecological Economics*, 70 (11), 1918–1925.

Sabel, C. F. and Zeitlin, J., eds. (2010) *Experimentalist Governance in the European Union*, Oxford: Oxford University Press.

Sbragia, A. (1996) 'Environmental Policy: The "Push-Pull" of Policy-making', in H. Wallace and W. Wallace, *Policy-Making in the European Union*, Oxford: Oxford University Press, 235–255.

Speth, J. G. and Haas, P. M. (2006) *Global Environmental Governance*, Washington, DC: Island Press.

Stringer, L. C. (2008) 'Reviewing the International Year of Deserts and Desertification 2006', *Journal of Arid Environments,* 72, 2065–2074.

Underdal, A. (2002) 'One Question, Two Answers', in E. Miles, A. Underdal, S. Andresen, J. Wettestad and E. Carlin (2002) *Environmental Regime Effectiveness: Confronting Theory with Evidence*, Cambridge MA: MIT Press, 3–45.

UNEP (2011) Bridging the Emissions Gap, United Nations Environment Programme (UNEP), Nairobi.

VanDeveer, S. D. (2004) 'Ordering Environments: Organizing Knowledge and Regions in European International Environmental Cooperation', in S. Jasanoff and M. Long-Martello, eds., *Earthly Politics: Local and Global in Environmental Governance*, Cambridge, MA: MIT Press, 309–334.

Annex

Outline of regimes covered in this volume

Masahiko Iguchi

Regimes covered are as follows (in order of appearance in this book):

1 Convention on Long-range Transboundary Air Pollution
2 Convention on the Protection of the Marine Environment of the Baltic Sea Area
3 Montreal Protocol on Substances that Deplete Ozone Layer and the Vienna Convention for the Protection of the Ozone Layer
4 UN Convention to Combat Desertification
5 The Convention on Biological Diversity and the Cartagena Protocol on Biosafety
6 Convention on the Prevention of Marine Pollution by Dumping of Wastes and Other Matter
7 International Convention for the Prevention of Pollution From Ships
8 Convention on the Future Multilateral Cooperation in North-East Atlantic Fisheries
9 Norwegian–Russian Joint Commission on Fisheries
10 Forest Stewardship Council
11 Marine Stewardship Council
12 Fair-trade Labelling Organization
13 E-Stewards Initiative
14 United Nations Framework Convention on Climate Change.

Convention on Long-Range Transboundary Air Pollution

The international responses to the issue

Background. The Convention on Long-range Transboundary Air Pollution (CLRTAP) was signed by 34 European countries as well as the United States and Canada in 1979 at Geneva, and came into force in 1983. Currently, there are 51 Parties to the Convention.

Objective. The objective of the Convention is to 'to protect man and his environment against air pollution and shall endeavour to limit and, as far as possible, gradually reduce and prevent air pollution including long-range transboundary air pollution' (Article 2 of the Convention).

Issue definition. The issue of 'air pollution' is defined as 'the introduction by man, directly or indirectly, of substances or energy into the air resulting in deleterious effects of such a nature as to endanger human health, harm living resources and ecosystems and material property and impair or interfere with amenities and other legitimate uses of the environment, and "air pollutants" shall be construed accordingly' (Article 1 of the Convention). The issue of 'long-range transboundary air pollution' is defined as 'air pollution whose physical origin is situated wholly or in part within the area under the national jurisdiction of one State and which has adverse effects in the area under the jurisdiction of another State at such a distance that it is not generally possible to distinguish the contribution of individual emission sources or groups of sources' (Article 1 of the Convention).

Decision-making structure. The Executive Body, the meeting of the representatives of the Parties to the Convention, is established to implement the fundamental principles of the Convention, and to review its ongoing work (Article 10 of the Convention). It also collaborates with other relevant international organizations and with international agreements on air pollution in other regions. In addition, an Implementation Committee has been established to oversee compliance with various obligations.

Developments. The Convention has been extended by following eight protocols, covering the major air pollutants:

1   The 1984 Protocol on Long-term Financing of the Cooperative Programme for Monitoring and Evaluation of the Long-range Transmission of Air Pollutants in Europe with 44 Parties (came into force on 28 January 1988).
2   The 1985 Protocol on the Reduction of Sulphur Emissions or their Transboundary Fluxes by at least 30 per cent with 25 parties (came into force on 2 September 1987).
3   The 1988 Protocol concerning the Control of Nitrogen Oxides or their Transboundary Fluxes with 34 parties (came into force 14 February 1991).
4   The 1991 Protocol concerning the Control of Emissions of Volatile Organic Compounds or their Transboundary Fluxes with 24 parties (came into force 29 September 1997).
5   The 1994 Protocol on Further Reduction of Sulphur Emissions with 29 parties (came into force on 5 August 1998).
6   The 1998 Protocol on Heavy Metals with 31 parties (came into force on 29 December 2003).
7   The 1998 Protocol on Persistent Organic Pollutants (POPs) with 31 parties (came into force on 23 October 2003).
8   The 1999 Protocol to Abate Acidification, Eutrophication and Ground-level Ozone with 26 parties (came into force on 17 May 2005).

Non-state actors

International organizations. As a secretariat to the Convention, the United Nations Economic Commission for Europe (UNECE) plays a main role in this issue. It is one of the five regional commissions of the UN, as the subsidiary body of the Economic and Social Council (ECOSOC) which operates under the General Assembly established in 1947.

The European Union (EU) has been implementing several initiatives since the mid-1990s, including the Auto-oil Programme, a new air quality framework directive, the Integrated Pollution Prevention and Control Directive, an acidification strategy, and the EU Clean Air Europe (CAFE) Programme between the EU and the Convention.

Organization for Economic Co-operation and Development (OECD) facilitated scientific knowledge association with the issue, as much of the framing and discourse for LRTAP issues was established within OECD technical cooperation beginning in the 1960s. Further, concerns about pollutants moving long distances and across borders, with serious and negative impacts in pollution-importing countries were internationalized and legitimized in OECD assessments – OECD coined the term 'long range transboundary air pollution'.

In addition, the United Nations Environment Programme has also played a role in the development of the Protocols. For instance, the 2001 Stockholm Convention on POPs negotiated under UNEP, resulted from the 1998 Protocol on POPs as a point of departure. The UNEP initiative on mercury, too, has been developed in relation to the 1998 Protocol on Heavy Metals.

Secretariat. UNECE has been providing the secretariat for the Convention. The role of the secretariat is 'to convene and prepare the meetings of the Executive Body', 'to transmit to the Contracting Parties reports and other information received in accordance with the provisions of the present Convention', and 'to discharge the functions assigned by the Executive Body' (Article 11 of the Convention). The secretariat is also participating in other regional cooperation initiatives, such as the Acid Deposition Monitoring Network for East Asia (EANET).

Science. The 'discovery' of acidifying precipitation by scientists in Western Europe and North America in the late 1960s and early 1970s led to the formation of CLRTAP. In particular, Swedish scientists and officials began to raise their concerns about pollutants moving long distances and across borders, which were internationalized and legitimized in OECD assessments. Further, Swedish and Norwegian scientists and officials raised awareness about the issue and encouraged other countries to establish international cooperation efforts by using the 1972 Stockholm conference and other smaller inter-state and scientific venues.

The Cooperative Programme for Monitoring and Evaluation of the Long-range Transmission of Air Pollutants (EMEP) programme was established in 1977, in order to provide scientific support to the Convention, such as atmospheric monitoring and modelling, emission inventories and emission projections, and integrated assessment modelling.

Three subsidiary bodies – the Working Group on Effects, the Steering Body to the EMEP and the Working Group on Strategies and Review – were established and report to the Executive Body each year.

The International Institute for Applied Systems Analysis (IIASA), an international research organization located in Austria, has been instrumental in

CLRTAP negotiations, by organizing and carrying out science. IIASA has been hosting the Centre for Integrated Assessment Modelling (CIAM), which is one of the core centres assigned to EMEP by the Convention since 1999. The role of CIAM is to prepare background materials for the annual meetings of the Task Force on Integrated Assessment Modelling (TFIAM), which was established by the Executive Body to assist the development of Protocols by proving scientific evidence. IIASA's Greenhouse Gas and Air Pollution Interactions and Synergies (GAINS) model, which is an extension of the Regional Air Pollution Information and Simulation (RAINS) model, has been instrumental to the development of Gothenburg Protocol of 1999 and its 2012 revision.

Environmental non-governmental organizations (NGOs). Since 1985, environmental NGOs have regularly attended Executive Body meetings of the Convention, disseminating information such as ECO Bulletins and 'Acid News' in the negotiation process. The ENGO delegation from World Wide Fund for Nature, Friends of the Earth and Greenpeace as well as various national environmental groups attended the Convention's meetings. The work of the Convention is continuously monitored by NGOs, primarily by the Swedish NGO Secretariat on Acid Rain, and reports to an informal network of national and international NGOs.

Business. Among the many industries monitored by the Convention and Protocols, the power industry and the automobile industry are the two biggest polluting industries that are under government control and have weak transnational connections. In contrast to the private sector and organizations with extensive transnational links, there were low incentives to assess their pollution control technology and hence technical knowledge diffusion is slow in these industries (Levy 1995).

Effectiveness

As the first regional environmental convention, CLRTAP has been instrumental in the reduction of key harmful pollutants in both Europe and North America. Over the past 30 years, the Convention has been extended by eight Protocols which target pollutants such as sulphur, nitrogen oxide, persistent organic pollutants, volatile organic compounds, ammonia, and toxic heavy metals. The Convention has contributed to drastically reduce the level of these pollutants:

- Between 1990 and 2006, SO_2 levels have dropped by 70 per cent within the European Union, and by 36 per cent in the United States.
- Between 1990 and 2006, NOx levels have dropped by 35 per cent within the European Union, and by 23 per cent in the United States.
- Between 1990 and 2006, Ammonia (NH_3) levels have dropped by 20 per cent in the European Union.
- Between 1990 and 2006, non-methane volatile organic compounds have decreased by 41 per cent in the European Union.
- Between 1990 and 2006, primary particulate matter (PM 10) has declined by 28 per cent in the European Union.

References

IIASA (n.d.) 'Convention on Long-range Transboundary Air Pollution (LRTAP)', Available from http://www.iiasa.ac.at/web/home/research/researchPrograms/MitigationofAirPollutionandGreenhousegases/Overview1.en.html (accessed 29 March 2013).

Levy, M. A. (1995) 'International Co-operation to Combat Acid Rain', in Helge Ole Bergensen, George Parmann, and Øystein B. Thommessen (eds.) *Green Globe Yearbook of International Co-operation on Environment and Development 1995,* Oxford: Oxford University Press, 59–68.

Sliggers, Johan and Kakebeeke, W., eds. (2004) *Clearing the Air: 25 Years of the Convention on Long-range Transboundary Air Pollution,* Geneva: United Nations.

UNECE (1979) *1979 Convention on Long-range Transboundary Air Pollution,* United Nations Economic Commission for Europe, available from http://www.unece.org/fileadmin/DAM/env/lrtap/full%20text/1979.CLRTAP.e.pdf (accessed 29 March 2013).

UNECE (2009) 'UNECE's Convention on Long-range Transboundary Air Pollution celebrates 30th Anniversary', online, available from http://www.unece.org/press/pr2009/09env_p29e.html (accessed 29 March 2013).

Related website

*   United Nations Economic Commission for Europe
    http://www.unece.org/env/lrtap/

Convention on the Protection of the Marine Environment of the Baltic Sea Area

The international responses to the issue

Background. The Convention on the Protection of the Marine Environment of the Baltic Sea Area (Helsinki Convention) was signed by seven Baltic coastal states in 1974 and came into force in 1980. With political changes and developments in international environmental and maritime law, a new 1992 Helsinki Convention was signed by all the states bordering on the Baltic Sea, and the European Community. The 1992 Helsinki Convention came into force in 2000.

Objective. Under the Convention, the contracting parties shall 'individually or jointly take all appropriate legislative, administrative or other relevant measures to prevent and eliminate pollution in order to promote the ecological restoration of the Baltic Sea Area and the preservation of its ecological balance' (Article 3 of the Convention).

Issue definition. 'Pollution' means introduction by man, directly or indirectly, of substances or energy into the sea, including estuaries, which are liable to create hazards to human health, to harm living resources and marine ecosystems, to cause hindrance to legitimate uses of the sea including fishing, to impair the quality for use of sea water, and to lead to a reduction of amenities (Article 2 of the Convention).

Decision-making structure. The governing body of the Convention is the Helsinki Commission (Baltic Marine Environment Protection Commission), also known as HELCOM. The present contracting parties to HELCOM are Denmark,

Estonia, the European Community, Finland, Germany, Latvia, Lithuania, Poland, Russia and Sweden.

Development. The 1974 Helsinki Convention was the first regional international agreement to limit marine pollution from both land- and sea-based sources, whether air- or water-borne. During the period of 1988 to 1992, enormous political and economic changes took place in the Baltic region and across Europe, with the collapse of the Soviet Union. This has led to updating of the 1974 Convention into a new 1992 Convention, which covers the whole of the Baltic Sea area, including inland waters as well as the water of the sea itself and the sea bed.

Non-state actors

International organizations. The integration of EU organizations and institutions in the Baltic region occurs at multiple levels of environmental governance from the ministerial level down into the national and subnational level bureaucracies. Furthermore, EU policy officially insists on the 'harmonization' of national environmental policy with EU policies as a condition of EU membership, which had an enormous impact on the Baltic states' environmental policy agendas. Moreover, the EU as an important Baltic actor and funder/donor also stimulated cooperation goals with the Baltic regime.

Secretariat. HELCOM functions as a secretariat to administer and implement the Convention. The Commission appoints an Executive Secretary, which shall be the chief administrative official of the Commission and shall perform the functions that are necessary for the administration of this Convention, the work of the Commission and other tasks entrusted to the Executive Secretary by the Commission and its Rules of Procedure (Article 21 of the Convention). HELCOM has also established itself as a centre of scientific and technical assessment in the early years of the Baltic cooperation regime, which provides a variety of environmental policy networks that address a range of issues including pollution from ships and ports, land-based pollution, and habitat protection.

Science. Scientists have been playing central roles in fostering the evolution of the Convention. Nordic state officials and marine scientists from around the region helped to drive state interest in establishing and maintaining early environmental cooperation in the Baltic Area. They had pointed out that pollutants discharged into the sea remain and accumulate for many years. By the late 1960s, concerns arose from scientists that the sea was dangerously degraded – especially because of increasing inputs and ambient levels of toxins, and increasing nutrients such as nitrogen and phosphorous (eutrophication) and the decreased oxygen levels – which led to the inclusion of air- and water-based pollutants and early technical focus on urban waste and industrial effluents in the 1974 agreement. Further, scientists networked with HELCOM activities to address some institutional deficiencies of the first Convention, and proposed the voluntary recommendations into the revised, binding treaty. They have also continued to influence important aspects of the political agenda, as they raised awareness about on-going challenges with both toxic inputs and nutrient loading and therefore played an important role in agenda setting.

Environmental Non-Governmental Organizations (NGOs). As a result of the engagement of active environmental NGOs in the issue, which often networked with the region's scientists, substantial progress has been made in reducing toxic inputs from sea and from land-based sources. NGOs from the Western and Northern Baltic states helped to build NGO capacity and regional NGO networks after the collapse of communist regimes in Eastern Europe and the Soviet Union.

Business. Business did not play a significant role in fostering the regional Conventions, but industrial sector representatives have participated more in regional networks since the early 1990s. The Convention established a permit system for industrial emissions.

Effectiveness

There have been a number of improvements made to the Baltic marine environment which resulted in the reduction of atmospheric nitrogen deposition, organohalogen compounds such as toxic dioxins and furans, and 20–25 per cent overall reduction of emissions of oxygen-consuming substances. It has also improved the monitoring of the state of the marine environment, and developed measures to eliminate all illegal discharges by ships into the Baltic Sea. In addition, seal and white-tailed eagle populations have recovered as a result of the Convention.

References

HELCOM (1993) *Convention on the Protection of the Marine Environment of the Baltic Sea Area, 1974*, available from http://www.helcom.fi/stc/files/Convention/convention1974.pdf (accessed 29 March 2013).

HELCOM (2008) *Convention on the Protection of the Marine Environment of the Baltic Sea Area, 1992*, available from http://www.helcom.fi/stc/files/Convention/Conv1108.pdf (accessed 29 March 2013).

Related website

*   Helsinki Commission
    http://www.helcom.fi/

The Vienna Convention for the Protection of the Ozone Layer and Montreal Protocol on Substances that Deplete the Ozone Layer

The international responses to the issue

Background. The Vienna Convention for the Protection of the Ozone Layer was adopted in 1985, and came into force in 1988. Since August 2012, 197 countries have ratified the Convention.

Objective. The aim of the Convention is to 'take appropriate measures in accordance with the provisions of this Convention and of those protocols in force to which they are party to protect human health and the environment against adverse effects resulting or likely to result from human activities which modify or are likely to modify the ozone layer' (Article 2, Paragraph 1 of the Convention).

Issue definition. The ozone layer is defined as 'the layer of atmospheric ozone above the planetary boundary layer', and 'adverse effects' are defined as 'changes in the physical environment or biota, including changes in climate, which have significant deleterious effects on human health or on the composition, resilience and productivity of natural and managed ecosystems, or on materials useful to mankind' (Article 1 of the Convention).

Decision-making structure. The Conference of Parties (COP) was established as the decision-making body. There have been nine meetings of the COP to date: COP1 in Helsinki, Finland in 1989; COP2 in Nairobi, Kenya in 1991; COP3 in Bangkok, Thailand in 1993; COP4 at San Jose in the United States of America in 1996; COP5 in Beijing, China in 1999; COP6 in Rome, Italy in 2002; COP7 in Dakar, Senegal in 2005; COP8 in Doha, Qatar in 2008; and COP9 in Bali, Indonesia in 2011.

Development. The Montreal Protocol on Substances that Deplete the Ozone Layer was adopted in 1987, in order to cut production and consumption of ozone-depleting substances (ODS) listed in Article 2 of the Protocol. It came into force in 1989, and 197 countries have ratified the Protocol. The Meeting of the Parties to the Montreal Protocol (MOP) was established as the decision-making body of the Protocol. The first MOP was held at Helsinki, Finland in 1989, and has been held annually. Since then, the following four amendments and adjustments to the Protocol have been adopted, which were gradually tightened to phase out ODS: the London Amendment in 1990 (with 196 ratifications by countries); the Copenhagen Amendment (with 196 ratifications by countries) and the 1992 Adjustments; the Montreal Amendments and Adjustments in 1997 (with 190 ratifications by countries); and the Beijing Amendment in 1999 (with 178 ratifications by countries).

Non-state actors

International organizations. International discussions on ozone layer depletion took place under the auspices of the United Nations Environment Programme (UNEP) and the World Meteorological Organization (WMO). UNEP was particularly important in the agenda-setting phase as it sponsored the Washington meeting in March 1977, where countries agreed on an 'International Plan of Action on the Ozone Layer' and established a Coordinating Committee of the Ozone Layer (COOL) to guide future international action on ozone and to assess ozone depletion. The UNEP Governing Council then launched the first meeting of the Ad Hoc Working Group in 1982, which led to the Vienna Convention in 1985. UNEP has also initiated the process of scientific assessment panels.

Secretariat. The Ozone Secretariat was established under the supervision of the UNEP offices in Nairobi, Kenya, and serves both the Vienna Convention for the Protection of the Ozone Layer and the Montreal Protocol on Substances that Deplete the Ozone Layer. The main duties of the secretariat include arranging and servicing the COP to the Convention and the MOP to the Protocol, as well as receiving, analysing, and providing data and information on the production and consumption of ODS to the Parties to the Protocol (Article 7 of the Convention).

Science. Prior to the negotiation of the Convention, scientists played an important role in agenda setting. Concerns that the Earth's stratospheric ozone layer could be at risk from ODS were first raised by Rowland and Molina in the early 1970s. Then, the US National Academy of Science confirmed scientific credibility of ozone depletion. Further, NASA launched the Ozone Trend Panel to assess existing data on the global impact of ozone depletion in 1986. The Assessment Panels were established in 1988, pursuant to Article 6 of the Montreal Protocol. The role of the Assessment Panels is to assess the scientific issues of ozone depletion, the environmental effects of ozone depletion, and the status of alternative substances and technologies and their economic implications. Currently, there are three panels: the Technology and Economic Assessment Panel (TEAP), the Scientific Assessment Panel (SAP) and the Environmental Effects Assessment Panel (EEAP). These panels carried out a periodic assessment at least every four years. They have released assessment reports in 1989, 1991, 1994, 1998, 2002, 2006, and in 2010.

Environmental non-governmental organizations (NGOs). A year after the Montreal Protocol, a series of environmental campaigns across the continent changed the corporate strategy in Britain, Germany and the United States. For instance, in Germany, Greenpeace and other campaign groups targeted Hoechst, one of Germany's biggest manufacturers. This resulted in Hoechst giving up initial opposition to a complete phase out of chlorofluorocarbon (CFC, one of the ODS), and declaring its support for an eventual phasing out of CFCs in 1988 (Falkner 2005). In the case of Britain, too, pressure exerted from British environmental groups, especially Greenpeace and Friends of the Earth, changed corporate strategy in 1988 (Bendick 1991). In the United States, Natural Resources Defence Council (NRDC) was instrumental in campaigning for removal of CFCs from aerosol cans in 1978.

Business. When the ozone hole was discovered in 1985, there were huge societal and political pressures on the US chemical industry. However, after 1986, the 'business support' appeared. DuPont and the Alliance for Responsible CFC Policy announced their support for international controls on CFCs in August 1986. In doing so, DuPont had invested in finding CFC alternatives from 1986 onwards. By establishing two industry programmmes to assess environmental accessibility and toxicity, DuPont invented two non-ODSs, hydrochlorofluorocarbon (HCFC) and hydrofluorocarbons (HFC) in 1988, and announced it would stop producing CFCs. On the other hand, companies have been lobbying their governments in order to protect their particular commercial interests and to safeguard their investment in HCFCs – which were classified as ODS in 1992 – for as long as possible (Falkner 2005: 124–125).

Effectiveness

The current ozone-depleting substances controls have been strengthened over time under amendments to the Montreal Protocol. Non-Article 5 parties (developed countries) were required to phase out the production and consumption of ODS, such as halons by 1994; CFCs, CTC, hydrobromochlorofluorocarbons (FCFC) and methyl chloroform by 1996; bromochloromethane by 2002; and methyl bromide by 2005. Article 5 countries (developing countries) were also required to phase out production and consumption of CFCs, halons and CTC by 2010; and methyl chloroform and methyl bromide by 2015. As for HCFC production and consumption, Article 2 countries were required to freeze the substance in 2004 and phase it out by 2020, while in Article 5 parties it has to be frozen by 2013 and phased out by 2030. As a result, the ozone-depleting potential of all controlled ODS decreased more than 93 per cent between 1986 and 2004 (UNEP 2005).

References

Benedick, R. (1991) *Ozone Diplomacy: New Directions in Safeguarding the Planet*, Cambridge, MA: Harvard University Press.

Falkner, R. (2005) 'The Business of Ozone Layer Protection: Corporate Power in Regime Evolution', in David L. Levy and Peter J. Newell, eds., *The Business of Global Environmental Governance*, Cambridge, MA: MIT Press, 105–134.

IISD (n.d.) 'Introduction to Ozone Regime', online, available from http://www.iisd.ca/process/ozone_regime_intro.htm (accessed 29 March 2013).

Natural Resources Defence Council (n.d.) 'About NRDC: Victories', online, available from http://www.nrdc.org/about/victories.asp (accessed 29 March 2013).

UNEP (2005) *Production and Consumption of Ozone Depleting Substances under the Montreal Protocol 1986–2004*, Nairobi: UN Environmental Programme.

UNEP (2009) *Handbook for the Vienna Convention for the Protection of the Ozone Layer*, 8th edn, United Nations Environmental Programme, available from http://ozone.unep.org/Publications/VC_Handbook/VC-Handbook-2009.pdf (accessed 29 March 2013).

UNEP (2009) *Handbook for the Montreal Protocol for the Protection of the Ozone Layer*, 8th edn, United Nations Environmental Programme, available from http://ozone.unep.org/Publications/MP_Handbook/MP-Handbook-2009.pdf (accessed 29 March 2013).

WMO (2010) 'Scientific Assessment of Ozone Depletion, World Meteorological Organization, Available from http://www.wmo.int/pages/prog/arep/gaw/ozone_2010/ozone_asst_report.html (accessed 29 March 2013).

Related website

*   United Nations Environment Programme Ozone Secretariat
    http://ozone.unep.org/new_site/en/index.php

UN Convention to Combat Desertification

The international responses to the issue

Background. The United Nations Convention to Combat Desertification (UNCCD) was adopted in Paris in 1994 and came into force in 1996. As of May 2012, 194 countries and the European Union are parties to the Convention.

Objective. The objective of the Convention is to 'to combat desertification and mitigate the effects of drought in countries experiencing serious drought and/ or desertification, particularly in Africa, through effective action at all levels, supported by international cooperation and partnership arrangements, in the framework of an integrated approach which is consistent with Agenda 21, with a view to contributing to the achievement of sustainable development in affected areas' (Article 2, paragraph 1 of the Convention). The 'affected areas' include Africa, Asia, Latin America and the Caribbean, the Northern Mediterranean, and Central and Eastern Europe (Annexes I, II, III, IV, and V to the Convention).

Issue definition. The issue of desertification is defined as 'land degradation in arid, semi-arid and dry sub-humid areas resulting from various factors, including climatic variations and human activities' (Article 1 of the Convention).

Decision-making structure. The Conference of the Parties (COP), which is the Convention's supreme governing body, has met ten times up to the present: COP1 in Rome, Italy (1997); COP2 in Dakar, Senegal (1998); COP3 in Recife, Brazil (1999); COP4 in Bonn, Germany (2000); COP5 in Geneva, Switzerland (2001); COP6 in Havana, Cuba (2003); COP7 in Nairobi, Kenya (2005); COP8 in Madrid, Spain (2007); COP9 in Buenos Aires, Argentina (2009) and COP10 in Gyeongnam, South Korea (2011). In addition, the Committee for the Review of the Implementation of the Convention was established at COP5.

Development. 'The 10-year strategic plan and framework to enhance the implementation of the Convention (2008–2018)' was agreed at COP8 in 2007. The strategic plan contains 'strategic objectives' and 'operational objectives' that guide the actions of short- and medium-term effects. The strategic objectives include: improving the living conditions of the affected populations; improving the conditions of affected ecosystems; generating global benefits through effective implementation of the UNCCD; and mobilizing resources to support implementation of the Convention through building effective partnerships between national and international actors. The operational objectives include: actively influencing relevant international, national and local processes and actors in adequately addressing desertification/land degradation and drought-related issues; supporting the creation of enabling environments for promoting solutions to combat desertification/land degradation and mitigate the effects of drought; and to become a global authority on scientific and technical knowledge pertaining to desertification/land degradation and mitigation of the effects of drought.

Non-state actors

International organizations. The issue of desertification was discussed at the United Nations Conference on Environment and Development (UNCED), held in Rio de Janeiro in 1992. The Conference called on the United Nations General Assembly to establish an Intergovernmental Negotiating Committee to Combat Desertification (INCD) to develop a Convention to Combat Desertification. The Convention was adopted at the fifth session of INCD.

As the home of the 1977 Plan of Action to Combat Desertification, the United Nations Environment Programme (UNEP) played a significant role in negotiations technically, financially and administratively. For example, UNEP, the United Nations Development Plan (UNDP), and the International Fund for Agricultural Development (IFAD) were instrumental in providing technical support for INCD.

The Organization for Economic Co-operation and Development (OECD) had also played an important role as a deliberative actor, and therefore helped to share the outcome of the negotiations. The Club du Sahel, a forum run by OECD to prevent drought in Sahel, acted as a funding organization and shaped the positions of some of the African countries.

Secretariat. The Secretariat of the UNCCD was established during the COP1. The functions of the secretariat include making arrangements for sessions of the COP and its subsidiary bodies established under the Convention, as well as compiling and transmitting reports submitted to it (Article 23 of the Convention). Also, it coordinates activities with other secretaries of relevant international environmental bodies and conventions, such as UN Framework Convention on Climate Change and the Convention on Biological Diversity.

Science. The International Panel of Experts on Desertification (IPED) was established in 1993 in Geneva to comment on the draft text of the Convention. The experts were appointed by the Executive Secretary of the INCD Secretariat. It functioned as the central mechanism for scientific input in the negotiations.

A Committee on Science and Technology (CST) was established under Article 24 of the Convention as a subsidiary body of the COP. It is composed of government officials competent in the field of combating desertification. Its role is to identify priorities for research, and to advise researchers to foster cooperation. In doing so, the so-called 'Group of Experts' provides current scientific knowledge regarding desertification and policy implications to the CST.

In addition, UNCCD Scientific Conferences, organized by CST, were held twice: the first was held in 2009; the second in 2012; and the third will be held in 2014.

Environmental non-governmental organizations (NGOs). Environmental NGOs were actively engaged in international negotiation on desertification. A total of 187 environmental and social NGOs actively participated in the UNCCD process from INCD1 to COP1. In particular, NGOs were instrumental in enhancing a linkage between global and local levels and encouraging local and national implementation policies, as well as strengthening capacity building for actions related to UNCCD.

Business. The business community was rarely engaged in the UNCCD negotiations as there were no business interests in protecting the world's drylands, and they were not put at risk by the Convention.

Effectiveness

According to Bauer (2007), implementation of the Convention has been rather slow, largely because of the issue's regional-specific character – many states are not affected by the issue of desertification and consequently there is less need for stringent global collective action to tackle the problem. As a result, the Convention has not been successful in attracting findings to implement its measures.

References

Bauer, S. (2007) 'Bureaucratic Authority and The Implementation of International treaties', in J. Joachim, B. Reinalda, and B. Verbeek, eds., *International Organizations and Implementation; Enforces, Managers, Authorities?* New York: Routledge pp. 62–74.

Corell, E. and Betsill, M. M. (2001), 'A Comparative Look at NGO Influence in International Environmental Negotiations: Desertification and Climate Change'. *Global Environmental Politics* 1:4, November 2001, pp.86–107.

Toulmin, C. (1994) 'Combating Desertification: Encouraging Local Action Within a Global Framework', in Helge Ole Bergensen, George Parmann, eds., *Green Globe Yearbook of International Co-operation on Environment and Development 1994*, Oxford: Oxford University Press, pp.79–88.

United Nations (1989) 'Plan of Action to Combat Desertification – A Implementation of the Plan of Action to Combat Desertification', Online, Available from http://www.un.org/documents/ga/res/44/a44r172.htm (accessed 29 March 2013).

UNCCD (n.d.) 'Text of the Convention including all Annexes', Online, Available from http://www.unccd.int/en/about-the-convention/Pages/Text-overview.aspx (accessed 29 March 2013).

UNCCD (2007) *ICCD/COP(8)/16/Add.1* Report of the Conference of the Parties on its eight session, held in Madrid 3 to 14 September 2007, United Nations Convention to Combat Desertification. Also available at http://www.unccd.int/Lists/OfficialDocuments/cop8/16add1eng.pdf (accessed 29 March 2013).

UNEP (n.d.) 'United Nations Conference on Desertification', Online, Available from http://www.unep.org/Documents.multilingual/Default.asp?DocumentID=65&ArticleID=1255&l=en (accessed 29 March 2013).

Related websites

•   United Nations Convention on Combat Desertification
     http://www.unccd.int/

The Convention on Biological Diversity

The international responses to the issue

Background. The Convention on Biological Diversity (CBD) was opened for signature in 1992 at the United Nations Conference on Environment and Development, and came into force in 1993. Currently, there are 193 Parties (168 Signatures) to the Convention. The Convention is not the first or the only international treaty to address conservation of all habitats, but it is the first to address conservation of *all* biological diversity and the first to include sustainable utilization of these resources. Other international agreements in this field include the Ramsar Conservation on Wetlands, the Convention on Migratory Species, the Convention on the Conservation of Antarctic Marine Living Resources (CCAMLR), International Convention for the Regulation of Whaling (ICRW), International Commission for the Conservation of Atlantic Tunas (ICCAT), and the Conservation on International Trade in Endangered Species of wild Fauna and Flora (CITES).

Objective. The objectives of the Convention is 'the conservation of biological diversity, the sustainable use of its components and the fair and equitable sharing of the benefits arising out of the utilization of genetic resources, including by appropriate access to genetic resources and by appropriate transfer of relevant technologies, taking into account all rights over those resources and to technologies, and by appropriate funding (Article 1 of the Convention).

Issue definition. Biological diversity is defined as 'the variability among living organisms from all sources including, *inter alia,* terrestrial, marine and other aquatic ecosystems and the ecological complexes of which they are part: this includes diversity within species, between species and of ecosystems. Biological resources include 'genetic resources, organisms or parts thereof, populations, or any other biotic component of ecosystems with actual or potential use or value for humanity' (Article 2 of the Convention).

Decision-making structure. The Conference of the Parties (COP) was established as a governing body to the Convention, and the first COP took place at Nassau, Bahamas in 1994 and held 11 times since: COP2 in Jakarta, Indonesia in 1995; COP3 in Buenos Aires, Argentina in1996; COP4 in Bratislava, Slovakia in 1998; COP5 in Nairobi, Kenya in 2000; COP6 in the Hague, the Netherlands in 2002; COP7 in Kuala Lumpur, Malaysia in 2004; COP8 in Curitiba, Brazil in 2006; COP9 in Bonn, Germany in 2008; COP10 in Nagoya, Japan in 2010; and COP11 in Hyderabad, India.

Development. At its first Extraordinary Meeting of the Conference of Parties to the Convention on Biological Diversity (EXCOP1) in 2000, the Cartagena Protocol on Biosafety to the Convention on Biological Diversity was adopted in order to 'contribute to ensuring an adequate level of protection in the field of the safe transfer, handling and use of living modified organisms resulting from modern biotechnology that may have adverse effects on the conservation and sustainable use of biological diversity, taking also into account risks to human health, and specifically focusing on transboundary movements' (Article 1 of the Protocol). The Protocol establishes an 'advance informed agreement' procedure that ensures countries are provided with the information necessary to make informed decisions before agreeing to the import of such organisms into their territory. It came into force in 2003, and currently there are 163 Parties (103 Signatures) to the Protocol.

At its tenth meeting of the Conference of the Parties to the Convention on Biological Diversity (COP10) in 2010, the Nagoya Protocol on Access to Genetic Resources and the Fair and Equitable Sharing of Benefits Arising from their Utilization (ABS) to the Convention on Biological Diversity was adopted. The objective of the Protocol is 'the fair and equitable sharing of the benefits arising from the utilization of genetic resources, including by appropriate access to genetic resources and by appropriate transfer of relevant technologies, taking into account all rights over those resources and to technologies, and by appropriate funding, thereby contributing to the conservation of biological diversity and the sustainable use of its components' (Article 1 of the Protocol). The Protocol will create a transparent legal framework by establishing more predictable conditions for access to generic resources, and by helping to ensure benefit-sharing between providers and users of generic resources. It will come into force 90 days after the fiftieth instrument of ratification, and currently there are 92 Signatures to the Protocol.

Furthermore, the Nagoya-Kuala Lumpur Supplementary Protocol on Liability and Redress to the Cartagena Protocol on Biosafety was adopted at COP-MOP5 at Nagoya, 2010. Its aim is 'providing international rules and procedures in the field of liability and redress relating to living modified organisms' (Article 1 of the Supplementary Protocol).

Non-state actors

International organizations. The United Nations Environment Programme (UNEP) was instrumental in setting up negotiations for biological diversity, and is responsible for the overall management of the Convention as a Secretariat. In 1988, it convened the Ad Hoc Working Group of Experts on Biological Diversity to explore the need for an international convention on biological diversity. In the following year, it established the Ad Hoc Working Group of Technical and Legal Experts to prepare an international legal instrument for the conservation and sustainable use of biological diversity. By 1991, these Ad Hoc Working Groups had become the 'Intergovernmental Negotiating Committee' (INC) that led to the creation of the CBD in 1992.

In the agenda-setting process of Cartagena Protocol negotiation, a number of international organizations, including UNEP, the UN Food and Agriculture Organization (FAO), the World Health Organization (WHO), and the UN Industrial Development Organization (UNIDO), worked with a group of 15 experts to prepare a background document on the need for a biosafety protocol for an *ad hoc* group of experts nominated by governments.

Secretariat. The Secretariat of the Convention on Biological Diversity was established to support the goals of the Convention. Its roles include preparing for, and servicing, meetings of the COP and other subsidiary bodies of the Convention, and to coordinate with other relevant international bodies (Article 24 of the Convention).

Science. The International Union for Conservation of Nature (IUCN) has been involved in the CDB since its drafting and through its further development. The IUCN is the 'largest professional global conservation network', with 1,200 members including more than 200 government and 900 NGOs, and almost 11,000 voluntary scientist and expert groups. 'The ICUN Red List', which is the inventory of the global conservation status of plant and animal species, provided information for the Convention of Biological Diversity as well as the Convention on International Trade in Endangered Species of Wild Fauna and Flora.

The Subsidiary Body on Scientific, Technical, and Technological Advice (SBSTTA), was established to assist COP by providing recommendations on the technical aspects of the implementation of the Convention. It is made up of government officials with expertise in relevant fields, observers from non-Party governments, the scientific community and other relevant organizations.

In the process of Cartagena Protocol negotiation, however, it faced no scientific consensus on the nature of biosafety. As a result, government delegates could not agree whether genetic modification was really a problem and negotiated in the face of scientific uncertainty and the role of precautionary decision-making.

Environmental non-governmental organizations (NGOs). During the CBD negotiation process, Environmental NGOs such as Greenpeace International, Friends of the Earth International and Third World Network, Worldwide Fund for Nature International, and Friends of the Earth International actively participated in this issue.

In the Cartagena Protocol negotiations, there were many environmental NGOs taking part. They tried to influence government representatives by lobbying delegates in the corridors, during lunch and other occasions. They also promoted their views, positions and policy-relevant information by organizing forums and handing out material to delegates, holding demonstrations and working on raising public awareness of the dangers of genetically modified organisms.

Business. Business has shown great interest in both the Cartagena Protocol on Biosafety and the Nagoya Protocol. In the biosafety negotiations, biotechnological and other relevant companies formed the Global Industry Coalition (GIC) to consolidate lobbying efforts, namely limiting the scope of the Protocol. In the Nagoya Protocol negotiations, too, various industries such as plant and animal breeding, horticulture, cosmetics, natural medicine, all types of biotechnology as well as the pharmaceutical industry were concerned with the consequences of the Protocol on their economic activities.

Recently, some businesses have engaged with environmental NGOs to initiate a sustainable programme on biodiversity. For instance, 'The Global Business and Biodiversity Programme' was established in 2003 between the private sector and the IUCN.

Effectiveness

Although there are 193 Parties to the Convention, the United States of America is still not a member. Nevertheless, the Convention endorsed the Plan of Action on Sub-national Governments, Cities, and other Local Authorities for Biodiversity at its tenth COP, thus allowing cities and sub-national governments to participate in the discussions.

References

Buck, M. and Hamilton, C. (2011) 'The Nagoya Protocol on Access to Genetic Resources and the Fair and Equitable Sharing of Benefits Arising from their Utilization to the

Convention on Biological Diversity', *Review of European Community & International Environmental Law*, 20, (1), 47–61.

CBD (1992) *Convention on Biological Diversity*. Available from http://www.cbd.int/doc/legal/cbd-en.pdf (accessed 29 March 2013).

CBD (2003) *Text of the Cartagena Protocol on Biosafety*. Available from http://bch.cbd.int/protocol/text/

CBD (2010) *Text of the Nagoya Protocol*. Available from http://www.cbd.int/abs/text/ (accessed 29 March 2013).

CBD (2010) *Text of Nagoya – Kuala Lumpur Supplementary Protocol on Liability and Redress to the Cartagena Protocol on Biosafety*. Available from http://bch.cbd.int/protocol/NKL_text.shtml (accessed 29 March 2013).

Rosendale, G. K. (1995) 'The Convention on Biological Diversity: A Viable Instrument for Conservation and Sustainable Use', in Helge Ole Bergensen, George Parmann and Øystein B. Thommessen, eds., *Green Globe Yearbook of International Co-operation on Environment and Development 1995*, Oxford: Oxford University Press, 69–81.

Related websites

- Convention on Biological Diversity
  http://www.cbd.int/
- International Union for Conservation of Nature (IUCN)
  http://www.iucn.org/about/

Convention on the Prevention of Marine Pollution by Dumping of Wastes and Other Matter

The international responses to the issue

Background. The Convention on the Prevention of Marine Pollution by Dumping of Wastes and Other Matter (known as the London Convention) was adopted in 1972, and came into force in 1975. This was the first major global treaty that protected the marine environment from unregulated dumping of waste. Currently, 87 countries are Parties to the Convention.

Objective. Its aim is to 'individually and collectively promote the effective control of all sources of pollution of the marine environment, and pledge themselves especially to take all practicable steps to prevent the pollution of the sea by the dumping of waste and other matter that is liable to create hazards to human health, to harm living resources and marine life, to damage amenities or to interfere with other legitimate uses of the sea' (Article I of the Convention). The main function of the Convention has been to provide a global basis for the application of sea disposal principles and a forum for discussion, negotiation and exchange of information on sea disposal and other related marine environmental issues.

Issue definition. The issue of dumping is defined as 'any deliberate disposal at sea of wastes or other matter from vessels, aircraft, platforms or other man-made structures at sea' and 'any deliberate disposal at sea of vessels, aircraft, platforms or other man-made structures at sea' (Article III of the Convention).

Decision-making structure. The governing body for the Convention is the Consultative Meeting of the Parties, which meets annually.

Development. In 1996, the Parties to the Convention adopted the 1996 Protocol (London Protocol), which came into force on March 2006, and there are currently 41 Parties to the Protocol. This Protocol was intended to eventually replace the Convention, as it prohibited all dumping, except for possibly acceptable wastes on the so-called 'reverse list'. Those are:

- Dredged material
- Sewage sludge
- Fish waste, or material resulting from industrial fish-processing operations
- Vessels and platforms or other man-made structures at sea
- Inert, inorganic geological material
- Organic material of natural origin
- Bulky items primarily comprising iron, steel, concrete and similar unharmful materials for which the concern is physical impact and limited to those circumstances where such wastes are generated at locations, such as small islands with isolated communities, having no practicable access to disposal options other than dumping CO_2 streams from CO_2 capture processes.

Non-state actors

International organizations. The International Marine Organization (IMO) acts as a secretariat to the Convention and the Protocol, and therefore administers the Convention. It also works closely with the Food and Agriculture Organization of the United Nations (FAO), the International Atomic Energy Agency (IAEA), the Intergovernmental Oceanographic Commission (IOC), the United Nations (UN), the United Nations Environment Programme (UNEP), the United Nations Education, Science and Cultural Organization (UNESCO), the World Health Organization (WHO), the World Meteorological Organization (WMO), and the Convention for the Protection of the Marine Environment of the North-East Atlantic (OSPAR).

In addition, the Convention and Protocol set up cooperative arrangements and advice complementary to other agreements, including the Basel Convention on Hazardous Wastes and their Disposal, the International Convention for the Prevention of Pollution from Ships (MARPOL), the UNEP Global Programme of Action for the Protection of the Marine Environment from Land-Based Activities, and the UNEP Regional Seas Programme.

Secretariat. The permanent secretariat is under the IMO, which is in London. Its role includes convening consultative meetings of the Contracting Parties, preparing and assisting in the development and implementation of procedures, and considering enquiries by, and information from the Contracting Parties, and providing recommendations to the Parties on questions related to, but not specifically covered by the Convention (Article XIV of the Convention).

Science. The Scientific Group on Dumping, comprising experts nominated by the Contracting Parties works on the technical issues of ocean dumping. Its role is to evaluate and review existing provisions and annexes in light of new scientific information. One of the milestones of its activity is the draft of 'Guidelines for the Assessment of Waste or Other Matters that May Be Considered for Dumping' (the Guidelines) for the 1997 Consultative Meeting, the year after the Protocol had been adopted.

With regard to the specific issue of dumping radioactive wastes at sea, which has been one of the contested issues at least from the 1980s, the Parties to the London Convention established the Intergovernmental Panel of Experts on Radioactive Waste (IGPRAD) in 1985 to address the issue.

As for the disposal of carbon dioxide into the sea, the Joint Group of Experts on the Scientific Aspects of Marine Environmental Protection (GESAMP) published a study of the scientific and technical issues in relation to the issue of climate change.

Furthermore, several research organizations and programmes are working closely with the Convention, including the Partnerships in Environmental Management for the Sea of East Asia (PEMSEA), the Arctic Monitoring and Assessment Programme (AMAP), the South Pacific Regional Environment Programme (SPREP), the Global Programme of Action for the Protection of Marine Environment from Land-based Activities (GPA), the International Ocean Institute (IOI), and the International Council for Exploration of the Sea (ICES).

Environmental non-governmental organizations (NGOs). Environmental NGOs, particularly Greenpeace International, have played an important role in the issue of marine pollution caused by dumping. It has participated in the seventh session of Commission on Sustainable Development in 1999 as an observer delegation, and urged states to ratify the Protocol. Further, it encouraged the Secretariat to cooperate with other regional seas programmes to adopt similar provisions. In addition, Greenpeace International organized a world-wide media campaign on the dumping of Brent Spar by Shell UK in 1995.

Business. Several industries, especially the oil, nuclear, and chemical industries are threatened by the Convention. In particular, the oil industry has formed the E&P forum (Oil Industry International Exploration and Production Forum). The E&P forum was established in 1974 as an international association to represent the interests of oil companies and the petroleum industry at the specialist agencies of United Nations, governmental and other international bodies concerned with regulating the exploration and production of oil and gas. The E&P Forum was represented at all the meetings of the IMO, the London Convention, and regional meetings such as the Convention for the Protection of the Marine Environment of the North-East Atlantic (OSPAR Convention).

Currently, some industrial associations are working closely with the London Convention. These include the World Association for Waterborne Transport Infrastructure (PIANC), the International Association of Dredging Companies (IADC), the World Organization of Dredging Associations (WODA), the Central Dredging Association (CEDA).

Effectiveness

High-level radioactive waste dumping has never been allowed under the Convention. A moratorium on low-level radioactive waste has been in place since 1983, which depends on the completion of scientific and technical studies as well as wider social scientific studies on radioactive waste dumping. With the completion of these studies, Parties to the Convention have agreed to ban the dumping of all radioactive wastes in 1993, and this legally binding prohibition came into force in 1994.

Dumping of industrial waste in the sea during the 1970s rose from 11 million to 17 million tons, but the quantity decreased and stabilized at about 8 million tons since the 1980s. Between 1992 and 1995, the quantity increased from 4.5 million to 6 million tons, and no dumping permits have been noted in reports submitted by Parties since.

For sewage sludge, the amount of sewage dumping increased from 12.5 to 17 million tons during 1970s, and then decreased to 14 million tons in 1985. From 1986, the amount remained at a steady level of about 20 million tons, and decreased to 12 million in the early 1990s due to the practice of several countries. However, the amount increased again from 12.5 to 16.25 million tons by 1994.

The annual amount of incineration at sea from the mid-1970s to the late 1980s was about 100,000 tons, and steadily decreased since then and was phased out early in 1991.

References

de Fayette, L. (1998) 'The London Convention 1972: Preparing for the Future', *The International Journal of Marine and Coastal Law*, 13 (4), 515–536.

IAEA (1974) *Convention on the Prevention of Marine Pollution by Dumping of Wastes and Other Matter,* available from http://www.iaea.org/Publications/Documents/Infcircs/Others/inf205.shtml (accessed 29 March 2013).

IMO (n.d.) *The London Convention and Protocol: Their Role and Contribution to Protection of the Marine Environment*, International Maritime Organization, available from http://www.imo.org/blast/blastDataHelper.asp?data_id=21278&filename=LC-LPbrochure.pdf (accessed 29 March 2013).

Parmentier, R. (1999) 'Greenpeace and the Dumping of Waste at Sea: A Case of Non-State Actors' Intervention in International Affairs', *International Negotiation*, 4, 433–455.

Stokke, O. S. (1998) 'Beyond Dumping? The Effectiveness of the London Convention', in H. O. Bergensen and O. B. Thommessen, eds., *Yearbook of International Co-operation on Environment and Development 1998/99*, London: Earthscan, 39–49.

Related website

- International Maritime Organization (IMO)
  http://www.imo.org/OurWork/Environment/SpecialProgrammesAndInitiatives/Pages/London-Convention-and-Protocol.aspx

International Convention for the Prevention of Pollution From Ships (MARPOL)

The international responses to the issue

Background. The MARPOL Convention was adopted in 1973 at the International Marine Organization (IMO) but has never come into force. In response to a spate of tanker accidents between 1976–1977, the Protocol was adopted in 1978 and entered into force in 1983, which absorbed its parental Convention. A new Protocol that amended the Convention and a new Annex VI was adopted in 1997 and came into force in 2005.

Objective. Its aim is the 'prevention of pollution of the marine environment by ships from operational or accidental causes' (IMO 2011). Therefore, the Convention includes regulations aimed at preventing and minimizing pollution from ships, both accidental pollution and that caused by routine operations.

Issue definition. The Protocol sets regulations for the prevention of pollution by oil, noxious liquid substances in bulk, harmful substances carried by sea in packaged form, sewage from ships, garbage from ships, and air pollution from ships.

Decision-making structure. The Marine Environment Protection Committee (MEPC) of the IMO functions as the decision-making body of the MARPOL.

Development. MARPOL consists of the following six annexes. Annex I, which came into force in 1983, covers prevention of pollution by oil from operational measures as well as from accidental discharge. Annex II, which came into force in 1983, details the discharge criteria and measures for the control of pollution by noxious liquid substances carried in bulk. Annex III, which came into force in 1992, contains general requirements for the issuing of detailed standards on packing, marking, labelling, documentation, stowage, quantity limitations, exceptions and notifications. Annex IV, which came into force in 2003, contains requirements to control pollution of the sea by sewage. Annex V, which came into force in 1988, deals with the prevention of pollution by garbage from ships. Annex VI, which came into force in 2005, sets limits on sulphur oxide and nitrogen oxide emissions from ship exhausts and prohibits deliberate emissions of ozone-depleting substances; designates emission control areas to set more stringent standards for SOx, NOx and particulate matter.

Non-state actors

Among the various non-state actors, IMO, which is responsible for prevention of marine pollution by ships, plays a key role in MARPOL since it serves as its Secretariat. Under Article 8 of the Protocol, the functions of the secretariat include informing all states which have signed the present Protocol about each new signature, the date of entry into force of the Protocol, and the deposit of any instrument of denunciation of the Protocol; and to transmit certified true copies of the present Protocol to all States which have signed the present Protocol.

Effectiveness

As of June 2012, there are 152 contracting states to Annexes I and II of MARPOL, with 99.20 per cent of world tonnage. As for Annex III, there are 137 contracting states with 96.59 per cent of world tonnage. There are 130 contracting states in Annex IV with 88.65 per cent of world tonnage. There are 144 contracting states in Annex V with 97.47 per cent of world tonnage. There are 70 contracting states in Annex VI with 93.29 per cent of world tonnage.

References

Admiralty and Maritime Law Guide (n.d.) Protocol of 1997 to amend the International Convention for the Prevention of Pollution from Ships of 2 November 1973, as modified by the Protocol of 17 February 1978, available from http://www.admiraltylawguide.com/conven/protomarpol1997.html (accessed 29 March 2013).

Socioeconomic Data and Applications Center (n.d.) *International Convention for the Prevention of Pollution from Ships, 1973*, available from http://sedac.ciesin.org/entri/texts/pollution.from.ships.1973.html (accessed 29 March 2013).

Socioeconomic Data and Applications Center (n.d.) Protocol of 1978 Relating to the International Convention for the Prevention of Pollution from Ships, available from http://sedac.ciesin.org/entri/texts/acrc/marpolp.txt.html (accessed 29 March 2013).

Related websites

*   International Maritime Organization (IMO) 'International Convention for the Prevention of Pollution from Ships (MARPOL)'
    http://www.imo.org/about/conventions/listofconventions/pages/international-convention-for-the-prevention-of-pollution-from-ships-%28marpol%29.aspx
*   International Maritime Organization (IMO) 'Status of Conventions'
    http://www.imo.org/About/Conventions/StatusOfConventions/Pages/Default.aspx

Convention on the Future Multilateral Cooperation in North-East Atlantic Fisheries and Norwegian–Russian Joint Commission on Fisheries

The international responses to the issue

Background. The Convention on Future Multilateral Cooperation in North-East Atlantic Fisheries (NEAFC) was signed in 1980 and came into force in 1982. The Joint Norwegian–Russian Fisheries Commission was established in 1976, as a bilateral fisheries management body between Norway and Russia.

Objective. The principal objective of NEAFC is to 'promote the conservation and optimum utilisation of the fishery resources of the North-East Atlantic area within a framework appropriate to the regime of extended coastal state jurisdiction over fisheries, and accordingly to encourage international cooperation and consultation with respect to these resources'. It also promotes the exchange of scientific information and data on the state of fishery resources in the area and management policies. The objective of Joint Norwegian–Russian Fisheries Commission is to manage cod, haddock and capelin in the Barents Sea.

Decision-making structure. The North-East Atlantic Fisheries Commission was established in 1982 under the NEAFC. Contracting parties to the Commission are Denmark, European Union, Iceland, Norway and Russian Federation. Its function is to recommend measures to contracting parties to promote the objectives of the NEAFC. Each contracting Party appoints to the Commission not more than two representatives. The commission holds annual sessions. The Joint Norwegian–Russian Fisheries Commission meets annually to adopt and allocate total quotas and other regulations for several stocks shared by the coastal states, which include the world's biggest cod stock, North-East Arctic cod.

Issue definition. The NEAFC covers all kinds of fishes, molluscs and crustaceans as well as any sedentary species that are not dealt with by other international agreements. The Joint Norwegian–Russian Fisheries Commission covers three types of fish – cod, haddock and capelin.

Development. NEAFC replaced the original North-East Atlantic Fisheries Convention of 1959, which in turn had replaced the 1946 Convention for the Regulation of Meshes and Fishing Nets and the Size Limits of Fish. Within NEAFC, there are two schemes currently operating with regard to control: the Scheme of Control and Enforcement (an electronic surveillance scheme to control the fishing activities of vessels in the Regulatory Area – outside the fishing zones of the coastal States) and the non-contracting party scheme to address the problem of non-contracting party fishing activity in the NEAFC Regulatory Area.

The development of the Joint Norwegian–Russian Fisheries Commission can be divided into three periods: before and after the end of the Cold War and after the millennium. Before the end of the Cold War, most of the discussion was focused on the size of total allowable catches for the three fish stocks, and whether the smallest permitted mesh size and the minimum length of fish could be increased. During the 1990s, discussions were centred on extensive coordination of technical management measures and general agreement about the annual total allowable levels of catch. In 2003, the Commission adopted a set of decision and action rules and a management rule for North-East Arctic cod. These include: 'average fish mortality should be kept below the precautionary limit over three-year periods; total allowable catches should not change more than 10 per cent from one year to the next; but exceptions can be made in situations where the spawning stock has fallen below declined critical levels' (Hønneland 2007).

Non-state actors

Among the several non-state actors, science plays a major role in both NEAFC and the Joint Norwegian–Russian Fisheries Commission. The International Council for the Exploration of the Sea (ICES), which was founded in 1902, to 'advance the scientific capacity to give advice on human activities affecting, and affected by, marine ecosystems', provides scientific advice to both NEAFC and the Joint Norwegian–Russian Fisheries Commission: NEAFC and NEAFC establishes conservation and management measures on the basis of advice from the Advisory Committee on Fisheries Management of ICES; the total allowable catch established by the Joint Norwegian–Russian Fisheries Commission is based on recommendations on catch levels given by the ICES, where both Norwegian and Russian scientists participate.

Effectiveness

The problem of illegal, unreported and unregulated (IIU) fishing has been the subject of discussion at NEAFC and the bilateral fisheries management between Norway and Russia. The NEAFC has developed tools to combat IUU fishing under the NEAFC Schemes of Control and Enforcement, and Norway and Russia have worked jointly to establish robust port state measures against IUU fishing. As a result, IUU fishing of cod in the Barents Sea, for example, has been reduced by 84 per cent between 2005 and 2008.

References

FAO (n.d.) 'North East Atlantic Fisheries Commission (NEAFC)', online, available from http://www.fao.org/fishery/rfb/neafc/en (accessed 29 March 2013).

Hønneland, G. (2007) 'Norway and Russia in the Barents Sea: Cooperation and Conflict in Fisheries Management', *Russian Analytical Digest*, 20, 9–11.

Norwegian Ministry of Fisheries and Coastal Affairs (2011) 'Fisheries collaboration with Russia', online, available from http://www.fisheries.no/resource_management/International_cooperation/Fisheries_collaboration_with_Russia/ (accessed 29 March 2013).

SEDAC (n.d.) Convention on Future Multilateral Cooperation in North-East Atlantic Fisheries (1980), online, available from http://sedac.ciesin.org/entri/texts/fisheries.north-east.atlantic.1980.html (accessed 29 March 2013).

Related websites

- Barents Portal
  http://www.barentsportal.com/barentsportal09/
- Convention on future multilateral cooperation in North-East Atlantic fisheries (NEAFC)
  http://ec.europa.eu/world/agreements/prepareCreateTreatiesWorkspace/treatiesGeneralData.do?step=0&redirect=true&treatyId=503
- International Council for the Exploration of the Sea
  http://www.ices.dk/Pages/default.aspx
- North–East Atlantic Fisheries Commission
  http://www.neafc.org/

Man and the Biosphere (MAB) Programme

The international responses to the issue

Background. The Man and the Biosphere Programme (MAB) of United Nations Educational, Scientific and Cultural Organization (UNESCO) was launched in 1971 as UNESCO's International Science Programme.

Objective. The aim of the MAB Programme is to 'set a scientific basis for the improvement of the relationships between people and their environment globally'.[1]

Decision-making structure. The main MAB governing body, the International Coordinating Council (ICC) of the Man and the Biosphere Programme, consists of 34 member states elected by UNESCO's biennial General Conference. The ICC meets annually, in order to guide and supervise the programme; review the progress; recommend research projects; assess priorities among policies and activities; coordinate the international cooperation of member states; coordinate activities with other international scientific programmes; consult with non-governmental organizations on scientific or technical questions; and also decide new biosphere reserves.

Development. The biosphere reserve network, which is internationally protected areas of terrestrial and costal/marine ecosystems or a combination thereof, was launched in 1974. This network is a key component of MAB's objective.

In 1983, the first International Biosphere Reserve Congress was held in Minsk (Belarus), jointly convened by UNESCO and United Nations Environment Programme (UNEP), in cooperation with Food and Agriculture Organization (FAO) and the International Union for Conservation of Nature (IUCN). As a result of this Congress, the 'Action Plan for Biosphere Reserves' was agreed and endorsed by UNESCO General Conference and by the governing body of UNEP.

In 1991, the Executive Board of UNESCO established an Advisory committee for Biosphere Reserves, which considered evaluating the effectiveness of the 1984 Action Plan, analyse its implementation and develop a strategy for biosphere reserves in the twenty-first century. In response to this, the Seville Conference was held in 1995, which adopted the 'Seville Strategy'.

The twentieth session of ICC and the Third World Congress of Biosphere that were held in Madrid in 2008, adopted the Madrid Action Plan. The plan set agendas for the MAB programme in the period 2008–2013, 'to develop mechanisms to encourage the sustainable development of biosphere reserves carried out in partnership with all sectors of society to ensure the well-being of people and their environment' (Madrid Action Plan).

Non-state actors

Among the various non-state actors, scientists play a key role in the MAB programme. As a matter of fact, MAB itself was launched as a loose network of biosphere reserves. The scientific network played a significant role during the 1995 Minsk Conference and 1995 Seville Conference. Even though the United States and the United Kingdom had withdrawn from UNESCO, scientists continued their activities in these countries.

Several international organizations – such as the United Nations Environmental Programme, the Food and Agriculture Organization of United Nations, the United Nations Development Programme, the World Meteorological Organization, and the World Health Organization – and NGOs, including the International Council for Science (ICSU), the International Union of Biological Sciences (IUBS), the World Conservation Union (IUCN), and the Scientific Committee on Problems of the Environment (SCOPE) were invited to the annual meeting of ICC.

Effectiveness

MAB relies on World Network of Biosphere Reserves for the implementation of its interdisciplinary work. As of July 2012, there are 598 biosphere sites registered in 117 countries (WNBR 2012).

References

United Nations Educational, Scientific and Culture Organization (1996) *Biosphere Reserves: The Servile Strategy and the Statutory Framework for the World Network*, UNESCO, Paris, also available from http://unesdoc.unesco.org/images/0016/001633/163301e.pdf (accessed 29 March 2013).

United Nations Educational, Scientific and Culture Organization (2008) *Madrid Action Plan for Biosphere Reserves (2008–2013)*, UNESCO, Paris, also available from http://unesdoc.unesco.org/images/0016/001633/163301e.pdf (accessed 29 March 2013).

Related websites

- United Nations Educational, Scientific and Culture Organization (UNESCO) Man and Biosphere Programme
  http://www.unesco.org/new/en/natural-sciences/environment/ecological-sciences/man-and-biosphere-programme/
- Directory of the World Network of Biosphere Reserves (WNBR)
  http://www.unesco.org/new/en/natural-sciences/environment/ecological-sciences/biosphere-reserves/world-network-wnbr/wnbr/

The Conservation on International Trade in Endangered Species of Wild Fauna and Flora (CITES)

The international responses to the issue

Background. The Convention on International Trade in Endangered Species of Wild Fauna and Flora (CITES) was opened for signature in 1973, and came into force on 1 July, 1975. Currently, there are 175 Parties to the Convention.

Objective. The aim is to ensure that international trade in specimens of wild animals and plants does not threaten their survival (Article 2 of the Convention). It divides species into the following three appendixes:

- Appendix I shall include all species threatened with extinction which are or may be affected by trade. Trade in specimens of these species must be subject to particularly strict regulation in order not to endanger further their survival and must only be authorized in exceptional circumstances.
- Appendix II shall include:
  (a) all species which although not necessarily now threatened with extinction may become so unless trade in specimens of such species is subject to strict regulation in order to avoid utilization incompatible with their survival; and
  (b) other species which must be subject to regulation in order that trade in specimens of certain species referred to in sub-paragraph (a) of this paragraph may be brought under effective control.
- Appendix III shall include all species which any Party identifies as being subject to regulation within its jurisdiction for the purpose of preventing or restricting exploitation, and as needing the cooperation of other Parties in the control of trade.

Issue definition. 'Species' means any species, subspecies, or geographically separate population thereof. It includes any animal or plant, whether alive or dead (Article 1 of the Convention).

Decision-making structure. The Conference of Parties (COP) was established to review the implementation of the Convention, which is held every two or three years.

Development. At the COP1 in Bern (Switzerland) in 1976, Parties established the first criteria for amending Appendixes I and II. At COP2 at San José (Costa Rica) in 1979, a permanent Standing Committee, was established to steer the work and performance of the Convention. Parties also formalized the relationship between CITES and the International Whaling Commission.

At the COP3 in New Delhi (India) in 1981, the Technical Committee, the forerunner of the Animals and Plants Committee was established. Parties also adopted the first standardized permit form, and the use of the CITES 'elephant' logo.

At COP4 at Gaborone (Botswana) in 1983, accession to the Convention of any organization of regional economic integration constituted by sovereign States, such as the European Economic Community (EEC), was discussed. However, insufficient numbers of the Parties have since accepted it, and this amendment has not yet come into force.

At COP5 in Buenos Aires (Argentina) in 1985, procedures were adopted for including species in Appendix III. At COP6 in Ottawa (Canada) in 1987, the Animals, Plants and Nomenclature Committee was formed.

COP7 at Lausanne (Switzerland) in 1989 and COP8 at Kyoto (Japan) in 1992 were largely focused on species issues and improving procedures on ranching, captive breeding and artificial propagation.

At COP9 in Fort Lauderdale (United States) in 1994, parties adopted the development of new criteria to amend Appendixes I and II, along with revised guidelines for inclusion of species in Appendix III. Moreover, Parties adopted

Resolutions on species not included in the Appendixes (sharks and edible-nest swiftlets).

At COP10 in Harare (Zimbabwe) in 1997, a Resolution was adopted on the relationship with the Convention on Biological Diversity. COP11 in Gigiri (Kenya) in 2000 and COP12 in Santiago (Chile) 2002, focused mainly on species issues. Parties adopted a Resolution on cooperation with the Commission for the Conservation of Antarctic Marine Living Resources (CCAMLR), and a decision on the establishment of a Memorandum of Understanding with the Food and Agriculture Organization of the United Nations (FAO).

At COP13 in Bangkok (Thailand) in 2004, Parties approved the listing of ramin, agarwood, the great white shark and the humphead wrasse in Appendix II, as well as the upgrading of the Irrawaddy dolphin from Appendix II to I.

At COP14 in The Hague (the Netherlands) in 2007, Parties approved the listing of the slender-horned and Cuvier's gazelles and the slow loris in Appendix I and Brazil wood, sawfish and eel in Appendix II.

At COP15 in Doha (Qatar) in 2010, Parties decided to list Kaiser's spotted newt, five species of tree frogs, the unicorn beetle, rosewood, holywood and several Madagascar plant species. COP 16 was held in Thailand, 3–14 March 2013.

Non-state actors

In the case of protecting the African elephant, the role of environmental NGOs was key in CITES. NGOs' pressure on states resulted in the initial move of African elephants, classified as a species from Annex II to Annex I. Activist NGOs have largely participated at the level of the Conference of Parties commenting on the information and recommendations made to CITES. Science was also important as CITES undertook an independent assessment in 1994 to change the listing process.

Furthermore, extensive support from the secretariat was also important in protecting the African elephant. The CITES Secretariat is administered by UNEP and is located in Geneva, Switzerland. The function of the secretariat is to arrange and service meetings of the Parties; perform the functions entrusted to it under the provisions of Articles XV and XVI of the present Convention; undertake scientific and technical studies in accordance with programmes authorized by the Conference of the Parties as well as contribute to the implementation of the present Convention, including studies concerning standards for appropriate preparation and shipment of living specimens and the means of identifying specimens; study the reports of Parties and to request from Parties such further information with respect thereto as it deems necessary to ensure implementation of the present Convention; invite the attention of the Parties to any matter pertaining to the aims of the present Convention; publish periodically and distribute to the Parties current editions of Appendixes I, II and III together with any information which will facilitate the identification of specimens of species included in those Appendixes; prepare annual reports to the Parties on its work and on the implementation of the present Convention and such other reports as meetings of the Parties may request; make recommendations for the implementation of the aims and provisions of the present Convention, including the exchange of information of a scientific or technical nature; and to perform any other function as may be entrusted to it by the Parties (Article 12 of the Convention).

Effectiveness

As of November 2011, roughly 5,000 species of animals and 29,000 species of plants are protected by CITES against over-exploitation through international trade.

References

CITES (2003) 'CITES World: Official Newsletter of the Parties, 3 March 2003', online, available at http://www.cites.org/eng/news/world/30special.pdf (accessed 29 March 2013).

ENB (2010) 'CoP15 Final', *Earth Negotiation Bulletin*, International Institute for Sustainable Development.

Sand, P. H. (1997) 'Commodity or Taboo? International Regulation of Trade in Endangered Species', *Yearbook of International Co-operation on Environment and Development* (06), 19–36.

Related website

*   The Conservation on International Trade in Endangered Species of Wild Fauna and Flora (CITES)
    http://www.cites.org/

The Forest Stewardship Council (FSC)

Background. The Forest Stewardship Council (FSC) was established in 1993 in order to promote the responsible management of the world's forests, by multi-stakeholders including the World Wide Fund for Nature (WWF), Greenpeace, Friends of the Earth (FoE), retailers, trade unions and indigenous interest groups.

Objective. Their main activity is to 'develop forest management and *chain of custody* standards, deliver trademark assurance and provide *accreditation* services to a global network of committed businesses, organizations and communities', which provides a link between responsible production and consumption of forest products.

Decision-making structure. The General Assembly, consisting of three chambers that represent business, social and environmental interests, is the governing body of FSC. Each chamber is given equal voting power, and representing North and South representation equally. Furthermore, FSC international secretariat is located in Bonn, Germany, that handles the operational work of FSC.

Development. The FSC has developed ten principles and criteria of forest management:

1 Compliance with Laws and FSC Principles. Forest management shall respect all applicable laws of the country in which they occur, and international treaties and agreements to which the country is a signatory, and comply with all FSC Principles and Criteria.

2 Tenure and Use Rights and Responsibilities. Long-term tenure and use rights to the land and forest resources shall be clearly defined, documented and legally established.

3 Indigenous People's Rights. The legal and customary rights of indigenous peoples to own, use and manage their lands, territories, and resources shall be recognized and respected.

4 Community Relations and Worker's Rights. Forest management operations shall maintain or enhance the long-term social and economic well-being of forest workers and local communities.

5 Benefits from The Forest. Forest management operations shall encourage the efficient use of the forest's multiple products and services to ensure economic viability and a wide range of environmental and social benefits.

6 Environmental Impact. Forest management shall conserve biological diversity and its associated values, water resources, soils, and unique and fragile ecosystems and landscapes, and, by so doing, maintain the ecological functions and the integrity of the forest.

7 Management Plan. A management plan—appropriate to the scale and intensity of the operations—shall be written, implemented, and kept up to date. The long-term objectives of management, and the means of achieving them, shall be clearly stated.

8 Monitoring and Assessment. Monitoring shall be conducted—appropriate to the scale and intensity of forest management—to assess the condition of the forest, yields of forest products, chain of custody, management activities and their social and environmental impacts.

9 Maintenance of High Conservation Value Forests. Management activities in high conservation value forests shall maintain or enhance the attributes which define such forests. Decisions regarding high conservation value forests shall always be considered in the context of a precautionary approach.

10 Plantations. Plantations shall be planned and managed in accordance with Principles and Criteria 1–9, and Principle 10 and its Criteria. While plantations can provide an array of social and economic benefits, and can contribute to satisfying the world's needs for forest products, they should complement the management of, reduce pressures on, and promote the restoration and conservation of natural forests.

Effectiveness

The FSC had certified 116 million hectares (2.9 per cent) of forest up to 2009, by applying its principles to certify sustainable forest management. On the one hand, certification occurred in 82 countries and is most widespread in countries such as Croatia, Ireland and Poland, where forests are owned publicly and where the use of the forest is primarily for wood products. On the other hand, effectiveness of certification to halt deforestation is still limited in developing countries because certification may be too expensive and there are no incentives such as export markets in these countries (Marx and Cuypers 2010; European Commission 2011).

References

European Commission (2011) 'How Effective Are The Forest Stewardship Council Certification Schemes?', online, available from http://ec.europa.eu/environment/integration/research/newsalert/pdf/226na6.pdf (accessed 29 March 2013).

FSC (1996) *Principles and Criteria for Forest Stewardship*, Oaxaca, Mexico: FSC. Also available from http://www.fscus.org/standards_criteria/ (accessed 29 March 2013).

Marx, A. and Cuypers, D. (2010) 'Forest Certification As A Global Environmental Governance Tool: What Is The Macro-effectiveness of The Forest Stewardship Council?' *Regulation & Governance* (4), 408–434.

Pattberg, P. (2005) 'What Role for Private Rule-Making in Global Environmental Governance? Analysing the Forest Stewardship Council (FSC)', *International Environmental Agreements: Politics, Law and Economics*, 5 (2), 175–189.

Related website

*   Forest Stewardship Council
    http://www.fsc.org/

Marine Stewardship Council (MSC)

Background. The Marine Stewardship Council was established in 1997 by multi-stakeholders including the World Wildlife Fund (WWF) and Unilever.

Objective. The mission of the MSC is 'to use our ecolabel and fishery certification programme to contribute to the health of the world's oceans by recognising and rewarding sustainable fishing practices, influencing the choices people make when buying seafood, and working with our partners to transform the seafood market to a sustainable basis'.[2]

Decision-making structure. The Board of Trustees, consisting of a maximum of 15 members, meets four times a year and governs the MSC. An advisory body to the Board, Technical Advisory Board and Stakeholder Council was established. These three bodies include representatives from industry, environmental groups and science, and from different geographical regions, therefore making MSC 'truly balanced and decisions reflect many sectors and interests'.[3]

Development. MSC had established a sustainable fishing standard. The standard was developed between 1997 and 1999 though an international consultation with more than 300 stakeholders that included eight regional workshops and two expert drafting sessions. The standard is based on the Food and Agricultural Organization of the United Nations' Code of Conduct for responsible Fisheries and other conservation instruments, and requires every fishery to meet the following three principles:[4]

- Principle 1: Sustainable fish stocks. The fishing activity must be at a level which is sustainable for the fish population. Any certified fishery must operate so that fishing can continue indefinitely and is not overexploiting the resources.
- Principle 2: Minimising environmental impact. Fishing operations should be managed to maintain the structure, productivity, function and diversity of the ecosystem on which the fishery depends.
- Principle 3: Effective management. The fishery must meet all local, national and international laws and must have a management system in place to respond to changing circumstances and maintain sustainability.

Effectiveness

According to WWF, more than 100 fisheries around the world are now MSC certified. This is equal to the supply of over 7 per cent of all the seafood we eat – 40 per cent of caught wild salmon, and almost 50 per cent of prime whitefish. In terms of the economic scale of MSC-certified seafood, it is estimated to be worth over US$2 billion annually.

References

MSC (2010) 'Fishery Standard: Principles and Criteria for Sustainable Fishing', online, available from http://www.msc.org/documents/scheme-documents/msc-standards/MSC_environmental_standard_for_sustainable_fishing.pdf (accessed 29 March 2013).

WWF (2011) 'Making Fishing Sustainable', online, available from http://wwf.panda.org/who_we_are/history/50_years_of_achievements/stories/?199902/Making-fishing-sustainable (accessed 29 March 2013).

Related website

- Marine Stewardship Council
  http://www.msc.org/?i18nredirect=true&set_language=en

Fairtrade Labelling Organization

Background. Fairtrade Labelling Organization International (FLO) was established in 1997. Currently, FLO has 25 members. Its headquarters are in Bonn, Germany.

Objective. The objective of Fairtrade International is to secure a better deal for producers, allowing them 'the opportunity to improve their lives and plan for their future',[5] and to offer 'consumers a powerful way to reduce poverty through their everyday shopping'.[6] To enable this, it set international Fairtrade standards, and supported Fairtrade producers.

The key objectives of the standards are to:[7]

- ensure that producers receive prices that cover their average costs of sustainable production;
- provide an additional Fairtrade Premium which can be invested in projects that enhance social, economic and environmental development;

- enable pre-financing for producers who require it;
- facilitate long-term trading partnerships and enable greater producer control over the trading process;
- set clear core and development criteria to ensure that the conditions of production and trade of all Fairtrade certified products are socially and economically fair and environmentally responsible.

Decision-making structure. Members of Fairtrade International meet once a year at the General Assembly, made up of 50 producer representatives. The function of the Assembly is to decide on membership issues, approve the annual accounts, and ratify new Board directors. The Board, elected by the General Assembly, comprises 14 members (five representatives from the Fairtrade Labelling Initiatives, four representatives from Fairtrade certified producer organizations, two representatives from Fairtrade certified traders, and three external independent experts). The Board appoints three committees which provide expertise and oversight in key areas: the Standards Committee which supervises the development of Fairtrade standards; the Finance Committee, responsible for supervising FLO's finances; and the Nominations Committee, which is responsible for recommending and reviewing appointments to the Board and the Committees.

Development. With the success of the first Fairtrade-labelled 'Max Havelaar' coffee, which was launched in the Netherlands in 1988, a number of independent Fairtrade bodies were created as national initiatives. To coordinate the monitoring and standards of these initiatives, a process of convergence among the labelling organizations started, and was formalized in 1997 by the creation of FLO. Currently, FLO has three producer networks (Fairtrade Africa, Coordinator Fairtrade Latin American and Caribbean, Network of Asian and Pacific Producers), 19 labelling initiatives covering 24 countries, and three marketing organizations. Furthermore, the following products carry the Fairtrade Mark: bananas, cocoa, coffee, cotton, flowers, fresh fruit, honey, gold, juices, rice, spice and herbs, sports balls, sugar, tea, wine, and composite products.

Effectiveness

The number of producer organizations has grown over time. There are 827 Fairtrade certified producer organizations in 58 producing countries, that represent over 1.2 million farmers and workers. Sales of Fairtrade certified products in 2009 amounted to approximately €3.4 billion worldwide, which is a 15 per cent increase between 2008 and 2009.

References

Fairtrade International (n.d.) 'Facts and Figures', online, available from http://www. fairtrade.net/facts_and_figures.0.html (accessed 29 March 2013).

Redfern, A. and Snedker, P. (2012) *Creating Market Opportunities for Small Enterprises: Experiences of the Fair Trade Movement*, Geneva: International Labour Office.

Related websites

- Fairtrade International
  http://www.fairtrade.net/
- Fairtrade Africa
  http://www.fairtradeafrica.net/
- Coordinator Fairtrade Latin American and Caribbean
  http://clac-comerciojusto.org/
- Network of Asian and Pacific Producers
  http://www.fairtradenap.net/

e-Stewards Initiative

Background. The e-Stewards initiative was created in 1997 by Basel Action Network (BAN), the US-based charitable non-government organization named after the Basel Convention.

Objective. The initiative was created in response to the growing e-waste crisis, with an aim to 'prevent the toxic materials in electronics from continuing to cause long-term harm to human health and the environment, particularly in countries with developing economies'.[8]

Decision-making structure. The e-Stewards Standard is governed by BAN. The certification, however, is accredited by a separate body called ANAB (ANSI-ASQ National Accreditation Board). As an advisory body, the e-Stewards Leadership Council was created in August 2010, comprising original equipment manufacturers, recyclers, businesses, government, collectors, and NGOs. The function of the Council is to provide an advisory oversight of the e-Stewards Initiative, including the certification, the standard and the marketing programme.

Development. In 2003, BAN launched e-Stewards Pledge Programme, which aims to encourage e-recyclers to commit to responsible recycling. As a result of the programme, over 40 e-recyclers in 100 locations across the US pledged to keep toxic e-waste out of developing countries, prisons, landfills and incinerators. In 2008, BAN initiated e-Stewardship Certification for e-recyclers, with an objective 'to enable individuals and organizations who dispose of their old electronic equipment to easily identify recyclers that adhere to the highest standard of environmental responsibility and worker protection'.[9] Its characteristics are as follows:[10]

- Encompasses a certified ISO 14001 environmental management system and R2 (Responsible Recycling) Practices.
- Prohibits all toxic waste from being disposed of in solid waste landfills and incinerators.
- Requires full compliance with existing international hazardous waste treaties for exports and imports of electronics, and specifically prohibits the export of hazardous waste from developed to developing countries.
- Prohibits the use of prison labour in the recycling of toxic electronics, which often have sensitive data embedded.

- Requires extensive baseline protections for and monitoring of recycling workers in every country, including developed nations where toxic exposures are routinely taking place.
- Is written for international use.

Effectiveness

The programme is expanding internationally and Redmetch UK became the first company outside the United States to achieve e-Stewards certification in October 2010. Furthermore, Santa Clara County, California, became the first local authority to approve the legislation requiring all e-waste to be processed by e-Stewards certified recyclers in 2011.

References

Basel Action Network (2010) 'BAN media release. California's Santa Clara County Commits to Highest Standard of Responsible E-Waste Recycling – "Silicon Valley" Government Becomes First in Nation to Join e-Stewards Initiative', Online, Available from http://ban.org/ban_news/2010/101014_santa_clara_county_commits.html (accessed 29 March 2013).
e-Stewardship Council (2010) 'FAQ: How e-Stewards Certification Works', online, available from http://e-stewards.org/wp-content/uploads/2010/03/FAQs-How-Certification-Works-1.pdf (accessed 29 March 2013).

Related websites

- E-Stewards
  http://e-stewards.org/
- Basel Action Network
  http://www.ban.org/

United Nations Framework Convention on Climate Change

The international responses to the issue

Background. The United Nations Convention on Climate Change (UNFCCC) came into force in March 1994. Currently, there are 194 parties to the Convention.

Objective. Its ultimate objective is to achieve 'stabilization of greenhouse gases in the atmosphere at a level that would prevent dangerous anthropogenic interference with the climate system' (Article 2 of the Convention), considering the following: 'human activities have been substantially increasing the atmospheric concentrations of greenhouse gases, that these increases enhance the natural greenhouse effect, and that this will result on average in an additional warming of the Earth's surface and atmosphere and may adversely affect natural ecosystems and humankind'.

Issue definition. The issue of climate change is defined as 'a change of climate which is attributed directly or indirectly to human activity that alters the composition of the global atmosphere and which is in addition to natural climate variability observed over comparable time periods' (Article 1 of the Convention).

Decision-making structure. In order to achieve this objective, the Conference of Parties (COP) was created as a supreme decision-body, which has met eighteen times to date: COP1 in Berlin, Germany in 1995; COP2 in Geneva, Switzerland in 1996; COP3 in Kyoto, Japan in 1997; COP4 in Buenos Aires, Argentina in 1998; COP5 in Bonn, Germany in 1999; COP6 in the Hague, Netherlands in 2000; COP6 in Bonn, Germany in 2001; COP7 in Marrakech, Morocco in 2001; COP8 in New Delhi, India in 2002; COP9 in Milan, Italy in 2003; COP10 in Buenos Aires, Argentina in 2004; COP11 in Montreal, Canada in 2005; COP12 in Nairobi, Kenya in 2006; COP13 in Bali, Indonesia in 2007; COP14 in Poznan, Poland in 2008; COP15 in Copenhagen, Denmark in 2009; COP16 in Cancun, Mexico in 2010; COP17 in Durban, South Africa in 2011; and COP18, in Qatar in 2012.

Development. In 1997, the Kyoto Protocol was formally adopted at COP3, held in Kyoto, Japan. It set binding targets for 37 countries and the European Union for reducing greenhouse gas emissions, on an average of 5 per cent against 1990 levels over 2008–2012. The Kyoto Protocol came into force in 2005. It offers states an additional means of meeting their target by three market-based mechanisms: emission trading, which allows countries that have emission units to spare to sell excess capacity to countries that have exceeded their targets; the Clean Development Mechanism (CDM), which allows a country with an emission-reduction/limitation commitment under the Protocol (Annex B Party) to implement an emission-reduction project in developing countries; Joint Implementation (JI), which allows a country with an emission reduction/limitation commitment under the Protocol to earn emission reduction units from an emission-reduction project in another Annex B Party to meet its Kyoto target.

The first Meeting of the Parties to the Kyoto Protocol (MOP1) took place in Montreal, Canada. In accordance with Kyoto Protocol requirements, Parties launched negotiations on the next phase of the Protocol (future commitments for industrialized countries) under the Ad Hoc Working Group on the Kyoto Protocol (AWG-KP).

In 2007, the Parties agreed on the 'Bali Action Plan' at COP13, held in Bali, Indonesia. The Bali Action Plan established the Ad Hoc Working Group on Long-term Cooperative Action under the Convention (LWG-LCA), to conduct 'a comprehensive process to enable the full, effective and sustained implementation of the Convention through long-term cooperative action, now, up to and beyond 2012, in order to reach an agreed outcome and adopt a decision' at COP15.

In 2009 at COP15 held in Copenhagen, Denmark, the 'Copenhagen Accord' was taken note of by the COP. Based on this agreement, countries submitted non-binding emission reduction pledges: the United States pledged 13 per cent against its 2005 level; the EU pledged 20–30 per cent reduction against its 1990 level; Japan pledged 25 per cent reduction against its 1990 level. Developing countries have also submitted their voluntary reduction targets: China pledged to reduce carbon intensity by 40–56 per cent compared to 2005; India pledged to reduce carbon intensity by 20–25 per cent compared to 2005; Brazil pledged 36.1–38.9 per cent reduction compared to business as usual; and South Africa pledged 34 per cent reduction compared to business as usual.

At COP17 held in Durban, South Africa in 2011, Parties to the Convention decided to launch a process to 'develop a protocol, another legal instrument or an agreed outcome with legal force under the Convention applicable to all Parties', through a subsidiary body under the Durban Platform for Enhanced Action, which shall 'complete its work as early as possible but no later than 2015 in order to adopt this protocol, legal instrument or agreed outcome with legal force at the twenty-first session of the Conference of the Parties and for it to come into effect and be implemented from 2010'. The agreements in COP17 also entail the continuation of the Kyoto Protocol, although only the EU is likely to commit among the major developed countries.

Non-state actors

International organizations. In 1979, the World Meteorological Organization (WMO), the United Nations Environment Programme (UNEP), the United Nations Educational, Scientific and Cultural Organization (UNESCO) and the World Health Organization (WHO) convened the First World Climate Conference in Geneva to 'assess the state of knowledge of climate and to consider the effects of climate vulnerability and change on human society'. This Conference led to the establishment of the World Climate Programme and its research component, the World Climate Research Programme. The second World Climate Conference was held in Geneva in 1990, and the third World Climate Conference was also held in Geneva in 2009. Recently, UNEP has released its 'Emission Gap Report', to suggest that to limit global warming to 2°Celsius, 9 gigatonnes of carbon dioxide equivalent must be reduced by 2020 from what has been pledged under the Copenhagen Accord.

Secretariat. The UNFCCC Secretariat has been located in Bonn, Germany since 1996. The role of the secretariat includes making arrangements for sessions of the Conference of the Parties and its subsidiary bodies established under the Convention and providing them with services as required, as well as compiling and transmitting reports submitted to it. Further, it ensures the necessary coordination with the secretariats of other relevant international bodies (Article 8 of the Convention).

Science. Prior to the UNFCCC negotiation, science played an important part in setting climate agenda. In 1988, the Intergovernmental Panel on Climate Change (IPCC) was established by UNEP and WMO to provide a world with 'a clear scientific view on the current state of knowledge in climate change and its potential environmental and socio-economic impacts'. In 1990, the IPCC and the Second World Climate Conference called for a global treaty in climate change, and the United Nations General Assembly began negotiations on a framework convention. It has released four assessment reports: the First Assessment Report (FAR) in 1990; the Second Assessment Report (SAR) in 1995; the Third

Assessment Report (TAR) in 2001; the Fourth Assessment Report (AR4) in 2007; and the Fifth in due course.

Environmental non-governmental organizations (NGOs). Climate Action network (CAN) is a network of environmental non-governmental organizations consisting of more than 700 NGOs in 95 countries, 'working to promote government and individual action to limit human-induced climate change to ecologically sustainable levels', by exchanging and coordinating development of NGO strategy at international, regional, and national levels. One of the notable activities of the CAN is to publish 'ECO', a daily newsletter on climate negotiations reflecting CAN's perspective since the Stockholm Environment Conference in 1972.

Business. Initially, business was sceptical on the issue of climate change. A group of US companies formed the Global Climate Coalition (GCC) in 1989, which opposed immediate actions to reduce greenhouse gas emissions. It was dissolved in 2002, mentioning that its missions have been successfully achieved, since 'The Bush administration will soon announce a climate policy that is expected to rely on the development of new technologies to reduce greenhouse gas emissions, a concept strongly supported by the GCC'. Recently, there are growing efforts in the business and voluntary sectors to reduce greenhouse gas emissions. For instance, in the steel industry, companies such as Alcoa, the Nippon Steel Corporation, and Norsk Hydro set their own emission reduction targets; and this is also evident in the cement and petroleum industries.

Businesses have established non-UNFCCC climate forums with their governments. In 2005, the United States, Japan, Australia, India, China and South Korea formed the Asian-Pacific Partnership on Clean Development and Climate (APP), an international, voluntary, public–private partnership. Canada joined in 2007. It has created eight task forces including: cleaner fossil energy; renewable energy and distributed generation; power generation and transmission; steel; aluminium; cement; coal mining; buildings and appliances.

Effectiveness

According to UNEP's 'The Emission Gap Report' (2010), the emission levels of approximately 44 gigatons of carbon dioxide equivalent (GtCO2e) in 2020 would be consistent with a 'likely' chance of limiting global warming to 2° Celsius. However, the pledges made to the Copenhagen Agreement would be 53 GtCO2e, thus leaving a significant emission gap of 9 GtCO2e, in order to limit global warming to 2° Celsius.

References

UNEP (2010) 'The Emission Gap Report', Nairobi: UNEP, also available from http://www.unep.org/publications/ebooks/emissionsgapreport/pdfs/EMISSION_GAP_REPORT_%20HIGHRES.pdf (accessed 29 March 2013).

UNFCCC (1992) *United Nations Framework Convention on Climate Change*, Available from http://unfccc.int/resource/docs/convkp/conveng.pdf (accessed 29 March 2013).

UNFCCC (1997) *Kyoto Protocol to the United Nations Framework Convention on Climate Change*, available from http://unfccc.int/resource/docs/convkp/kpeng.pdf (accessed 29 March 2013).

World Meteorological Organization (n.d.) 'World Climate Conference', online, available from http://www.wmo.int/pages/themes/climate/international_wcc.php (accessed 29 March 2013).

Related websites

- United Nations Framework Convention on Climate Change (UNFCCC)
  www.unfccc.int
- Climate Action Network
  http://www.climatenetwork.org/
- Global Climate Coalition
  http://web.archive.org/web/20040927082141/http://www.globalclimate.org/
- Intergovernmental Panel on Climate Change (IPCC)
  http://www.ipcc.ch/

Notes

1 MAB website (accessed on 30 August 2012) http://www.unesco.org/new/en/natural-sciences/environment/ecological-sciences/man-and-biosphere-programme/
2 MSC website (accessed on 16 August 2012) http://www.msc.org/about-us/vision-mission
3 MSC website (accessed on 16 August 2012) http://www.msc.org/about-us/governance/structure
4 Direct quote from MSC website (accessed on 16 August 2012) http://www.msc.org/about-us/standards/standards/msc-environmental-standard
5 Fairtrade International website (accessed on 16 August 2012) http://www.fairtrade.net/what_is_fairtrade.html
6 Ibid.
7 Direct quote from Fairtrade International website (accessed on 16 August 2012) http://www.fairtrade.net/aims_of_fairtrade_standards.html
8 e-Stewards website (accessed on 16 August 2012) http://e-stewards.org/about/
9 e-Stewards website (certification) (accessed on 16 August 2012) http://e-stewards.org/certification-overview/
10 Ibid.

Index